D1477244

PROFESSOR K. H. CONNELL
Reproduced from a line drawing by Raymond Piper
Property of Mrs Hanna Connell

IRISH POPULATION, ECONOMY, AND SOCIETY

Essays in Honour of the late
K. H. Connell

Edited by
J. M. GOLDSTROM
and
L. A. CLARKSON

CLARENDON PRESS · OXFORD
1981

Oxford University Press, Walton Street, Oxford OX2 6DP

London Glasgow New York Toronto
Delhi Bombay Calcutta Madras Karachi
Kuala Lumpur Singapore Hong Kong Tokyo
Nairobi Dar es Salaam Cape Town
Melbourne Auckland

and associate companies in
Beirut Berlin Ibadan Mexico City

Published in the United States by
Oxford University Press, New York

© *The several contributors listed on*
pages ix and x, and, so far as the
residual copyright in the whole work is
concerned, Oxford University Press, 1981

British Library Cataloguing in Publication Data
Irish population, economy and society.
  1. Connell, K.H.
  2. Ireland - Social conditions - Festschriften
  I. Goldstrom, J.M. II. Clarkson, L.A.
  III. Connell, K.H.
  941.5   HN398.17

  ISBN 0-19-822499-0

Filmset by DBM Typesetting (Oxford)
Printed in Great Britain
at the University Press, Oxford
by Eric Buckley
Printer to the University

Preface

Kenneth H. Connell, 1917-1973

These essays are in homage to the scholar, K. H. Connell, who, because he died relatively young, did not receive a Festschrift. They are also in affectionate memory of the man.

When Connell came to the Queen's University of Belfast he was motivated by more than academic ambition. He believed, simply, that to understand Irish history one had to work at an Irish university. 'Ideally', he remarked, not altogether tongue in cheek, 'one should be born and bred in the bogs.' He arrived an established scholar, having relinquished a Fellowship at Nuffield College, Oxford (prior posts were at Aberystwyth, Liverpool, and the London School of Economics). He was to add further to his achievements while at Queen's with a visiting professorship at the National University of Australia and a visiting Fellowship of All Souls College, Oxford.

His influence pervades modern Irish scholarship, as many of these essays demonstrate. Connell had given fresh impetus to the course of demographic studies with *The Population of Ireland*; his academic achievement at Queen's University was to place the study of Irish peasant society on a firm historical basis, using the conventional techniques available to the economic and social historian, and making imaginative use of oral history and literary sources. Yet the volume of his printed work, as the bibliography below shows, was surprisingly modest. This is partly explained by the way he wrote—slowly, painstakingly, working passages and phrases until every nuance was to his satisfaction. Elegance of style was woven into the erudition. 'My pencil is my only research assistant', he remarked drily, adding that 'a paragraph a day is a good day's work'. It should be borne in mind, also, that every article he published represented years of gestation, and much of his research remained unfinished. His undergraduate lectures on Irish economic history, which from modesty he forbade new assistant lecturers to attend, were said to have been polished pieces of prose. Most scholars would have put such lectures into printed form.

When it comes to the man as distinct from the scholar, we remember him as one to whom principles were paramount. If he felt an injustice had been perpetrated, he would fight to rectify it, regardless of personal cost. He loved controversy—it was 'good for the adrenalin'. Perhaps that explains the pleasure he took in securing the appointment of Michael Drake as lecturer in the department after the latter had published a critique that disputed the thesis of *The Population of Ireland*. Connell relished academic confrontation, and the two enjoyed several happy seminars in the mid-1960s locked in dispute.

Whilst there were few colleagues whom Connell did not at some time infuriate because of his refusal to compromise upon a principle, his charm and warmth made him many friends. Those who enjoyed the Connell family hospitality knew him as a host who was always concerned to put at ease the young, the new, and the shy—whom he brought into his wide circle; he never stinted the time he gave to students and visitors to the department.

The extent of Connell's friendships in the academic world was something of a problem when the shape of this collection of essays was under consideration. The range of possible topics was exceedingly wide and the list of possible contributors embarrassingly long. The broad selection principle invoked was that contributions should focus on the theme of Ireland's economy and society. This was in deference to Connell's life long commitment to the subject.

J. M. Goldstrom

CONTENTS

III   The Irish Overseas

IV   Policies, Policy-Makers, and Development

Contributors

L. A. Clarkson — Reader in Economic and Social History, Queen's University, Belfast

Brenda Collins — Junior Fellow, Institute of Irish Studies, Queen's University, Belfast; former student, Queen's University, Belfast

E. Margaret Crawford — Research Student, London School of Economics; former student, Queen's University, Belfast

L. M. Cullen — Professor of Modern Irish History, Trinity College, Dublin

M. Daly — Late Lecturer in Economic and Social History, Queen's University, Belfast

Alun C. Davies — Senior Lecturer in Economic and Social History, Queen's University, Belfast

Cyril Ehrlich — Professor of Economic and Social History, Queen's University, Belfast

D. E. C. Eversley — Senior Research Fellow, Policy Studies Institute, London

J. M. Goldstrom — Senior Lecturer in Economic and Social History, Queen's University, Belfast

E. R. R. Green — Late Director, Institute of Irish Studies, Queen's University, Belfast

H. D. Gribbon — Honorary Research Fellow, Department of Economic and Social History, Queen's University, Belfast

D. S. Johnson — Lecturer in Economic and Social History, Queen's University, Belfast

Líam Kennedy

Joseph Lee

Peter Roebuck

Lecturer in Economic and Social History, Queen's University, Belfast; former lecturer in Continuing Education, New University of Ulster; formerly Visiting Research Fellow, Queen's University, Belfast

Professor of History, University College, Cork

Senior Lecturer in History, New University of Ulster

Introduction

K. H. Connell and Economic and Social History
at Queen's University, Belfast

In 1853 T. E. Cliffe Leslie was elected to the chair of Jurisprudence and Political Economy in the Queen's College,
Belfast. In 1953 Kenneth Hugh Connell was appointed to the
senior lectureship in economic and social history in the Queen's
University, Belfast. The links between the two events a century
apart are tenuous but not totally missing. Cliffe Leslie was
among the most important proponents of historical economics
in the British Isles; and since historical economics is one of the
roots from which the modern study of economic history has
grown, he can therefore be numbered as one of the founders
of the discipline. Historical economics developed in the third
quarter of the nineteenth century as a reaction to the increasingly
abstract theorizing of deductive economics. Cliffe Leslie's own
dissatisfaction sprang from 'the distinctive needs of Ireland, for
which economic orthodoxy did not appear to have a solution';
and much of his work was directed towards forging an economics
of a greater practical value.[1]

Connell, by contrast, belonged to a well-established discipline. He was, nevertheless, the first professional economic
historian to be appointed to a lectureship in economic history
in Ireland (although not the first scholar to hold a lectureship
entitled economic history) and his *Population of Ireland 1750-1845*
was 'the first book by a professional economic historian to tackle
a major theme affecting Irish society at large'.[2] And like Cliffe
Leslie, his intellectual interests were conditioned by the requirements of the society in which he worked. '[Not], to me', he wrote
in 1969, 'is Irish economic and social history an exotic growth
in an Irish university. The basic education any university offers

---

[1] G. M. Koot, 'T. E. Cliffe Leslie, Irish Social Reform, and the Origins of the
English Historical School of Economics', *History of Political Economy*, vii (1975), 312-36.
Quotation at p. 320.
[2] Anon., 'Kenneth H. Connell 1917-1973', *The Economic and Social Review*, 2nd Ser.
vi (1974), 1.

in economic history should surely be adapted to the provenance and experience of its students and to the expertise of its teachers. Basic education that strikes home in Aberystwyth might be a bore in Kampala: the standard British base (if it exists) is hardly best for Belfast. Irish economic history, properly taught, might be peculiarly rewarding for the bulk of our students, for their country and its schools.'[3]

There is another similarity between Cliffe Leslie and Connell: their scholarly influence has been better appreciated outside the institution that housed them and has grown after their deaths. In the late nineteenth century Cliffe Leslie's importance in both historical economics and economic history was over-shadowed by the German historical economists and such English scholars as Thorold Rogers, Toynbee, Ashley, and Cunning-ham.[4] Within Queen's College, Belfast, he had only a slight impact. He lived in London for nine months in the year and when in Belfast taught mainly jurisprudence. A single course in political economy was offered to Arts students but competed with history and metaphysics.[5] To judge from the question papers in the subject nothing of a particularly historical nature was taught. Economic history occasionally appeared in the general courses offered by the professors of history. Thus in April 1879 third-year Arts' students were asked to 'give some account of the regulations affecting Irish manufactures and Commerce in the 17th and 18th centuries'.[6] (Students a century later are asked to do much the same thing).

Belfast of course was not out of line with developments in Britain, where economic history began to find a home in history syllabuses during the 1870s. The Cambridge Historical Tripos, for example, contained a paper entitled 'Political Economy and Economic History' for the first time in December 1876.[7] Appointments specifically in economic history came at the end of the century. The first anywhere in the English-speaking world

---

[3] Typescript Departmental Memorandum, 27 May 1969. Connell never gave an inaugural lecture. Had he done so this might well have been his text.

[4] Koot, pp. 335-6; N. B. Harte (ed.), *The Study of Economic History* (London, 1971), pp. xiii-xiv, xix-xxii.

[5] T. W. Moody and J. C. Beckett, *Queen's Belfast 1845-1949: The History of the University* (London, 1959), p. 173.

[6] *Belfast: Queen's College Calendar 1880* (Belfast, 1880), p. 18.

[7] Private communication from N. B. Harte; also Harte, p. xviii.

was Sir William Ashley's chair at Harvard in 1892; the first in Britain was a lectureship at the London School of Economics in 1904. Belfast was not far behind. In 1910 a Faculty of Commerce was established in the newly constituted Queen's University and H. O. Meredith, who had held the second British lectureship in economic history—at Manchester between 1905 and 1908—came from Cambridge to the chair of economics. Possibly as a result of Meredith's interest in economic history a lectureship in the subject was created, the fifth such post in the United Kingdom, and an economic-history paper introduced into the commerce degree.[8]

The lectureship was held for less than a year by R. L. Jones, almost as briefly by J. F. Rees, later to become distinguished in the universities of Edinburgh, Birmingham, and Wales, and from 1912 to 1919 by Conrad Gill, well known to Irish historians for his book on the linen industry. From 1919 until 1948 the post was a joint lectureship in economic history and political science held by Joseph Lemberger. The two subjects were then split, the economic-history lectureship being occupied by H. G. Koenigsberger, now professor of history at Cornell, who was in turn succeeded by K. H. Connell in 1953. Initially a single course on the economic history of Britain and Ireland in the eighteenth and nineteenth centuries was offered; but in Gill's time there were two courses on England and Ireland divided at 1760. Not surprisingly, the recommended reading on England for pass students included the standard texts of Cunningham, Meredith, and Mantoux (in French); and on Ireland, Alice Murray's *Commercial and Financial Relations between England and Ireland from the Period of the Restoration* (1903), a book still on reading-lists today. Honours' students had to read, in addition, Ashley, Hewings, Leonard (poor relief), Unwin, and Dowell (taxation) on England; the only additional reference for Ireland was Alice S. Green's *Making of Ireland and its Undoing, 1200-1600* (1908).[9]

Irish economic history was thus taught in the university in the years before the First World War, although it occupied a subordinate place in the courses. After the war an outline course on British and Irish economic history from the eleventh century

---

[8] Moody and Beckett, pp. 405-6; Harte, pp. xxv, xxvi, xxxvi.

[9] These details are taken from the annual *Calendars* of Queen's University, Belfast.

was offered as late as 1926 in the B. Com. Sc. degree, but it then dropped out of sight. Thereafter the staple diet was British and - increasingly - European economic history. There were no Irish texts among the comprehensive reading-lists, not even the well-known works of George O'Brien. Whether the ignoring of Irish economic history was the result of the establishment of a separate government of Northern Ireland in 1920 or the product of Lemberger's greater involvement in political science[10] is impossible to determine. At all events the position continued into the post-war years. Koenigsberger provided medieval and modern courses on West-European economic history without any Irish content, and these Connell inherited in 1953.

Unlike Cliffe Leslie, Connell was a prominent figure in the academic community in Belfast: his delight in controversy and his distinctive physical appearance could hardly have made him otherwise. Yet his writing was better known beyond Queen's. He was, in the words of an anonymous obituary, probably 'the best known Belfast scholar in the broad field of Irish studies, and outside Ireland almost certainly the most widely known living Irish historian'.[11] Within the university academic recognition came slowly. For nine years he taught economic history (non-Irish) in the department of economics, but in 1962 became the head of an independent department of economic history, still with the rank of senior lecturer. A reader-ship followed in 1966 and a chair the year after. With the establishment of the department, the first full course of Irish economic history in the history of the university was introduced: 'Irish Economic Development since 1750'. With some modifi-cations to title and time-span this remains the introduction to Irish economic and social history for undergraduates.

Nine years seems a long time to establish an undergraduate course in a subject that Connell regarded as so important. Two reasons go some way towards explaining the delay. First, as Connell remarked in 1969, 'Irish economic history has suffered because, for many years, nobody with appropriate qualifications applied for a job'.[12] The appointment of Mrs Miriam Daly to

[10] Lemberger was primarily a political scientist. When the two subjects were split in 1948 he became lecturer in political science.

[11] Anon., p. 1.

[12] Memorandum, 27 May 1969.

a lectureship in Irish economic history in 1969 helped change this position; and she carried a heavy burden of teaching in the subject until her tragic death in June 1980. The second reason is suggested by the rubric of the course printed in the *Calendar* in 1962-3 and subsequent years: 'with no recommended outlines of the subject-matter of this course, students' reading must range in contemporary materials and monographs'.[13] The problem of adequate introductory reading still exists, although it is less acute today than it was in the early 1960s. Irish economic and social history has progressed a long way in twenty years.

The role of Connell and the department he created during this evolutionary process has been important but not straightforward. As several of the essays that follow point out, *The Population of Ireland, 1750-1845* (1950) was a seminal work both in Irish economic history and in demographic history more generally. It provided a series of population estimates between 1687 and 1821 which has served as the framework for the rest of eighteenth-century Irish economic history ever since. Its explanation of population growth, stressing high levels of nuptiality and marital fertility rather than a falling death-rate, stimulated historians in Britain and elsewhere to reconsider the reasons offered for population growth in their own countries during the eighteenth and early nineteenth centuries. As for the central role assigned by Connell to diet in the mechanics of demographic change, it was, as Cullen observes below, a novel departure in a book published in 1950. A clutch of elegant articles on population, diet, and marriage carried Connell from *The Population of Ireland* to *Irish Peasant Society* (1968), containing four essays on sex, drink, and religion. Its impact is more difficult to assess. His colleague at Queen's, Professor Michael Roberts, remarked shortly after its publication that it was a work greater than the sum of its parts. Taken together, they constitute a sustained exploration of the psychology of a peasantry suffering profound economic and social upheavals. Few Irish scholars have so far followed Connell along this path, although it is familiar enough to Continental historians.

In some ways, though, the influence of the Queen's department was initially less than that which might have been expected

---

[13] *The Queen's University of Belfast Calendar, 1962-63* (Belfast, 1962), p. 256.

from the only independent department in the whole of Ireland. In part this was because much of its teaching continued to be in non-Irish and particularly in British economic history: the 'British base'. The problem here is one that faces all teachers in countries whose histories have been closely bound up with and influenced by Britain: in Australia no less than in Ireland finding the right balance between domestic and British history in undergraduate courses is a nice point of judgement. Connell believed the balance in Belfast was tilted too much towards Britain. 'By strengthening our appeal to research students in Irish economic history; by improving and extending our under-graduate teaching; by dealing with the Irish overseas by developing relevant comparative studies, we might contribute notably not only to Irish historiography but to the study and writing of British - and general - economic history.'[14] That he did not always persuade his departmental colleagues was due not to the merits of the case, but to his way of arguing it, which was not always diplomatic.[15] He was, moreover, to quote again from the anonymous obituary, 'a loner, not a leader' in aca-demic matters, who would have been 'pleased, but amused somewhat cynically, in seeing himself described or cast in the role of creator of a school'.[16]

Still, by a process of osmosis more than by stern direction the study of Irish economic and social history has grown at Queen's in the last decade or so and the authors of the fourteen essays and the bibliography that follow all have some association with Connell or the department. Five, Clarkson, Daly, Davies, Ehrlich, and Goldstrom, were colleagues at the time of his death and another, Johnson, joined the department shortly after. Gribbon and Kennedy have held research appointments and taught in the department, the former in Connell's time and the latter since. Cullen, Green, and Lee have been associated with the department through what Connell once called the rockier road of external examining—a road he smoothed with lavish hospitality. Roebuck's association is as co-editor of *Irish Economic and Social History*, the journal of the Economic and

---

[14] Memorandum, 27 May 1969.

[15] See R. M. Hartwell, 'Kenneth H. Connell—an Appreciation', *Irish Economic and Social History*, i (1974), 12.

[16] Anon., p. 3.

Social History Society of Ireland which Connell helped to found and whose president he was when he died. Eversley is a link with Connell's days at the London School of Economics and a fellow-enquirer into Irish demography. But perhaps Connell would have found the greatest satisfaction in the contributions of Collins and Crawford, both former students of the department: ultimately the measure of any academic community is the quality of the students it produces.

The essays in the present collection fall into four groups. The first, 'Demography and Diet', contains papers dealing with themes that were central to Connell's own work. Those by Clarkson and Lee examine numbers. Connell's estimates of the population of Ireland during the eighteenth century have become an article of faith for historical demographers although controversy has raged over his explanations of population growth. Clarkson's essay calls attention to the frailty of Connell's figures—a point that he made himself but which users of his work have frequently ignored—and suggests that population growth after 1750 was sharper than Connell suggested. That the hypothetical figures of Clarkson's paper should not become a new orthodoxy is soon suggested by a reading of Cullen, who sees the post-1750 period as the continuation of more than a century of rapid population growth, punctuated by a few brief pauses. We are, as Lee observes, among 'the swirling hazards of eighteenth century population estimates' where travellers should tread warily. And if they think they have reached firm stepping-stones when they get to the censuses of 1821, 1831, and 1841 they are mistaken, for Lee has thrown slippery suspicion upon them. The 1821 census has usually been regarded as an underestimate, that for 1831 as an overestimate, and that for 1841 as a monument to the census-takers' skills, but Lee suggests they all understate the true population in some degree. His conclusion that 'Connell's famous Table 4 [in *The Population of Ireland*] may itself require revision below, as well as above the "census figures" line' is a measure of the uncertainty that still surrounds Irish population history.

In an area of speculation a solid body of data is worth having, and for this reason alone Eversley's paper on the Irish Quakers commands attention. The Quakers were a peculiar people, not least for the care with which they kept their demographic data.

They can hardly be regarded as a representative group in Irish society, yet some features of their behaviour identified by Eversley, notably their young marriages and high marital fertility, seem to set them apart from their English counterparts and closer to the ways in which the generality of the Irish are assumed to have behaved. No doubt Connell, forever suspicious of new fashions and technologies—even typewriters—would welcome this computerized support for his thesis.

The essays by Cullen and Crawford are concerned with diet, a subject which plays a vital role in Connell's explanations of Irish population growth. In a complexly argued paper Cullen explores the relationship between population, dietary changes, and commercialization, implying although never explicitly stating, that the rapid population growth from the seventeenth century was connected with the variety and richness of Irish diets. That changes in diet over time, and particularly the growing dependence on the potato after 1750, were complicated events linked with commercialization rather than with pauperization, is a thesis worthy of further investigation. So, too, are the medical consequences of the dairy-based diets of the pre-potato period. What hazards to health were associated with a diet dominated by butter and milk? The question is prompted by Crawford's essay on Indian meal and pellagra. A dietician as well as a historian, she raises issues of wider relevance than the possible presence in nineteenth-century Ireland of a hitherto unsuspected disease. Connell, in *Irish Peasant Society*, explored the connections between poverty and the sexual and drinking habits of the Irish. The association between economic conditions, food, and health should prove an equally fruitful field for Irish social historians of the future.

The second group of essays, on rural economy and society, also treats matters central to Connell's writings. His heroes, the peasants, are not considered directly, but his villains, the landlords, appear in the persons of the Chichester family, eventually to become earls and marquesses of Donegall. But as Roebuck shows, they were not so much villains as victims: sometimes of their own follies, sometimes of demographic accidents, and nearly all the time of the peculiar problems— peculiar by English standards, that is—of administering great estates in Ireland. Roebuck's paper is thus within the recent revisionist tradition on Irish landlordism. Connell's treatment of landlord attitudes and behaviour was always the weakest part of his work and it is not surprising that it is being substantially modified.

With the essays of Goldstrom and Kennedy we move away from the problems of land ownership to those of land use in the nineteenth century. Goldstrom discusses the issue in the wider context of the effect of the Great Famine on Irish economic and social development, arguing that it was a catalyst speeding up changes already in train and not a watershed between two very different kinds of society. Kennedy agrees, though on other matters there are differences of emphasis, if not of substance. For example, Kennedy suggests that patterns of regional commodity specialization were more firmly established before the Famine than Goldstrom implies; while their views of the influence of railways on the commercialization of agriculture are clearly different. There are also differences between Goldstrom and Lee, on the size of the population in 1841. These—and other—inconsistencies have been kept as a reminder that Irish economic history is still in its formative years and prone to conflicts of facts and interpretations.

In his unpublished memorandum cited above, Connell called for comparative studies of the Irish overseas as a means of contributing to the understanding of non-Irish as well as of Irish economic history. The two essays by Collins and Green illustrate his point. They also illustrate two types of Irish emigration. Collins's migrants to Paisley and Dundee were poor farmer-weavers whose livelihoods were undermined in Ireland by the collapse of their dual occupations and who moved to textile regions in Scotland in search of work. In examining the reasons for their choice of Paisley or Dundee and their impact on the host communities, she adds to our knowledge of Scottish as well as of Irish history. Green's single emigrant, Thomas Barbour, was a member of the much smaller groups of professional and commercial men who left Ireland in the nineteenth century. Some were the 'briefless barristers' and classical scholars produced in over-abundance by Trinity College, Dublin, and who departed to establish legislatures, judiciaries, and institutions of learning in far-flung colonies; others, like Barbour, were economic men seeking opportunity and profit wherever it might occur. From Green we learn as much about America as we do about Ireland.

The final four essays examine subjects less central to Connell's main interests, but important nevertheless. They have been called collectively 'Policies, Policy-makers, and Development', a catch-all category, possibly, but pointing to the common thread running through all four. Each deals, in different ways, with visionaries or schemers, idealists or pragmatists, hoping to make Ireland a better, or at least a different, place. Gribbon examines the writings and life of Thomas Newenham, well known to readers of Connell's work for his calculations of Ireland's population in 1804. Verbose and muddle-headed, he advocated Catholic emancipation, opposed the Act of Union, and harangued Englishmen on how best to manage Ireland. He achieved little but articulated the views of many Anglo-Irishmen of his time. Arguably William Dargan, driving force behind the Dublin international exhibition in 1853, achieved little of lasting value either, save for the forerunner of the National Gallery. Hard-headed business man though Dargan was, Davies in his essay shows that Ireland's Crystal Palace was built on vain hopes and empty rhetoric. Ireland's economic problems in mid-century were those of a country suffering de-industrialization in the face of competition from an economically more powerful neighbour; such problems were incapable of solution by an exhibition of imported machinery, handicrafts, and *objets d'art*. The agricultural co-operative movement of the late nineteenth century was at least more practical in its intentions, although Ehrlich in his essay on Plunkett questions the economic rationale on which it was based. Plunkett himself emerges as a high-minded, arrogant idealist concerned with the condition of Ireland but contemptuous of the mass of Irishmen. Finally, Johnson in his paper on the Belfast Boycott takes us into the twentieth century, into a world of political manœuvering motivated by principles no less high-minded and fanciful than those inspiring Newenham, Dargan, and Plunkett.

The essays in this volume give some indication of the way Irish economic and social history is developing. They are not the whole story of course. Since the end of the 1950s Professor L. M. Cullen in the history department of Trinity College, Dublin, has, almost singlehanded, established a strongly revisionist school of Irish economic history, particularly of the eighteenth century, challenging older judgements, including those of Connell. Elsewhere in Ireland, in Britain and overseas, a steady flow of publications from the 1960s has extended our understanding of the subject.[17] In the department of economic and social history at Queen's University much of what Connell hoped to achieve in 1969 is now in being. The seed sown by Cliffe Leslie in the third quarter of the nineteenth century but largely dormant for a hundred years is yielding fruit. In large part because of the scholarly writings of K. H. Connell and the department he created, Irish economic and social history is being taught and is proving rewarding to its students, their country and its schools.

L. A. Clarkson

[17] See L. A. Clarkson, 'The Writing of Irish Economic and Social History Since 1968', *Economic History Review*, 2nd Ser. xxxiii (1980), 100-11.

1. Irish Population Revisited, 1687-1821*

L. A. Clarkson

I

K. H. Connell's *Population of Ireland* offered a revised set of estimates of population between Petty's figure for 1687 and the first census of 1821, and advanced an explanation of population growth that emphasized the importance of early marriage and rising fertility. Since its publication, debate has concentrated almost entirely on the mechanics of population growth. The estimates have been practically unchallenged, although Connell himself pointed out 'that all, and especially those for the century before 1780, may remain seriously inadequate'.[1] Yet his individual estimates are not consistent with one another;[2] and an examination of the assumptions underlying their construction reveals how fragile they are. This essay attempts to show that alternative estimates can be produced by making plausible changes in the assumptions. The results suggest a markedly higher rate of population growth after 1750 than Connell implied and fit into the wider pattern of Irish economic history at least as well as his. Paradoxically, though, the rejection of Connell's figures strengthens the case for accepting some of his arguments relating to the causes of population growth.

* Versions of this essay were read to the Annual Conference of the Irish Economic and Social History Society, Professor F. J. Fisher's Graduate Seminar, Institute of Historical Research, London, and the Staff Seminar, Department of Economics, Salford University. I am grateful for comments I received and also from my colleague A. C. Davies. I am grateful, too, to D. Dickson of Trinity College, Dublin, for allowing me to refer to his unpublished work on the hearth-money returns.

[1] K. H. Connell, *The Population of Ireland, 1750-1845* (Oxford, 1950), p. 25. One early reviewer implied that they were beyond criticism: 'There is only one main line of criticism ... which is useful, or indeed permissible. In contrast to his extremely careful and judicious examination of statistics [Connell] indulges from time to time in vast generalizations about social organization and conditions ...', W. L. Burn, *Economic History Review*, 2nd Ser. iii (1950-1), 257.

[2] Calculation of annual growth-rates in each of his fourteen sub-periods produces highly erratic figures than cannot be explained on demographic grounds.

The first serious inquirer into population in pre-census Ireland was Sir William Petty. He made calculations for 1672, 1676, and 1687, using the hearth-money returns to establish the number of houses in Ireland and multiplying that number by an estimate of mean houseful size. Practically every subsequent investigator has used the same method. The 1821 Census Commissioners printed sixteen estimates, all but three based on the hearth-money. These, together with thirteen others, Connell replaced by calculations of his own because he thought that both the house-counts and the multipliers were wrong.[3]

The main problem with all estimates based on the hearth-money returns is that the tax was sometimes evaded and not always efficiently or honestly administered. Furthermore, collectors did not always record the number of exempt hearths, and house-counts derived from the returns, therefore, are understatements. To establish the extent of their deficiency Connell assumed that the average annual number of houses built in Ireland between the two census years, 1821 and 1831— approximately 10,000—could be applied to all years between 1791 and 1821. He therefore subtracted 300,000 from the number of houses recorded in the 1821 census to obtain the true number for 1791. This procedure indicated that the house-counts for 1791 and 1790 derived from the hearth-money should be increased by 20 per cent, and that for 1788 by 25 per cent.[4] The house-count for 1785 required more serious surgery for the hearth-money returns for that year were extremely defective. 'It would, perhaps, not be too rash to estimate the deficiency of the 1785 return as appreciably over 50 per cent', although 50 per cent was the adjustment he made. He raised the rest of the eighteenth-century house-counts by the same amount, 'which at least does not exaggerate the omissions from the returns of earlier years.'[5] Coming to Petty, Connell believed

---

[3] Census of Ireland, 1821, *Accounts and Papers*, P.P. 1824, XXII 417. Connell's additions to the Census Commissioners' list brought the total numbers of years covered to twenty-four, five years having more than one estimate, most of the additions coming from contemporary literary sources (Connell, *Population of Ireland*, pp. 4-5). His revised estimates, however, centred on only fifteen years, all of them being years for which hearth-money returns were extant (pp. 5, 25). For a detailed discussion of the construction of the traditional pre-census estimates, see pp. 255-60.

[4] Connell, *Population of Ireland*, pp. 12, 25.   [5] Ibid., p. 13.

his work to be 'very insecurely based', and the calculation for 1687, therefore, was increased by two-thirds.[6]

Having dealt with the estimates of house numbers in pre-census Ireland, Connell turned to the size of the houseful. The 1821 Census Commissioners, without explanation, used a multiplier of six, ignoring other figures that were available.[7] Connell reviewed estimates from twenty-three printed sources between Petty and the incomplete census of 1813, ranging in size from 4.36, calculated by Arthur Dobbs for County Antrim in 1725, to 6.23 for the whole country, derived from the hearth-money returns for 1788 by Gervase Bushe.[8] Dobb's figure was abandoned on the curious ground that it was the result of a private enquiry and therefore suffered 'from the householder's reluctance to give a full return.'[9] Connell also discarded Bushe's calculation, although with extreme reluctance, for it was apparently based on a careful examination of the hearth-money returns, a source which Bushe, as First-Commissioner of the Revenue, knew intimately. But it was higher than the mean houseful size of 5.95 revealed by the census of 1821 and it seemed implausible to Connell that houses became less crowded between 1788 and 1821.[10] He finally settled on a series of multipliers, starting with Petty's 5.5 for 1687, declining gradually to 5.2 in 1732, rising again to 5.65 in the 1780s and 1790s, and so to the census figure for 1821.[11]

Connell's revisions had the effect of spreading pre-Famine population growth more evenly through the eighteenth and early nineteenth centuries than the traditional figures. In particular, the increase between 1781 and 1841 was brought closer to British experience.[12] This result had two important implications. First, since Irish and British population growth seemed of roughly similar size, then perhaps similar explanations should be sought on both sides of the Irish Sea.[13] Second, broadly

[6] Ibid., pp. 259-60.   [7] Census of Ireland, 1821, 417.

[8] Connell, *Population of Ireland*, pp. 14-24.   [9] Ibid., p. 24.

[10] Ibid., pp. 18-19, 21.   [11] Ibid., p. 25.

[12] Less than 100 per cent in Ireland compared to around 88 per cent in Britain. Ibid., p. 24.

[13] This point was made by Connell himself in his 'Some Unsettled Problems in English and Irish Population History', *Irish Historical Studies*, vii (1951), 225-34. It was taken up, on the English side, by H. J. Habakkuk, 'English Population in the Eighteenth Century', *Economic History Review*, 2nd Ser. vi (1953), 117-33, from which much modern work on English population history has stemmed.

identical demographic experiences apparently produced very different economic experiences. 'In England the rapid growth of population provides one essential part of the explanation of the coming of the industrial revolution. In Ireland it did even more than largely determine the magnitude of the catastrophe of the Famine.'[14] This suggested, in turn, peculiar circumstances operating in Ireland, but not in England, which Connell identified as the effects of an oppressive landlord system. Thus were established fruitful lines of enquiry, both in British and Irish history, but on insubstantial foundations.

II

Connell believed that his adjustments to the house-counts for 1790 and 1791 were conservative, for had he assumed not a constant *number* of houses built between 1791 and 1821 but a constant *rate* of building, then the gap between the hearth-money estimates and the projections from 1821 would have been even greater.[15] Yet it is possible that the annual number of new houses built was declining rather than rising from the end of the eighteenth century. Such a decline is implicit in Connell's own arguments about the slackening pace of subdivision of land, which was a pre-condition of building in rural areas. Subdivision was gradually checked by landlords, at least from the end of the Napoleonic Wars, although, admittedly, not very effectively.[16] As early as 1789 Bushe had argued that house building was becoming more difficult because of rising costs and insecure tenures that made tenants reluctant to build.[17] His view conflicted with other contemporary opinion;[18] but it is supported in the case of one town, Armagh, when more stringent clauses in building leases from the late 1760s resulted in the housing stock growing more slowly than the population.[19]

---

[14] Connell, 'Unsettled Problems', p. 225.
[15] Connell, *Population of Ireland*, p. 12.
[16] Ibid., pp. 169-83.
[17] G. P. Bushe, 'An Essay Towards Ascertaining the Population of Ireland', *Transactions of the Royal Irish Academy*, iii (1789) [1790], 153.
[18] Connell, *Population of Ireland*, pp. 14-15.
[19] L. A. Clarkson, 'Household and Family Structure in Armagh City, 1770', *Local Population Studies*, xx (1978), 22-3; J. Stuart, *Historical Memoirs of the City of Armagh* (Newry, 1819), 450-1.

In the absence of more certain published calculations Connell's adjustments for 1788, 1790, and 1791 have been accepted, although without any great confidence. However, his treatment of the pre-1785 house-counts was certainly too radical. Much of the contemporary discussion of the mal-administration of the hearth tax was focused on the 1780s, not on the whole of the eighteenth century and recent research suggests that collection was more efficient earlier in the century than it was in the 1780s. Administration was thrown awry, less by the laxity of officials, than by the spread of cottages on marginal land from the mid-century onwards which made collection more difficult. Possibly the returns for 1753 were more accurate than those for 1791.[20] If, therefore, the deficiency in the 1791 house-count was 20 per cent as Connell suggested, a smaller adjustment ought to be made to the 1753 figure and, by implication, to the rest of the early eighteenth-century estimates. For the purpose of this essay a hypothetical addition of 15 per cent has been adopted.

What of the seventeenth century? The hearth-money had been widely evaded when first introduced, but organization was improved in 1665; and the fact that it was farmed until 1706 meant that farmers 'had every incentive to collect the tax to the last penny.'[21] It seems implausible that Petty, with his intimate knowledge of Irish conditions and his passion for

[20] Work on the hearth-money returns is being undertaken by David Dickson of Trinity College,Dublin. My statement that the 1753 returns may be more accurate than those for 1791 is based on his paper, 'Irish Population in the Eighteenth Century: Some Reconsiderations' read to the Irish Historical Society in November 1973. A summary of the paper appears in 'Abstracts of Papers Read to the Irish Historical Society and the Ulster Society for Irish Historical Studies in 1973 and 1974' prepared by the Ulster Society for Irish Historical Studies (typescript, Belfast, no date [1974]). Since this present essay was written David Dickson has allowed me to read another paper: D. Dickson, S. Daultrey, C.Ó Gráda, 'Eighteenth Century Irish Population: Old Sources and New Speculations'. I have not been able to make use of this paper, but it sets out in detail the reasons why the hearth-money returns between 1753 and 1791 are misleading. It also suggests that a considerably smaller adjustment is required to the 1791 house-count than Connell or I assumed. This would have the effect of increasing the rate of growth between 1791 and 1821 shown in my Figure 1 and Table 3. It would also depress the growth-rates for the years before 1791, though they would depend on the scale of adjustments required to the earlier house-counts. Throughout I have followed Dickson in giving 1753 as the date of the hearth-money, when Connell and others give 1754.

[21] T. J. Kiernan, *History of the Financial Administration of Ireland to 1817* (London, 1930), p. 261.

political arithmetic, would use the house-count for 1687 without adjustment, knowing it to be 'two-thirds deficient'. Admittedly a recent scholar has remarked that 'the major features of Petty's exercises in political arithmetic were a somewhat cavalier attitude towards facts and a reliance on over-lengthy chains of deduction from initially dubious material'; but the same authority also describes him as 'a master of statistical techniques and a paragon of carefulness' compared with his predecessors.[22] Interestingly, Petty's near-contemporary, Gregory King, thought him prone to exaggeration.[23] That the house-count for 1687 requires revision to take account of exemptions and evasions is clear, but the scale of adjustment is uncertain. The hypothetical 15 per cent employed for the eighteenth century may be too low, just as Connell's 66 per cent appears unreasonably high. For the purposes of this paper an addition of 30 per cent has been adopted, a guess admittedly, but no less firmly based than Connell's.

Turning now to the multipliers, Connell's are possibly somewhat high for much of the eighteenth century. Three types of evidence have been used to gauge the average size of housefuls in pre-census Ireland: opinions of hearth-money collectors, casual impressions, and local investigations. The first have been widely quoted, but their reliability is questionable, for the collectors were unpopular and their clients unco-operative. Bushe lamented in 1789 that 'to the hearth-money collector the people frequently refuse an answer [when asked to state the number of occupants in the house]. The wealthy, or their servants, often think the question impertinent, and the poor often suspect that it is asked with some bad design.'[24] These difficulties, he thought, would lead to underrecording, but they could have produced inflated guesses of houseful size. Bushe's own calculations are probably no more than elaborate guesswork.[25]

[22] M. J. Cullen, *The Statistical Movement in Early Victorian England* (Hassocks, Sussex, 1975), p. 6.
[23] G. S. Holmes, 'Gregory King and the Social Structure of Pre-industrial England', *Transactions of the Royal Historical Society*, 5th Ser. xxvii (1977), 53.
[24] Bushe, p. 149.
[25] Bushe's mean houseful size of 6.23 was calculated from a sample of 14,108 houses containing 87,895 persons. The houses were taken from sixteen counties, the counties being chosen according to the intelligence of the hearth-money collectors; from each

Impressionistic evidence is even more unreliable. For example, the Revd John Howlett made an estimate of not less than 5.5 in 1786 without ever setting foot in the country.[26] Arthur Young, on the other hand, did visit Ireland and remarked several times on the large housefuls, although he was careful to note the paucity and unreliability of the data.[27] In 1804 Thomas Newenham used Young's authority to support

---

county the first 5 per cent of entries of single-hearth, double-hearth, new, and pauper households were selected. The sample is therefore not a random one and may be biased by some unknown ordering of the original data. Bushe also calculated the mean houseful size for each of the sixteen counties. The mean of the county means is 6.28 and the standard deviation 0.37, giving a coefficient of variation of 5.89 per cent. This is suspiciously low, as a comparison with other Irish and English data suggests:

Place	Number of Means	Mean of Means	Standard Deviation	Co-efficient of Variation (%)
One hundred English communities, 1574-1821	100	4.82	0.67	13.90
Thirteen districts in County Cork, 1804	13	6.33	0.83	13.11
Forty-six townlands, Barony of Portnehinch, Queen's County, 1819	46	5.53	0.68	12.30
Sixteen Irish counties, 1788 (Bushe)	16	6.28	0.37	5.89

Sources: England: P. Laslett, 'Mean Household Size in England Since the Sixteenth Century', in P. Laslett and R. Wall, eds., *Household and Family in Past Time* (Cambridge, 1972), 133; County Cork: T. Newenham, *A Statistical and Historical Inquiry into the Progress and Magnitude of the Population of Ireland* (London, 1805), facing p. 252; Portnehinch: W. Shaw Mason, *Survey, Valuation, and Census of the Barony of Portnehinch* (Dublin, 1821), Table 2; Irish Counties, 1788: Bushe, facing p. 143. One of two conclusions seem to follow: either the sixteen Irish counties investigated by Bushe were remarkably homogeneous in their houseful size despite their geographical diversity; or his data are estimates, not precise findings, clustering around a predetermined norm. Such a norm may have been cemented in Bushe's mind by conditions on his own estate at Kilfaine, County Kilkenny which had been visited a decade earlier by Arthur Young. For his benefit Bushe had lined up his haymakers. With their families there were 144 of them living in 22 cabins: a mean of 6.5. Arthur Young, *Tour in Ireland (1776-9)*, ed. A. W. Hutton (London, 1892), i, pp. 78-9.

[26] J. Howlett, *An Essay on the Population of Ireland* (London, 1786), p. 16; Joseph Lee, 'Introduction' to *The Population of Ireland Before the 19th Century* (Farnborough, Hants, 1973), no pagination. (This volume contains reprints of works by J. Howlett, G. P. Bushe, W. Shaw Mason, and T. Newenham).

[27] Young, i, pp. 78-9, 191, 290; ii, p. 121.

his belief that mean houseful size was as high as six,[28] ignoring the work of Daniel Beaufort, who earlier had guessed the national average to be 5.5.[29] While Newenham was writing, the first of the county *Statistical Surveys* commissioned by the Dublin Society were appearing, several giving figures of mean houseful size of between five and six.[30]

There are several reasons for believing that the observations of men such as Howlett and Young were exaggerated. First, they were attracted by eye-catching large housefuls which obscured the presence of small ones. This tendency was reinforced by a particular interest in the labouring population coupled with a belief that labourers bred large numbers of children. In this respect Arthur Young was very influential since his views on the subject were widely quoted.[31] Observers of Irish conditions, especially, possessed an inbuilt belief that housefuls in Ireland were larger than in England, a belief strengthened at the end of the century by a desire to frighten Englishmen with the spectre of a rapidly growing population in Ireland.[32] Newenham was typical in asserting 'that the average number of persons in each house in Ireland exceeds the average number in each house in [England]',[33] an opinion repeated by Townsend in his work on County Cork. While noting that mean houseful size exceeded eight in parts of Cork City, was over six in other towns, and that 'five to a house is the usual computation of country residents, and, in general, it seems to be a fair average', Townsend nevertheless preferred to use the estimate of six of 'my friend' Newenham.[34] A writer who was rare in resisting the lure of large numbers was Patrick Duigenan who dismissed Bushe's calculations as 'too great' and mocked other 'grossly exaggerated' guesses made 'with a view to bearding Great Britain'.[35]

[28] Newenham, p. 248.

[29] D. A. Beaufort, *Memoir of a Map of Ireland* ... (London, 1792).

[30] For a discussion of the findings of the *Statistical Surveys*, see Connell, *Population of Ireland*, p. 20.

[31] R. Wall, 'Mean Household Size in England from Printed Sources', in Laslett and Wall, pp. 171-2; Clarkson, p. 25.

[32] Lee, 'Introduction' to *Population of Ireland Before the 19th Century*.

[33] Newenham, p. 247; Connell, *Population of Ireland*, p. 14.

[34] H. Townsend, *Statistical Survey of the County of Cork* (Dublin, 1810), p. 86.

[35] P. Duigenan, *A Fair Representation of the Present Political State of Ireland* (Dublin, 1800), pp. 237-9. Duigenan's own estimate of houseful size was 'not more than four, if so many'.

The more extreme estimates of houseful size are implausible on theoretical grounds. High mean houseful sizes usually occur in societies possessing high fertility, low mortality, and extended family structures.[36] Levels of fertility and mortality in pre-Famine Ireland are matters of intense discussion; but even assuming high fertility and low mortality, mean houseful size is unlikely to be much in excess of five unless it is further assumed that extended families are widespread.[37] Such an assumption was made by Connell, but not by eighteenth-century observers. As Lee has noted, 'every commentator on the question of household size as far back as Petty assumed the existence of the nuclear family, even in what was, arguably, the least "western" of Western European societies, still less than a century removed from tribalism in Petty's time.'[38] Perhaps Petty and others were imposing English patterns on to Irish society; on the other hand it is possible that even in tribal Ireland the normal resident group had been the nuclear family. The only study of family structure so far published for an eighteenth-century Irish community demonstrates that the nuclear family was common.[39]

Mean houseful size may be inflated by the presence of servants and lodgers. In Ireland both the proportion of houses containing servants and the average size of the servant group were lower than in England.[40] The position regarding lodgers is obscure. The Census Commissioners in 1821 stated that 'lodgers ... when of full age, and maintaining themselves from their own resources' constituted separate families; but if it appeared that lodgers worked for the head of the house or were otherwise maintained by him, they should be included as part of his houseful.[41] Earlier surveys seem to have been unaware of the distinction. Newenham dealt in housefuls, treating all

[36] T. K. Burch, 'Some Demographic Determinants of Average Household Size: An Analytical Approach', in Laslett and Wall, pp. 96-7.
[37] Ibid., Table 2.1.
[38] Connell, *Population of Ireland*, p. 16; Lee, 'Introduction' to *Population of Ireland Before the 19th Century*.
[39] Clarkson, p. 19.
[40] Laslett, 'Mean Household Size', in Laslett and Wall, pp. 153, 155; Clarkson, pp. 18, 28-9; F. J. Carney, 'Aspects of Pre-Famine Irish Household Size: Composition and Differentials', in L. M. Cullen and T. C. Smout, eds., *Comparative Aspects of Scottish and Irish Economic and Social History, 1600-1900* (Edinburgh, 1977), p. 36.
[41] Census of Ireland, 1821, pp. 424-5.

inmates of a house as members of a single, co-resident, group.[42]
Bushe wrote of 'number of houses' and 'number of souls' and
the high figures he cited for Dublin and Cork, showing between
10 and 13 persons per house, suggest that he was thinking of
housefuls including lodgers.[43] Most users of the hearth-money
returns apparently thought the same way and probably all
early Irish estimates were confused in their treatment of the
problems posed by the presence of lodgers.[44]

To resolve the matter of houseful size it would be useful to
have analyses of population listings of the kinds undertaken in
England.[45] Unfortunately such listings are rare in Ireland and
the only one so far studied for the eighteenth century, that for
Armagh City in 1770, produces a very low mean household
size of 3.9.[46] We are forced to rely instead on contemporary
investigations of local communities which may be prone to the
same problems besetting the estimates of hearth-money collectors and casual observers. One of the earliest was undertaken by Arthur Dobbs in 1725. 'From several Returns made
to me of the Number of Persons in each Family, in a great
many contiguous Parishes in the County of Antrim, I find the
Medium to be 4.36 to a Family.'[47] Far from rejecting this as a
prying piece of private enterprise, as Connell did, it deserves
serious consideration. Dobbs was writing of his own county,
his calculation of the second decimal place suggests a statistical
care uncommon at the time, and, more important, he was
aware of regional differences: 'from a different way of living in
the several Provinces and in Cities and great Towns, there may
be more in a Family in some parts of the Kingdom than in the
County from whence I took my Estimate.'

Confirmation of this observation is provided by the Religious
Census of 1766. Church of Ireland incumbents were required
to make a return of the numbers of Catholic and Protestant
householders in their parishes, but some gave the numbers of

[42] Newenham, pp. 247-52.

[43] Bushe, p. 148.

[44] For a discussion of this question relating to seventeenth-and eighteenth-century
England, see Wall in Laslett and Wall, pp. 159-66.

[45] Laslett, 'Mean Household Size', in Laslett and Wall, pp. 125-58.

[46] Clarkson, pp. 14-31.

[47] Arthur Dobbs, *An Essay on the Trade and Improvement of Ireland*, Part II (Dublin,
1731), p. 9.

inhabitants as well. Table 1.1 shows that the unweighted mean houseful size in these parishes was 5.38, but this figure was inflated by the presence of Cork City which accounted for 35 per cent of houses and 43 per cent of inhabitants. Excluding Cork, the mean was 4.71, or 5.07 if the doubtful case of Urney is also omitted.[48] The mean of means (5.06) may be a better

Table 1.1   Houseful[1] size in various parishes of Ireland, 1766

Place	Number of houses	Number of persons	Mean houseful size
Lurgan and Munster-Connaught, Co. Cavan	604	2967	4.91
Urney and Annagelliffe, Co. Cavan	1433	3845	2.66
Killashee, Co. Longford	360	2065	5.74
Donneraille, Co. Cork	602	3506	5.82
Templetrine, Co. Cork	148	843	5.70
Killbrogan, Bandon, Co. Cork	605	3018	4.99
Ballymodan, Bandon Bridge, Co. Cork	869	4660	5.36
Cork City (13 parishes)	4977	33016	6.63
Tullynakill, Co. Down	139	767	5.52
Greyabbey, Co. Down	351	1786	5.09
Balteagh, Co. Derry	363	1667	4.59
Clonleigh, Co. Donegal	735	4062	5.53
Drumbo, Co. Down	395	2370	6.00
Faughanvale, Co. Derry	850	3916	4.61
Collon, Co. Louth	195	911	4.67
Augherloo, Co. Louth	167	838	5.02
Killmegan, Co. Down	680	3282	4.83
Bright, Co. Down	216	1074	4.97
St. Mary's, Drogheda	659	2581	3.92
Total	14348	77174	5.38
Total (minus Cork)	9371	44113	4.71
Total (minus Cork and Urney)	7938	40268	5.07
Mean of means			5.06
Mean of means (minus Cork)			5.00
Mean of means (minus Cork and Urney)			5.13

Source: Public Record Office, Ireland, M 2476. I am grateful to David Dickson for bringing this source to my attention.
    [1] The document refers to 'families', but in the context it seems that houses and housefuls are meant.

[48] The mean houseful size for Urney and Annagelliffe of 2.66 is so low that it suggests that there may have been a transcription error in the source.

indicator for the country as a whole, although it is composed from only nineteen returns. The alternative means of means, excluding Cork, and excluding Cork and Urney, are also close to five. This may be compared with the substantially higher figure of 5.82 for the early nineteenth century derived from the results of ten local surveys reported by the authors of the *Statistical Surveys* (Table 1.2); and the 5.68 calculated by Carney from the surviving census-enumerators' books for 1821.[49]

Table 1.2   Mean size of families, households or housefuls according to the Statistical Surveys

Date	Unit	Place	Mean
1801	Houseful	Castle McAdam, Co. Wicklow	5.56
1802	Houseful	Annahilt, Co. Down	5.25
1802	Family	Ballintoy, Co. Antrim	4.98
1802	Family	Ballyaghan, Co. Londonderry	5.19
1802	Family	Aghanloo, Co. Londonderry	4.79
	Household		5.27
1803	Family	Ballintoy, Co. Antrim	5.13
1807	Houseful	Wexford Town	9.0
1807	Houseful	Country parish, Co. Wexford	6.29
1807	Family	Larne, Co. Antrim	5.43
	Houseful		5.97
1808	Houseful	¦ Carrickfergus, Co. Antrim	6.98
		Mean of means	5.82

Sources : J. Dubourdieu, *statistical Survey of the County of Antrim* (Dublin, 1812), pp. 442-3, 482, 488.
Idem, *Statistical Survey of the County of Down* (Dublin, 1802), p. 244.
G. V. Sampson, *Statistical Survey of the County of Londonderry* (Dublin, 1802), pp. 293-4.
R. Frazer, *Statistical View of the County of Wexford* (Dublin, 1807), p. 72.

The above discussion suggests that regional rather than national multipliers ought to be established; but that if the latter are used they should be weighted averages of regional figures. We are a long way yet from possessing such data; still, if we wish to estimate pre-Famine population in Ireland, some assumptions about houseful size must be made. For much of

[49] Carney, 'Aspects of Pre-Famine Irish Household Size', in Cullen and Smout, p. 37.

the eighteenth century of multiplier of 5.0 seems more appropriate than Connell's slightly higher figures. A more difficult problem is to decide by how much this figure should be increased at the end of the eighteenth century. In the calculations that follow alternative assumptions of mean houseful size for 1791 of 5.0, 5.25, and 5.50 are employed.

III

It is convenient to recall the argument so far. Connell's revisions of the house-counts before 1788 are too great and his houseful multipliers too high. In their place, more modest, though hypothetical, adjustments to the house-counts and lower multipliers have been suggested. These suggestions need testing by empirical research; nevertheless, it is useful to see what a different picture of pre-Famine population growth they produce. The results are set out in Table 1.3 and Figure 1.1. The years used in the Table are those indicated in the previous discussion: 1687 as the date of Petty's final population estimate; 1753 and 1791 as years on which consideration of the reliability of the house-counts has centred; 1821 as a census year. It seemed desirable, also, to divide the long first period; this has been done at 1725, the date of Arthur Dobb's careful discussion of the population of Ireland.

One difficulty immediately eased by the new population estimates in Table 1.3 is the rate at which population grew during the seventeenth century. By projecting back from Connell's revised estimate of nearly 2.2 million for 1687, Cullen arrived at a population of 1.4 million in 1600.[50] Unfortunately this is at odds with other estimates for 1600, some of which go as low as half a million. As Canny has pointed out, non-demographic evidence suggests that Ireland was sparsely populated in 1600, whereas Cullen's estimate indicates a high density of population in the cultivatable regions.[51] If, however, Cullen were to lower his figure to, say, 1.1 million, he is implying a rate of growth during the seventeenth century considerably higher than that which apparently occurred anywhere else in

---

[50] L. M. Cullen, 'Population Trends in Seventeenth Century Ireland', *Economic and Social Review*, vi. 2 (1975), 149-65.

[51] N. P. Canny, 'Early Modern Ireland: An Appraisal Appraised', *Irish Economic and Social History*, iv (1977), 64.

Table 1.3   The Population of Ireland

1.3.1   The number of houses in Ireland, 1687-1791

Year	Number according to the hearth-money returns	Number according to Connell	Hypothetical
1687	260 000	431 600 (+ 66%)	338 000 (+ 30%)
1725	386 229	579 343 (+ 50%)	444 163 (+ 15%)
1753	395 439	593 158 (+ 50%)	454 755 (+ 15%)
1791	701 102	841 322 (+ 20%)	841 322 (+ 20%)
1821	1 142 000 (census)	-	-

1.3.2   The Houseful Multiplier

Year	Connell	Hypothetical
1687	5-6	5.0
1725	5.25	5.0
1753	5.38	5.0
1791	5.65	{5.0 (a) 5.25 (b) 5.50 (c)
1821	5.95 (census)	5.95 (census)

1.3.3   Population Estimates
(000)

Year	Traditional	Connell	Hypothetical
1687	1300 (Petty)	2167	1690
1725	1679* (Dobbs)	3042	2221
1753	2373 (Hearth-Money)	3191	2274
1791	4207 (Hearth-Money)	4753	{4207 (a) 4417 (b) 4627 (c)
1821	6802 (census)	6802	6802 (census)

* Arthur Dobbs's own estimate; not the figure attributed to him by the Census Commissioners in 1821.

1.3.4   Annual Growth-Rates (%)

Period	Traditional	Connell	Hypothetical
1687-1725	0.68	0.90	0.72
1725-53	1.20	0.17	0.08
1753-91	1.56	1.05	{1.63 (a) 1.76 (b) 1.89 (c)
1791-1821	1.67	1.20	{1.61 (a) 1.45 (b) 1.29 (c)

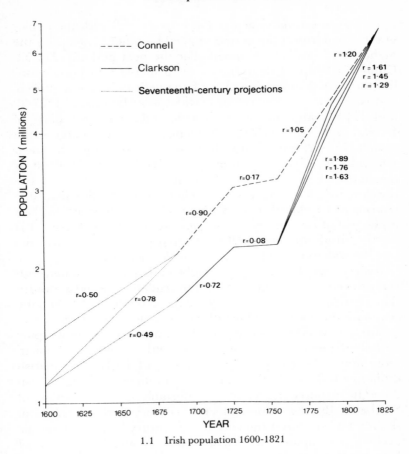

1.1   Irish population 1600-1821

Western Europe. But if seventeenth-century projections were worked back from a lower figure of 1.7 million the difficulty is resolved, for an increase from 1.1 million to 1.7 million between 1600 and 1687 requires an annual growth-rate of just under 0.5 per cent, well within the range of pre-industrial experience. To put the point another way, an estimated population of around 1.7 million in 1687 is more consistent with the demographic developments of earlier periods than the higher figure suggested by Connell.

Moving into the first half of the eighteenth century, the lower growth-rate between 1687 and 1725 suggested by the

hypothetical estimates accords at least as well with the demographic patterns of the period implied by other evidence as the
higher rate shown by Connell. For the next period, 1725-53,
Connell's figures reveal only a small increase in population;
but the virtual stagnation of the hypothetical figures is entirely
consistent with the occurrence of widespread famines in 1727-30
and 1740-1, and the severe dearths affecting some parts of
Ireland in the early 1750s.[52] Problems, however, emerge in the
period 1753-91, when the rate of growth of population—between
1.6 and 1.9 per cent per annum—is very high and difficult to
match elsewhere in Europe. This raises the possibility that the
revisions in Table 1.3 are wrong; if not, we need to find plausible
reasons why Ireland's population growth should be higher than
in the rest of Europe. Before suggesting reasons, however, it is
worth considering how well very rapid population growth fits
into the wider view of Irish economic development.

Irish economic history of the eighteenth and early nineteenth
centuries contains a conundrum. Put crudely: how did a country
that participated so vigorously in the growth of the Atlantic
economy during the eighteenth century become, in the nineteenth, a byword for poverty, backwardness, and demographic
decline? Cullen and Smout have recently posed the problem
more subtly by comparing the course of Irish and Scottish
economic history. At the end of the seventeenth century Irish
domestic exports per capita comfortably exceeded those of
Scotland. By the mid-eighteenth century Ireland was still
slightly ahead, but at the end of the century Scottish domestic
exports per capita were substantially greater than those of
Ireland. If we can use domestic per capita exports as a proxy
for per capita incomes, Scotland enjoyed a higher rate of
economic growth than Ireland from the 1750s onwards and the
two economies diverged even more sharply after 1800 as Ireland
failed to achieve the 'classic take-off'.[53]

[52] V. Morgan, 'A Case Study of Population Change over Two Centuries' Blaris,
Lisburn 1661-1848', *Irish Economic and Social History*, iii (1976), 12-15. M. Drake,
'Population Growth and the Irish Economy', in L. M. Cullen, ed., *The Formation of
the Irish Economy* (Cork, 1968), 72-3; idem, 'The Irish Demographic Crisis of 1740-41',
in T. W. Moody, ed., *Historical Studies*, vi (Dublin, 1968), pp. 101-24; J. M. Beckett,
The Making of Modern Ireland, 1603-1923 (1966), pp. 174-5; L. A. Clarkson, 'Portrait of
an Urban Community: Armagh 1770', in D. W. Harkness and M. O'Dowd, eds.,
The Town in Ireland: Historical Studies, xiii (Belfast, 1981), p. 91.

[53] L. M. Cullen and T. C. Smout, 'Economic Growth in Scotland and Ireland', in
Cullen and Smout, pp. 3-8, 54.

Why? An older generation of historians emphasized the harmful effects of English policy towards Ireland. Today, greater emphasis is put on the influence of factor endowments, market opportunities, and cultural values. Of particular importance is agricultural development. The striking feature about Ireland, according to Cullen and Smout, was its 'failure to start an agricultural revolution before the middle of the nineteenth century'.[54] To say this, of course, merely pushes the problem back a stage, to the reasons for the absence of an agricultural revolution. Those suggested include the indifference to agricultural improvement by an alien and largely absentee landlord class, and the difficulties caused by a conservative and impoverished peasantry. These influences are more understandable against a background of a very rapidly growing population. With an abundance of labour in Ireland the introduction of capital-intensive methods into agriculture was unlikely, for output could be increased by applying more labour to the cultivation of land. The English agricultural revolution was particularly marked by the reorganization of tenancies into more compact units, resulting in more efficient use of land, labour, and capital. How could Irish landlords carry out such reorganization when faced with a tangle of undertenants of whose existence they neither knew nor approved? Thompson, reviewing Maguire's book on the Downshire estates, remarks that there was something Canute-like in the attempts of the third Marquess, a business-minded if not benevolent man, to stem the rising tide of subdivision and subletting.[55] The Canute-theory of Irish economic history is hardly new, but the higher the tide, the stronger its appeal.

The new population estimates presented in Table 1.3 show a slight slowing-down of population growth in the period 1791-1821, although growth remains high by English standards. The extent of the retardation depends on what adjustments are made to the 1791 house-count and what assumptions are made about mean houseful size, and possibly it was very small indeed or even non-existent. A small decline is entirely consistent with studies of pre-Famine population carried out since Connell

---

[54] Ibid., p. 16.
[55] F. M. L. Thompson, Review of W. A. Maguire, *The Downshire Estates in Ireland 1801-1845* (Oxford 1972) in *Irish Economic and Social History*, ii (1975), 75-6.

wrote. Cousens, for example, argued that the increase in population was retarded by delayed marriage 'at least since the Napoleonic wars'; and the work of Crotty, Carney, and others has confirmed the importance of the years immediately following 1815 as a watershed in Irish population history. Land-hunger and the increasing resistance of landlords to subdivision combined to curb natural increase and to raise the levels of emigration out of the country.[56]

It seems, therefore, that rates of growth of population higher than those implied by Connell fit neatly into the general picture of Irish economic history in the late eighteenth and early nineteenth century. An analysis of the 1821 census carried out by Ó Gráda, showing that Ireland's population was distinctly younger than the population of England and Scotland, also supports the case for high growth-rates. Such a young age structure is consistent with rates of population growth of between 1.5 and 2.0 per cent per annum for some decades prior to 1821.[57]

Connell's main explanation of population growth was the conjunction of early marriage and high fertility; he examined, but rejected, the possibility that falling mortality was an important part of the explanation.[58] Nevertheless, the question of mortality requires re-examination, for if population in Ireland grew appreciably faster than population in England, the burden of explanation may have to rest both on lower mortality and on higher fertility.

The Irish Census of 1841 showed that the death-rate in Ireland had been lower during the 1830s than had been the

[56] S. H. Cousens, 'The Restriction of Population Growth in Pre-Famine Ireland', *Proceedings of the Royal Irish Academy*, lxiv, Section C, no. 4 (1966), 85-99; quotation at p. 98; R. D. Crotty, *Irish Agricultural Production: Its Volume and Structure* (Cork, 1966), pp. 37-41; F. J. Carney, 'Pre-Famine Population: The Evidence from Trinity College Estates', *Irish Economic and Social History*, ii (1975), 35-45.

[57] Cormac Ó Gráda, 'Demographic Adjustment and Seasonal Migration in Nineteenth-Century Ireland', unpublished paper prepared for the Conference of French and Irish Economic Historians on Rural Society, Dublin, 1977, revised 1978, pp. 3-5. I am grateful to him for providing me with a copy of this paper and also of another, 'The Population of Ireland 1700-1900: A Survey', forthcoming in *Annales de démographie historique*. In fairness to Ó Gráda and myself it should be added that we had been working independently and from different directions towards broadly similar conclusions. See also Crotty, pp. 37-8.

[58] Connell, *Population of Ireland*, chapter VII.

case in England. Connell considered the Irish evidence unreliable, but Razzell has shown that Irish age-specific mortality
levels under 35 years were all below the levels for comparable
age groups in England.[59] This does not mean, of course, that
the position has been similar in still earlier decades, nor that
mortality in Ireland had been declining from the late eighteenth
century, but it does imply that there had been causes at work
for some time in Ireland keeping the death-rate comparatively
low.

One possibility is that diets improved, or that food supplies
became more regular, with the introduction of potatoes. The
timing of their diffusion into Irish diets is a controversial matter[60]
and a comparison with the Scottish Highlands may be helpful
at this point. Potatoes were introduced into the Highlands after
the failure of the grain harvest in 1740-1 and their cultivation
spread rapidly from about 1780 in response to population
growth. Potatoes enlarged the supply of food in three ways:
as a high-yielding crop rich in calories; as a cleansing crop used
in arable rotations aimed at producing grain; and as feed for
animals, especially pigs. The increased supply of food permitted
a continuing increase in population which, without potatoes,
would otherwise have been halted by Malthusian crises or
retarded by high rates of emigration.[61]

A second probable reason for lower mortality in Ireland was
its comparatively small degree of urbanization. In 1840-1
mortality was higher in the urban civic districts of Ireland than
in rural areas; and in Britain, likewise, urban mortality was
higher than rural mortality. Since Ireland was less urbanized
than England, the urban-rural differences could explain much
of the gap between the crude death-rates of the two countries.[62]
The gap had possibly widened during the decades before 1840-1

[59] Ibid., p. 189; P. E. Razzell, 'Population Growth and Economic Change in
Eighteenth- and Early Nineteenth-Century England and Ireland', in E. L. Jones and
G. E. Mingay, eds., *Land, Labour and Population in the Industrial Revolution: Essays
Presented to J. D. Chambers* (London, 1967), p. 268.

[60] K. H. Connell, 'The Potato in Ireland', *Past and Present*, xxiii (1962) 60-1;
M. Drake, 'Marriage and Population Growth in Ireland, 1750-1845', *Economic History
Review* 2nd Ser. xvi (1963), 312-13; L. M. Cullen, 'Irish History Without the Potato',
Past and Present, xi (1968), 79. See also Chapter 4, below.

[61] M. Flinn, ed., *Scottish Population History From the 17th Century to the 1930s*
(Cambridge, 1977), pp. 421-38.

[62] Connell, *Population of Ireland*, pp. 191-4; Razzell, pp. 268-9.

because urban growth had occurred more swiftly and on a larger scale in England. In Ireland, Dublin was a large city of approaching 200,000 at the end of the eighteenth century, suffering all the problems of urban squalor and high mortality, but it grew to only 233,000 by 1841. Cork, similarly, was a city of around 80,000 in 1800, but increased little thereafter. Ireland's only industrial city was Belfast, growing rapidly from less than 20,000 at the end of the eighteenth century to 75,000 by 1841. From the end of the Napoleonic wars, in effect, Ireland's urbanization took place overseas.

The pattern of urbanization in Ireland was significant in another way. Irish towns were generally small. Apart from Dublin, Cork, Limerick, Belfast, Drogheda, and Waterford, none were bigger than about 6,000 and the majority were much smaller.[63] Communities of this size were better able to cope with the problems of urban growth, even though that growth might be quite rapid for a time. For example, the population of Armagh quadrupled between 1770 and 1821, when it was almost 8,500. Yet Stuart, the historian of the town, wrote in 1819 that 'severe dysentries, agues, asthmas, putrid fevers and epidemic diseases' earlier afflicting the population had either disappeared or 'are comparatively of rare occurence'. The explanation he offered was the draining of marshy ground in the town, but there was also improved standards of building, street paving, and cleansing, and the provision of piped water in 1793.[64] In Connell's view, 'it is fanciful ... to suppose that improved public hygiene could have any significant influence in Ireland',[65] but this judgement may not be true for small towns, although admittedly in 1800 they contained only around 6 per cent of the population.

The lower level of urbanization in Ireland compared to Britain operated less to pull mortality down than to prevent it increasing by the movement of people from regions of low to regions of high mortality.[66] The treatment of disease, on the

[63] L. M. Cullen, *An Economic History of Ireland Since 1660* (London, 1972), p. 85; L. A. Clarkson, 'An Anatomy of an Irish Town: The Economy of Armagh', *Irish Economic and Social History*, v (1978), 27-8.

[64] Clarkson, 'Economy of Armagh', p. 29; Stuart, pp. 473-4, 503-5.

[65] Connell, *Population of Ireland*, pp. 186-7.

[66] Urban death-rates were rising in Britain at least from the 1820s. See Flinn, ed., pp. 17-19; B. Hammond, 'Urban Death Rates in the Early Nineteenth Century', *Economic History*, i (1928), 419-28.

other hand, may have had a more positive effect. There are two main developments to consider: the spread of hospitals and dispensaries; and the introduction of innoculation and vaccination against smallpox. On the first point, Connell concluded that, although every county except Waterford possessed an infirmary by 1821, there were too few of them to have had much effect on mortality. Furthermore, McKeown, although not writing specifically of Ireland, condemned the quality of treatment received in hospitals.[67] Such criticisms may need to be muted. The hospital in Armagh, for example, was established by public subscription in 1766, and in 1774 was housed in specially built premises still in use today. Originally containing fourteen beds, by 1819 it had twenty-two beds and admitted about 160 patients a year, in addition to dispensing medicines, supplying minor surgical treatment, and giving vaccinations to several hundred outpatients.[68]

There is disagreement about the effects of innoculation against smallpox, which was a major cause of death in eighteenth-century Ireland. According to Connell the reduction of smallpox mortality was the 'greatest contribution made by medical advance to the growth of the population of Ireland'.[69] The reduction, he believed, came from vaccination at the beginning of the nineteenth century, not from innoculation, which had been widely available from the 1760s, but which was more likely to have spread than prevented the disease by causing secondary infections. A similar view is taken by McKeown, but Razzell insists that innoculation reduced mortality in country districts from the 1770s onwards. Once again the recent work on Scotland is suggestive, for there innoculation 'was used with sufficient regularity in some rural districts to reduce the impact of the disease', the scattered nature of settlements preventing secondary infections.[70] Since settlement

---

[67] Connell, *Population of Ireland*, chapter VIII; T. McKeown, *The Modern Rise of Population* (London, 1976), pp. 13-14.

[68] Stuart, pp. 532-5.

[69] Connell, *Population of Ireland*, p. 208.

[70] Connell, *Population of Ireland*, pp. 213-20; McKeown, pp. 11-13; Razzell pp. 269-74; Flinn, ed., p. 16. For a perceptive and not totally dismissive medical assessment of Razzell's arguments see the review of his *The Conquest of Smallpox: The Impact of Innoculation on Smallpox Mortality in Eighteenth Century Britain* (Firle, Sussex, 1977), by P. Froggatt in *Irish Historical Studies*, xxi (1978), 230-2.

patterns in Ireland were more akin to those in Scotland than in England, the contribution of innoculation may have been similar.

Taken together the influences leading to lower mortality seem incapable of totally explaining the higher rate of population growth in Ireland and we are forced, therefore, to consider the explanations emphasized by Connell himself. Essential to his case was a falling age of first marriage, especially from the 1780s, made possible by the combined influences of subdivision of farms, reclamation of previously uncultivated land, and the extension of potato cultivation. A decline in the age of marriage led to a rise in marital fertility. Possibly, too, fecundity increased because of the nutritional benefits of the potato, and nuptiality may also have risen; but these were subsidiary matters. Both Connell's main points—falling age of marriage and high marital fertility—have been severely criticized, notably by Drake,[71] yet the evidence of the censuses of 1821 and 1841 indicates that fertility in pre-Famine Ireland was high; according to Tucker, marital fertility in 1841 was 21 per cent greater than in England.[72] Furthermore, Lee points out that labourers married younger than others—frequently in their low twenties—and this class was becoming much larger in the century before the Famine.[73]

A fresh element in the discussion has been added by Ó Gráda who argues that literary evidence indicates that relatively early marriage was common in Ireland back to Petty's time.[74] This suggestion raises two problems. First, why was the normal age of first marriage relatively low in Ireland even in the seventeenth century? It is not difficult to think of a possible answer along the same lines as Connell's explanation for early marriage a century later: that land was so abundant and tenancies so easy to obtain that there was little need for young men and women to postpone marriage until they inherited their parents' holdings. Connell, of course, stressed the importance in the late eighteenth century of the growing demand for cereals in Britain leading to the creation

[71] Drake, 'Marriage and Population Growth in Ireland', pp. 301-13.

[72] Ó Gráda, 'Demographic Adjustment', pp. 2-5; G. S. L. Tucker, 'Irish Fertility Ratios before the Famine', *Economic History Review*, 2nd Ser. xxiii (1970), 280.

[73] Joseph Lee, 'Marriage and Population in Pre-Famine Ireland', *Economic History Review*, 2nd Ser. xxi (1968), 283-5.

[74] Ó Gráda, 'The Population of Ireland 1700-1900', p. 5.

of new, small, grain farms. A century earlier, this pressure did not exist, but there was a general scarcity of tenants and young couples wishing to marry and seeking land as an economic basis to marriage could find it.[75]

The second problem is to explain why population growth apparently accelerated from the middle of the eighteenth century, even though a young age of marriage may have prevailed for more than half a century before. Once more, it is not difficult to guess at an explanation: that some time during the third quarter of the eighteenth century mortality declined as a result of the dietary and medical developments already discussed. If the saving of lives occurred principally among children,[76] then the effects would be cumulative as increasing proportions of children survived to become parents themselves. Further rises in the birth-rate and decreases in the death-rate would result from the changing age structure of population.

Ultimately the growth of population in Ireland in the way postulated would slow down. The supply of cultivatable land was finite, market conditions changed and became unfavourable to the further creation of grain farms, and landlords tried to put a brake on subdivision. In the absence of an expanding industrial sector to absorb the surplus population, Irish men and women emigrated in increasing numbers, in the process tending to remove the most fertile groups from society. And when, finally, the potato failed, uniquely high rates of population growth were followed by a fall in population, on a scale likewise unique among major European countries.

[75] It may be remarked in passing that the explanation offered here postulates the same link between economic conditions and the timing of marriage that recurs throughout Connell's discussions of marriage in Ireland. Recent work on the history of marriage and the family suggests that the whole question needs to be considered in a broader framework.

[76] Morgan has shown that in the parish of Blaris (Lisburn), County Antrim, child mortality was falling from the 1760s (Morgan, pp. 11, 15-16). A similar picture is emerging from a study of the Church of Ireland registers for the parish of Armagh (Public Record Office, Northern Ireland, T 679/140).

2. On the Accuracy of the pre-Famine Irish Censuses *

Joseph Lee

The first statutory census of the population of Ireland in the nineteenth century was taken between 1813 and 1815. Plagued by administrative difficulties, it remained officially 'incomplete', and has generally been considered unreliable.[1] While dismissing the 1813-15 census, demographic historians have relied heavily, if hesitatingly, on the decennial censuses of 1821, 1831, and 1841 as guides to pre-Famine developments. They have, too, generally accepted the verdict of the 1841 census commissioners—in effect, Thomas Larcom—concerning the relative reliability of these censuses.[2] Larcom praised the 'able' introduction to the 1821 census, though he felt that the recorded population, 6,801,827, might be an underestimate because of the inevitable pioneering difficulties.[3] He expressed more serious reservations about the quality of the 1831 census, and felt the recorded population, 7,767,401, may have been an overestimate, partly because 'it was taken in different places at different times, extending over a considerable period' and 'the enumerators considered that they would be paid—and in many cases were paid—in proportion to the numbers they enumerated, the obvious tendency of which would be to augment the total numbers'.[4] In neither case, however, did Larcom feel that the results were sufficiently erroneous to require extensive revision.[5] His verdict has been endorsed by scholars impressed

---

* I am grateful to R. Dudley Edwards for advice on sources, and to William O'Sullivan, Trinity College, Dublin, for help with the Shaw Mason papers.

[1] K. H. Connell, *The Population of Ireland, 1750-1845* (Oxford, 1950), pp. 2, 20-1; Peter Froggatt, 'The Census in Ireland of 1813-15', *Irish Historical Studies*, xiv (1965), 227-35.

[2] Connell, p. 3; S. H. Cousens, 'The Regional Variation in Emigration from Ireland between 1821 and 1841', *Transactions of the Institute of British Geographers*, (1965), 15; R. B. McDowell, *The Irish Administration* (London, 1964), p. 285.

[3] *Report of the Commissioners appointed to take the census of Ireland for the year* 1841 H.C. 1843 (504), XXIV, viii, lii. (Henceforth cited as Census of Ireland, 1841).

[4] Ibid., p. viii.   [5] Ibid.

by his professionalism and desperate for firm numerical footing after navigating the swirling hazards of eighteenth-century population estimates. Larcom's own 1841 census was generally considered reliable until Tucker's important critique, which suggested that it underestimated the number of young children by at least 150,000.[6] More recently, one local census, that of the Trinity College estates in 1843, has been analysed by Carney,[7] whose important findings are already exerting considerable influence on wider views about probable population movements between 1841 and the onset of the Famine.[8]

This paper, due to limitations of both knowledge and space, discusses only the 1821 and 1831 censuses in some detail, before casting a glance at the 1841 and 1843 returns. It is hoped, however, that even this partial investigation may draw attention to some important neglected problems.

William Shaw Mason, a pluralist office-holder,[9] organized both the 1813-15 and the 1821 censuses.[10] His technique for deducing the total population from the incomplete 1813-15 returns 'by the aid of comparative calculations founded on previous enquiries and on the partial results of the Act'[11] suggests that he was no demographer. The technique was devised by Mr Patrick Lynch, 'the author of several ingenious treatises relative to Ireland'. It is based on the simple device of projecting forward rates of change in the number of houses deduced from the returns of 1777 and 1791. 'From the number of houses returned to parliament in 1791, he deducted that of the houses returned in 1777, and thence inferred that as the intervening term of fourteen years between 1777 and 1791, is to the difference or increase of houses thus found, so is the interval of twenty three years, viz. from 1791 to 1814 to a fourth number; which, added to the number of houses in 1791,

[6] G. S. L. Tucker, 'Irish Fertility Ratios before the Famine', *Economic History Review*, 2nd Ser., xxiii (1970), 267-84.

[7] F. J. Carney, 'Pre-Famine Irish Population: The Evidence from the Trinity College Estates', *Irish Economic and Social History*, (1975), 35-45.

[8] See, for instance, F. M. L. Thompson's review of *Irish Economic and Social History* in *Irish Historical Studies*, xx (1977), 496.

[9] McDowell, p. 9.

[10] Froggatt, pp. 228-9, 234.

[11] *Abstract of answers and returns, pursuant to act 55 Geo. 3, for taking an account of the population of Ireland in 1821* H. C. 1824 (577), XXII, vii. (Henceforth cited as Census of Ireland, 1821).

should give a number equal to that of the houses in 1814 ...
The number of houses multiplied by 5.78 or 5 ¾ persons to a
house, will give the number of souls.'[12] One has some sympathy
for Lynch and Mason. Demographic historians have not
flinched from resorting to similar devices. But the technique is
based on the assumption of unchanging household size, and of
an unchanging rate of growth of population between 1777 and
1814. Neither assumption can be accepted uncritically, and
both betray a lack of sophistication compared with some earlier,
not to mention later, students of the subject.

Mason substituted for demographic knowledge a voracious
curiosity about social matters, combined with a habitual
optimism that led him to discount easily warnings about the
probable reliability of his sources, both in respect of his census
work and of his *Statistical Account*.[13]

Mason claimed to have digested the multiple lessons of the
unsatisfactory 1813-15 census, and to have greatly improved
the procedures for the 1821 census, with whose general accuracy
he declared himself 'perfectly' satisfied, 'for I took every pains
to ensure accuracy', although 'at the time I undertook it, it was
thought a hopeless attempt'.[14] The main improvement over
1813-15 was the transfer of the appointment of enumerators
from the grand juries to the resident magistrates 'aided by the
advice of a permanent legal Coadjutor, selected from among
the practising Barristers'.[15] Whatever improvement resulted
must have been mainly due to the barristers, agents of central
government intended to compensate for local laxity. The
resident magistrates were in the main the same people as the
grand jurors, and even Mason himself conceded elsewhere that
the transfer was 'more a change of office than of person'.[16]
Mason claimed to have taken six months to examine the qualifications of the enumerators, which hardly suggests complete

[12] William Shaw Mason, *A Statistical Account or Parochial Survey of Ireland* (Dublin, 1819), vol. iii, p. xlviii.

[13] William Shaw Mason, *A Statistical Account or Parochial Survey of Ireland*, 3 vols. (Dublin, 1814, 1816, 1819).

[14] *Minutes of Evidence taken before the Select Committee of the House of Lords, appointed to enquire into the state of Ireland* H.C. 1825 (521), IX, 294, Ev. W. S. Mason. (Henceforth cited as Lords' Enquiry).

[15] Census of Ireland, 1821, p. ix.

[16] Ibid., p. viii; William Shaw Mason, *Parochial Survey*, vol. iii, p. xxv.

confidence in the new procedures.[17] That several of the enumerators initially recommended by the magistrates resigned
'from a consciousness of their own inadequacy'[18] after unfortunate trial runs, to be replaced by others 'deemed more capable'[19]
(by a vague procedure), scarcely suffices to establish full confidence in the conscientiousness of the magistrates. Even then,
Belfast had to be retaken because of the inadequacy of the
original enumeration,[20] and the sense of public duty of the
enumerators in two Cork baronies did not prevent them from
withholding their returns until their fees were settled.[21]

Relatively well-informed contemporaries did not share
Mason's confidence in the calibre of the enumerators. When
Thomas Newenham, doubtless recollecting his own problems
in conducting local surveys for his population work,[22] found
that 'the number of houses for Youghal published in a Cork
newspaper is identical with the number returned to the Irish
parliament in 1800',[23] he suggested that 'recourse to my enquiry might in some instances assist in detecting that negligence on the part of the enumerators which I confess I have
always apprehended'.[24]

Mason's confidence in his enumerators may therefore carry
little more conviction than his confidence in his correspondents
for the statistical surveys. He professed to have found the clergy
of the Established Church 'very attentive to my communications',[25] though only 54 of the 2,400 parishes were covered
in his three volumes. Allowing his claim to have gathered sufficient material for one or two more volumes, this would still
amount to only a 4 per cent return by the 'very attentive' vicars.[26]

---

[17] Lords' Enquiry, p. 294.   [18] Census of Ireland, 1821, p. xiii.

[19] Ibid.   [20] Ibid., p. xiii.   [21] Ibid.

[22] Thomas Newenham, *A Statistical and Historical Inquiry into the Progress and Magnitude
of the Population of Ireland* (London, 1805), *reprinted in The Population of Ireland before the
19th Century*, with an Introduction by Joseph Lee (Farnborough, 1973).

[23] Shaw Mason Papers, Trinity College, Dublin, (henceforth TCD), MSS 1734,
Thomas Newenham to W. S. Mason, 12 October, 1821. I have followed the attributions
etc. in the invaluable Calendar compiled by the late Mrs Maureen Wall.

[24] Ibid. Newenham had earlier expressed scepticism about some of the enumerators
(TCD MSS 1734, Newenham to Mason, 19 June, 1821). So had E. W. N. Dawson,
recording his pleasure on hearing—from Mason—'that the census of population is
proceeding so successfully, I had my fears upon that subject ...' (Ibid., Dawson to
Mason, 3 August 1821).

[25] Lords' Enquiry, p. 296.   [26] Ibid.

He conveniently overlooked the comment from Patrick Lynch that 'the clergy are ... lazy drones',[27] so inferior in education and knowledge to their Scottish counterparts—who provided Sir John Sinclair with information for his statistical survey of Scotland, which Mason used as a model—that they were incompetent to undertake comparable parish surveys.[28] Little wonder that G. R. Dawson, to whom Mason dedicated the third volume of his *Survey*, professed to think highly of the compilations *'when the accuracy with which they are made can be relied upon'*.[29]

Even where the enumerators shared Mason's relish for the task, they faced formidable objective difficulties. There was considerable local hostility, which can hardly have been assuaged by the widespread resort to local tax-collectors as enumerators.[30] The local knowledge which these were deemed to possess must have been balanced, to some extent, by the suspicion their motives were likely to arouse. No list of 1821 enumerators, except for Donegal,[31] has hitherto come to hand. A national list of the 1,308 enumerators engaged in 1831 does survive, and suggests that a disproportionate number of the enumerators, as one might expect, belonged to the 'ascendancy', even if many may have been lumpen-ascendancy.[32] It is not clear, however, just how intimate their local knowledge would have been in all cases, nor how much trust would have been reposed in them by the populace at large, even where they were not tax-collectors. Shortly before, the archdeacon of Westport had apparently met a wall of silence in his endeavours

---

[27] Shaw Mason Papers, TCD, MSS 1733, Patrick Lynch to W. S. Mason, 5 September, 1817.

[28] Ibid., T. L. O'Beirne (Bishop of Meath) to W. S. Mason, 13 November, 1817.

[29] Ibid., George Dawson to W. S. Mason, 29 September 1816. Emphasis in original.

[30] Census of Ireland, 1821, p. ix.

[31] State Paper Office (henceforth SPO) OP 527/14, 'A copy of the accounts of the enumerators and others as settled from their affidavits with the compensation awarded to each claimant', January 30, 1822.

An Account, in detail, of the expenses incurred under the Population Act in Ireland, in making the last census H.C., 1830-31 (93), XIV, which might have been expected to list the payments to enumerators, consists of a return of excise payments, which prompts delicious speculations.

[32] *An account in detail, of the expenses incurred under the Population Act in Ireland, in making the census of 1831* H.C., 1833 (442), XXXIX, 2-11.

to extract information for Shaw Mason's *Statistical Survey*.[33] Appeals to the Catholic clergy in cases of disputation suggest the seriousness of the problem as much as its alleged successful resolution.[34]

Probably even more important was the absence of adequate measurements of area, or precise data on many townland or even parish boundaries. 'No list of the parishes or minor subdivisions could be procured' for County Cork.[35] Nor had the boundaries of townlands ever been ascertained in Kerry, where they were collected for the first time in the course of the census[36] —a procedure hardly designed to reassure Kerrymen, even then not universally renowned for their unfailing trust in human nature. Confusion between the boundaries of civil, Protestant, and Catholic parishes produced, on Mason's own admission, 'much difficulty in the progress of the Census'.[37] In view of this confusion it is difficult to accept without qualification Mason's claim that 'it has been ascertained that no parish whatever has been omitted'.[38] This did not convince the 1831 census commissioners, who recorded 54 parishes, with a then population of 43,000, for which no returns were apparently made in 1821.[39] The 1831 list need not be considered infallible, for that census had its own difficulties. But the general claim gains credence from the fact that sixteen of the missing parishes were located in County Cork, which obviously presented special topographical problems in 1821.[40] Mason further noted that in some counties (number unspecified) the census returns were taken by baronies instead of by parishes, and that this had affected the accuracy of the returns due to the lack of local knowledge by the enumerators of such relatively extensive areas.[41]

Mason hoped to use the census 'to obtain a statement of the number of Acres in every Townland throughout Ireland'[42] instead of relying on Beaufort's estimate of twelve million Irish

---

[33] Shaw Mason Papers, TCD, MSS 1733, Thomas Grace to Patrick Lynch, 15 August 1817.

[34] Census of Ireland, 1821, p. xii.   [35] Ibid.

[36] Ibid.   [37] Ibid., p. x.   [38] Ibid.

[39] *Census of the population, 1831, with comparative abstract as taken in 1821* H.C. 1833 (23), XXXIX, 3-41 (henceforth cited as Census of Ireland, 1831).

[40] Census of Ireland, 1821, p. xiii.

[41] Ibid., pp. xi, xv.

[42] Ibid., p. xiii.

acres for the size of the country. The handling of this problem by both the enumerators and Mason himself may cast light on their general procedures. The enumerators' returns came to only 6.8 million acres, a glaring underestimate, as Charles Grant did not hesitate to point out.[43] Mason himself referred to the results with majestic blandness: 'this attempt, as was to have been expected, had not complete success'.[44] He was not going to allow his confidence in the enumerators to be undermined by trivial oversights of this nature. He himself divided Beaufort's 12 million acres into 8 million arable, 2.5 million plantation and bog, and 1.5 million mountain and waste. But the conjectural nature of his approach seems evident from the fact that the 8 million appears to be written, as an afterthought, over an original 7.5 million, and the 2.5 million written over an original 2.0 million.[45] Latter-day 'guestimators' will not permit their sympathy for Mason's dilemma to blind them to the casualness of his techniques.

The diligence of the 1821 enumerators can be further gauged from their response to the request to distinguish the population of villages from those of parishes in the 'general observations' column on their schedules.[46] Only detailed local knowledge will suffice to test the accuracy of the returns, which seem to have varied widely from parish to parish. This writer has not ventured in any systematic manner beyond his native parish. But he has sadly to report that in the parish of Killiney in the barony of Corca Dhuibhne in the County of Kerry the enumerator did not deign to notice the existence of those far-famed cradles of culture, Castlegregory and Killiney village, which in 1831 were to have recorded populations of 970 and 263 respectively.[47] A certain residual doubt concerning the dedication of that enumerator must lurk in the historian's mind.

Mason's introduction overlooks the fate of the directive that the clerks of the peace of the counties and the town clerks should copy all the enumerators' returns and lodge them safely

---

[43] Shaw Mason Papers, TCD, MSS 1735, Charles Grant to W. S. Mason, 26 February 1822.

[44] Census of Ireland, 1821, p. xiii.

[45] Shaw Mason Papers, TCD, MSS 1735, W. S. Mason to Charles Grant 16 March 1822.

[46] Census of Ireland, 1821, p. xiii.

[47] Census of Ireland, 1831, p. 162.

'among the county records', before dispatching them to the chief secretary.[48] Neither the financial incentive contained in the Act, nor the threat of fine for failure to comply,[49] sufficed to rouse the local authorities to action. These provisions were hastily repealed less than a year after the census, because 'great delays have occurred ... and such copies have not in many instances been made'.[50] If local authorities chose to ignore an uncongenial provision, it is not inconceivable that they also failed to subject the enumerators' returns to exhaustive scrutiny before authorizing their dispatch to Dublin Castle.

Certain of the census procedures themselves militated against comprehensive coverage. The census was taken viva voce over a two-month period, beginning on 28 May and lasting at least until 28 July.[51] In addition, census directions concerning categories such as 'visitors' and 'beggars', were either ambiguous, non-existent, or futile.[52] Interpreters had to be used in Irish-speaking areas.[53] Seasonal labourers were likely to be increasingly on the move throughout the period. The 1841 commissioners recorded 58,000 seasonal labourers, on their own admission a considerable underestimate, leaving Ireland for Britain in the summer of 1841.[54] In addition, there was a regular internal migration flow of seasonal labourers from west to east.[55] It remains unclear if, or where, they were counted. Shaw Mason's introduction does not consider the issue.

The different totals returned at various times by Mason do not increase confidence in the absolute accuracy of the 1821 returns. His first estimate, dated 28 November 1821—'it is only this day we first began to see the light'—was 6,648,033.[56]

---

[48] 55 Geo. III, c.xx.   [49] Ibid.   [50] 3 Geo. IV, c.v.

[51] Census of Ireland, 1821, p. 387; SPO, OP 527/14, William C. Spence, Lifford: *Accounts of the enumerators* ..., records many enumerators claiming for more than fifty days' work.

[52] Census of Ireland, 1821, Appendix I, p. 387. National Library of Ireland (hereafter NLI) MS 12788, p. 7.

[53] SPO, OP 527/14.

[54] Census of Ireland, 1841, p. xxvi.

[55] Cormac Ó Gráda estimated there may have been 35,000-40,000 seasonal migrants to Britain, and a further 35,000-40,000 internal seasonal migrants by the mid-1830s; 'Seasonal Migration and Post-Famine adjustment in the West of Ireland', *Studia Hibernica*, xiii (1973), 51.

[56] Shaw Mason Papers, TCD, MSS 1734, Mason to Thomas Newenham. (I follow Mrs Wall's attribution), 28 November 1821.

The light brightened twice more, to the extent that two different final totals were actually published in parliamentary papers, without adequate clarificatory comment. The first, in 1822, amounted to 6,846,949.[57] The final official return in 1824 was 6,801,826.[58] It is true that the 1822 returns, dated as early as 22 February, contained the qualification that 'though generally accurate, they are in some instances defective; but not to such a degree as materially to affect the results'.[59] Only sixteen of the county and towns-of-county returns had been verified by the magistrates at that stage. Though verification by the magistrates did not ensure complete clerical accuracy, most of the subsequent changes in these 'verified' returns were minor, except in the case of Meath, whose total was subsequently reduced by nearly 20 per cent. More disturbingly, the decline of 45,000 recorded between the two published figures represents the net conclusion of wider variations at the provincial level, as Table 2.1 indicates.

Table 2.1

	1822	*1824*	
Leinster	1 785 702	1 757 492	− 28 210
Munster	2 005 363	1 935 612	− 69 751
Ulster	2 001 966	1 998 494	− 3 472
Connaught	1 053 918	1 110 229	+ 56 311
TOTAL:	6,846,949	6,801,827	− 45,222

The situation becomes more complex when the roughly 5 per cent decline in the reported Connaught total appears to coincide with an increase in the number of recorded houses from 191,267 in the 1822 returns to 197,408 in the 1824 returns. It is unfortunate that the introduction to a census that appeared to a committee of the London Statistical Society 'to have been by far the most perfect in its machinery and method of any that has yet been executed in these islands'[60] should contain no comment on this particular issue.

[57] *Abstract of the population of Ireland according to the late census*, H.C. 1822 (36), XIV.
[58] Census of Ireland, 1821.
[59] *Abstract of the population of Ireland ...*, 1822 (36), XIV, 2.
[60] Quoted in Froggatt, p. 234.

What conclusions can be reasonably inferred from this account? Whatever the possible answers, it is certainly time for scholars to begin quantifying Larcom's verdict on the 1821 census of 'rather below than above the truth'.[61] The administration of the 1821 census, though presumably a marked improvement on that of 1813-15, still fell far short of perfection. Early censuses notoriously tend to underrate population. The underrepresentation in the English census of 1801 may have been at least 5 per cent, in that of 1811 3 per cent, and in that of 1821 1 per cent.[62] A 1 per cent underenumeration in Ireland would imply a real population of about 6,870,000. A 3 per cent underenumeration would imply a population in excess of 7 million. A 5 per cent underenumeration, far from inconceivable, would imply a population of nearly 7.2 million. If one applies Tucker's conclusions concerning the underenumeration of children in the 1841 census to 1821, when at least the same degree of underenumeration probably occurred, about 120,000 infants were overlooked. Perhaps 30,000 seasonal labourers, beggars, and visitors escaped the enumerators' attention. How many suspicious and/or remote inhabitants were silently missing from the returns? In the light of the above discussion, it may be hazarded that a figure comfortably in excess of 7 million —I suggest 7.2 million— is more plausible than the official return of 6.8 million.

The 1831 census has long suffered from the derision of Larcom's comments. It was inferior in certain respects to the 1821 census, though this may have been the result more of English administrative pressure, determined to restrict the Irish census to the level of the less ambitiously conceived English census, than of Dublin Castle indolence.[63] Enumerators were no longer required to return the names of all the inhabitants, only of household heads. The census has, however,

---

[61] Census of Ireland, 1841, p. viii.

[62] J. T. Krause, 'Changes in English Fertility and Mortality, 1781-1850', *Economic History Review*, 2nd Ser. xi (1958), 60. The earliest Scottish censuses also probably involve some underenumeration, though perhaps relatively slight. See Michael Flinn, ed., *Scottish Population History* (Cambridge, 1977), p. 52.

[63] 1 Will. IV, c. xix. Shaw Mason had been obliged to follow Rickman's presentation style in publishing his 1821 returns, in much less ambitious form than he wished. (TCD, MSS 1735, W. S. Mason to Charles Grant, 25 January, 1823; Sir John Newport to W. S. Mason, 7 August, 1823).

been singled out for unfair criticism in other respects. The viva-voce principle, and the collection over a period of time, simply continued the practice of 1821, and indeed of contemporary English censuses, on which the Irish procedures were compulsorily based. They were in no way unique to the 1831 census.

It is the suggestion that enumerators expected to be paid by results that has earned the amused condescension of posterity.[64] No attempt seems to have been made to quantify the probable degree of exaggeration, beyond Larcom's own concession that it was scarcely sufficient (but how could he know?) to affect the order of magnitude. Was it 1 per cent? 5 per cent? 10 per cent? 50 per cent? What are the parameters of plausibility? What was to stop an ambitious enumerator inflating his figures really remuneratively?

The fact is that there was nothing unique about the specified payments procedures in 1831. The relevant clauses in the Act were taken from those in the relevant Act for the 1821 census, which in turn were based on the corresponding English Acts.[65] Enumerators were to be generally paid by the day, not by the head.[66] It does seem clear that in practice different procedures were adopted in different localities in 1831.[67] If the rumour that payment by results gained credence among some enumerators (how many?), it is not inconceivable that much the same had occurred in 1821—confusion about payments procedures in Cork points in this direction—and indeed in 1813, where Shaw Mason records a case of the enumeration of infants in the womb.[68] In both cases, however, the national total probably lies well above the recorded figure, in 1813 by general admission. Why should not the same hold true in 1831?

The simplest way to enhance enumerators' earnings was not by inflating the population, which required laborious clerical work, uncongenial filling-out of forms, possible recrimination from Dublin Castle, and perjury, but by simply limiting the

---

[64] See McDowell, p. 283, where all enumerators, as distinct from some enumerators, were allegedly paid according to the numbers returned.

[65] 1 Will. IV, c. xix; 11 Geo. IV, c. xxx; 52 Geo. III, c. cxxxiii.

[66] Ibid.

[67] *Expenses incurred ... in Making the Census of 1831* H.C. 1833 (442), XXXIX, 2-11.

[68] Mason, *Parochial Survey*, iii, p. xxiv, note.

number of enumerators. The number officially recorded for 1831 did differ alarmingly from county to county, suggesting that certain magistrates were more alert to the potential than others. Kerry, with a recorded population of 263,000, had only nine recorded enumerators, whereas Louth, with a recorded population of 125,000, had thirty eight.[69] Limiting the number of enumerators was likely to result in an underestimate of population, particularly if they left themselves with too much ground to cover. They may of course have subcontracted much of their work. In either case, the degree of casualness apparently involved will not automatically have resulted in an inflation of the real population.[70]

The 1831 enumerators certainly did not take full advantage of the inflationary opportunities allegedly available. Fourteen villages are recorded as no longer in existence—in some cases obviously erroneously—compared with 1821.[71] If the Commissioners of Public Instruction noted in 1835 that some townlands had been double counted, and included in more than one parish, they also noted cases where townlands had been completely overlooked. There seems to be no consistent direction in the errors.[72] The Commissioners, incidentally, unlike Larcom 'had every reason to be satisfied' at the 'general correctness' of the 1831 census.[73]

The coincidence of rates of population change in neighbouring baronies within counties, and even across county-boundaries, is instructive. The whole south-east area, including the Wexford baronies of Forth, Bargy, and Shelbourne (an actual loss of population), Gaultier in Waterford (another loss, bordering Shelbourne), and the south Kilkenny baronies of Kells (another loss), Ida, Iverk, and Knocktopher, recorded very slow over-all growth. These baronies were presumably enumerated by different officials, even within the counties,

---

[69] *Expenses incurred ... in Making the Census of 1831* H.C. 1833 (442), XXXIX, 2 ff.

[70] The financial incentives did not prevent some returns being still outstanding as late as June 1833. Ibid.

[71] Census of Ireland, 1831, pp. 3-41, notes. Examples include Tinnahinch and Castletown, which reappear in 1841.

[72] *First Report of the Commissioners of Public Instruction in Ireland* H. C. 1835 (45), XXXIII, 5.

[73] Ibid., p. 6. Unfortunately, this too must be taken with a grain of salt. It was in the commissioners' interest to express satisfaction with the 1831 Census. Otherwise they might have been expected to do much more work themselves.

much less between them. Wexford had 46 official enumerators for 10 baronies, Waterford 20 for 8, and Kilkenny County 78 for 12.[74] It seems unlikely that results emanating from so many different sources could have been so consistent, unless they came fairly close to recording reality, or at least achieved a fairly consistent degree of either overenumeration or under-enumeration with, in the circumstances, underenumeration appearing the more plausible alternative.

Considerable consistency also prevails in this respect else-where. The two Carlow baronies to record losses, Forth and Idrone East, border on each other. Offaly East, the sole Kildare barony recording a decline, borders on Talbotstown Upper, the sole Wicklow barony showing a fall. The two Westmeath baronies to lose population, Farbill and Moyashel and Maghera Dernan, bordered on each other. So did the two Limerick baronies to record declines, Kenry and Pubblebrien. The four Cork baronies to record losses, Carbery West (Eastern Division), Ibane and Barryroe, Kinalmeaky, and Courceys, though narrowly separated from each other by intervening strips, were all clustered on the south coast. Baronies which lost population in apparent isolation included Stradbally in Queens County (Laois), and Ardagh in Longford. In both cases, how-ever, the neighbouring baronies of Cullinagh and Granard respectively, recorded only marginal increases.

Must suspicion then be confined to the apparently fastest-growing baronies? Suspicion certainly must attach to some of these cases, pending more detailed investigation. Even here, however, rates of growth varied widely between parishes within 'problem' baronies. A few examples must suffice to illustrate the variety of local conditions to be taken into account before convincing conclusions can be drawn.

The barony of Lower Ormond in Tipperary recorded a 30 per cent rate of increase, from 34,700 in 1821 to 45,000 in 1831, before slowing down to an 11 per cent rate of increase in the 1830s to reach a population of 50,000 in 1841. Within the barony, however, the parish of Finoe actually recorded a loss from 1,730 to 1,399 between 1821 and 1831. Knigh rose only from 1,407 to 1,447, Loughkeen and Ballyloughnane jointly

---

[74] *Expenses incurred ... in Making the Census of 1831* H.C. 1833 (442), XXXIX, 2 ff.

from 2,609 to 2,691. The most important factor contributing to the apparent increase was a return of 4,506 for the parish of Modreany and the village of Cloughjordan, for which no return was apparently recorded in 1821. Their omission reduces the rate of growth in the barony from 30 per cent to 14 per cent over the decade.

Mayo recorded the fastest rate of growth of any county between 1821 and 1831. Within Mayo, the barony of Costello recorded the highest rate of growth, 36.8 per cent, with population rising from 32,900 to 45,000. Only two parishes in the barony, however, Kilbeagh and Aghamore, record implausibly fast rates. There was no return for the parish of Bunin Adden in 1821, which had 1,199 inhabitants in 1831. Nor, however, was this parish recorded in 1841. Whether it was a figment of an ambitious enumerator's imagination, or does in fact reflect local reality behind changing nomenclature or boundaries, awaits further investigation.[75] The barony of Loughrea in Galway recorded an increase of more than 50 per cent, more than double the county average of 23 per cent. But fifteen of the twenty parishes lay partly outside the barony. One would need to know precisely how these were allocated in 1821 before dismissing the increase as impossibly rapid. The barony of Ballinahinch in Galway also shows a very rapid growth of nearly 50 per cent. Of its four parishes, Ballindoon recorded a relatively slow growth of about 16 per cent. In the much faster-growing parish of Omey, the sharp rise in the population of Clifden town accounted for nearly half the increase. This was the decade of the Nimmo road, when literary evidence suggests that Clifden mushroomed.[76] The other two parishes remain a problem, though in all cases the recorded 1841 population was higher than that of 1831. In view of the degree of movement occurring in this area as a result of improved communications, and in view also of the distinct possibility of significant underenumeration in this remote and trackless region in 1821, it seems

[75] A village (not a parish) approximating phonetically to Bunin Adden exists just outside the barony, across the county border in Sligo. I am indebted to John Coakley for this information. It seems doubtful in the circumstances if the 1831 enumerator was consciously faking his results. The population he returns for Bunin Adden was much the smallest for any Costello 'parish'.

[76] T. W. Freeman, *Pre-Famine Ireland* (Manchester, 1957), pp. 107, 244, 267.

premature, pending detailed local investigation, to assume automatically that the error lies with an inflated 1831 return.

Even where neighbouring baronies record suspiciously divergent rates of growth between 1821 and 1831, it cannot be assumed that the faster rate must have been inflated. Consider Table 2.2.

Table 2.2

Barony	Population (000)		
	1821	1831	1841
Ibrickane	16.2	20.5	25.2
Inchiquin	16.2	18.6	21.2
Carrigallen	23.0	26.1	28.3
Drumahaire	23.4	31.6	35.8

In Clare, the neighbouring baronies Ibrickane and Inchiquin recorded similar populations in 1821. Ibrickane pulled suspiciously ahead in 1831, but the difference appears to be confirmed by the 1841 census, where the returns are compatible with the 1831 figures. The same appears to be the case with the experience of the neighbouring baronies of Carrigallen and Drumahaire in Leitrim.

The 1831 enumerators faced fewer difficulties concerning topographical boundaries, but presumably confronted much the same degree of hostility and suspicion as their 1821 predecessors. Seasonal labourers, visitors, and beggars were probably overlooked to much the same degree. It is clear also that at least some of the clerks engaged in the final compilation failed to enjoy total job satisfaction. The returns are riddled with transcription errors and inconsistencies of detail.[77] The 1831 enumerators, for instance, were required to return villages separately from parishes. The 1821 enumerators were not, but were requested to include in their observations column 'names of towns and villages in each townland...'[78] The 1831 clerks overlooked these returns, however incomplete, in compiling their comparative abstract for 1821 and 1831, as a result of

[77] Compare, for instance, the population figures for the parishes of Moorstown Kirk and Graystown in Tipperary as recorded in the main text, (pp. 192-3) and in the *Comparative Abstract* (see footnote 39 above), pp. 27-8.

[78] Census of Ireland, 1821, p. 385.

mechanically entering 'no return' for 1821 against the names of all their separately returned villages.[79]

Nevertheless, the abiding impression of the 1831 census does not justify its casual dismissal in comparison with that of 1821. George Hatchell, the census commissioner, who was appointed after Shaw Mason came under a cloud,[80] dispensed with an introduction to the census report. This may have been interpreted as an implicit confession of inadequacy, particularly when contrasted not only with Mason's introduction to the 1821 census but also with Larcom's magisterial introduction to that of 1841. It may be, however, that Hatchell was simply more alert than Mason to the inherent problems of census-taking in Ireland, and had a more modest self-image. His cryptic comment that 'the number of acres given for each province is taken from the best authorities extant; it being quite impracticable to obtain a correct return from the respective enumerators of the acreable contents of each parish'[81] faced the problem more realistically than the optimistic Mason. Hatchell's instructions to his enumerators were a sensible adaptation to Irish circumstances within the limits permitted by the Act, which enjoined him to follow English example, and he had the good sense to instruct his enumerators always to check with the clergy.[82]

The variations in household size between 1821 and 1841 do seem to suggest an unlikely rate of increase in the 1820s, casting further suspicion on the 1831 returns. These are normally quoted as in Table 2.3:

Table 2.3[83]   Household size

1821	5.95
1831	6.21
1841	5.9

---

[79] Among the numerous examples see, for instance, the treatment of Abbeyleix; or of Benmore, Finuge, and Kilflyn in the barony of Clanmaurice, Co. Kerry.

[80] McDowell, p. 10.

[81] Census of Ireland, 1831, p. 342.

[82] The Census volume does not contain the instructions. They can be found in 'Population, Mohill Estate, 1831', NLI, MS 12788.

[83] Connell, p. 17.

The correct figures, however, appear to be as follows:

Table 2.4[84]   Household size

1821	5.95
1831	6.21
1841	6.15

This brings the 1831 figure more into line with that of 1841, and in turn casts some doubt on the now suspiciously low 1821 figure, reinforcing reservations about the possible extent of underenumeration in that census.

In the light of the above considerations, it seems that whatever tendency to inflation may have marked the 1831 proceedings was more than counterbalanced by other tendencies making for underenumeration. The recorded population was 7.767 million. Allowing, for argument's and convenience's sake, an 'inflationary' excess of 67,000, would reduce this to 7.7 million. It is suggested that this should be increased by about 140,000 to cover, on the Tucker principle, children overlooked by the enumerators. A further 1 per cent for general underenumeration (a conservative assumption, I think) would add a further 80,000. This suggests a real population of about 7.9 million in 1831.

The 1841 census marked a breakthrough in Irish census techniques. The commissioners, under Larcom's inspiration, no longer relied on a viva-voce enquiry spread over a couple of months. Instead, the enumeration referred to a single day (June 6) and the returns were to be made, wherever possible, by the householders themselves. Larcom dispensed with enumerators appointed by the magistrates. He obviously did not share Mason's confidence in them. Instead, he relied on the constabulary supplemented, where necessary, by other agents of central government like coastguards. Some hostility was still encountered, but much useful additional information was collected, and the census was almost certainly more accurate than any earlier efforts.

Larcom was a more professional demographer than either Shaw Mason or Hatchell. He nevertheless apparently failed to anticipate the difficulty caused by holding a census on a Sunday,

[84] Calculated from Census of Ireland, 1841, pp. viii, xv.

the great visiting day in Ireland, and a day specifically avoided by the 1821 and 1831 enumerators.[85] 'Visitors' accounted for 15 per cent of the total population recorded in 1841.[86] At the national level they cancel each other out, and many in any case were lodgers and relatives.[87] But the smaller the unit of analysis, the more it is likely to be distorted by genuine visitors from neighbouring townlands or parishes. At the local level this makes the 1841 census a treacherous base for comparative purposes. It has been noted elsewhere that Larcom, for all his sophistication and dedication, fails to make allowance for other problems such as the underrecording of infants,[88] age clustering,[89] and, in the agricultural statistics, returns in Irish rather than English acres.[90] The 1841 census schedule, with its wide range of questions, was the first to be actually presented to household heads for their perusal. It must have been a traumatic experience for many of them. The outcome of the 1971 Irish census, which resulted in significant underenumeration due apparently to the extra trouble imposed on householders by its ambitious design, serves as a warning of the way in which private initiative can silently sabotage the best-laid public plans. It seems possible, despite Larcom's heroic efforts, that the 1841 census suffers from adult underenumeration of at least 1 per cent. This would raise the real total to over 8,250,000. Adding the 150,000 or more extra children detected by Tucker would bring the total to just over 8.4 million.

It is therefore tentatively suggested that the real population of Ireland that should have been recorded by the censuses was as in Table 2.5:

Table 2.5

	Census figures (millions)	Real figures
1821	6.802	7.2
1831	7.767	7.9
1841	8.175	8.4

[85] Census of Ireland, 1821, Appendix II, p. 338; NLI, MS 12788, Enumerators' oath, following p. 8.

[86] Census of Ireland, 1841, p. xii.   [87] Ibid.   [88] Tucker, *passim.*

[89] Joseph Lee, 'Marriage and Population in Pre-Famine Ireland', *Economic History Review*, 2nd Ser., xxii (1968), 288 ff.

[90] P. M. Austin Bourke, 'The Agricultural Statistics of the 1841 Census of Ireland. A Critical Review', *Economic History Review*, xviii (1965), 376-91.

When oversights of the type mentioned could occur even in the case of as able and conscientious a commissioner as Larcom, it is doubtful if any purely private undertaking could have achieved complete success. The census of the estates of Trinity College, Dublin, was held in 1843. The main estate agent claimed that he appointed 'competent' persons for this purpose. It is impossible to test this claim of competency, but it appears that the census was taken on a viva-voce basis and spread over a period of time.[91] The enumerators seem to have been at least as unaware as Larcom of the tendency towards underenumeration of children. Trinity College had considerable holdings in Kerry. For what it is worth, the proportion of children aged under twelve months to those aged 'between 2 and 4' was 52.3 per cent in the Trinity College survey, compared with 54 per cent for all Kerry in 1841. When so much unreliability attaches to the total figures recorded at these ages, it seems premature to base any conclusion about trends on differences of this sort. In addition, unless it was conducted on a June Sunday, the Trinity College returns at townland level can hardly be compared confidently with those recorded in 1841. There were in 1841 495 'visitors' to the rural part of Aghavallen parish, and 94 to Ballylongford town, both on the estate. But we do not know the direction of net movement. It might reinforce the case for population decline or it might not. It may be that to some extent movements of visitors help explain gyrations in townland populations at this time. Thirteen per cent of townlands on the Trinity estates experienced population falls of more than 20 per cent, and 30 per cent of more than 10 per cent. Eleven per cent experienced population growth of more than 20 per cent, 18 per cent of more than 10 per cent, and 27 per cent of more than 5 per cent. Movements of this apparent magnitude over a two-year period would have to be confirmed by a good deal more local evidence to carry full conviction.

It is not to detract from Carney's illuminating study to suggest that it may run the risk of being asked to bear a burden of interpretation which the underlying fragility of the source material renders excessive. The interpretation may be correct.

---

[91] *Report from H.M. Commissioners of Inquiry into the State of the Law and Practice in respect to the Occupation of Land in Ireland* H.C. 1845 (606), XIX, pp. 301 ff., Ev. Maurice Collis.

But no generalization concerning changes in population trends between 1841 and 1845 can be based on this evidence at present.

This preliminary enquiry suggests that much remains to be learned about the administrative and the demographic history of the pre-Famine censuses. Connell's famous Table 4[92] may itself require revision below, as well as above, the 'census figures' line. The implications of such a revision cannot be pursued here. First it must be established, through more detailed enquiry, whether the revised estimates suggested in this paper can themselves survive further scrutiny. What does seem clear is that whatever the population of Ireland may have been in 1821, 1831, and 1841, it was not that recorded in the censuses.

[92] Connell, p. 25.

3. The Demography of the Irish Quakers, 1650-1850*

D. E. C. Eversley

I

Introduction

Since 1960, Richard Vann of Wesleyan University, Connecticut, and the present author have been working on the registers of the Society of Friends (Quakers) with a view to establishing the course of the demographic transition (decline in mortality followed by decline in fertility) in that relatively small but well-documented sub-group within the British and Irish nonconformist populations. It was not until 1967 that there was any real prospect of analysing the material described below by modern methods, and not until 1977 that the first reliable tables became available from the computers operated by the Cambridge Group for the History of Population and Social Structure (Campop). This chapter describes very briefly the earliest results of this research, and confines itself mainly to a comparison of the fertility of the English (Southern Rural) and Irish Quakers. Space constraints forbid the detailed explanation of the methods used, and the compressed tables present some generalizations which have restricted validity. It is hoped to publish the full material within a year from the appearance of this volume.

Material and location

Membership of the Society of Friends (Quakers) could, and still can, only be acquired either by birthright or by convincement. Births and convincements were recorded at the local

* The full acknowledgements to the very large number of people who helped to extract and process the information on which this paper is based will appear in our forthcoming report. For this chapter, the author wishes to thank Clare Currey for abridging the text from the fuller manuscript, and constructing the compressed tables from the fifty originals on which they are based. Gail Hickman typed the manuscript.

Richard Vann read the manuscript and suggested numerous improvements, not all of which have been incorporated into the text.

level. Births and deaths were entered into special registers at
the Monthly Meeting level. Marriages took place in Meeting
and were witnessed by those present; the certificates were
preserved and the event also recorded in Monthly Meeting
registers. Great care seems normally to have been exercised in
the keeping of these records. Conversely, the privilege of membership was formerly strictly guarded and when members fell
into laxer ways, or 'married out', they were usually disowned.
When Friends moved to another Meeting, a complex procedure marking transfer of membership was followed. The
change was supposed to be recorded.

There is some internal evidence that registration was not as
good in the Southern Rural Quaker population, as it was in
Ireland. Some underrecording is possible, but it is doubtful
whether this would invalidate the findings presented here.
Separate registers survive virtually in their totality both for
Ireland and for the rest of the British Isles. The Irish Quakers,
however, kept in addition to the separate chronological records
of events, 'Family Lists', which record the marriage of a couple,
the children born to them, and usually which of those children
died in childhood or, if they survived, whom they married.[1]

It will be seen that the material is immensely rich. Moreover,
it was easily accessible to researchers: the Act of Parliament[2]
which created civil registration in Great Britain was only par-

---

[1] Isabel Grubb, *Quakers in Ireland 1654-1900* (London, 1927), p. 85; John Stephenson
Rowntree, *Quakerism past and present, being an enquiry into the causes of its decline in Great
Britain and Ireland,* (London, 1852). (Discipline was revived in 1760 in England, and
this led to a fresh fall in numbers. See chapter 6, pp. 117 ff. and chapter 7, pp. 144
ff.) There were also complaints about Irish laxity. Irish Friends themselves were
concerned at slipping standards: see Rufus M. Jones, *The Later Periods of Quakerism,*
vol. i, (London, 1921), pp. 295-9. William Savery was shocked by Irish 'secret
infidelity': see p. 280; Richard T. Vann, *The Social Development of English Quakerism
1655-1755* (Cambridge, Mass., 1969); O. C. Goodbody, *Guide to Irish Quaker Records
1654-1860* (Dublin, 1967), pp. 6 ff. for the method of reporting sufferings and other
important events to Monthly Meeting, and the transmission of these records to the
National Meeting at Dublin from 1669. It is not clear at what stage these details
began to be regularly reported to London; E. M. Milligan in *Britannica on Quakerism*
(London, 1965), p. 6 - cf. Thomas Holm and James Fuller, *A Compendious View of the
Extraordinary Suffering of the People called Quakers*, 2 vols. (Dublin, 1753).

[2] 3 & 4 Victoria, cap. 92. For details of English Quaker practice, see William
C. Braithwaite, *The Beginnings of Quakerism* (Cambridge, 1955, 2nd ed. revised by
H. J. Cadbury), pp. 144 ff. and note, p. 558; *Lists of Non-Parochial Registers and
Records in the Custody of the Registrar-General of Births, Deaths and Marriages* (Wm. Clowes
for HMSO, London, 1841).

tially applied in Ireland and the nonconformist churches there were not obliged to deliver up their registers to the Public Record Office. Richard Vann has already presented the first results of the analysis of the English Quaker registers, based on the chronological index volumes ('Digests') in Friends House, London, while access to the Irish material was provided by Olive Goodbody, Historian of Ireland Yearly Meeting in Dublin.[3]

Irish Quakers emerge from the records as a peculiar group.[4] Many of them initially were 'in humble circumstances' but by the end of the period studied (1850) they appear as middle to upper middle class, affluent, travelling a great deal but not hazardously, making money and reinvesting it rather than spending it too ostentatiously, marrying probably as much for business as for romantic reasons. The registers (and the original marriage certificates with fuller information about brides and grooms and their parents) make it clear that we have practically no labourers, and at least after 1700, no identifiable gentry. William Penn, perhaps the most celebrated Quaker with Irish associations, was an altogether exceptional case.[5] Some of the early converts were humble artisans, others were army officers. Later the two outer ends of the social spectrum disappear.

Reliability

The Irish Quakers, intensely conscious of their English identity (for very few were of Irish origin) often adhered to the strict customs and practices prevalent in the early years of English Quakerism after their co-religionists in England had to some

---

[3] 'The early registers are variously named: Family Lists, Lineage Books or registers, e.g., Mountmellick: Book of Mountmellick Meetings from 1667, Sufferings, Family-Lists, Marriage Certificates, Testimonies, etc.', Goodbody, p. 8; for inventory of Family Lists for all Irish Monthly Meetings, see Goodbody, p. 31. The words 'Family List' do not occur very often, but the 'digests' often contain similar information.

[4] John Rutty, *A History of the Rise and Progress of the People called Quakers, in Ireland, from the Year 1653 to 1700* (London, 1811, 4th ed.) pp. 72 ff.; Braithwaite, pp. 210-23; Grubb, pp. 20-30, 36-9; T. C. Barnard, *Cromwellian Ireland: English Government in Ireland* (Oxford, 1974). For the distribution of Quakers in Ireland, see the end-paper map in Isabel Grubb, 'Social conditions in Ireland in the seventeenth and eighteenth centuries as illustrated by early Quaker records', (unpublished MA thesis, University of London, 1916). Copy in Friends House Library, London.

[5] William Penn, *My Irish Journal 1669-1670*, ed. Isabel Grubb (London, 1952); Rutty, pp. 112-15; Grubb, 'Social conditions ...', pp. 31 ff.

extent abandoned them. The records were kept with loving care, and are therefore quite different from Anglican registers which were often kept by absentee incumbents or, as during the Commonwealth period, not at all, and where the entries of even conscientious priests were not subject to the elaborate ritual of cross-checking which was typical of the persecuted and community-conscious Quaker laity, the Registering Officers later called Registrars.[6]

It should also be pointed out that Quakers did not practise baptism: therefore the records refer always to births. Lord Hardwicke's Marriage Act, such an important watershed in Anglican registration, was unnecessary for the Quakers who already carefully recorded every marriage. Other factors affecting the accuracy of Anglican registration, such as bad weather or the absence of the incumbent postponing baptism and therefore the recording of a birth, or the problems created by the existence of both public and private baptisms, do not arise. The Quaker material is more accurate, over a longer period of time, than all but the best of the Anglican registers, and much less fragmentary than the Roman Catholic and non-conformist records in general.

Whereas Anglican registers always refer to single parishes, and therefore make it impossible to reconstitute a family's demographic history if it changed its parish of residence, Quaker records were collected into Monthly, and then Quarterly Meeting records, so that thanks to the Family Lists and the Friends House Digests it is usually quite easy to complete records even if people moved around a great deal. By contrast, however, frequent 'disownment' or voluntary resignations connected with the application of Church Discipline, and, in the eighteenth century, a high propensity to emigrate to North America mean that individuals and families are more often lost to the record system altogether. This made it necessary to

---

[6] Before 1836, these were often the Clerks of the Meeting: from 1837, Registrars of Marriages were appointed under the Civil Registration Act. Religious Society of Friends, *Church Government* (London Yearly Meeting, 1968), pp. 885, 910, 912-13, 917. For details of Quaker marriages and their validity, see Braithwaite, pp. 144-6. Act for Registering Births, Marriages and Deaths in England, 6 & 7 Will. IV, cap. 85, as amended by the Act of 1837, cap. 35. s. 2, Marriages of Jews and Quakers. Further confirmation of the validity of Quaker marriages can be found in 10 & 11 Victoria, cap. 58.

apply very strict analytical tests to make sure that the statistics relate only to families 'in observation', i.e. still 'at risk', e.g. of dying before reaching adulthood. This often meant that a promising family reconstitution form could be only partially used (e.g. for early birth intervals), since no inferences could be made about the later history of people who were no longer Quakers or had gone to Pennsylvania.

Analysis method

Broadly, the analysis was undertaken in this way: for the whole of Ireland, we produced about 2,500 family reconstitution forms (see Table 3.1 for breakdown by Monthly Meeting areas). Of these, 1,755 or just over 70%, were useable as a whole or in large part, but only 1,330 (53%) were used in the majority of calculations, after excluding certain estimated dates. The distribution both of the higher and the lower figure by decennial period is shown in Table 3.2.

Table 3.1   Family Reconstitution Forms, Ireland

Distribution of Family Lists transcribed

Cork	441
Dublin	438
Limerick	207
Lurgan	35
Mote	64
Mountmellick	733
Newgarden	46
Tipperary	143
Waterford	81
Wexford	202
Wicklow	94
	2 484

Source: Reconstitution forms (FRF's) held in the library of Friends House, London, in 1977.

Table 3.2   Marriages by Decennial Period

	1st round	2nd round
Before 1650	23	12
1650-59	48	21
1660-69	66	38
1670-79	115	82
1680-89	142	112
1690-99	158	119
1700-09	157	119
1710-19	151	117
1720-29	102	82
1730-39	103	87
1740-49	98	78
1750-59	100	78
1760-69	69	55
1770-79	91	66
1780-89	80	54
1790-99	62	42
1800-09	44	35
1810-19	41	25
1820-29	24	19
later	81	89
	1 755	1 330

For England and Ireland together, we made up some 12,000 forms of which something over 8,000 found their way into the final analysis by areas. In the Tables, comparisons have been confined to Quaker families of southern rural England (SRUR). SRUR covers Southern Quarterly Meetings (Norfolk, Cambridgeshire and Huntingdonshire, Bedfordshire and Hertfordshire, Buckinghamshire, Berkshire and Oxfordshire Quarterly Meetings, and a random sample from Sussex of approximately 15 per cent) with the exception of London and Middlesex, and the Norwich and Bristol registers. The forms, containing over 100,000 separate events, were analysed according to the methods originating in France[7] which prescribed the measures to be taken, and the later advances in computerized analysis which are attributable especially to Roger Schofield and his colleagues of the Cambridge Group.[8]

In the text reference is made repeatedly to the OMNIQUAK program which incorporates all Quaker families in Britain and Ireland. For space reasons, none of these tables are reproduced. They are larger because the much greater number of cases enabled the total to be divided into seven cohorts (from 1675 to 1850) instead of the four which was the maximum deemed feasible for Ireland and the other regions. This information for twenty-five year periods makes it possible to pinpoint more accurately the important turning-points of the demographic transition: the fall in mortality, and the fall in fertility.

II

1. *The approach to fertility*

In lay language, we refer to fertility by talking about birth-rates. In historical demography, such rates are often not available, because to establish them we need to know the total size of the population, as well as the number of annual events. In any case, the crude birth-rate does not really tell us anything about reproductive behaviour. The analysis of fertility therefore, as presented here, is dictated both by the nature of the material

---

[7] M. Fleury and L. Henry, *Nouveau Manuel de dépouillement et d'exploitation de l'état civil ancien* (Paris, 1965); E. A. Wrigley, ed., *An Introduction to English Historical Demography* (London, 1966).

[8] E. A. Wrigley and R. S. Schofield, *The Population History of England, 1541-1871: a Reconstruction* (London, 1981).

and the need to produce statistics which tie in over-all numbers with the behaviour of individual couples. A start is made by looking at the age at marriage, and this is followed up with an analysis of age and duration-specific fertility rates, total family size, and birth intervals. Other measures of fertility are possible but have here been omitted. Although general mortality is excluded from this chapter, it ends with an examination of infant and child mortality rates (to see whether differences in numbers of births in large families, for instance, would lead, eventually, to more young people surviving to reproductive age), and also some very rough comparisons of adult expectation of life at various ages so as to test the possibility that chances of marriages surviving intact throughout the reproductive period may have influenced fertility patterns. Other tests of alternative hypotheses were made, but are here omitted. It should only be stated that none of them invalidate the conclusion presented in part III.

2.   *Ages at marriage (Table 3.3)*

John Hajnal[9] destroyed the myth that our western populations married very early, and the author's information bears him out. Malthus reckoned in his *Essay on Population* that the best way of limiting fertility was to postpone marriage until the husband was in a position to support a family, and it would seem that our Quakers did just this: not only do they marry late, but their morality forbade pre-marital intercourse, and no illegitimacy is recorded. The view that marriage was 'early' survives in traditional Quaker historiography; it is not known what gave rise to this myth.

Irish Quaker marriages, however, did take place considerably earlier than those in England. For all cohorts, Irish Quaker men married about two years earlier than the Southern Rural men and about eighteen months earlier than those recorded in OMNIQUAK (among whom are numbered the Irish contingent, so the differences are bound to be smaller). Irish Quaker women married nearly four years earlier than English Quakeresses, and over two years earlier than those in OMNIQUAK.

---

[9] J. Hajnal, 'European marriage patterns in perspective' in D. V. Glass and D. E. C. Eversley, eds., *Population in History* (London, 1965), pp. 101 ff.

Time trends, it will be noticed, are not significant. The conclusion must be that Irish Quaker women had, throughout the two centuries under consideration, four extra years compared with their English cousins to bear children. These years, moreover, are those when fecundity is greatest, and this fact is reflected in their fertility. Basically, the Irish women started reproducing at twenty-four and finished at the menopause, while the Southern Rural women did not begin to reproduce until they were twenty-eight.

Traditionally, it is assumed that in earlier centuries total fertility was reduced by the premature deaths of parents, mothers in childbirth in particular. First marriages were therefore separated from later marriages for the purpose of analysis. It was found, however, that men who remarried were over forty, on average, when they remarried, and their brides were fifteen years younger in Ireland, so that they had the opportunity to produce more children. In England, men were also over forty when they remarried, but their wives were only nine years younger. In both cases, they produced fewer children than the bachelors who married spinsters, but overall these remarriages are not important enough to depress fertility rates.

Irish Quakeresses, therefore, whether marrying for the first or second time, married significantly earlier than the English ones, and had a longer childbearing life.

At this stage, no interpretation of these statistics can be attempted. Most 'economic' theories of marriage (and indeed the whole Malthusian system)[10] are based on the age at marriage of the male partner, and for them the difference was only two years. The English Quakers chose women nearer their own age (an age difference of 1.8 years) than did the Irish (3.8 years). If the conventional account of Irish Catholic marriages before the Famine was correct,[11] one might say that the Quakers were

---

[10] J. Ermisch, 'The relevance of the Easterlin hypothesis and the new home economics to fertility movements in Great Britain', *Population Studies* 33 (1979), 39-58; D. Freedman *et alia*, 'Fertility, aspirations and resources: a symposium on the Easterlin Hypothesis', *Population and Development Review*, 2 (1976) 411-78.

[11] K. H. Connell, *The Population of Ireland 1750-1845* (Oxford, 1950); K. H. Connell, 'Some unsettled problems in English and Irish population history, 1750-1845', *Irish Historical Studies*, vii (1951), 225-34; S. H. Cousens, 'Emigration and demographic change in Ireland, 1851-61' *Economic History Review*, xiv (1961), 275-88; Michael Drake, 'Marriage and population growth in Ireland, 1750-1845', *Economic History*

Program No: 90L

Table 3.3 Ages at marriage by sex and marriage rank

| | All marriages: mean ages of men and women | | | | First marriages only[1] | | | | Second or later marriages only[2] | | | | | | |
| | SRUR | | EIRE | | SRUR | | EIRE | | SRUR | | | EIRE | | |
	Men	Women	Men	Women	Men	Women	Men	Women	M	F1	F2	M	F1	F2
1650-99	29.9 (158)	26.4 (182)	28.7 (209)	23.7 (161)	28.6 (78)	24.9 (111)	27.2 (104)	22.7 (99)	38.8 (13)	29.6 (13)	33.0 (6)	35.1 (10)	25.3 (13)	30.4 (8)
1700-49	29.6 (432)	28.0 (452)	29.8 (278)	24.1 (245)	28.1 (267)	26.3 (302)	27.6 (116)	23.2 (135)	38.3 (17)	31.0 (23)	39.9 (15)	42.7 (15)	27.3 (17)	31.2 (5)
1750-99	31.6 (442)	28.8 (457)	29.9 (121)	25.4 (124)	30.0 (321)	27.5 (334)	28.8 (76)	24.9 (88)	45.0 (26)	36.9 (29)	36.3 (13)	50.8 (5)	28.1 (6)	31.1 (3)
1800-49	32.4 (227)	30.2 (263)	30.2 (69)	25.8 (54)	31.7 (185)	29.8 (216)	29.3 (58)	24.9 (49)	40.1 (11)	32.9 (12)	43.6 (8)	37.5 (5)	26.6 (3)	47.6 (1)
All Cohorts	30.8 (1259)	28.5 (1354)	29.6 (697)	24.5 (599)	29.6 (851)	27.3 (963)	28.1 (370)	23.8 (386)	41.3 (67)	33.3 (77)	38.5 (42)	41.3 (38)	26.7 (39)	31.8 (17)

Notes: One or both spouses age of marriage known—all dates accepted.

[1] The 'First Marriages' referred to are those where it is assumed the husband was a bachelor (in the absence of any contrary information) and it is known that the bride was a spinster.

[2] The figures for men in all cases refer to those married for the second time or later.
The first figure for women (F1) refers to the single women whom these men married.
The second figure (F2) for women refers to those women who married presumed bachelors only.
Figures in brackets denote the number of cases studied.

in some way influenced by those around them: but this is hard to believe since they did not otherwise conform to the social conventions of the host population.

It would be interesting to know whether the well-attested rise of the age at first marriage of the Irish Catholics, after 1846, is also present amongst the Quakers, but the figures available are too small to draw any firm conclusions.

Whether the slightly earlier Irish marriage age was connected with easier availability of land, or trading and professional opportunities, or less anxiety about living standards in general, cannot be deduced from the published histories.

A final word on the mythical early marriages: under 2% of both Irish and Southern Rural Quaker men married before they were twenty. (For OMNIQUAK, the figure is 1.3%). But 20% of Irish Quaker brides, compared with 8% of the Southern Rural ones, and 9.4% of OMNIQUAK, were under twenty.

3.   *Age and duration-specific marital fertility rates and birth intervals*

(a)   *Birth according to age.* This is an ambitious calculation. Basically, what has to be known for each cohort of women married, and each area, is: how many women-years in total were lived during the period in question, and in the area, by women whose husbands were still alive? How many children were born to these women, by five-year age groups of mothers? Does the age at which women marry affect their fertility at particular ages?

Table 3.4 compresses the available information: it shows how many children were produced by women of certain age groups, regardless of the age at which they had been married. Thus, the first line of the table is to be read like this: in the Southern Rural population, women under twenty produced 357 children per thousand complete years lived (in the married state), and there are twenty-seven cases on which to base this assertion. In Ireland, the same age group produced 424 children, and there are fifty-eight known cases. Thus it cannot only be seen that Irish fertility was higher, but also by looking at the comparative

---

Review, xvi. 2 (1963), 301-13; Michael Drake, 'The Irish demographic crisis of 1740-41' in T. W. Moody, ed., *Historical Studies*, VI (London, 1968); Joseph Lee, 'Marriage and population in pre-famine Ireland', *Economic History Review*, xxi 2nd Ser. (1968), 283-95.

Table 3.4   Fertility rates at different ages of the mother   Program 90VW
(births per thousand women years lived)

		SRUR		EIRE	
1650-99	>20	357	(27)	424	(58)
	20-24	373	(204)	443	(341)
	25-29	368	(372)	438	(474)
	30-34	315	(435)	421	(534)
	35-39	238	(407)	360	(419)
1700-49	>20	212	(52)	386	(83)
	20-24	378	(535)	488	(483)
	25-29	412	(1093)	460	(718)
	30-34	330	(1277)	442	(690)
	35-39	257	(1280)	343	(610)
1750-99	>20	282	(39)	410	(39)
	20-24	450	(566)	598	(184)
	25-29	425	(1357)	502	(314)
	30-34	367	(1680)	470	(345)
	35-39	264	(1680)	426	(282)
1800-49	>20	-	-	-	-
	20-24	393	(163)	514	(74)
	25-29	418	(512)	445	(173)
	30-34	387	(730)	437	(184)
	35-39	306	(735)	366	(131)
All	>20	268	(127)	401	(187)
Cohorts	20-24	406	(1468)	496	(1097)
	25-29	413	(3334)	461	(1724)
	30-34	353	(4122)	441	(1808)
	35-39	267	(4102)	362	(1480)
	40-44	127	(3651)	175	(992)
	45-49	21	(3305)	40	(816)

Notes: (1) All marriage ranks. Date of end of marriage
known and unknown.
(2) Figures in brackets denote number of cases on
which calculations are based.

size of the case groups, the important over-all effect of earlier
marriage can be observed. The highest values occur in the
second half of the eighteenth century. In the unpublished
detailed tables, the highest figures available are for the age
group 20-24, in Ireland, and relate to women also married
under twenty: we have eighty-six such cases and they produced
640 children per thousand women-years. The corresponding

group in Southern England (145 cases) produced 476 children in the same period. There are also high values in the first and the last cohorts, with the peak fertility occurring everywhere when the young brides of 1750-99 were between twenty and twenty-four years old. So as far as the small numbers available for 1800-49 allow it, it can be said that in Ireland as in England, the young brides showed their maximum reproductive performance in the last half of the eighteenth century. It is also noticeable that for *all* Irish mothers married between twenty and twenty-four, fertility was highest at the end of the eighteenth century.

It seems then, that some sort of peak in fertility, whatever the age at marriage, occurred some time between 1775 and 1825. (The figures for our two populations refer to half-centuries. The supposition that the point of this occurrence can be more precisely dated is based on the 25-year periods which are the basis of the OMNIQUAK records). The great majority of the figures show that the last cohort had lower age-specific fertility rates than the preceding ones, and this occurred with few exceptions, even in Ireland.

If a comparison is now made between the experience of particular age groups over time, the same picture emerges. If, for example, one looks simply at all women who were between twenty-five and twenty-nine one finds once again the highest values occurring in the last fifty years of the eighteenth century. The differential for Ireland remains at almost every point.

(b)   *Births within marriage.* There are two ways of measuring fertility in relation to the course of married life—duration-specific fertility rates, and birth intervals. While the two measures are not identical, it is true that for any group of women whose fertility is relatively high throughout marriage, duration-specific rates will not drop very much at least during the first fifteen years of marriage, and birth intervals will not lengthen: the reverse will be true for women whose fertility is low. Table 3.5 shows duration-specific fertility rates according to the mother's age at marriage.

Looking first of all at the over-all distribution, it is found that, as would be expected, there is a heavy concentration in the first fifteen years of marriage, and higher values for the

Program 90VW

Table 3.5 Duration-specific marital fertility rates

no. of years married	(1) Women married aged under 20 years		(2) Women married aged 20-24 years		(3) Women married aged 25-29 years	
	SRUR	EIRE	SRUR	EIRE	SRUR	EIRE
1650-99						
0-4	398 (181)	448 (174)	440 (75)	439 (173)	380 (234)	476 (286)
5-9	329 (143)	413 (143)	351 (57)	353 (139)	296 (189)	449 (227)
10-14	242 (120)	315 (108)	245 (49)	373 (118)	248 (153)	396 (169)
15-19	90 (89)	113 (53)	250 (40)	387 (93)	80 (137)	317 (104)
20-24	-	-	-	295 (44)	-	88 (68)
1700-49						
0-4	408 (510)	496 (226)	330 (203)	456 (241)	406 (684)	481 (491)
5-9	315 (425)	436 (226)	361 (180)	394 (193)	376 (561)	441 (379)
10-14	233 (344)	285 (130)	201 (144)	400 (140)	267 (461)	397 (292)
15-19	56 (287)	133 (90)	128 (109)	360 (125)	141 (405)	243 (222)
20-24	-	-	53 (95)	187 (107)	25 (325)	56 (160)
1750-99						
0-4	429 (750)	554 (130)	455 (145)	583 (96)	458 (853)	554 (186)
5-9	328 (668)	534 (103)	382 (136)	575 (80)	366 (738)	432 (155)
10-14	211 (570)	311 (74)	292 (120)	419 (62)	306 (641)	377 (122)
15-19	74 (499)	67 (60)	207 (92)	435 (33)	182 (521)	271 (96)
20-24	-	-	81 (86)	-	49 (446)	157 (51)

(Contd.)

Table 3.5 (contd.)

no. of years married	(1) Women married aged under 20 years		(2) Women married aged 20-24 years		(Women married aged 25-29 years)	
	SRUR	EIRE	SRUR	EIRE	SRUR	EIRE
1800-49						
0-4	436 (374)	450 (80)	200 (25)	514 (35)	443 (327)	463 (95)
5-9	355 (321)	407 (59)	333 (15)	500 (30)	381 (278)	356 (90)
10-14	230 (248)	314 (35)	333 (15)	520 (25)	327 (220)	459 (61)
15-19	69 (203)	114 (35)	267 (15)	733 (15)	126 (182)	150 (40)
20-24	-	-	-	-	43 (138)	-
All Cohorts						
0-4	421 (1815)	487 (640)	382 (448)	480 (550)	430 (2098)	491 (1038)
5-9	330 (1557)	438 (495)	366 (388)	423 (447)	364 (1766)	423 (876)
10-14	223 (1282)	297 (357)	247 (328)	406 (350)	289 (1475)	401 (654)
15-19	70 (1078)	107 (243)	184 (256)	399 (271)	149 (1245)	259 (467)
20-24	-	-	68 (221)	219 (183)	37 (1030)	77 (310)
25-29	-	-	35 (198)	46 (152)	-	-

Notes: Basis of calculation the same as for age-specific fertility. Number of cases in brackets. (-) denotes too few cases to make any reliable observations.

three lowest age-at-marriage groups. Of the nearly 3,000 children for whom there is information in the Irish population, 80% were born within the first fifteen years of marriage, to women who married under the age of thirty. The OMNIQUAK figures are even more striking: 90% of children were born during the first fifteen years of marriage and 88.8% to women who married under thirty.

Again, Irish values are higher for all durations and at all marriage ages, just as they are for age-specific fertility rates. The rate of decline of fertility from the earliest years of marriage is slower. The conclusion must be reached again that the English Quakers did not have as many children early in marriage as they were biologically capable of having. Whether the Irish figures constitute some sort of limit cannot be determined and certainly the rates drop in the later stages of marriage.

What about time trends? In Ireland, the decline in the last half-century under observation is most marked for all women in the first ten years of married life. Whilst the resulting fertility is still well above the English level, especially for those who married young, some restriction of fertility can be seen even here.

(c) *Birth intervals.* While it is theoretically possible for a woman to have a child every year between puberty and menopause, in practice this does not happen. There are four main reasons:

1. Although lactation is not a completely effective means of contraception, it does inhibit conception.
2. Frequency of intercourse declines, and after a woman is thirty, intercourse would have to be frequent or accurately timed to coincide with the ovulation period to produce conception.
3. Deliberate prevention of conception.
4. Many pregnancies end negatively—in our period through spontaneous abortion (miscarriage), and much later through deliberate abortion. Unrecorded still births would also reduce the apparent frequency of live births.

In practice all four play their part. From Table 3.6, actual birth intervals can be measured. The lactation theory can be tested by observing whether or not a second child follows more rapidly a sibling that died in infancy than one that survived (the calculations have been arranged to take into account the fact that one must be sure that the conception of the next child took place *after* the death of the previous one). It is possible of course that there was an unrecorded taboo on intercourse while the woman was breast-feeding—but there is no known written or oral evidence for such a custom.

The English and Irish Quakers have close socio-economic similarities. In the case of the north-west English Quakers who form the greater part of the NRUR population (not considered here in detail) they can be said to belong to the same 'genetic pool' as the western and north-western Irish Quakers—they were often members of the same families when Quakers first came to Ireland, and later there was much intermarriage. The Gloucestershire and Somerset Quakers (not part of the SRUR universe) were related to the south-west Irish Quaker families.

Table 3.6   Birth intervals in months by birth rank,   Program 90XY
             and wife's age at marriage (mean values only)

		SRUR			EIRE	
	Under 25	25-34	All ages	Under 25	25-34	All ages
1650-99						
-1	21.8	24.3	22.8	14.2	15.2	14.4
1-2	29.0	24.9	27.7	23.5	22.7	23.2
2-3	27.6	24.7	26.6	24.3	24.7	24.2
3-4	30.6	30.5	30.5	25.7	28.1	26.2
4-5	35.6	28.8	32.2	36.4	29.7	35.2
and later						
1700-49						
-1	21.3	19.6	19.9	16.5	14.8	15.9
1-2	24.2	25.6	25.2	23.7	22.5	23.3
2-3	24.7	26.3	25.5	25.1	27.0	25.6
3-4	27.2	27.4	27.2	25.7	24.0	25.1
4-5	27.6	26.8	27.3	25.4	26.8	25.7
and later						
1750-99						
-1	19.8	18.6	18.9	16.7	14.9	16.1
1-2	26.6	22.7	24.0	21.3	19.2	20.4
2-3	25.1	25.3	25.5	20.1	21.1	20.3
3-4	24.9	29.4	27.5	22.0	23.0	22.8
4-5	26.1	24.5	25.3	23.5	26.1	24.1
and later						

Table 3.6 (contd.)

	Under 25	SRUR 25-34	All ages	Under 25	EIRE 25-34	All ages
1800-49						
-1	21.3	18.3	19.5	16.5	15.5	16.0
1-2	24.6	21.1	22.3	24.4	20.9	22.9
2-3	26.1	25.2	25.4	26.0	23.5	24.7
3-4	41.4*	24.3	29.2	27.3	25.6	26.3
4-5 and later	27.4	25.6	26.4	22.9	25.3	23.6
All cohorts						
-1	20.8	19.6	19.8	16.3	15.1	15.9
1-2	25.9	23.5	24.7	23.4	21.6	22.7
2-3	25.5	25.5	25.7	24.00	25.4	24.3
3-4	28.2	28.1	28.0	25.2	25.5	25.3
4-5 and later	27.8	25.8	26.9	27.8	27.4	27.7

Notes: Rows denote the interval measured: the first relates to time between marriage and first birth, the next between first and second births, and so on, and the last one relates to the interval between the fourth and fifth or any subsequent interval.

The program is based on the following number of cases overall:

	SRUR	EIRE
Mar - 1	650	507
1-2	546	474
2-3	449	421
3-4	371	372
5 +	957	1205
	2973	2979

* based on the evidence provided by only 15 births.

Yet despite these affinities the two groups show quite different rhythms. This is in all probability due to a restriction of fertility on the part of the English Friends. Underregistration could affect the number of live births, but not the age at marriage. Even in Ireland, the average family sizes recorded hide some diversity: a mean of six children implies that there must have been a good many with only two or three children. (This has been confirmed by looking at the standard deviations of the means shown here.) Whether it was through abstinence or other means of birth control, many had small families, but much more so in England than in Ireland.

Contrasting Ireland and the Southern Rural population over time, what is particularly noticeable is the very short mean elapsed time between marriage and first birth—this is not above sixteen months for any cohort or age at marriage in Ireland, and never less than eighteen months for the Southern Rural group. The interval between the first and the second child is never more than just two years in Ireland, and again on average about two months more in Southern England. On the average for all cohorts and all ages at marriage, Irish values are between two and four months shorter than the English ones.

The over-all picture is of course affected by the fact that a far higher proportion of the Irish women come into the first category (married under twenty-five) than do the Southern English women.

One last observation is required. Conception and birth are not interchangeable categories. Miscarriages were frequent, and the very low number of still births so recorded in the Quaker Family Lists suggests that this negative outcome of pregnancy may have been underrecorded. (Even in modern populations this is still held to be the case, especially in the case of illegitimate children and in rural societies.) Miscarriages are sometimes a question of general health: they are supposed to occur more frequently when a woman has had many children in quick succession, and during periods of general sickness, food shortages, especially bowel disorders, and possibly vitamin E deficiency. We might therefore have two phenomena outside the questions of lactation, age-related fecundity, and deliberate restrictions: women may on the whole have become healthier since the mid-seventeenth century and therefore more pregnancies may have ended positively, and the Irish women may have had a better diet than their English counterparts.

(d) *Conclusion*. Whichever way the matter is looked at, a rise of fertility can be seen from the earliest cohorts to a peak generally occurring between 1775 and 1825, and a fall thereafter. But within marriage the rise and fall appears quite clearly, and this is important because for this purpose the strict Malthusian explanation at the local level (i.e. changes in the age at marriage as regulators of fertility) can be excluded. Since the figures refer to marriages which are in being, expectation of life has nothing to do with these changes. Basically, it is what young couples married for the first time accomplish in the first fifteen years of marriage which most strongly affects the total (and to a lesser extent how sharp the cut-off is after the woman reaches thirty-five, or after they have been married fifteen years). It is quite possible, of course, that the rise up to the end of the eighteenth century is the result of more pregnancies ending positively, i.e. a reduction of accidental miscarriages (scarcely, in this case, deliberate abortions). But once the peak is reached, the reduction cannot be due to more miscarriages. Only four explanations are possible: abstinence, the use of contraceptives, a significant change in breast-feeding patterns, or coitus interruptus. And since this is the unsolved question in the case of all populations whose fertility declines from a peak, whether temporarily as at Colyton,[12] or permanently as is the case with the French population, from the end of the eighteenth century onwards, the cause is unlikely to be discovered here.

4. *Completed family size*

It will have become clear from the sections on marriage age and on age- and duration-specific fertility that the family size of the Irish Quakers must have been noticeably larger than that of their English cousins. Although the rules of analysis restrict the size of the sample, and the Irish sample is small, the differences are so large that, taking the information here with the evidence about age at marriage and the age- and duration-specific rates (which make use of births which cannot be taken into account for some calculations of completed fertility), the figures shown make sense. Table 3.7 summarizes the information. The statements which follow are taken from the more detailed tables distinguishing families by the age of marriage of the wife.

For the women married under twenty, Irish family size was 9.8 children per marriage, and 5.7 for the Southern Rural Quakers. For Ireland, the average figure rises throughout the 200 years, reaching 15.5 children per marriage at the end— but this is a freak result, based on only two marriages for which this information is given. The figures for 1700-49 are

[12] E. A. Wrigley, 'Family limitation in pre-industrial England', *Economic History Review*, xix, 1 (1966), 82-109.

Table 3.7 Family size

Program 92 TS

All ages at marriage[1]

Values for marriages when both partners were single irrespective of age at marriage (i.e. supposed first marriages)[2], and all marriage ranks

	SRUR		EIRE		SRUR		EIRE	
	Complete	All	Complete	All	GE = 1/ = 1	All	GE = 1/ = 1	All
1650-99	4.3 (74)	4.0 (109)	6.4 (38)	5.4 (67)	4.6 (32)	4.0 (55)	5.9 (17)	5.1 (32)
1700-49	4.3 (218)	4.0 (331)	7.4 (78)	6.1 (131)	4.5 (118)	4.0 (185)	8.0 (35)	6.2 (65)
1750-99	4.4 (315)	4.3 (444)	6.5 (34)	6.1 (62)	4.2 (168)	4.2 (241)	6.8 (26)	6.2 (53)
1800-49	3.9 (132)	3.7 (182)	6.6 (17)	5.6 (27)	3.4 (80)	3.2 (108)	6.9 (14)	5.9 (23)
All Cohorts	4.3 (739)	4.1 (1066)	6.9 (170)	5.9 (291)	4.2 (398)	3.9 (589)	7.1 (94)	6.0 (176)

Notes: [1] First column shows only those families whose fertility was completed (i.e. both parents survived to end of fertile period), second column shows all families. All marriage ranks.
The numbers in parentheses refer to the totals of marriages which were analysed to calculate the ultimate family size.

[2] The 'First Marriages' referred to are those where it is assumed that the husband was a bachelor (in the absence of any contrary information) and it is known that the bride was a spinster. The notation for this is GE = 1/ = 1, GE standing for 'greater than or equal to'.

perhaps more useful, referring to twenty couples: they show 9.4 children per marriage, compared with 7.3 for all Quakers and 4.7 for the Southern Rural.

Turning to the rather more numerous cases of women married between twenty and twenty-four, the Irish over-all average is 7.9 (for sixty couples) compared with 6.7 (OMNI-QUAK) and 6.0 (SRUR). For this group there is the expected maximum of 8.7 children in 1750-99, 6.6 for SRUR, and 7.7 for OMNIQUAK (for 1775-99).

For women aged 25-29 at marriage, the maximum of 6.9 is reached in the case of Irish women in 1700-49, but 5.5 for SRUR in 1800-49 and 6.0 for OMNIQUAK in 1825-49. Whilst this shows a clear 'lead' for the Irish marriages in all periods, the rather earlier peak compared with the rest of the Quakers should be taken in conjunction with the fact that these late marriages were rarer in Ireland than elsewhere.

Table 3.7 summarizes average family size for all ages of women's marriages by cohort. Numbers here are rather larger, and more reliable. Differences are clearly the outcome of a combination of age at marriage and reproductive behaviour within marriage. The difference between Ireland and the rest of the Quaker universe remains striking. The ninety-four families resulting from first marriages for whom all the relevant information is available, and who completed their fertility (i.e., where we know that neither parent died), produced 7.1 children each. Even when adding in those whose child-bearing life was interrupted by the death of one of the partners, and other incomplete families, 176 cases in all, the average is still 6.0. For SRUR the figures are 4.2 and 3.9 respectively, and for OMNIQUAK 4.7 and 4.5. This last figure is perhaps the best over-all measurement we have, since it refers to 1,261 first-marriage families for whom all the required information is available—and this average is not startling when set against figures from other sources. A good reference-point might be the 1911 English fertility census. A figure of 4.5 live births for women married once is very near the top level of fertility reached by cohorts of women born in the nineteenth century and still living in 1911.

Looking at the time series, the Irish peak figure occurs very early, in 1700-49. For SRUR there is very little difference for the first three cohorts, and a fall in the last one. Taking the shorter periods of twenty-five years for the OMNIQUAK population, the peak occurs, as expected, in 1775-99.

The difference between completed and uncompleted fertility does not significantly alter the size of the difference between the two populations. Those women who married very early were also most likely to die before they had completed their fecund life: those who married under twenty were exposed to more years of danger, both from general diseases and those associated with childbirth. So the longer they live and the more children they have, the greater the chance that one or other partner will die before fertility is complete. Thus for all Irish cohorts, just over half the women married under twenty survived to the end of their reproductive age, and these 31 produced 9.8 children each. If we take the other 28 families into account, where one or other partner dies, the percentage reduction is the same for OMNIQUAK. It is therefore the age of the mother at marriage which has more effect on total fertility than the morality levels for particular periods. We conclude that the greater difference between completed and uncompleted fertility cases in Ireland is due to the preponderance of young marriages, and the higher average number of children born to each couple. And since the reduction of the fertile period through premature death is less for older married women than for the younger ones, the much higher age-specific rates for the younger women are seen to be not as important as the fact that duration-specific rates are always high for the first ten years of marriage, whatever the age of the woman when she started.

However, the younger they start, the more children they have in the earliest period, and the higher the values for succeeding age-periods. Thus, 35.4% of Irish Quaker women married before 20 produced 3 children before they were 25. Of the same cohort, 33.3% repeated this achievement between 25 and 29, and 32.3% between 30 and 34. For the next higher age group at marriage (those married between 20 and 24) the figures are 34.8%, 29.6%, and 17.1%, a much steeper falling-off in fertility in later quinquennial groups for the later starters. This underlines the significance of early marriage.

It is worth looking also at those who had no children ever, and also at the proportion who had no children in particular

age groups. The proportion altogether childless is about 10%
(roughly the same as the supposed current extent of involuntary
sterility).

But when it comes to the end of child-bearing for those who
did have some children, the picture is very different. Our figures
again strongly support the view that family limitation was prevalent in the Southern English population, whereas the Irish
population showed a decline in fertility reasonably consistent
with the hypothesis of little control of reproduction. For example, of those Southern Rural women aged 30-34, who had
married under 20, 34.5% had no children in that quinquennium
of their lives, whereas the figure for Ireland was only 12.9%.
OMNIQUAK records prove that there is an observable time
trend for all Quakers and once again the Irish stand out as the
group who did not stop having children even if they married
early. The contrast is perhaps greatest for the 35-39 age group,
with only just over 10% of those who had been married about
twenty years (i.e. before the age of twenty) having no children
at all, compared with values between 30% and 60% for the
rest of the population in that quinquennial age group.

5. *Mortality*

(a) *Infant and child mortality*. Infant mortality in the Quaker
universe was low. Table 3.8 shows a relatively high infant
mortality rate until 1725 after which it fell drastically for the
rest of the century and still further in the nineteenth century.
National British rates in the second half of the nineteenth
century fluctuated between a low of 130 and a high of 163; by
this standard, rates were low in the Quaker population, and
consistently lower in Ireland except in the eighteenth century.

We calculated, in addition to the simple infant mortality
rates shown here, the relationship between infant mortality
and fertility. There is a view that the death of a previous born
child accelerates the birth of the next. Whether this is due to a
hormonal function related to lactation, or whether parents who
had lost a child would be more eager to replace it, or even
whether there was some unrecorded taboo on intercourse
during breast-feeding, is not known. The first theory is however the likeliest. Whilst we were trying to measure the birth
intervals in the two cases (where the previous child was still

Table 3.8   Infant and child mortality rates

per 1000 live born (0-1)
per 1000 surviving (other age groups)

		SRUR Male	SRUR Female	EIRE Male	EIRE Female
1650-99	0-	133	101	121	95
	1-4	116	96	105	106
	5-9	49	35	18	45
	10-14	19	25	26	23
1700-49	0-	135	114	132	102
	1-4	106	89	171	148
	5-9	28	25	54	49
	10-14	13	21	35	21
1750-99	0-	125	117	121	95
	1-4	76	80	143	130
	5-9	33	30	34	44
	10-14	20	20	29	11
1800-50	0-	93	83	59	39
	1-4	51	48	48	71
	5-9	35	35	36	23
	10-14	0	26	39	8
All Cohorts	0-	126	108	116	90
	1-4	91	82	127	119
	5-9	35	30	35	43
	10-14	15	22	30	17

alive, and where it had died), we first established the very low over-all infant mortality rates: in only 100 cases out of every 1,000, the previous child was dead when the next was conceived. The figures confirm the hypothesis up to a point: birth intervals were shorter where the previous child was dead. However, the loss rate was very small, and therefore the larger number of children born is not due to high infant mortality (a statistical consequence of shorter birth intervals where infant mortality is high). In any case, the difference was of the order of one and a half months: large enough to be seen as statistically significant, but too small to affect differences, for instance, in age- or duration-specific fertility rates.

(b) *Infant mortality and the age of the mother, and maternal death risks.*
The OMNIQUAK and Southern Rural families bear out the

accepted theory that the risk to a child slightly increases with the age of the mother, but the EIRE figures show no such rise. As regards the risks to mothers, we have only 214 births to mothers over 40 and 29 to those over 45, and their mortality risk was low: 89 and 69 per thousand births respectively. (OMNIQUAK shows a slightly higher risk: 164 per thousand for the 171 mothers giving birth when over 45.)

(c)   *Child mortality*. The Table gives mortality rates for children after the first year of life as well. These figures must be read as indicating how many died out of each 1,000 survivors from the previous age group—so that *total* child mortality cannot be calculated by summing the four individual rates. However, in rough terms one can see how small were the losses of children before they reached the quinquennium in which they might get married. Significant losses here occur only in the 1-4 age group, which reach their maximum for OMNIQUAK in 1700-24 and for EIRE in the first half of the eighteenth century, whilst those for SRUR decline throughout. It is difficult to account for the relatively heavy losses of small Irish children, but the result cannot be a statistical accident: we are dealing with over 2,500 births in that cohort. It is just possible that the crises of 1725/9 and 1740/1 raised child mortality temporarily.

These figures will not fit into the historical experience of developed countries, chronologically, nor are such rates encountered in less developed countries today. What part was played in all this by inoculation, by a sensible diet, by the cult of fresh air and exercise for which no records exist until much later, or by good medical practice available to all patients, is not known.

It must be emphasized that the low rates of loss of babies and children was the common experience of our Quaker families even in the seventeenth century. They must therefore have expected most of those born to survive to adulthood, so that the usual nineteenth century explanation of the onset of family limitation (fears engendered by the change in infant and child mortality) cannot apply here.

However, it is possible that standards changed, and that different opinions prevailed in England, so that a survival rate which disturbed few people in 1700 might be seen as a threat in Southern England by 1775 and in Ireland by 1825. Our figures would not be inconsistent with such a hypothesis. By 1800, seven out of eight daughters born to Irish Quaker parents would one day need a dowry, and given the uncertain economic growth rates, and the dangers inherent in partible inheritance (which was not uncommon), a threshold point would be reached sooner or later. Since we have no Irish material for the period after 1850, the only statement that can be made with any certainty is that the need to restrict the size of families was not felt before that date. In contrast, family limitation was clearly practised in Southern England before that date (unless it is supposed that the reduction in births was mainly due to under-registration).

6.   *Expectation of life of adults*

Life-tables can be constructed for modern populations if a great deal of information is known—mainly how many people are alive at each single year of age, at the beginning of a calendar year, and what proportion of them die in the following year. For the Quaker populations, this is much harder to calculate, because we do not really know how many people were 'in observation' at the beginning of each year, though it is known how many died, at a specific age, during a year. We have constructed life-tables which incorporate various techniques for estimating survival chances and, leaving aside some intermediate values, we have calculated expectations of life, for particular cohorts, at certain ages: these are shown in Table 3.9, giving values at four stages in the lives of men and women—the youngest 20-24 (or in some cases 25-29), 30-34, 40-44, and 50-54. The technical reason for sometimes not quoting figures for the youngest group is that for any group which started with fewer than 100 'person-years' lived in a quinquennium, the death risk is too small to place any confidence in it, so that the Table starts with the first cohort of sufficient size.

In this table, the last cohort apparently has a shorter life expectation, especially at younger ages. It is not clear to us why this should be so. Where life-tables are calculated by the 'reverse survivor' method, we can be misled by a truncation effect: that is, since the computer works from the age at death of people

Table 3.9   Expectation of life of adults in certain age groups

Program 92 MO

	(1) 20-24				(2) 30-34				(3) 40-44				(4) 50-54			
	SRUR		EIRE		SRUR		EIRE		SRUR		EIRE		SRUR		EIRE	
	M	F	M	F	M	F	M	F	M	F	M	F	M	F	M	F
1650-99	28.9*	25.9	34.1*	28.0	27.2	24.4	29.9	26.4	23.0	21.8	23.8	24.4	17.3	16.8	17.9	18.8
1700-49	37.0	31.4	33.9*	30.6	29.6	29.3	30.8	28.3	24.0	24.8	25.6	24.0	18.4	19.3	18.6	19.3
1750-99	42.0	37.3	32.7*	33.7	33.9	31.2	29.6	29.0	27.0	26.0	23.1	24.1	20.1	20.2	19.2	19.8
1800-49	35.4	-	-	29.1*	33.9	34.4	29.0	28.8	27.5	28.9	23.1	26.3	21.4	23.5	17.6	18.3
All Cohorts	37.5	30.9	37.9	30.7	30.2	28.7	30.2	28.1	24.9	24.7	24.3	24.3	18.9	19.4	18.5	19.3

Notes: Derived from known dates of death only.
* Starred figures refer to next higher age group, i.e. 25-29.
- Numbers too small for calculation.

dying in a particular year, out of all those 'in observation', the last cohort is biased by having too many deaths of young people in its span. However, the Family Lists did record the deaths of many people after 1850, and these were certainly calculated for the Southern English population in respect of all those born before 1850, so that no computational error should arise. If there were environmental reasons for these changes, they are not known to us. The 1846 famine did not touch the Irish Quakers directly or indirectly—of that we are certain. It is exceedingly unlikely then that the later Quakers had worse prospects than the earlier ones, and an inspection of the seven OMNIQUAK cohorts confirms that view.

Once again, the results are fairly startling by modern standards. In no cohort was the expectation of life for either men or women less than a number of years which would see them comfortably through their fertile period. Over time, the figures improve, but not as dramatically as they do for children. Thus, for EIRE, a woman aged 20-24 in 1650-99 had a life expectation of 28 years on known deaths only, or 36 years on 'averaged' assumptions. By 1750-99, these figures had improved by six years on known deaths and not at all on the estimated averages. The improvement was rather higher for the Southern Rural women, from nearly 26 to 37 years, and for Southern Rural men from nearly 29 to 42 years. But these rates still betoken fairly slow changes. For the higher age groups, the improvement is correspondingly less still, until at 50-54 only the Southern Rural women can show a real increase of about six years in their expectation of life.

In other words, once the Quakers had got over the perils of childhood (such as they were), they could expect to live to what was then considered a ripe old age.

One cannot very easily make direct comparisons with modern life-tables. However, if one compares the life expectations of men and women, especially those over thirty, both in Southern England and in Ireland, with those shown in the English life-tables for 1950-2, one can easily see that the differences cannot be great. This applies more strongly for adults over thirty, and it is most striking for the penultimate cohort in the OMNI-QUAK program (i.e. 1800-24) where one can say that, by and large the Quakers had the same sort of life expectation as English people of all classes more than a century later.

More detailed comparisons are not needed here. It is sufficient to state that such health sets the Quakers apart, once again, from the rest of the inhabitants of the UK and Ireland. The implications are far-reaching—for example the expectation of inheritance could not play a large role in the decisions of young people to marry. (In fact young people normally obtained a portion or settlement from their parents on marriage, whatever their age, and they did not therefore have to wait for their parents to die.) Had partible inheritance (of land) prevailed, Quaker wealth would have dwindled rapidly with such large families. However, we know that they prospered in trade and manufacture, that increasingly in the nineteenth century they took up professional careers, that those without good prospects emigrated to England or America, and that in the rural areas young people moved on, as they did in the United States, to farm new lands elsewhere (a fact underlined by the establishment of new Meetings). Our main interest in these statistics is once again concerned with fertility: Quaker couples married late, though earlier in Ireland, and most of them would be alive, and of course together. This, like the high survival rates for children, should have meant early birth control. This has been demonstrated for the Southern Rural population, but not for Ireland.

III

Conclusion

The debate about the changes in size, structure, and vital statistics of pre-registration populations continues, and even with the publication of now massive volumes of evidence, especially about the industrialized countries of Western Europe, some of the most important questions remain unanswered. The Irish aspects of these questions have been identified as being more intractable than most, partly because of the paucity of pre-census and pre-registration material. All that can be agreed is that the population of Ireland grew at an increasing rate until some time in the mid-nineteenth century without any apparent connection with any widening of the country's economic base (unless the spread of the potato culture is considered to come under that heading), and that after 1846 the population decreased more or less abruptly through a combination of death, emigration, postponement of marriage, and, just possibly, some limitation of fertility within marriage. It has often been suggested that the Irish pre-Famine population had a level of fertility otherwise only known in connection with a few highly selective groups known not to practise contraception, mainly the Hutterites.[13]

The Quaker group studied here was not segregated, like the Hutterites, but lived amidst the Irish peasant and urban labouring population. We cannot give reliable information about the main Irish groups—the Catholics in the southern and western provinces, and the Protestants in Ulster; but we do have information about the English Quakers. These can properly be compared with the Irish Friends not only because they are members of the same 'genetic pool' (the main groups came from north-western England in both cases, and they were often cousins) but also because they resembled each other closely in their socio-economic composition and life-style.

Our calculations show that the Irish Quakers had a very different demographic regime from that of the English ones. They married earlier (especially the women), their childbearing period lasted longer, their birth intervals were shorter, and their marriages remained intact a little longer because both partners survived. The fertility rates are accordingly different in kind, as well as in degree, from those of the English Quakers. The 'tempo' of fertility is that of an entirely different sort of population, and it fits no known model of modern populations in the developed world. The fact that their infant and child mortality rates were quite significantly lower than those of the English Quakers leads to ultimate average family sizes which would have alarmed Malthus had he known them.

If what we have shown here is correct, and we believe it is, we are faced with some unanswered questions. It would appear that not only the English Quakers, but also the English population observed in the Anglican registers of parishes, which

[13] C. Tietze, 'Reproductive span and rate of reproduction among Hutterite women', *Fertility and Sterility*, 8 (1957), 89-97; Mindel C. Sheps, 'An analysis of reproductive patterns in an American isolate', *Population Studies*, 19, 1 (1965), 65-80.

the Cambridge Group has subjected to the process of family reconstitution, all practised 'moral restraint' in that they married later, and what Malthus later called 'prudential restraint' within marriage. The Irish material causes us to ask: what was there about life in eighteenth- and nineteenth-century England that made it desirable to limit family size?

Secondly, can we assume that the Irish Quaker pattern of nuptiality and fertility was similar to that of their Irish Catholic and Protestant neighbours? It certainly seems that the Irish population at large and the Irish Quakers have demographic patterns more nearly alike than other possible pairings such as that of Irish Protestants with English Protestants, or of English Quakers with Irish Quakers. If this is so, the question of the social mechanisms involved in bringing about such similarities elude us totally: propinquity does not create similarity. (The British colonial populations did not have fertility patterns closer to those of the native Asian and African populations than to those of their families at home.)

This investigation has apparently resulted in an inescapable set of alternative conclusions: either the Irish Quakers were a very peculiar sect indeed, achieving some unnaturally high fertility rates, and everybody else is 'normal' for the supposed pre-birth-control centuries, or the Irish Quakers represent something nearer the biological maximum and everybody else, except the Irish peasantry, was already restricting their fertility, by what Malthus described as 'un-natural practices', or 'vice', or just abstinence. This confirms E. A. Wrigley's conclusions in 1966, before the days of the computer, that, to judge by Colyton (Devon), English rural or small-town populations had adopted family limitation at certain times. (In recent years, the Cambridge Group has begun to regard the Colyton experience as atypical.)

Fertility has been stressed because the differences there are the most striking. But mortality appears to have been significantly lower for the Irish Quakers (though we are on less sure ground here). Why was this? Could the reasons have applied to the Irish population in general? The poor Irishman's diet of potatoes is said to have been healthy—but the Quakers probably did not live on potatoes. Oral tradition suggests a diet of white bread, a lot of meat, small beer until that became morally questionable, and thereafter, tea and coffee. Were their doctors better than the English? Did their isolated settlements keep illness at bay? Is a warm wet climate an encouragement to longevity? It seems to us rather that it was some local influence, hitherto disregarded, that reduced the incidence of certain diseases in Ireland and that the Quakers, as well as the rest of the population, benefited from this.

Family size was extraordinarily large by western-European standards. How was 'subsistence', to use the language of Malthus, so readily available for Irish Quakers compared with the English? Is it possible that Irish society was less competitive than its counterpart in England? If we accept the 'reference groups' for the Irish Quakers (as well as the English) to be the ordinary farmers and, in the towns, the merchants and professional people, they certainly (to judge by their houses) lived more modestly in Ireland than in England.

But this is pure speculation, and is mentioned only to support our contention that the facts can speak for themselves and do not entitle us to make causal inferences.

The demography of the Irish Quakers then is intrinsically valuable because it throws a great deal of light on their life and death in pre-census and pre-registration times. But it is even more important because it helps to focus more sharply important questions as yet unanswered for populations of all classes and persuasions, and in different countries, round about the time of Malthus. If we could finish with one single question which links our own investigations with those of Kenneth Connell and his contemporaries, it is this: if it is true that Malthus's direst fears were realized in Ireland in 1846, and if his thought processes can now be seen to echo the practice of English populations in his lifetime, why were the Irish Quakers immune, why did they have large families, and why did they not pay the price eventually? After the universal dearth and sickness of 1725-9 and 1740-1, the Irish Quakers multiplied undeterred by any fear of catastrophe. They remain a singular phenomenon on the demographic map of Europe, and we have no plausible explanation for their high fertility, or their low mortality, let alone their apparently improvident marriage patterns.

4. Population Growth and Diet, 1600-1850*[1]

L. M. Cullen

K. H. Connell's *The Population of Ireland, 1750-1845* has a three-fold importance in demographic studies. It analysed and revised existing estimates of Irish population; it advanced an explanation for the accelerated population growth of the late eighteenth century; and it put population growth in a dietary context. No other account of population growth in modern European history has related the phenomenon so exclusively to diet and particularly to the potato. Just as Connell's emphasis on a falling age of marriage as a cause of population growth was novel, stimulating a general reappraisal of the birth-rate as a factor in the demographic revolution,[2] so his emphasis on diet was precocious. It foreshadowed the subsequent widening interest in the subject among social historians; and linked diet not, as might be expected, to the death-rate but to the birth-rate. Connell's conclusions on marriage ages and the role of the potato have been catalysts for a continuing discussion of both subjects which is far from concluded, and his revised estimates of population have been accepted by historians for thirty years, even by those who have taken issue with him on other points. Any changes in his estimates will thus affect not only the profile of population growth, but the trends of both trade and general development which have been studied within the demographic framework established by Connell.

Connell's book was mainly concerned with late eighteenth and early nineteenth century Ireland: the terminal dates are very specifically 1750 and 1845. However, estimates of population for the years before 1750, based on the hearth tax, were

* I am grateful to D. Dickson for comments on an earlier draft of this paper, and greatly indebted to my wife, on whose expert knowledge of aspects of the evolution of cooking I have drawn.

[1] Part of this article dealing with diet draws on a section in L. M. Cullen, *The Emergence of Modern Ireland 1600-1900* (London, 1981).

[2] R. M. Hartwell, 'Kenneth H. Connell - an Appreciation', *Irish Economic and Social History*, i (1974), 7-13; M. Drake, 'Professor K. H. Connell', *Irish Historical Studies*, xix (1974), 83-5; Anon., 'An Appreciation - Kenneth H. Connell', *Economic and Social Review*, vi (1974), 1-4.

reworked to make it possible to appraise the direction and force of post-1750 growth, although the pre-1750 trends were little discussed. Connell saw population after 1750 accelerating from previously low rates of growth, even though his own estimates for 1687 and 1712 indicated that population at least between these years was growing rapidly. The reason for the lack of discussion seems to lie in his belief that his revised population estimates for the earlier years understated the true position,[3] even though he adjusted the traditional population estimates for 1687 by a larger margin than later ones. Before his death, Connell was of the opinion that Irish population at the outset of the eighteenth century was greater than he had earlier suggested.[4] Consequently, the rate of growth of population during the first half of the eighteenth century would be slower than implied, not only by traditional estimates, but by his own revisions. If so, the post-1750 growth becomes all the more remarkable.

In reality, of course, Irish population rose sharply between 1600 and 1712. It may have doubled[5] (from 1.4 million to 2.8 million), a scale of increase that is to be compared with the increase of 156 per cent occurring between 1750 and 1845. If the estimate for 1600 is excessive, as has been argued,[6] the increase between 1600 and 1712 would of course be even greater. Thus it would seem that the whole period 1600-1845 was one of rapid population growth with only the sub-period 1712-54, when on Connell's estimates the rate of growth was very modest indeed, standing out as exceptional.

In fact the years 1712-54 have no special significance in either economic or political history. By contrast, the earlier period, 1687-1712, was one of profound economic difficulties when the only exceptional factor conducive to population growth was the influx of Scottish Presbyterians in the 1690s. Even that inflow, which occurred at the highest rate ever experienced in Irish history, was partially offset by a massive emigration from

---

[3] K. H. Connell, *The Population of Ireland, 1750-1845* (Oxford, 1950), pp. 24-5, 260.

[4] Anon., *Economic and Social Review*, op. cit., 4.

[5] L. M. Cullen, 'Population Trends in Seventeenth-Century Ireland', *Economic and Social Review*, vi (1975), 149-165; L. M. Cullen, 'Economic Trends, 1660-91' in T. W. Moody, F. X. Martin, and F. J. Byrne, eds., *A New History of Ireland*, iii (Oxford, 1976), pp. 388-90.

[6] N. P. Canny, 'Early Modern Ireland: An Appraisal Appraised', *Irish Economic and Social History*, iv (1977), 64-5.

Ireland between 1687 and 1690 as James II's reign became increasingly intolerant of Protestants. Possibly Connell's population estimates for 1687 (2.2 million) and 1712 (2.8 million) overstate the true increase in population, for his revisions to the traditional figures are highly problematic. A crude comparison of the gross yield of the hearth tax over the period may, on balance, be more helpful. Between 1685 and 1711-13 the gross yield rose by 22 per cent, against the 29 per cent increase shown by Connell's population estimates.[7] The actual increase in the gross produce might in fact have been smaller for the hearth tax was farmed in 1685 and the yield in that year might therefore have been understated, compared to the yield in 1711-13 when the tax was collected directly. Nevertheless there was an increase, conceivably small, suggesting an underlying growth of population. The only likely halt to population growth was between 1687 and 1691; and there was possibly a pause also in the very depressed first decade of the new century when the yield from the hearth tax stagnated, even after it was directly collected from 1706.

During the first half of the eighteenth century the underlying strength of demographic forces is obscured by specifically demographic events such as famine in the late 1720s, the sickly 1730s, and the crisis of the first half of the 1740s. It is also obscured because Connell had only four hearth-counts for the years 1725-54, two of them for the relatively depressed years 1726 and 1732, and none at all for the years between 1732 and 1754.[8]

A further difficulty in judging population trends in this period arises from the change in administration of the hearth tax. In 1706 it was directly collected for the first time and the quality of the returns under the new system was initially probably better than it became later in the century. However Connell assumed a constant scale of deficiency throughout the first eighty years of the century and his revised population estimate for 1712 therefore may be an overstatement. If so, it would have the effect of exaggerating the rate of growth of population between 1687 and 1712. Conversely, it would conceal a faster rate of growth within the first half of the eighteenth century, particularly if

[7] Cullen, 'Population Trends', 151.
[8] Connell, p. 25.

administrative inefficiency set in from an early date as it did in the case of the excise duty, which like the hearth-money was a significant tax in every revenue district.[9]

Although Connell's population figure for 1712 (and much more problematically for 1687) may be too high, it is important not to assume too readily that there was a marked increase in the efficiency of collecting the hearth tax from 1706. Net revenue rose by only 13 per cent between 1705 and 1706 as the result of moving from farming to direct collection and thereafter the yield rose very modestly in the next six years. The collection of the tax was made difficult by the desperately low prices and chronic shortage of cash characteristic of this period: the tax which was resented by poor taxpayers even eighty years later, must have been even more resented at this time, as the difficulties in acquiring either the income or silver or both to make payment possible were much more acute. The large omissions evident in the population returns by the parish clergy of the Church of Ireland in 1766 are a reminder of the limitations of even a non-fiscal operation, and of the difficulties in both administrative and cultural circumstances of making a comprehensive return of every household in the island.

Whatever the uncertainties, the evidence suggests growth of the population before 1750. Net produce from the hearth-money rose by 14 per cent between 1711 and 1720, the gross produce by 9 per cent between 1719-20 and 1727-8 and by a further 5 per cent by 1739-40 on the eve of the demographic collapse of the early 1740s, which brought the tax yield down to the level of the early 1720s. The upturn in population in the 1750s was therefore not abnormal. Thus the entire period from 1687 to the 1750s was one of growth, but almost certainly with some recession at the outset of the 1690s and possibly in the first decade of the eighteenth century. Before 1687 there was more certainly a period of growth, the rise in the 1650s and 1660s being especially sharp. Since the population figure for 1672 is understated relative to that of 1687, the rate of growth between

[9] *Irish Commons Journal*, iv, app. LXXXIX-XCIX; Public Record Office of Ireland, A registry of reports by Edward Thompson esq., anno 1733. The hearth-money returns for 1701-5 and 1727-31 (app. XCV-XCVI) give a misleading impression of growth as the earlier ones are incorrectly described as the gross produce of the collection.

1652 and 1672 was more rapid than in 1672 to 1687.[10] The years 1600-40 and 1652-9 were periods of high immigration, times, probably, when population growth was greatest: as immigration tended to rise when internal conditions were most benign, the natural increase was probably also sharpest in these years.

Growth in the seventeenth century as a whole appears to be as great as in the eighteenth century, especially if the initial population in 1600 is put at a relatively low level. Even if population growth seems slower after 1672, the contrast is less significant than it appears at first sight, because by then immigration had ceased to play an important role. Immigration recovered for some years at the end of the 1670s, but the only sustained influx thereafter was in the 1690s, caused more by internal crisis in Scotland than by the attractions of Irish conditions. Immigration to rural Ireland for all practical purposes dried up in the first decade of the eighteenth century, when natural increase was also halted. Thereafter, immigration was confined to artisans coming to east-coast towns and cities, numerically important and qualitatively significant, but insufficiently large to give immigration the massive role it had played intermittently in the preceding century.

Changes in immigration could thus largely account for the apparent swings in seventeenth-century growth rates. If this is the case, the birth-rate would have been relatively stable, and in fact likely to have been very high. Contemporaries not only from England but from the Continent, struck by the difference in Irish conditions, commented on the pleasure the Irish took in begetting children.[11] In more modern language what they were saying was that the birth-rate was very high compared with that in their own lands. The implication of this is that Ireland was unaffected by the demographic revolution which had affected western Europe in or before 1500 in which the marriage age rose progressively to around twenty-seven for males and twenty-five for females. Irish marriage ages would

---

[10] Cullen, 'Population Trends', 152.

[11] Letter of 10 November, 1645 from Dean of Fermo to Rinnuccini's brother, quoted in *Irish Times,*, 29 August, 1979; G. O'Brien, ed., *Advertisements for Ireland*, (Dublin, 1923), p. 43; N. A., *Four letters originally written in French relating to the Kingdom of Ireland* (Dublin, 1739), pp. 21-2.

probably have been around 20-22 years in the early seventeenth century. The ages a century later were probably not significantly different. If one were to hypothesize a much lower marriage age, close to puberty, in 1600, it would be difficult to explain the subsequent sharp rise in population for it would imply that the accelerating growth of population over two centuries occurred against a background of rising marriage ages: a situation which is inherently impossible. Rather, the growth of population after 1600 is likely to have taken place in conditions of a high and relatively stable birth-rate and of low marriage ages (with some fluctuation of course not excluded). A rising birth-rate was therefore not important in relation to any acceleration of population growth.

This would suggest that in the eighteenth century a decline in the death-rate was the more likely cause of the rise in population. Of course the fact that the birth-rate was already high is important. If the reduction of the death-rate were concentrated on the young (0-5 years) then a sharp rise in the number of marriages would follow some twenty years later. Ó Gráda has put forward a persuasive case for an abrupt rise in the age of marriage in Ireland several decades before the Great Famine.[12] His argument gains plausibility if the long-term background was one of relatively low marriage ages and of a decisive fall in the death-rate around 1750 leading, in the absence of any short-term change in birth-rates at that stage, to a greatly increased number of marriages some twenty years later. At some later date, probably between 1800 and 1820, pressures would have begun to make it increasingly difficult to adhere to traditional marriage ages.

The growing population in the mid-eighteenth century is related in a complex way to the expansion of trade and the increase in domestic industry. While population growth could have encouraged economic development in various ways, better economic conditions could also have helped to keep the birth-rate high. The dramatic growth in domestic employment in the textile industries from the late 1740s would be quite important in this context. The rate of growth of foreign trade was uniquely high in the third quarter of the century, and

[12] C. Ó Gráda, 'Demographic adjustment and seasonal migration in nineteenth-century Ireland' in L. M. Cullen and F. Furet, eds. *Towards a Comparative Study of Rural History* (Paris, 1980).

national income may have risen sharply also. Even wages for domestic service, traditionally very stable, rose sharply in the late 1760s. These changes meant a movement from purely subsistence conditions, and if people were better off it was because earnings had been monetized or monetized earnings had been increased. Year-to-year fluctuations in the hearth-money returns, which reflected mobility in difficult years by the poor rather than mortality, declined in number from the end of the 1740s[13] as cash savings enhanced people's ability to survive difficult seasons. The change was nation-wide, affecting even the most remote areas. Higher prices for young livestock benefited smallholders and the increase in domestic service in farm households took away the surplus children, especially females of the poorest families, once they reached the age of eight or nine.

The commercialization of the Irish economy was reflected in growing sales of butter and pork by smallholders at the cost of forgoing consumption of these commodities within the household or by compensating for the loss by keeping more poultry. In such conditions commercialization often made more headway through necessity among the poor than among the better off who were slower to change their ways. Farmers continued to eat butter and pork; the poorer families ate less of these goods. Weavers were quicker to take up tea-drinking than were farmers. Whiskey production had formerly been poorly commercialized, much of it produced privately in anticipation of rare festive occasions. After mid-century, rural people began to buy it in quantity, an industry, legal or clandestine, coming into being. Even in good years, cottiers and labourers were increasingly food buyers in the spring. If their own food supply failed, the income that bought whiskey, tea, or tobacco, could be switched to food.

The role of the potato in mid-century is more complex than it appears at first sight. It cannot be linked simply to population growth for population had been growing over a century and a half and probably more rapidly in the seventeenth than in the first half of the eighteenth century. Moreover, the significance

---

[13] L. M. Cullen, 'Economic and Social History, 1691-1800' in T. W. Moody, F. X. Martin, and F. J. Byrne, eds., *A New History of Ireland*, vol. iv, forthcoming.

acquired by the potato in mid-century—Connell's emphasis on it was not misplaced because its use did increase sharply after mid-century—is not related simply to subsistence or to poverty. It is related to commercialization and to the urge to increase cash incomes, not solely to pay rents, but to buy the conventional luxuries of good years or the food that was dramatically helping people to improve their condition in the bad years. What is most striking about the Irish economy is its high degree of commercialization and how increasingly foods which in other societies were consumed within the family were sold. Commercialization which affected the diet of the poor early in the eighteenth century affected the better-off farmers as time went by. At the end of the century, farmers were uprooting orchards in County Armagh because of the demand by weavers for plots at high rents. High prices attracted farmers to sell more of their own produce: some evidence seems to suggest that the high prices of the Napoleonic era had a marked catalysing effect. By the end of the nineteenth century, even comfortable farmers were selling their own bacon and eating imported fat American bacon. Population growth in Ireland can thus be seen not simply in terms of food supply but of the interplay between food supply and commercialization. So typical did food purchases become that foods which had no commercial outlet at all but which were immensely useful to poor families where they were available—certain sea fish, pike, other coarse lake and river fish, and the less sought-after varieties of shell fish—acquired a social stigma and were quickly abandoned by individual families or whole districts as circumstances permitted them to switch to more expensive bought foods.

Irish diet must first be looked at both in terms of its distinctive features which mark it off from other national diets, and of its internal social distinctions resulting from the ability of better-off families (farmers as opposed to cottiers) to resist the blandishments of commercialization and retain some of the original features of their diet. Reduced to crude statistical terms, Irish diet has even today several significant distinctive features. The per capita consumption of butter is the highest in the world, meat consumption per capita is also relatively high— even without taking into account the fact that incomes in most major meat-eating countries are substantially higher—and the range of meats consumed is uniquely wide, spread across beef, pork, and mutton in almost equal proportions. The fact that at one and the same time Irish consumption of meat and butter is very high and per capita consumption of the potato also the highest in the world, suggests the complexity of the diet.

The present high butter consumption was greatly exceeded in the past in rural Ireland: as late as 1600 Irish diet was based primarily on milk, both liquid and in its many solid and semi-solid forms, a dependence even at that time already uncommon as a general pattern in Europe. The Norman invasion in the twelfth century had also introduced a quite different dietary pattern. As the conquest was incomplete and the colony receded in the fourteenth and fifteenth centuries, the two patterns over-lapped and in the march or frontier lands even fused—the butter-based tradition of Gaelic Ireland and the tradition in the Norman areas of gruels and puddings based on cereals, peas, and beans and of bread often of mixed cereals and sometimes even incorporating beans. In Ireland, probably more than half the oats were consumed in the form of porridge.[14] In the old Anglo-Norman areas peas and beans loomed large in the diet, and in these areas, as in the Gaelic areas, the scant evidence seems to suggest a greater prominence of gruels and porridge than of bread in the diet as late as the early seventeenth century. It is clear that the relative absence of bread struck outsiders. Even in the English Pale, the author of *Advertisements for Ireland* in 1623 observed that all their corn was 'eaten up by their peasants that attend their tillage and husbandry before half the year be spent'.[15] Peas and beans of course supplemented this diet; and in the Pale as much more heavily outside it, milk was immensely important in the diet. By contrast with England and lowland Scotland, the wetter Irish climate favoured dairying. As early as the twelfth century the chronicler Geraldus Cam-brensis who accompanied the Normans to Ireland observed that the unceasing rain made the reaping of the harvest diffi-cult,[16] and Boate in 1652 reflected the attitude of the new

---

[14] A. T. Lucas, 'Irish Food Before the Potato', *Gwerin*, iii (1960), 8, 30.

[15] *Advertisements for Ireland*, p. 33.

[16] J. J. O'Meara, ed., *The Topography of Ireland by Geraldus Cambrensis*, (Dublin, 1951), 14-15.

English settlers in observing that the danger to the Irish harvest was not from scorching dryness but from excessive rain.[17]

It is not surprising therefore that diet especially among the Gaelic population should have depended on milk and milk products. Butter, whey, and curds constituted the main items in their summer diet, and the autumn harvest of oats, supplemented by butter, formed the winter food supply. Butter was regarded as a winter food, and the practice of burying tubs of butter was a means of saving food for the lean days before the supply of milk resumed with the fresh pastures of late spring. As late as 1802 in County Tyrone, many parts of which were remote and comparatively unchanged, the 'maxim of the common people is, to live on buttermilk in summer, and reserve the butter for winter'.[18]

Outsiders had been impressed in the seventeenth century by the consumption of milk and butter, especially by the prodigal use of butter as a food in its own right rather than as a garnish. Some echoes of this can be detected centuries later, as for instance in the fact that duck eggs with a generous helping of butter were an alternative to meat every second day in the dinner of farmworkers fed by a farmer in north County Dublin.[19] Moreover, butter had often been added in large lumps to broths, or was mixed in quantities with oatmeal and roasted in front of the fire. The latter practice was described by Gernon in 1620 as one of the foods of the 'baser cabbins',[20] but it became archaic. Cheese consumption, which was well established in medieval times, was still widespread in the seventeenth century, although subordinate to butter and curds. It collapsed in the eighteenth century, though a tradition of cream cheese lingered on, especially in comfortable homes, well into the nineteenth century. Vegetables and 'salads' entered upper-class diets but with the exception of cabbage, were not a significant component of popular diets. Cabbage had always been important and as late as 1830 the diarist Humphrey O'Sullivan noted that in the

---

[17] G. Boate, *Ireland's Natural History* (London, 1652), pp. 167-8.
[18] J. McEvoy, *Statistical Survey of ... Tyrone* (Dublin, 1802), p. 81.
[19] L. J. Kettle, *Material for Victory: the Memoirs of Andrew J. Kettle* (Dublin, 1958), p. 5.
[20] Luke Gernon, 'A Discourse of Ireland', *c*.1620, in C. L. Falkiner, *Illustrations of Irish History* (Dublin, 1904), p. 360.

lean summer of that year the poor of Callan were surviving in part on cabbage.[21]

The main consumption of cereals must have taken place in the winter and early spring before the supply of milk resumed. Thus, given the complex seasonal pattern, important though milk was in the diet, its supremacy could easily be overstated. Conversely, the importance of bread could be underestimated, because while porridge was more important, bread was well-established even if overshadowed in the day-to-day diet of ordinary people by porridge. The comment of foreign observers was that bread was little used, not that it was unknown. In fact, bread, easily portable, was essential for the military hosting, for the ambulant worker, or for the traveller, a fact no less evident to the largely potato-eating poor of the rural country-side in the early nineteenth century.

A diet of milk and butter presupposes an abundance of dairy cattle and is typically found in thinly populated countries with little foreign trade. As population increases, access to land and cattle for many of the poorer members of a community is limited, and at the same time the growth of trade in butter gives it a commercial value and transfers it from the countryside. The impressive growth of population and trade in Ireland in the seventeenth century thus operated to alter the basis of Irish diet quite independently of other factors. The growth of trade in butter from an almost non-existent level presupposed a more varied diet and a greater dependence on other foods during the winter months; and for the very poor, reduced even in favourable circumstances to the possession of a single cow, an even greater reliance on non-dairy products. The greater emphasis on porridge as opposed to bread in much lower-class diet in eighteenth-century rural Ireland seems to be a reflection of unchanged attitudes inherited from earlier times, but the presence of bread, whether oaten, barley, wheaten, or mixed, in lower-class diet in many regions, reflects complex internal patterns or frontiers in bread-baking of native, Anglo-Norman, or more recent origin. The decline in butter and milk, especially in the diets of the poor, explains both the increased reliance on bread and porridge, and the growing dependence on the potato.

[21] M. McGrath, ed., *Diary of Humphrey O'Sullivan*, 4 vols., (Dublin, 1936-7), vol. iii, p. 313.

The early potato's keeping qualities were very indifferent and its value as a supplement to the butter or winter food, which was now becoming scarce, for the labourer or cottier, was obvious. As grain supply was modest and difficult to stretch out over the entire year, the potato promised to take the place of or supplement the winter supply of butter, and, by economizing oats consumption in winter, to guarantee more effectively the food supply from the spring onwards. It is clear that the changes in diet in the seventeenth century were interrelated, especially for the poor, and that the objective, consciously or unconsciously, in responding to economic pressures, was to use every available food between grain, potatoes, and butter to secure a supply of food over the entire year.

The contrast between Irish and outside conditions was arresting to foreign visitors who were more numerous from the outset of the seventeenth century and who made a closer acquaintance with the countryside, whether on military service or in travel, than the few and perfunctory visitors of the past. The striking contrasts in diet led them to seize on it as they did on hygiene as yardsticks of comparative civilization. From Moryson to Jouvin de Rochefort to Dinely and Dunton, not to mention lesser fry, a series of close observations emerged.[22] Gernon's *Discourse of Ireland*, *c.*1620, has some invaluable though little quoted observations on food, especially significant, made as they were by an English-born resident of Irish ancestry with a particularly keen and not unsympathetic insight into Irish life-styles.[23] Significantly, the comments of such observers are much more specific for the seventeenth century than for the eighteenth century, precisely because Irish diet was more singular at that stage: later comments are as a rule more banal, their only observations drawn by the prominent place of potatoes. Even the *Statistical Surveys* commissioned by the Dublin Society at the outset of the nineteenth century are not on balance very helpful. The most penetrating comments come

---

[22] Fynes Moryson, *An Itinerary …* (London, 1617); Gernon's *Discourse*, Bodley's *Visit to Lecale* and De Rochefort's *Description* as reproduced in Falkiner; Dinely's *Tour*, National Library of Ireland, MS 392; Dunton's account as reproduced in E. MacLysaght, *Irish Life in the Seventeenth Century* (Cork, 1950, 2nd ed.). See also *The Present State of Ireland* (London, 1673) and 'Of the Irish', Bodleian Library, Locke MS c.31, f.40. I am indebted to D. Dickson for the latter reference.

[23] Gernon, cited in Falkiner.

from those observers who made close contact with the people, and stayed on occasion in their cabins. Of these, the most remarkable come from the unpublished diaries of the Frenchman, Coquebert de Montbret.[24] By the 1830s study of poverty as a general problem tended to overshadow diet as an issue in its own right: published accounts were noticeably less specific than earlier writings, although the reports of the Commission on the State of the Poor in the 1830s have never been analysed as closely as they merit for their information on lower-class diets at that date. Several problems have made the study of Irish diet difficult. The first is the marked seasonal variations in the pattern, which accounts for much of what at first sight is contradiction in contemporary sources. Another is the fact that outside visitors were accustomed to the ready availability of bread at any hour: the unleavened oatcakes of the Irish countryside were usually baked just ahead of their immediate consumption. The diaries of Humphrey O'Sullivan in the 1820s and 1830s are a rich source providing a series of observations over several years which illustrate both the diet of the modest *notables* of a poor country town and its hinterland, and the precarious diet of the very poor.[25] Evidence on diet begins to become more substantial from the middle of the eighteenth century. Labourers' accounts in estate records, for instance, illustrate in the cash advances for food purchases the shift in spring from potatoes to meal. Dietary patterns sometimes over long periods

[24] In the Bibliothèque Municipale, Rouen, and Bibliothèque Nationale, Paris. The Paris diaries are also available on microfilm in the National Library of Ireland. I am much indebted to Síle Ní Chinnéide for information from the diaries over many years. See also the following by S. Ní Chinnéide: 'A Frenchman's impressions of Limerick Town and People in 1791', *North Munster Antiquarian Journal*, v (1948), 96-101; 'Coquebert de Montbret's impressions of Galway City and County in the year 1791', *Journal of the Galway Archaeological and Historical Society*, xxv (1952), 1-14; 'A Journey from Cork to Limerick in December 1790', *North Munster Antiquarian Journal*, xiv (1971), 65-74; 'A New View of Eighteenth Century Life in Kerry', *Journal of the Kerry Archaeological and Historical Society*, 6 (1973), 83-100; 'A New View of Cork City in 1790', 'A Frenchman's Impressions of County Cork in 1790', parts I and II, *Journal of the Cork Historical and Archaeological Society*, lxxviii (1973), 1-13, 117-23, lxxix (1974) 14-25; 'An Eighteenth-Century French Traveller in Kildare', *Journal of County Kildare Archaeological Society*, xv (1974), 376-86; 'A Frenchman's Tour of Connaught in 1791', Parts I and II, *Journal of the Galway Archaeological and Historical Society*, xxxv (1976), 52-66; xxxvi (1979), 30-42; 'A view of Kilkenny City and County in 1790', *Journal of the Royal Society of Antiquaries of Ireland*, civ (1974), 29-38; 'A Journey from Mullingar to Loughrea in 1791', *Journal of Old Athlone Society*, ii (1978), 15-23.

[25] Diary of Humphrey O'Sullivan, op. cit.

are reflected in the account books of congregations of religious orders. As early as 1690-1 the experiences of French and Danish troops in Ireland document the quite unfamiliar problems their commissariats had to face.

The process under way in the seventeenth century was not the one of contraction of food supply seen by Salaman[26] but of change to a more varied diet and change from simple foods like porridge to bread. In particular since much oatmeal was consumed as porridge, easier to make and less novel in traditional diets than bread, it seems quite likely that many countrymen under the commercial pressures of the age may have come to use the potato without ever having consumed bread regularly.

A Danish soldier recorded in 1691 lying in quarters in Cork with an old man who said to him that he had eaten no bread other than potatoes for sixteen years.[27] From what we know of eating habits and the keeping qualities of the potato, this seems impossible at this period. It does not imply an exlusively potato diet in the way that the quotation has usually been interpreted, but a diet in which there were seasonally other constituents. To a lowland Scot, Englishman, or Dane, for whom bread was the staff of life, a diet lacking it would have seemed scarcely comprehensible. A poem by the Gaelic poet Seán O Neachtain shows how, in fact, a diet characterized by the consumption of potatoes was not as restricted as it might look at first sight: the poem, incidentally to its main purpose, contrasts the diet of the lowland people of the Dublin and Kildare plain, consisting of grain, peas, and beans in the form of porridge, and to a lesser extent bread, with the upland people of the Dublin and Wicklow mountains beyond Tallaght, who had a potato diet. The contrast did not lie in poverty; the upland people's potatoes which were said to last from the first of August till St. Patrick's day were accompanied by 'ever-lasting happiness and roast meat'.[28] It also implies reliance on other foods, presumably grain, very probably oats, for the remainder of the calendar. The potato's importance increased undeniably in the eighteenth century, no longer supplementing but even replacing bread or

[26] R. N. Salaman, *The History and Social Influence of the Potato* (Cambridge, 1949).
[27] K. Danaher and J. J. Simms, eds., *The Danish Forces in Ireland 1690-91* (Irish Manuscripts Commission, Dublin, 1962), p. 15.
[28] R. McKay, ed., *An Anthology of the Potato* (Dublin, 1961), p. 26.

porridge in the diet of the poor, and becoming prominent even in regions where it had made little headway before 1700. In the closing years of the eighteenth century the potato began to spread very rapidly throughout Europe, but with initial greater reliance on it at the outset, dependence on it remained more marked in Ireland.

Changes in diet and foot in Ireland since the 1880s are part of a widespread revolution in rural Europe; the gradual evolution of the Irish diet between 1600 and 1880, however, had few European parallels. The dependence on butter as opposed to cereals and, within cereal consumption, the reliance on porridge as opposed to bread, testified to the limited evolution attained by Irish diet by 1600 compared to that of other countries which had experienced the changes centuries previously. The sustained evolution of diet after 1600 resulted in the presence to a remarkable degree of archaic and modern elements simultaneously. The Irishman of the mid-nineteenth century was likely to be familiar with potatoes, oaten or wheaten bread, maize, and butter in substantial quantities. The belated evolution of the Irish diet gave it a fossilized character with the survival in comfortable rural households of a heavy consumption of milk and butter. Diet is conditioned by several underlying influences, a factor of special relevance to Ireland, because of its comparatively belated transition. First, there is the evolution from primitive to more modern diets, effectively the replacement of 'moist' diets based on butter, puddings, or porridges by more solid diets based on bread. A butter-based diet was the diet of a relatively primitive people. Survival on the milk of the dairy herd was more economical than reliance on meat which entailed the large costs of rearing replacement animals to maturity. Frugal in its approach to livestock husbandry and implying summer abundance and winter penury, it was therefore easily associated with poverty. Second, the evolution of diet was powerfully influenced by commercialization: while country people produced a wide variety of products, foods once widely consumed were often abandoned by necessity or choice as they acquired an enhanced price. The gradual decline in the consumption of butter in Ireland is intimately linked to commercialization, which created markets. As late as 1687 Sir William Petty thought the growing exports of butter were the produce of dairies maintained by English settlers in Ireland;[29] by implication the native Irish ate their own butter instead of sending it to market. The very fact that butter production expanded in the Cork region in the 1720s and 1730s at a time when nationally exports temporarily fell, suggests that the cumulative consequences of commercialized butter production outweighed diversification of food supply and that the process of popular dietary impoverishment in that region advanced significantly in those two decades. In the Cork and Kerry region which had experienced a sustained growth in dairying from 1720 to 1775, Young thought the conditions of labourers worse than elsewhere in the kingdom, many or most of the labourers having no cow and having to buy milk.[30] The situation worsened subsequently in the dairying regions of Cork and Waterford, and at the outset of the nineteenth century, while milk was already rare in the diet of labourers, the diet even of middle-sized farmers seemed sparing.

The high monetary value of beef and the importance of cattle in inland trade is reflected in the fact that throughout rural Ireland, pork and mutton were the meats most widely consumed. The wide availability of pork is in part explained by the growing importance of potatoes and the fact that potatoes as a largely non-commercial crop made easier the fattening of a pig. Pig-meat was invariably cheapest in the season after potatoes had become available, and when potatoes were particularly abundant, the pig population rose sharply. The feeding of pigs on potatoes developed only in the eighteenth century after potatoes had ceased to be a garden crop and had become a field one. As late as 1729 the writer Arthur Dobbs clearly envisaged pigs as fed simply on 'thrash'.[31] Pigs fed on grain or beach mast were necessarily something of a luxury, although a prized one, as the numerous references to them in the source material for early historic and medieval Ireland show.[32] In

[29] W. Petty, *Treatise of Ireland* (1687) in C. H. Hull, *Economic Writings of Sir William Petty* (Cambridge, 1899), ii, 594.

[30] Arthur Young, *Tour in Ireland 1776-79*, A. W. Hutton, ed. (London, 1892), i, pp. 340-1, 369, 456.

[31] Arthur Dobbs, *Essay on the Trade and Improvement of Ireland*, (1729-31) in n.a., *A Collection of Tracts and Treatises Illustrative ... of Ireland* (Dublin, 1861), ii, p. 349.

[32] Lucas, pp. 15-16.

consequence, even as late as the 1670s the traveller Dinely regarded the consumption of pork as confined to 'people of condition'.[33] The spread of potatoes brought about a dramatic change by reducing the cost of pigkeeping and transforming pork from a relative luxury into the most universal and cheapest meat. Pork exports themselves rose—although the pork trade was slow to become commercialized, and began to be so extensively only from the last three decades of the eighteenth century. The cheapness of potatoes ensured that the supply of pig-meat kept ahead of export trade. Since many pigs were produced for home consumption even in cottier households, much pig production took place outside the market context. No doubt commercialization did lead to the withdrawal of pork from the consumption of households, and in addition the proportion of labourers and cottiers not keeping a pig increased sharply in pre-Famine Ireland. But the majority of rural households still kept a pig for their own consumption at the end of the eighteenth century and the practice was so general that pork or bacon became the popular form of meat. In a prosperous region like Kilkenny and Waterford in 1790, at a time when the pig trade was still only in the early stages of commercialization and when labourers still had access to sufficient land for potatoes, Coquebert de Montbret, a French visitor, had not seen a cabin with fewer than two or three pigs.[34]

Changes in Irish diet were thus in no small measure determined by the forces of commercialization. The major exporter in Europe of beef and butter in the eighteenth century, Ireland became very rapidly an exporter of grain and flour in enormous quantities to Britain in the early nineteenth century. Exports, rising to a million quarters, soared to two million quarters, and even to three million quarters at their peak in the 1830s. Such a vast and rapid change taking place within a comparatively short period implied significant reorganization in Irish agriculture, notably the increased importance of root crops, in Ireland almost invariably potatoes, in crop rotations if soil fertility was not to be undermined. The spread of the potato

[33] National Library of Ireland, MS 392, p. 269. See also W. Petty, *Political Anatomy of Ireland* 1672 in C. H. Hull, i, 174.
[34] S. Ní Chinnéide, 'A Frenchman's Impressions of County Cork in 1790, part ii', *Journal of the Cork Historical and Archaeological Society*, lxxix (1974), 15.

diet is a complex phenomenon. In the century and a half preceding the 1770s everybody made some use of the potato, even
if only for the poor did it become increasingly the staple of
life. Moreover, the linking of the spread of the potato in its
early stages in Ireland to the native population is very much
open to question. It was grown by immigrant English even
in their first generation in Ireland in the early seventeenth
century. They remained attached to it when they emigrated to
the new world, just as much as did the Irish merchants in
French ports for whom a basket of potatoes was a prized delicacy.
The potato itself, uncommercialized though it was, was devoid
of social stigma: only sole dependence attracted ridicule. The
more general dependence on the potato in the early decades of
the nineteenth century is related to commercialization as much
as to poverty, and for the classes above the cottier and labourer
must be seen as a process of substitution between grain and
potatoes rather than between potatoes and non-grain items in
the diet. It is not at all evident that meat consumption was
altered. Indeed the growing supply of potatoes, cheap in good
years because their market was local, promoted a rapid expansion in pig production, bacon compensating in the diet for
the decline in mutton.

In families above the labourer and cottier levels, heavy potato
consumption thus came late. The belief that the potato debased
Irish diet is subject to much qualification, especially as it was
resorted to by all classes and was a versatile item which enhanced the variety of the diet. The changes in Irish diet in the
late eighteenth and nineteenth centuries were very complex.
Beans and peas virtually disappeared as field crops. Maize
meal was already making its appearance in Irish diet ahead of
the rest of the British Isles and in particular ahead of the Great
Famine with which its use as a food in Ireland is popularly
associated. Its first recorded use as a food in Ireland is in
County Wicklow in the hard season of 1800-1,[35] and it was
extensively consumed in Callan in County Kilkenny in the bad
years at the end of the 1820s and early 1830s.[36] Contemporaries
certainly thought that the potato was driving or already had
driven field crops such as beans, peas, and vegetables out of

---

[35] R. Fraser, *General View of the Agriculture of Wicklow* (Dublin, 1801), p. 56.
[36] *Diary of Humphrey O'Sullivan*, especially i, 51; ii, 181, 285, 315; iv, 41-3.

popular diets,[37] although the decline in beans had in fact been a progressive and long-drawn-out process already in its final stages in 1800. There were other reasons affecting the decline in beans as a field-crop, for they were thought to encourage weeds and in consequence to leave the ground dirty; they were also, it was said, disliked by females for more intimate personal reasons 'to escape a mark, which they are said to impress on the person'.[38]

Irish diet originally had a marked regional character. The most fundamental contrast was between the regions with a diet heavily dependent on butter and milk in all their forms, and the old Anglo-Norman regions which relied more on peas, beans, and grain. The latter regions, largely the Pale, the entire south-east, and much of the Shannon estuary, especially the rich lands along the Fergus on the Clare side where beans were still cultivated extensively as late as 1808, given their comparative wealth, had at least in stable conditions little need to adopt new foods, and in a culinary sense seem to have been the most conservative regions in Ireland. Dried peas and beans preserved well, and supplemented the grain supply. This diet buttressed with milk and butter from May onwards, was sufficient to provide an all-year-round supply of food. In the cereal and pulse region the period of scarcity was the late spring and early summer before the new crops arrived. This accounted for the emphasis on peas and beans which supplemented the grain supply and which because they ripened early helped to ensure that the food supply could be eked out over the critical months before the next year's grain harvest. This also accounts for the emphasis in traditional diets on bere, or winter barley, which ripened as early as July, well ahead of the other cereals in this region.

In contrast to the cereal-pulse regions where scarcity was a feature of the summer, winter was the season of scarcity in milk regions: cows went dry in the autumn, and the widespread practice of burying butter in wicker baskets in bogs is testimony

---

[37] W. Tighe, *Statistical Survey Relative to the County of Kilkenny* (Dublin, 1802), pp. 479-80; *Munster Farmer's Magazine*, May 1819, vi, pp. 114-5; *Diary of Humphrey O'Sullivan*, i, 277. I am indebted to D. Dickson for the reference from the *Munster Farmer's Magazine*.

[38] W. Shaw Mason, *Statistical Account, or Parochial Survey of Ireland*, iii (Dublin, 1819), p. 410; R. Fraser, *Statistical Survey of the County of Wexford* (Dublin, 1807), p. 79.

to the necessity of storing food for the winter and spring before the resumption of grass growth in April when the cows calved and the milk supply began again. The dairying regions were coming out of crisis therefore at a time when in cereal-pulse districts the supply of cereals and pulses was beginning to run out. The potato, until the late-keeping varieties of the closing decades of the eighteenth century appeared, did not keep well, and had to be consumed in the winter and spring: many early accounts of the potato emphasize it as a food item from August to March, St. Patrick's day being the traditional divide. In the dairying districts with their winter food shortage, the incorporation of the potato which had to be consumed immediately was therefore particularly attractive. It is hardly accidental that most regions where the potato was tithed were in Munster, much of whose economy was based on dairying from an early date. Similarly, Kilkenny, where dairying loomed large in the economy, and where resistance to the tithe proved longest and fiercest in the dairying south of the county, was the only Leinster county where the potato paid tithes. It is tempting to assume that the imposition of tithe on the potato took place in those areas where the potato first became prominent and that tithe was not extended to it as it became important in other areas simply because of the halt called to the aggressive tithing policy of the Church of Ireland by growing lay resistance which culminated in the disputes of the 1720s and 1730s. The results of this resistance have usually been seen as selfish, as reflected in the celebrated resolution by the Commons in 1735 against the levying of the tithe on dry cattle. One of the indirect results of the resolution may however have been of more popular benefit—to halt the spread of a tithe on potatoes to other counties. Potato tithe was still a local issue in some areas in the middle decades of the century, emphasizing the fact that the tuber was only acquiring significance at a relatively late date. The fact that outside Munster and Kilkenny the potato was untithed, while cereals and pulses paid tithes, must itself have enhanced the attractions of the potato for people on the margin of subsistence.

Whatever its regional distinctions, Irish diet in its way was varied. While the Danish soldiers in Ireland in 1690-1 were struck by the comparative absence of bread, they were clearly impressed by the availability of other foods, and by the possibilities of substitution between foods. Such observations in the middle of a military campaign are in their own way remarkable; for they indicate the way in which Irish diet was evolving. The emphasis in the literature has exaggerated the poverty of Irish diet; in the seventeenth century it was becoming more varied and while the potato was the dominant new element it was not the sole one. Thus, to take one illustration, while beans and peas declined in their traditional locations, they actually spread in the poorer regions of mid-Ulster, almost certainly in consequence of imitation of the diet of English settlers in Armagh who brought a more varied diet to Ulster to supplement the narrow existing one of the region. With its extensive use of beans, grain, potatoes, and butter, Irish diet had a variety of products to help it over the difficult months of spring and summer. Ireland escaped famine entirely in the 1690s and in the first decade of the eighteenth century, although both Scotland and Denmark were stricken in the 1690s and France in the 1690s and again in 1709. Famine remained a feature of relatively backward societies that failed to advance quickly beyond a secure threshold of sufficiency in food supply, but later Irish food difficulties should not be assessed without taking into account the fact that Scandinavia experienced severe famine as late as the early 1740s, France nearly experienced it in 1788, and Finland, at the time still a relatively backward country, as late as 1867.

The fact that famine was experienced in Ireland twice in the eighteenth century—in 1728-9 and 1740-1—and near famine in three years—1745, 1757, and 1783-4—reminds us, however, of the countryman's continuing need or interest in varying and supplementing his food supply. A country with a wet climate was particularly vulnerable to harvest failure, and in fact the one year of near-famine without a bad harvest also occurring in the immediately preceding year came in the wake of the torrential rains of the summer of 1744, which ruined the grain and destroyed the hay that would have helped to carry livestock over the winter in good condition. There is some evidence, impressionistic because seventeenth-century sources are poor, that near-famine was more common in the eighteenth century in Ireland than in the seventeenth century. If this is correct, one of the reasons for it may have been the decline in a butter diet. A larger population meant inevitably a significant increase in the number of families with few, if any, dairy cattle. Until the middle of the century many of these families were able to rent grazing for a single cow or two, but the milk supply from one or two cows was not sufficient to provide a very large surplus of butter for the winter. The critical period of shortage for a primitive dairying community was the winter and spring; in May, on the other hand, when the food supply of cereal districts was running out, the resumption of grass growth ensured an abundant supply of food. Because the ownership of dairy cattle became less general, the proportion of the population at risk in the spring rose sharply, and a short grain or potato supply after the harvest heralded a critical shortage in the following spring. On the whole, food supplies seem to have deteriorated somewhat in Ireland after the relatively halcyon 1690s and the first decade of the eighteenth century, whereas in both Scotland and France the community successfully put famine behind it after 1699 and 1709 respectively, though the margin of survival was still often painfully slender in individual seasons. This margin was the more critical for Ireland because as cow ownership, more significant in Ireland than in drier France or colder Scotland, ceased to be universal, there was a decline in family availability of food in the spring to face the traditional shortages of grain and potatoes in the late spring. The fact of an emerging milk and butter shortage added greatly to the interest of the poor in having potatoes, because the earliest potatoes were available at the beginning of August two months ahead of the staple cereal of the poor districts, the late ripening oats. With its cloudy summer, ripening of all cereal crops tended to be later than in the drier climates of lowland Scotland, England, and France. The habit of late harvesting was thus well established and persisted even in the years when sunshine could guarantee an earlier one. An attachment of the Irish countryman to a late harvest was noted by many contemporaries, and is attributable to the habits created by the uncertain harvests more than to the insouciance which observers commented on. It was of course also promoted by the fact that many smallholders could gather their own harvests only after working on the harvests of large farmers or gentry or after their return from migrant harvest work to the south or east.

In the last analysis Ireland remained a poor society, as the distress caused by food failure in 1782-4 after the harvests of 1782 and 1783, and in 1800 and 1801, or regional crises as in South Munster in 1793, suggested. Its incomes were low at the outset of the seventeenth century, even ahead of sustained population growth—its archaic butter-based diet is conclusive proof of that—and poverty therefore preceded population growth. The relationship between population growth and incomes in Ireland as in other countries is a complex affair. Well behind western Europe in culture, behaviour, and development in 1600, the scope for rapid expansion was considerable. In the process, Ireland became a highly export-oriented country, coincidentally with its sustained demographic expansion which, if the period 1600-1845 is taken as a whole, has few parallels within pre-industrial Europe. Growth of trade and population associated with low incomes necessarily promoted a rapid commercialization of any food surpluses within the economy and a persistent process of substitution between foods. In particular the potato, bulky and with poor keeping qualities, which did not lend itself to easy transport or to the speculative carrying-forward of stocks, remained relatively uncommercialized and became increasingly important in diet. Only after 1850 can one detect significant dietary changes in other countries. Before 1850 comparative stability was the norm even if we range as far afield as Brittany or Finland. In Brittany, one of the poorest parts of France, cow ownership remained universal into the early decades of the nineteenth century, whereas it had long ceased to be so in Ireland. A growing dichotomy existed between the farmers and the substratum on the fringe of commercialized agriculture, who were experiencing an alarming impoverishment in their diet from the 1770s. A century later Synge made a perceptive comment on the penury of Irish living standards compared with those of Brittany.[39]

The ultimate proof of Ireland's precarious position was its Great Famine of 1845-8, the last true famine in western Europe, the significance of which has been understated because the

---

[39] R. Tracy, ed., *The Aran Islands and Other Writings by John M. Synge* (New York, 1962), p. 274.

emphasis on the potato has tended to obscure certain under-lying similarities to earlier famines in Europe at large.

Finland's famine in 1867 is of course later: for climatic reasons, a terrible season in which the snows did not end till June, prevented the planting of rye. The Finnish failure, compared with the Irish, was more climatic than economic— all food production was affected, and Finland's diet, rye-based for centuries, had in contrast to Ireland's long been stable. The difference between the 1740 famine and the Great Famine was that in the earlier famine the entire population was at risk; in the later it was much more a regional and social disaster. Things had changed for the better in part because of commercialization itself, but it was still a society in which a relatively high pro-portion of the population was at risk; the real significance of the Famine is the anachronistic condition of Ireland which remained closer to the past than any other society in Europe despite the many changes and the intensely complex evolution of its diet. It was the importance of a subsistence crop and the loss of flexibility it entailed in food supply for the poorest classes and regions that left them vulnerable when faced with the abrupt and novel appearance of potato blight.

The rapid growth of Irish population by European standards becomes very evident if the seventeenth and eighteenth centuries are taken together. Even today's high birth-rate and the slow-ness of the fall in the crude birth-rate over the last century is a reflection of characteristics archaic by European standards. Population growth is of course statistically difficult to study before the era of modern census-taking from 1821. In such circumstances the sustained change in Irish diet from 1600— and the resulting lack of stability in the dietary pattern in comparative terms—is interesting not only in its own right but also because it helps to make it possible to appreciate the dis-tinctive demographic profile of seventeenth- and eighteenth-century Ireland.

5. Indian Meal and Pellagra in Nineteenth-Century Ireland*

E. Margaret Crawford

Indian meal was initially introduced into Ireland as a food substitute for the labouring poor when their staple food, the potato, was in short supply. It is derived from maize by grinding and milling the whole maize grain. The cultivation of maize originated in the New World, but was soon brought across the Atlantic by explorers in the sixteenth century and became established in Mediterranean countries, where climatic conditions were suitable for its growth. Maize is generally much more resistant to drought than wheat, and in addition gives a higher yield per acre. It matures quickly, so that a good crop can be grown in a short season. Maize has for these reasons acquired the reputation of being a poor man's cereal, and in many societies where it has become the staple food the population has been subject to pellagra, a deficiency disease associated with a diet dominated by Indian meal.

Some historians have been under the impression that Indian meal was first imported into Ireland in 1846 to alleviate the crisis of the Great Famine. According to Cecil Woodham-Smith, 'Indian corn was purchased because doing so did not interfere with private enterprise. No trade in Indian corn existed: it was virtually unknown as a food in Ireland ... and was neither imported nor bought and sold.'[1] J. S. Donnelly Jr. is of the same opinion, stating that the grain was 'introduced in order to meet the catastrophic emergency of the famine'.[2] There is, however, ample evidence of Indian meal being eaten by the poor prior to 1846. In the *Statistical Survey of the County of Londonderry*, the Revd Vaughan Sampson, when writing about

* I would like to thank L. A. Clarkson for his advice during the preparation of this paper for publication. My thanks also go to T. C. Barker and Dr Peter Froggatt for their comments on an earlier draft.

[1] C. Woodham-Smith, *The Great Hunger* (London, 1962), p. 50.

[2] J. S. Donnelly Jr., *The Land and the People of Nineteenth Century Cork* (London, 1975), p. 245.

the cost of provisions and labour in 1800, noted that in 'the latter end of July a schooner ... arrived with a cargo of Indian meal'.[3] In the same year John Handcock of Lisburn imported from Philadelphia a consignment of '200 tons of Indian meal, the first sample of that article ever seen in Ulster ... sold at cost price to the more distressed families in Lisburn'.[4] The cause of this distress was a poor yield of potato and grain crops, and in the emergency the government intervened by granting bounties on the importation of grains, including Indian corn and meal.[5] The customs ledgers confirm the arrival of sizeable amounts into several Irish ports, as can be seen in Table 5.1:

Table 5.1   Indian corn imports into Ireland
(in barrels)

	1799	1800	1801	1802
Belfast	-	2 024	4 287	16
Cork	-	1 341	3 779	-
Dublin	-	8 284	2 977	-
Newry	-	630	1 559	-
Londonderry	-	1 125	-	-
Total	-	13 404	12 602	16

Indian meal imports into Ireland
(cwt)

	1799	1800	1801	1802
Belfast	-	1 096	21 553 ½	-
Cork	-	2 280 ¾	15 867	-
Dublin	-	9 760 ¾	51 796 ¼	-
Newry	-	6 883	12 799 ¼	262
Londonderry	-	-	19 457 ¼	-
Sligo	-	-	17	-
Waterford	-	-	22 410 ½	-
Killybegs	-	-	2 465 ¾	-
Kinsale	-	-	4 061 ¾	-
Total	-	20 020 ½	150 428 ¼	262

Source: Public Record Office, London, Cust 15/103, 104, 105, 106.

[3] G. V. Sampson, *Statistical Survey of the County of Londonderry* (Dublin, 1802), p. 316.
[4] W. J. Green, *A Concise History of Lisburn and Neighbourhood* (Belfast, 1906), p. 23.
[5] *Journal of the House of Lords*, XLIII (1801), 140.

Between 1803 and 1826 there are no records of imports of Indian corn or meal into Ireland. However, it was brought in again in the distressed year of 1827. Humphrey O'Sullivan, a schoolteacher in Callen, County Kilkenny, noted in his diary on 12 May 1827 that 'Indian meal has come in from America: many people like it well: it will keep down the cost of living for the poor.'[6] Again on 27 June 1827 he wrote, 'we were distributing Indian meal to-day ... the spirit of the Gael is very much broken'.[7] Such references suggest that Indian meal was eaten at this time, only when crops failed in Ireland. During the 1830s and the early years of the 1840s imports amounted to little more than an annual trickle. However, from 1846 Indian meal became an important part of the labourers' staple diet, a fact confirmed by the establishment of a large though fluctuating import trade, dietary surveys, a study of workhouse diets, and contemporary observations.

Table 5.2 and Figure 5.1 show the course of importation of Indian corn and meal into Ireland between the Famine and the end of the nineteenth century. Following a rapid growth in the Famine years, imports fluctuated around a gradually rising trend, with the average level of the Famine years not being regularly exceeded until the 1880s.

Table 5.2   Averages of Indian corn and meal
imports to Ireland 1840-99 (in cwt)

1840-44	..	..	29 432
1845-49	..	..	5 833 014
1850-54	..	..	4 490 183
1855-59	..	..	2 754 022
1860-64	..	..	5 109 497
1865-69	..	..	4 001 033
1870-74	..	..	5 118 860
1875-79	..	..	8 199 613
1880-84	..	..	6 003 693
1885-89	..	..	6 367 079
1890-94	..	..	7 983 721
1895-99	..	..	9 477 956

Sources: *Returns of ... Grain or Flour imported into
Ireland* ..., P.P. 1849 (588), L, 404;
Returns ..., P.P. 1852 (537), LI, 484-5;
Return ..., P.P. 1857-8 (101), LIII, 467; and in
Parliamentary Papers annually thereafter.
See also P. M. Austin Bourke, 'The Irish Grain Trade
1839-48', *Irish Historical Studies*, xx (1976-7), 156-69.

[6] S. J. McGrath, ed., *The Diary of Humphrey O'Sullivan*, vol. i, (London, 1936), p. 51.
[7] Ibid., p. 79.

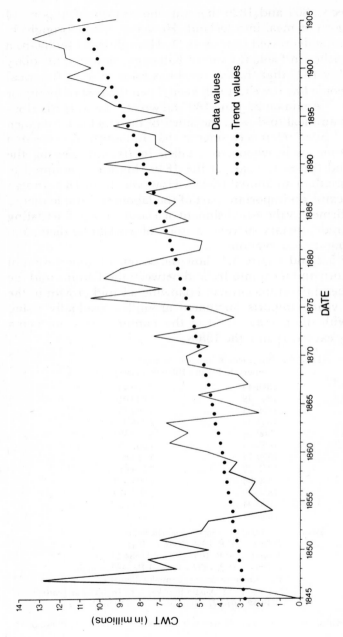

Figure 5.1   Imports of Indian corn at principal Irish ports 1845-1905

Unfortunately statistics of direct importation are not a totally reliable measure of human consumption of Indian meal. Some may have come into Ireland from British ports, for which few figures are available between 1851 and 1904. However, the bulk of Indian corn imports originated in North America and there was no particular advantage in bringing it first into Britain and then reshipping it to Ireland. When statistics of cross-channel trade were published again from 1904, the proportion of total imports coming from Britain was small.[8] There was also an insignificant re-export trade in Indian corn from a few Irish ports.[9]

More important, Indian meal was also used for feeding livestock and poultry. Large quantities, for example, were imported into Great Britain where it was used almost exclusively for livestock feedstuff. By the end of the nineteenth century maize products were the most important of all the animal feedstuffs bought by British farmers.[10] However, the position was very different in Ireland where an abundance of grass reduced the need for imported feed. Furthermore, the mild winters permitted the extensive outwintering of cattle and sheep, a practice that remained general until the twentieth century.[11] Winter grass might be supplemented by hay and root crops, but rarely, it seems, by imported feeds. A little Indian meal was fed to pigs, but there is abundant evidence that domestic pigs were fed principally on potatoes; some Indian meal was also used in commercial pig-meat production by the twentieth century, but in small amounts, otherwise it produced an oily, soft, yellow carcase.[12] Probably more substantial amounts of Indian meal were fed to poultry and it is likely that much of the upward trend in imports was associated with the increase in poultry

[8] *Report on the Trade in Imports and Exports at Irish Ports during the year 1904*, P. P. 1906 [Cd. 3237], CXIV, 655; and in Parliamentary Papers annually thereafter.

[9] Ibid.

[10] T. W. Fletcher, 'The Great Depression of English Agriculture 1873-1896', *Economic History Review*, 2nd Ser. xiii (1961), 420; E. M. Ojala, *Agriculture and Economic Progress* (Oxford, 1952), pp. 212-13, 215. Ojala assumed that all United Kingdom maize imports were for animals.

[11] J. O'Donovan, *Economic History of Livestock in Ireland* (Cork, 1940), pp. 142, 164, 249; Donnelly, p. 140; Raymond D. Crotty, *Irish Agricultural Production* (Cork, 1966), p. 70.

[12] O'Donovan, pp. 266-7; Ministry of Agriculture, Fisheries and Food, *Rations for Livestock*, Bulletin No 48 (London, 1970), p. 38.

numbers in Ireland and with the growth of an egg trade with England and Scotland.[13]

The rising trend in imports shown on the Graph reflects the growing need of livestock and poultry, but in the present context the peaks above the trend are more significant. Except for 1876[14] the peaks coincide with the subsistence crisis of the Great Famine, and the subsequent lesser subsistence crises of 1859-64, 1872, 1879-80, and 1890 when there was acute shortage of food for both people and livestock. In these years a large, though indeterminate, part of the increase in imports was to provide food for human consumption.

The attraction of Indian meal as a substitute for the potato was its cheapness: it was one of the cheapest foods by which human life could be sustained. Although it could not be grown in Ireland, imported Indian meal cost less than home-grown oatmeal. Sampson quoted the price of Indian meal in 1800 as 2*s*. a peck (2½*d*. per lb), and oatmeal at 4*s*. 6*d*. a peck. The price differential continued; O'Sullivan gave the price of Indian meal in 1827 as 3*d*. a pottle (a small wicker basket), and oatmeal at 5*d*. a pottle. In March 1846—at the height of the Famine—Indian meal was released on to the market by the government at 1*d*. per lb, rising to 2½*d*. per lb in 1847, by which time private enterprise had taken over. Meanwhile oatmeal prices were considerably higher, and certainly far beyond the pocket of the labouring poor. This pattern continued throughout the nineteenth century. A report from the Poor Law Inspectors on agricultural labourers' wages noted that in 1850 the price per ton of Indian meal was £7 10*s*., and for oat-

---

[13] J. H. Tuke, *The Condition of Donegal. Letters reprinted from The Times* (London, 1889), p. 17; *Second Report by Mr Wilson Fox on the Wages, Earnings and Conditions of Employment of Agricultural Labourers in the United Kingdom*, P. P. 1905 [Cd. 2376], XCVII, 608. An indication of the importance of Indian meal in egg production comes from the following incident occurring in the fictitious community of Ballygullion in the early years of the twentieth century: "Ould Miss Armitage up at the Hall was on for encouragin' poultry- farmin'; an' give a prize for the best layin' hen in Ballygullion ... Deaf Pether of the Bog's wife was an aisy winner if her hen hadn't died an' nothin' would satisfy her but it was poisoned; though divil a all killed it but the gorges of Indian male the ould women kept puttin' intil it. Ivery time the hen laid she gave it an extra dose av male ...; an' wan day ... she put a charge intil it that stretched it out stiff in half an hour". (Lynn Doyle [pseud. Leslie A. Montgomery], *Ballygullion* (Belfast, 1908; new edn., 1976), p. 51.

[14] The peak of 1876 is difficult to explain. A possible explanation may be the 20 per cent drop in the price of imported Indian meal in that year.

meal £10 per ton. W. N. Hancock, writing of the Irish economy in 1863, stated that 'the present price of ...[Indian meal] is ... from seven shillings to seven shillings and six pence per cwt., being about half the price of oatmeal.'[15] Even in the twentieth century the relationship remained unchanged, as evidenced by the contract food prices for Armagh Poor Law Union, 1910-1914:

Table 5.3   Contract food prices for
            Armagh Poor Law Union
            1910-1914

	Oatmeal (per ton)	Indian meal (per ton)
1910	£10 0s. 0d.	£6 18s. 4d.
1911	£ 9 17s. 6d.	£6 17s. 6d.
1913	£11 5s. 0d.	£6 16s. 0d.
1914	£11 12s. 6d.	£6 10s. 0d.

Source: Public Record Office,
         Northern Ireland, BG II/BJ/1

   The importation of Indian corn from America at the time of the Great Famine was not without difficulties, even though it had been shipped in before. Indian corn could not be processed like other grain; it was particularly hard, and in the Southern States of America, where it was a staple food, it was not ground but chopped in steel mills. Indian corn was also susceptible to sweating and overheating; it therefore required to be unloaded and ground into meal immediately upon arrival at port. But mills where intensive grinding of corn could be carried out were not readily available, since they were frequently being used to mill home-grown grain for the export market. During the Famine large quantities of old and dry corn of inferior quality were received, which added to the problems. These technical difficulties of milling into a digestible form, and the ignorance of the population of the correct method of cooking the food initially inhibited widespread use. As Wilde pointed out: 'the poor were totally unacquainted with the mode of preparing either Indian meal or rice for food: indeed in many instances, they ate the former raw. Some had no fuel, others

---

[15] W. N. Hancock, *On the Supposed Progressive Decline of Irish Prosperity* (Dublin, 1863), p. 79.

were too hungry to carry it home, and all were ignorant of the mode of preparing it either as stirabout or bread.'[16]

Inadequately ground and incorrectly cooked Indian meal caused intestinal disorders. The flint-hard grain was both sharp and irritating, it could pierce the intestinal wall, and eaten by a starving people produced agonizing pain. Little wonder it was so unpopular with the Irish, who called it 'brimstone' on account of its bright yellow colour. Indeed, so strong was the feeling against this particular food that even workhouse paupers sometimes refused to eat it. According to Woodham-Smith, 'attempts to introduce ... [Indian meal] into workhouses to replace potatoes caused riots'.[17] The refusal of the paupers at the Limerick workhouse in 1846 to eat stirabout made of Indian meal can perhaps be attributed to the fact that this particular workhouse served a larger quantity of Indian meal in its daily menu than any other workhouse. However, as the 1846 season advanced, and other food became very scarce, the population was compelled to overcome its dislike of Indian meal; indeed so widespread did its consumption become, that supplies were very quickly exhausted.

From the Famine onwards contemporary comment and dietary studies testify to the importance of Indian meal in the diet, particularly in years of economic difficulty. Two surveys of household diets were carried out in nineteenth-century Ireland, one in 1859 and the other in 1863. These were years of exceptional weather conditions resulting in failure of potato and grain crops, forcing the poor to rely on Indian meal.[18] The survey of 1859 was undertaken on the instruction of the Poor Law Commission. Information was collected from all Irish counties, with the exception of Longford and Carlow. Details of 213 labourers' family diets were obtained, 162 of these giving the quantity of various foods consumed. One hundred and one families (62 per cent) had Indian meal as part of their daily menu, consuming on average 8 lb per adult per week. In certain areas both its prevalence and the quantity consumed

---

[16] William Wilde, 'The Food of the Irish', *Dublin University Magazine*, xliii (1854), 138.

[17] Woodham-Smith, p. 68.

[18] J. S. Donnelly Jr., 'The Agricultural Depression of 1859-64', *Irish Economic and Social History*, iii (1976), 48-9.

was greater. Within the south-east of Ire.,
drawn from Dublin to Limerick, 84 per ce
families ate on average 10 lb of Indian meal pe
W. P. O'Brien, a Poor Law Inspector, rep
counties of Cork, Limerick, and Waterford that
enters largely into the present dietary of the wor,
This is usually of good quality, and is made use of
shape of stirabout and griddle-cakes.'[19]

The second survey was undertaken in 1863 by Dr Ldward
Smith, who investigated the diets of the lowest-paid labourers
throughout the United Kingdom. Smith's Irish sample involved
only fifty-two families and these were regionally biased, the
majority coming from the west of Ireland. However, the survey
was very detailed and gives a good indication of the importance
of Indian meal. Smith noted that 'maize or Indian corn meal
is used exclusively in this division of the kingdom',[20] where it
was a prominent item of food in the daily diet of the poor, particularly in the summer months during the hiatus between the
previous year's potato crop and the new season's potatoes. The
survey showed that forty-eight of the fifty-two families studied
bought Indian meal, and consumed on average 10½ lb per
adult per week. The popularity of Indian meal he explained
was 'not due to any preference for its flavour, nor altogether to
a belief in its nutritive qualities, but because of its furnishing
in the absence of potatoes, the largest amount of nourishment
at the smallest cost'.[21] The following examples of menus from
Smith's survey illustrate the extent of its adoption by the
Irish:

A County Tipperary family, 1863:
weekly food for six persons

Flour	7 lb	Potatoes	196 lb
Indian meal . . .	56 lb	Skimmed milk .	24 pt

[19] *Annual Report of the Commissioners for Administering the Laws for Relief of the Poor in Ireland* (Dublin, 1860), p. 80. (Reprinted from Parliamentary Papers.)

[20] *Sixth Report of the Medical Officer of the Privy Council, 1863*, P. P. 1864 [3416], XXVIII, 289.

[21] Ibid., p. 289.

A County Galway family, 1863:
weekly food for three persons

Flour	14 lb	Oatmeal	14 lb
Indian meal ...	70 lb	Milk	12 pt

A County Armagh family, 1863:
weekly food for five persons

Bread	18 lb	Buttermilk	42 pt
Flour	14 lb	Milk	3 ½ pt
Oatmeal	20 lb	Butter	2 lb
Indian meal ...	14 lb	Tea	4 oz
Potatoes	28 lb	Coffee	4 oz
Eggs	24	Bacon	1 ½ lb
Sugar	1 ½ lb	Meat	1 ½ lb

The Armagh example suggests that in the relatively prosperous province of Ulster diets were more varied and nutritious than in the west, but, nevertheless, Indian meal remained a useful adjunct to other foods.

Other evidence of the consumption of Indian meal among the Irish peasantry abounds. Henry Coulter, a touring correspondent for *Saunder's Newsletter*, writing from Ballina, County Mayo, in 1862 commented: 'many of the small farmers and their families are at present subsisting exclusively on Indian meal or oatmeal. Some are getting their own oats ground, but the majority are selling them and applying the proceeds to the purchase of Indian meal, which is becoming a common article of diet with the Irish peasantry.'[22] Heavy dependence on Indian meal was reported from the west of Ireland in 1879-80,[23] and over a decade later the inspectors of the Congested Districts Board, collecting data for the Base Line reports, noted widespread consumption of Indian meal amongst the peasantry of the west of Ireland. Unfortunately the inspectors did not state the quantities eaten; it is, therefore, impossible to ascertain if Indian meal was a dominant item in the diet, although one or

[22] H. Coulter, *The West of Ireland* (Dublin, 1862), p. 246.
[23] See below, p. 128.

two comments indicate that it was. At Desertegney, County Donegal, for example, the inspector observed, 'several shop-keepers and other residents inform me that Indian meal stir-about is in many families the substitute for potatoes, when the supply of the latter fails'.[24]

Other comments in the Base Line reports, however, suggest that oatmeal was supplanting Indian meal in popularity by the 1890s. At Islandeady, County Mayo, it was said that 'Indian meal is not much favoured except by the very poor people, and oaten meal, the use of which at one time had almost died out, is now again much used'.[25] And at Joyce County and Carna in County Galway the inspector noted that 'oatmeal is also used, and ... the people are gradually ceasing to take Indian meal'.[26] These and similar remarks reflected rising wage rates and more regular employment, permitting the purchase of the higher-priced oatmeal. The very poorest class still had to depend heavily on cheap Indian meal, but the better off were turning to the more expensive grains. Indeed, as early as 1882 the Earl of Shannon's agent, William B. Leslie, had urged small farmers to imitate the Scottish custom of making oatmeal the principal food instead of the less nutritious Indian meal.[27]

When we come to the Board of Trade dietary surveys, published in 1905, lack of detail makes it impossible to estimate the amount of Indian meal consumed by the Irish at the turn of the century, since it is grouped with flour and oatmeal. Nevertheless, sample diets of agricultural labourers reveal that the food still figured in the rural Irish diet, as indicated by the following example from County Galway:

Breakfast: Tea and Soda Bread
              or
              Indian Meal Porridge and Milk
Dinner: Potatoes and Milk, sometimes Eggs
Tea: Soda Bread and Tea[28]

---

[24] Congested Districts Board, *Inspectors' Local Reports (Base Line Reports)*, *1892-8* (Dublin, 1898), p. 33. Deposited in Trinity College, Dublin.

[25] Ibid., p. 364.

[26] Ibid., p. 442.

[27] *Cork Constitution*, 4 December, 1882.

[28] *Second Report by Mr Wilson Fox on Wages*, P. P. 1905 [Cd. 2376], XCVII, 607.

It is remarkable, though, that in the three dietary surveys carried out among Irish urban populations, in 1903-4, Indian meal does not appear, with the exception of a single case in Dublin in which polenta—a porridge made of maize meal, eaten in Italy—is recorded. Sir Charles Cameron, Public Health Inspector for Dublin, writing about the diet of Dublin's poor in 1904, noted that 'Indian meal, formerly much employed in the dietary of the poor , now rarely enters into their cuisine'.[29]

The explanation for the disappearance of Indian meal from diets of town dwellers was the availability of cheap bakers' bread and the inadequacy of cooking facilities in the Dublin tenements. The preference for ready-made bread rather than Indian-meal stirabout which required cooking is clearly understandable. Furthermore, populations in towns had access to a wider variety of foods, as demonstrated by the dietary surveys; certainly town dwellers were greater bread eaters than their rural counterparts. In many rural districts home-grown potatoes still provided a major part of the peasant's diet at the end of the century, and Indian meal remained a cheap substitute during the summer months preceding the potato harvest, especially in years when potato yields were poor.

Wherever maize is the major element of a poor-quality diet pellagra is likely to be present. Pellagra is a vitamin-deficiency disease, caused by a lack of nicotinic acid (niacin)—one of the B complex vitamins—in the diet. As early as the eighteenth century a few eminent physicians believed that pellagra was a nutritional-deficiency disease, but there was a strong body of influential opinion preventing such a belief becoming widespread. The eighteenth-century Spanish physician Casal believed that pellagra was a nutritional disease, but political and economic considerations made the thesis unacceptable. 'It was more reassuring to believe that the victims had some hereditary taint ... or that they had an infection.'[30]

Maize, the poor man's cereal, became the staple food of many peasant societies long before it intruded into Irish diets: in the eighteenth century the very poor inhabitants of Asturias in Spain and the peasants of northern Italy, chiefly those from

---

[29] C. Cameron, *Reminiscences of Sir Charles Cameron* (Dublin, 1913), p. 169.
[30] D. A. Roe, *A Plague of Corn* (London, 1973), p. 2.

the Plain of Lombardy, subsisted on it; in the nineteenth century it was the support of the peasants of south-west France, Austria, Romania, Egypt, and the Turkish empire; and in the early decades of the twentieth century the share-croppers of the Southern States of America depended on it. In all these maize-eating countries there was a high incidence of pellagra; whereas in nineteenth-century Ireland there is no record that the disease existed among the peasantry. Was Ireland one community where the link between maize and pellagra was broken? Or was the disease prevalent, perhaps from time to time, with merely subclinical symptoms, but not recognized, and hence not diagnosed as such? To answer these questions a detailed examination of the symptoms of pellagra is required, together with a more precise consideration of the role of Indian meal in the aetiology of the disease.

The nutrient value of maize resembles that of other cereals in general, but differs in important respects. Maize *corn* is a moderate source of nicotinic acid, though maize *meal* (i.e. Indian meal) is a poor source; but what is of particular interest, is that in some cereals, particularly maize, the greater part of the nicotinic acid is present in a bound unabsorbable form, as niacytin (Kodicek), and is therefore nutritionally unavailable. Man is not entirely dependent on dietary sources of nicotinic acid; it may also be synthesized from the amino acid, trypto-phan, a protein constituent, but the amount of tryptophan contained in maize is low. Zein, the principal protein in maize, is an imperfect protein,[31] lacking in the essential amino acid, lysine, and containing very little tryptophan. This defect is important in the relationship between maize and pellagra. A diet may contain a low nicotinic-acid level, but if that diet includes foods with enough tryptophan pellagra would be averted. Experiments suggest that on average about sixty milli-grams of tryptophan will convert to one milligram of nicotinic acid. Thus, the nicotinic-acid equivalent—i.e. the nicotinic-acid content of the diet plus one-sixtieth of the tryptophan

---

[31] Proteins are composed of units called amino acids. Those amino acids which cannot be synthesized by the human body must be supplied by dietary proteins, and are known as essential amino acids. Many common dietary proteins are deficient in one or more of these essential amino acids, and are, therefore, incomplete or im-perfect; hence the name 'imperfect protein'.

content of the diet—is a better measure than nicotinic acid alone.[32] Table 5.4 gives a practical demonstration of the principle, using an example of a diet from Smith's dietary survey.

Table 5.4   Per capita nicotinic acid equivalent of a County Galway family diet 1863

	Quantity	Nicotinic Acid	Tryptophan	Nicotinic Acid Equivalents*
	(g/ml)	(mg)	(mg)	(mg)
Bacon	3	0.11	11.00	0.29
Butter	20	-	-	-
Flour	137	2.67	215.78	6.27
Herring	2	0.05	3.47	0.11
Indian meal	274	(5.48)**	220.57	3.68
Milk skimmed	343	0.27	169.79	3.10
Oatmeal	137	1.37	232.35	5.24
Sugar	10	-	-	-
		9.95		
	less	5.48**		
		4.47		18.69

*   Nicotinic acid equivalent = available nicotinic acid + $\dfrac{tryptophan}{60}$.

** Unabsorbable nicotinic acid.

Dietary analysis based on R. A. McCance and E. M. Widdowson, *The Composition of Foods*, Medical Research Council, Special Report Series, no. 297 (HMSO, London, 1960; new edn., 1978); United States Department of Agriculture, *Composition of Foods*, Agricultural Handbook, no. 8 (Washington DC, 1950).

This diet provides an excellent example of how a regimen deficient in dietary nicotinic acid can in effect provide sufficient available nicotinic acid to achieve the 'Recommended Daily Intake' (RDI) of 18 mg for an adult male. But many Irish labouring families did not have such a variety of fare. For the poorest, potatoes and buttermilk alternated with Indian meal and buttermilk. In many cases during the summer months when diets consisted of Indian meal and buttermilk, not even the tryptophan conversion-factor could raise the nicotinic-acid level to the recommended level. Table 5.5 shows the position of a labourer in 1859, the example taken from the Poor Law Commission Survey of that date.

[32] M. K. Horwitt *et al.*, 'Tryptophan-Niacin Relationships in Man', *Journal of Nutrition*, 60 (Supplement 1), (1956), 1-43.

Table 5.5   Per capita nicotinic acid equivalent of a County Tipperary
labourer's diet 1859

	Quantity	Nicotinic Acid	Tryptophan	Nicotinic Acid Equivalents*
	(g/ml)	(mg)	(mg)	(mg)
Indian meal	720	(14.4)**	579.6	9.66
Buttermilk	480	0.5	237.6	4.46
				14.12

* Nicotinic acid equivalent = available nicotinic acid + $\dfrac{\text{tryptophan}}{60}$.

** Unabsorbable nicotinic acid.

In the short term low levels of nicotinic acid are not a cause for alarm, since it is a storable vitamin, but once stores become depleted, which takes about 60 to 180 days, symptoms of nicotinic-acid deficiency—pellagra—will soon appear.

In good seasons, therefore, when the potato harvest was ample, Indian-meal consumption low, and supplies of milk and eggs were adequate, the likelihood of pellagra was remote; for although the nicotinic acid available from Indian meal and potatoes was relatively small and mainly in a bound unabsorbable form, the provision of foods in the diet such as milk and buttermilk in sufficient quantities provided adequate nicotinic acid by the synthesis of the amino acid, tryptophan. In the famine conditions of 1845-8, however, once Indian meal was released on the market, the peasantry had little else to eat for a considerable length of time. Whether they developed symptoms of pellagra is unclear. Because of the debilitated health of the labouring classes prior to the importation of Indian meal, it is impossible to attribute the ailments of the malnourished peasantry to one particular deficiency disease; their physical condition bore the marks of multiple deficiencies. However, the regional famine of 1879-80 provides us with a better opportunity for discovering whether pellagra was associated with maize eating in Ireland, as it was in other countries.

The subsistence crisis of 1879-80 affected the west and southwest of the country. There the potato had been restored to its old dominance in the diet after the failures of the Great Famine, with the additional supplement of Indian meal for a considerable part of the year. During three to six months, in fact, Indian meal was the major food item. In the particular season of 1879-80, the potato crop was a total failure, as too were the grain crops. During the previous three years the produce of both the potato and grain crops had been remarkably low,[33] and consequently the poorer sections of the population were totally dependent on Indian meal for longer than usual. This long dependence combined with a shortage of milk—many cows in the region being either sold or dry of milk because of shortage of grass—created conditions particularly conducive to pellagra. Illness which was described at the time as being of a febrile nature was prevalent in the distressed district, and in many cases was diagnosed as typhus. It is conceivable, though, that the ailment was in fact pellagra, since the two diseases have a superficial resemblance to each other.

One can investigate the possibility of pellagra among the peasantry from two directions. The medical reports of the epidemic may be examined in an attempt to make a retrospective diagnosis, a dangerous and difficult approach, at best resulting in only tentative conclusions. A safer method is to evaluate the nutritional status of the subsistence diet during the distress period, and to compare it with diets used to induce pellagra in scientific studies.

Despite the perils of the medical approach a cautious appraisal is of value. One of the key medical sources is the report of Dr Stewart Woodhouse and Dr C. J. Nixon on the outbreak of fever, to the Local Government Board in 1880. They noted that the fever was typhus, which they described as maculated (i.e. spotted), the patients having what Dr Woodhouse termed 'characteristic rose coloured spots';[34] he also recorded symptoms of diarrhoea and abdominal tenderness. In some cases the symptoms were constipation rather than diarrhoea, together with a more or less constant development of head symptoms,

---

[33] G. Sigerson, 'Final Report on Destitution Diseases in the West', in *The Irish Crisis of 1879-80, Proceedings of the Dublin Mansion House Relief Committee*, 1880 (Dublin, 1881), p. 162. Sigerson's Report had originally been published, with others, in August 1880 under the title *Report of the Medical Commission of the Mansion House Committee*, Dublin (City Printing and Lithographing Co. Ltd.), 1880. It differed from the version cited here in not having the footnotes, which were added after August 1880.

[34] *Ninth Annual Report of the Local Government Board for Ireland: Relief of Distress*, P. P. 1881, XLVII, 344.

and a marked degree of emaciation. Both doctors remarked that the symptoms presented in these fever patients were unlike those exhibited by the fever victims of the 1847-8 outbreak. According to Dr Woodhouse, 'of famine [typhus] or relapsing fever, such as was described in 1847-48, I found no cases whatever, nor could I hear of any case in which the symptoms at all resembled it'.[35] This raises the possibility that these doctors were not looking at typhus. Indeed many of the symptoms they described have a similarity to the symptoms of pellagra, although few doctors in Ireland at the time had sufficient knowledge to diagnose it.

The clinical manifestations of pellagra are popularly described as dermatitis, diarrhoea, and dementia—the three D's—though not all pellagra victims exhibit skin symptoms, some having only a disturbance of the digestive tract, making the certain diagnosis of pellagra in such cases difficult. The first stage of pellagra is manifest by abdominal pain, followed by diarrhoea, or, sometimes, by the reverse condition of constipation. Returning to the medical reports of the fever outbreak in 1880, the symptoms described correspond closely to those of pellagra. The dermatological symptoms of pellagra commence with distinctive redness on the skin, hence the name 'mal de la rosa' sometimes given to the disease. This progresses to the peeling of the skin, leaving a brown pigmentation. In the case of the diagnostic signs of typhus, a pink rash also appears, later turning purple or brown: the similarity to pellagra is very close. Possibly if the condition of the skin in the two diseases could be directly compared a difference would be discernible, but with a retrospective study this is impossible, and so only the possibilities can be looked at.

Yet another comparison exists between the clinical manifestations of pellagra and the fever symptoms described in the Local Government Medical Reports. Classical symptoms of pellagra in an advanced stage are severe neurological disturbances, with psychic phenomena, and a downhill phase of wasting. In 1880 Dr Nixon reported 'a more or less constant development of head symptoms, and a marked degree of emaciation'[36] among the sick. The resemblance between these

---

[35] Ibid., p. 344.
[36] Ibid., p. 348.

symptoms and the classical indications of pellagra is striking. However, too much stress should not be placed on this medical evidence. The clinical presentations are rather non-specific and arguments could be mounted for a number of diseases using these data.

Doubts that the disease described in the Local Government Medical Reports really was typhus are roused also by the timing. Typhus is recognized as a disease of winter months. The human-body louse is the main vector of the disease, so that when the atmospheric temperature falls and people huddle together to keep warm the contagion is easily spread. The medical reports of the fever outbreak in 1880 show the months of greatest prevalence to have been April, May, and June, the season characteristically associated with the onset of pellagra symptoms. 'Usually the rather vague symptoms of distress began shortly after Christmas, with more definite signs of the disease appearing in the spring. Erythema might occur as early as March or April or as late as June.'[37] Meteorological observations for the year 1880 suggest that summer temperatures were normal with a mean temperature in July of 57°F, and 60.5°F in August, which was comparable with the average temperature for these months of 58°F to 60°F: hardly conditions necessitating huddling together to keep warm.

An infinitely stronger case for the prevalence of pellagra in Ireland during the 1879-80 crisis can be built based on dietary evidence. An independent inquiry by Dr George Sigerson and Dr J. E. Kenny for the Dublin Mansion House Relief Committee, strongly deplored the population's reliance on Indian meal and believed the food to be a cause of disease. Reporting on the district of Ballaghadereen, County Mayo, both doctors noticed that all the families in which the illness appeared had been compelled to subsist on supplies of Indian meal. Other inhabitants of the area who were not in receipt of relief meal were not attacked by disease. In Faheens, near Swineford in County Mayo, the circumstances were exactly the same: disease victims were those whom want had forced to appeal to the local relief committee for sustenance, which was in the form of Indian meal. While Drs Woodhouse and Nixon in the Local Government Medical Report suggested that a predisposing

---

[37] W. Etheridge, *The Butterfly Caste* (Connecticut, 1972), p. 7.

cause of the fever outbreak was the inferior quality of the food, particularly dependence on Indian meal for longer duration than usual, Dr Sigerson had no doubt that reliance entirely on Indian meal was a major cause of the population's ill health. He observed:

Many of those whom we found stricken with fever and other diseases had been compelled to subsist for four, five or six months on Indian meal, generally insufficiently boiled: as adjuncts, they had very rarely any milk; in one or two districts, weak coffee; in some sweetened water; and in not a few cases, water only. Now the absolute necessity of a mixed dietary has been shown by experiment.[38]

James H. Tuke, travelling in County Donegal and the province of Connaught in 1880, made some pertinent observations. Of the poorer inhabitants of Dunfanaghy, County Donegal, he noted, 'there is a general absence of actual sickness, but a low condition and breaking out of skin disease, betokening low diet etc.'[39] On conditions in Muckish and Cresslough, Tuke cited a case of a family which a year or two previously was in good circumstances. 'Now, the man is miserably dressed ... They crowded around a miserable fire, cooking the stirabout and Indian meal cakes, all more or less affected with skin disease, very bad and infectious, the result of low diet; all looked thin, pale and wretched, and evidently wanted noursihment.'[40] Although it could be argued that the skin condition in such descriptions was the manifestation of various diseases, including nutritional diseases, the high proportion of the western population dependent solely on relief supplies of Indian meal[41] makes it plausible to suggest that skin eruptions among the peasantry in this area were symptomatic of pellagra.

[38] Sigerson, p. 166. County Mayo was heavily dependent on relief rations of Indian meal in 1879-80 and in the parish of Knock 77 per cent of the population existed on relief rations in March 1880 (*The Irish Crisis of 1879-80*, Appendix IX). This, coupled with the widespread reporting of pellagra-type symptoms in the county, raises the possibility that the fifteen villagers who saw the Apparition at Knock in August 1879 were suffering from the effects of an Indian-meal diet.

[39] J. H. Tuke, *Irish Distress and its Remedies. The Land Question. A Visit to Donegal and Connaught in the Spring 1800* (London, 1880, 4th ed.), p. 35.

[40] Ibid., pp. 36-7. Pellagra is not infectious, but it was thought to be so.

[41] *The Irish Crisis of 1879-80*, Appendix IX. This Appendix provides figures of the number of persons in distress in each county. When assessed as a percentage of total population, over 50 per cent in the counties of Galway, Leitrim, Mayo, and Sligo were in distress, and in receipt of relief rations.

In the early decades of the twentieth century, an American physician, Goldberger,[42] produced pellagra experimentally in subjects by feeding them a diet very high in carbohydrates and low in protein, the protein source being of cereal origin. The major constituent of the diet was Indian meal in the form of mush (maize porridge), grits (coarse maize), corn bread, and biscuits. Rice, sweet potatoes, green vegetables, pork fat, syrup, sugar, and coffee were also included in the diet. An evaluation of the nicotinic-acid equivalent of this regime (Table 5.6) reveals the Goldberger diet to be deficient, particularly remembering that nicotinic-acid is water soluble and 15-25 per cent may be lost in cooking:

Table 5.6   Per capita nicotinic acid equivalent of a Goldberger diet

	Quantity (g/ml)	Nicotinic Acid (mg)	Tryptophan (mg)	Nicotinic Acid Equivalents* (mg)
Buttermilk	44.8	0.04	22	0.40
Cornmeal	249.4	(4.98)**	201	3.35
Grits	46.8	(0.90)**	38	0.62
Wheat flour	138.5	2.70	218	6.34
Rice	21.8	0.32	21	0.68
Syrup	42.1	-	-	-
Sugar	75.8	-	-	-
Potatoes	165.0	1.32	30	1.83
Turnips	38.7	0.15	-	0.15
Cabbage	92.5	0.14	6	0.24
Pork fat	126.8	-	-	-
Turnip greens	69.4	0.10	27	0.55
				14.16

* Nicotinic acid equivalent = available nicotinic acid + $\dfrac{\text{tryptophan}}{60}$.

** Unabsorbable nicotinic acid.

This strengthens the case for suspecting the presence of pellagra among those Irish peasants existing solely on relief rations of Indian meal, as a comparison of Goldberger's diet with the Irish relief rations demonstrates:

[42] J. Goldberger and G. A. Wheeler, 'The Experimental Production of Pellagra in Human Subjects by Means of Diet' in M. Terris, ed., *Goldberger on Pellagra* (Baton Rouge, 1964), p. 54. Goldberger's subjects were 'volunteer' convicts.

Table 5.7   Comparison of per capita nicotinic acid equivalent
of Irish relief rations and Goldberger's diet

	Quantity	Nicotinic Acid	Tryptophan	Nicotinic Acid Equivalents*
	(g)	(mg)	(mg)	(mg)
Full rations				
Indian meal	960	(19.2)**	773	12.88
Reduced rations				
Indian meal	240	(4.8)**	193	3.22
Goldberger's diet				14.16

* Nicotinic acid equivalent = available nicotinic acid $+\dfrac{\text{tryptophan}}{60}$.

** Unabsorbable nicotinic acid.

Goldberger's volunteers developed 'pellagra sine pellagra' (i.e. non-dermatological symptoms) after two months. Considering that in Ireland Indian-meal diets contained considerably less nicotinic-acid equivalent, that many people relied upon Indian meal for longer than the American volunteers—Nixon mentions eight months—, and that in numerous cases less than the stipulated ration was provided,[43] the likelihood of pellagra being present becomes increasingly plausible.

It would be inappropriate for an essay of this kind to end on anything other than a cautious note. It is certain that Indian meal was eaten occasionally in Ireland before the Famine, and regularly in Ireland from the Famine until the end of the nineteenth century. We cannot be certain, though, that the poor man's cereal brought with it the poor man's disease. Pellagra may have existed during the Famine, and dietary analysis strongly suggests that it was present in the west of Ireland in 1879-80. Contemporary medical observations on the matter are scarcely conclusive, although the last word may be left with a medical man. In a footnote to his medical report, published in 1881, Dr Sigerson alluded to 'one case of an adult near Killala [who] presented some symptoms which resembled those of the first stage of pellagra. But the subject is one that requires continued observation.'[44]

[43] Sigerson, p. 133.
[44] Ibid., p. 166.

6. Landlord Indebtedness in Ulster in the Seventeenth and Eighteenth Centuries *

Peter Roebuck

I

In Ireland landlord indebtedness reached acute proportions before the mid-nineteenth century. By 1844 responsibility for some 1,322 properties with a combined annual rental of nearly £1 million was vested in the courts of Chancery and Exchequer because of otherwise unmanageable debts. After the Famine many landowners were keen to cut their losses in the face of falling rent receipts, rising expenditure, and a rush of anxious creditors determined to foreclose on mortgages. Keen to bring new men, capital, and enterprise into the Irish landed system, the government passed the Encumbered Estates Act in 1849 which produced a huge transfer of property—some five million acres or about a quarter of the country's total land area— during the next thirty years. The measure failed to attract British investors, but it was the first of the series of legislative departures which finally created peasant proprietorship in this century.[1] Thus, the importance of landlord indebtedness as an initial stimulant of legislative change is beyond dispute.

The reasons for this indebtedness seem obvious enough. The fall in agricultural prices during the second decade of the nineteenth century produced heavy rent arrears which were mitigated only by abatements or reductions of rent. Thereafter owners were unable or unwilling to reduce their expenditure;

* Although I alone am responsible for the views expressed here, I gratefully aknowledge comments on an earlier version of this essay from W. H. Crawford, D. Dickson, W. A. Maguire, and A. P. W. Malcomson; and from those who attended the Irish Economic and Social History Society's Conference at Cork in September 1977, and a History Staff Seminar at the University of Newcastle-upon-Tyne in January 1978. I am also indebted to those who deposited the manuscripts which I consulted, and to the staffs of the various repositories where I worked.

[1] J. S. Donnelly Jr., *Landlord and Tenant in Nineteenth-Century Ireland* (Dublin, 1973), pp. 18-19, 48-52.

this, together with a failure to appreciate the deep-seated nature of contemporary economic trends, raised the profile and widened the incidence of debt. Yet we know that landlord indebtedness had a longer pedigree than this. Over a decade ago D. Large concluded that 'it may well be that already by 1815 indebtedness was a serious matter for many landowning families', and other research has identified many landowners who were heavily indebted much earlier, despite the significant rise in levels of rent achieved on the bulk of Irish estates during the eighteenth century.[2] It is also clear that two features of the Irish landed system central to the problem of indebtedness were prevalent at an early date. Long leases prevented landowners from realizing the current rental value of their property other than infrequently; and the existence of middlemen between owners and occupying tenants, while insuring against proprietorial losses in difficult years, tended overall to depress head rentals, particularly on more substantial properties.[3] Undoubtedly many landowners in Ireland were in financial difficulties by the later eighteenth century, if not before.

This paper examines the difficulties of one landowning family, the Donegalls, and in the light of their and others' experience, attempts to identify major causes of landlord indebtedness in Ulster between 1600 and 1815. Like many of their contemporaries the Donegalls exhibited a tendency towards indebtedness from the time they were established in Ulster. This was due not so much to the fecklessness or extravagance so readily highlighted by earlier historians, as to other, largely impersonal factors, relating both to their income and to their expenditure, which set them and many other Irish landowners apart from

---

[2] D. Large, 'The Wealth of the Greater Irish Landowners, 1750-1815', *Irish Historical Studies*, xi (1966), 44; A. P. W. Malcomson, *John Foster: The Politics of the Anglo-Irish Ascendancy* (Oxford, 1978), pp. 12-15, 18-21; C. Clay, *Public Finance and Private Wealth: The Career of Sir Stephen Fox 1627-1716* (Oxford, 1978), pp. 164, 177, 193, 287-8, 290, 305, 322-3. For Ulster landowning families, see for example M. J. Craig, *The Volunteer Earl* (London, 1948), pp. 140-1, 152, 204-5; W. A. Maguire, *The Downshire Estates in Ireland 1801-45* (Oxford, 1972), pp. 85-94; Public Record Office of Northern Ireland, Belfast (hereafter PRONI), D 623/45 (Abercorn); D 526/84 (Massereene); D 691/21/ B/22 (Bayly); D 1375/3/26/43-44 (Antrim).

[3] L. M. Cullen, *An Economic History of Ireland since 1660* (London, 1972), pp. 77-82; D. Dickson, 'Middlemen', in T. J. Bartlett and D. Hayton, eds., *Penal Era to Golden Age: Essays in Eighteenth-Century Irish History*, Ulter Historical Foundation, Historical Series (Belfast, 1979).

most other contemporary proprietors in these islands. By weakening or undermining the finances of landed economies these factors eroded the control and authority which the greater proprietors endeavoured to exercise in their respective localities, and thereby contributed to the problems associated with the land question in nineteenth-century Ireland.

II

The collapse of the Donegall estate began in the early nineteenth century although the structure had been crumbling for a long time. The second Marquess, both before and after his succession in 1799, was remarkably improvident and dissipated his inheritance in the 1820s by granting, for cash in hand, leases for lives renewable for ever. Nevertheless his debts continued to grow and the third Marquess was left to preside over the sale in the Encumbered Estates Court of much of the rest of the property.[4] However, while this suggests that mismanagement and extravagance were the twin causes of the family's ultimate decline, it is clear that the second Marquess's problems were not entirely of his own making.

The first Marquess outlived two wives and married again in 1790; his bride was only twenty-two years of age to his fifty-one and for the thirty years by which she outlived him the estate was charged with her jointure. At the Marquess's death in 1799 the fittings in the mansion he had built at Fisherwick Park in Staffordshire were sold, and the shell demolished so that the building materials could be used to raise money; much timber was cut and the park and gardens were converted to arable. Capability Brown's work alone had cost over £16,000— 100,000 trees had been planted, and according to one report the Marquess had 'expended £20,000 on books not yet opened, and £10,000 on shells not yet unpacked'.[5] Earlier, in the 1770s, he had altered the terms of the leases of some of his Ulster property in order to raise rents and levy fines, and thereby

---

[4] W. A. Maguire, 'The 1822 Settlement of the Donegall Estates', *Irish Economic and Social History*, iii (1976); 'Lord Donegall and the Sale of Belfast: A Case History from the Encumbered Estates Court', *Economic History Review*, 2nd Ser. xxix (1976), 570-84.

[5] William Salt Library, Stafford, M 521/5; D. Stroud, *Capability Brown* (London, 1975), pp. 151-3, 225; V. Gibbs *et al.*, eds., *The Complete Peerage* (London, 1910-59), vol. iv, pp. 391-2.

finance activities at Fisherwick. This contributed substantially to the Hearts of Steel disturbances in County Antrim with which the Marquess has long been infamously associated. Significantly, however, the latest analysis of that episode refutes many of the accusations made against Donegall in older, second-hand accounts.[6] Nothing like the £100,000 suggested by Bigger was sought in fines; nor was most of the property let to middlemen over the heads of existing occupying tenants. The chief grievance stemmed from the disappointed expectations of some undertenants who had hoped to become direct tenants of Donegall, and who were supported by further substrata of lessees whose own rents were increased following rent improvements at the level of the head tenants. Most of the latter found they had not obtained bad bargains; in relation to its size, the Ulster estate income prior to Donegall's intervention had been absurdly low. Moreover, in 1760 he had inherited what was, financially and in other respects, a parlous situation.

His predecessor, the fourth Earl of Donegall, had succeeded forty years earlier in 1716, following a lengthy minority. From the start his regime proved disastrous. The Earl was 'extremely weak and, though he was taught the Latin, Greek and French languages, yet could never by any possible means be taught the use of figures, even common addition, though the utmost endeavours [were] used for that purpose'. The Earl's guardian, the Dowager Countess, 'knowing the oddity of her son's character, was desirous as soon as he came of a competent age to have him married and his estate settled in the strictest manner to avoid the injuries that the family might receive by his Lordship's being imposed on'. Accordingly, within six months of attaining his majority, the Earl married, though his bride was reputedly almost equally feeble-minded. A post-nuptial settlement placed the estate under three trustees but thereafter matters quickly deteriorated. The trustees quarrelled and became estranged, alternately refusing to act, pursuing individual policies, or individually being rendered impotent by each others' actions. The Earl oscillated, relying at different times on various of the parties, though never kindling

---

[6] I am grateful to W. A. Maguire for allowing me to use material from his article 'Lord Donegall and the Hearts of Steel', forthcoming in *Irish Historical Studies*.

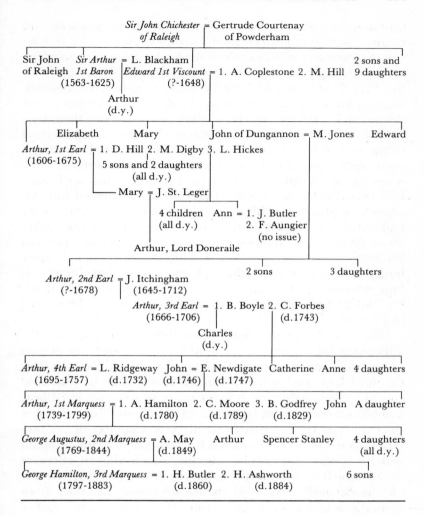

Fig. 6.1   Abbreviated pedigree of the Chichester (Donegall) family

Sources: V. Gibbs *et al.*, eds., *The Complete Peerage* (London, 1910-59), vol. iv, pp. 389-95; J. Lodge, *Peeerage of Ireland*, rev. M. Archdall (Dublin, 1789), pp. 314-41.

confidence in any of them. The ricochet of accusations and counter-accusations which soon surrounded the family is difficult to penetrate: an estate which the Earl obtained by marriage was sold cheaply and the money embezzled; the Earl was drawn into 'fraudulent contracts'; the Dowager's jointure was stopped, whereupon she retired to rooms in Kent; and property was deliberately underlet for large fines, which were then misappropriated. After his wife's death in 1732 the Earl spent most of the rest of his life as a lodger with friends in England. A veritable log-jam of suits in Chancery eventually restored some order but not before several unsuccessful petitions for lunacy had been filed against him. Everyone had believed him incapable of producing children and in 1724 the Wexford estate had been settled on his brother. In 1752 a private act of Parliament allowed the resetting of property in Belfast, but the property was so ruinous that tenants were granted lengthy building leases, so that, although rents were then increased, they remained at the same level for many years. At his death the Earl's entire estate was under the direct control of the court of Chancery.[7]

The first Marquess inherited this difficult situation but the difficulties did not stem solely from his predecessor; the origins of his problems were more remote. The fourth Earl's father, the third Earl, had succeeded in 1692. Although he displayed considerable imagination in financing improvements in Belfast, a public career early in life removed him from Ulster. He was elected to the Irish Parliament and, as a supporter of William III, gained a military command in 1697. On arriving in Spain with his regiment in 1704 he was appointed a Major-General of the Spanish forces. In the following year, on board HMS *Panther* off the Spanish coast and in circumstances divorced from domestic realities, he made a will. He confirmed the earlier provision of a jointure of £1,200 for his wife, and increased the amount allocated for his daughters' portions from £6,000 to £13,000. Moreover, as all his children (two sons and five daughters) were under age, he made arrangements for their

[7] PRONI T 2873/2 (quotations); D 509/45; William Salt Library, M 521/1; PRO London, C 11/192/16; 12/377/19; 33/395/205, 263, 295-6, 307; 33/397/317, 328, 453, 501; 101/4968; House of Lords Record Office, Manuscript Estate Bill of the 4th Earl of Donegall, 13 February 1752.

maintenance; the total sum was not to exceed £600 per annum, decreasing proportionately as they married or came of age. The Earl also granted a legacy of £500 to a half-sister, one of £300 to his brother, and an annuity of £200 to his younger son. The will was executed in the Earl's thirty-ninth year when his public career was prospering; perhaps he felt it to be no more than a precaution. Within a year, however, he was killed in action. Had his property been relatively unencumbered the Earl's bequests might be described as generous, perhaps ambitious, though not as extravagant; but, as he had frankly admitted, this was not the case. He was heavily indebted: the sum involved, exclusive of the above provisions, was at least £23,500. In addition the Earl's mother still enjoyed the Wexford estate which she had brought into the family in 1660. Even more remarkable is the will's reference to 'debts, legacies, portions and annuities' which had remained unpaid since the second Earl's death in 1678. Estate accounts for the ensuing minority indicate that even then the family's property would have qualified as encumbered under the Act of 1849.[8]

These debts derived in part from the first Earl's lack of a male heir. His first marriage had produced a daughter; a second, five sons and two daughters, all of whom died young or were stillborn. Even before this wife's death he despaired of rearing a son, for his earldom was granted with a special remainder to his brother. A third marriage in 1651 produced five children, of whom only a daughter survived. By the late 1650s the Earl's despair began to be reflected in dispositions of his property. There was nothing he could do to keep the earldom in his branch of the family, but what happened to the estate was another matter. He docked the entail on his property and left all of it to his daughters and their heirs. On his death in 1675 his nephew, who then inherited the earldom, but held only 1,300 acres at Dungannon, challenged these dispositions. The case lapsed on the latter's death in 1678, but not before he had left a costly will in anticipation of success. The debts which thereby burdened the third Earl could not be paid out of the

[8] *Complete Peerage* vol. iv, pp. 390-1; J. Lodge, *Peerage of Ireland*, rev. M. Archdall (Dublin, 1789), pp. 338-9; PRO London, T 1/108, no. 12, f. 59; PROB 11/504/246, f. 177; C 107/16 are the estate accounts, copies of which are at PRONI Mic 4b and T 455/1-2.

main estate; indeed, could not for the time being be paid at all. On coming of age he resumed the legal battle and in 1692 won, earlier disentailing processes being reversed 'for manifest errors therein'. Instead of proceeding to the appeal stage the various parties hammered out a compromise. By this the third Earl, in return for recognition of his claim to the entire property, allowed his great-uncle's descendants substantial sums and life-interests in much of the estate. Fortunately the last of these interests ran out in 1700, just before his military career gathered momentum. Thus, the optimism of his disastrous Spanish will grew out of a few years of unfamiliar prosperity.[9]

The first Earl's lack of a male heir was not his only problem. His second marriage in 1631, to the Earl of Bristol's daughter, was welcomed by his father, Viscount Chichester, as the family's position was then on the wane following the death in 1625 of ex-Lord-Deputy Chichester. Except for Dungannon, the entire estate was settled on the pair for a portion of £5,500. The Viscount then searched for a blue-blooded bride for his younger son, John, though only Dungannon remained available for settlement. In offering his daughter's hand in 1638 Viscount Ranelagh drove a hard bargain. In addition to Dungannon, and for a portion of only £2,000, Viscount Chichester agreed to purchase property up to £1,000 per annum in value for settlement on the couple. At the Viscount's death in 1648 no additional land had been purchased and a penalty of £10,000 for non-performance of covenants in the marriage settlement was due for forfeit. Meanwhile, the family had lost control over its Ulster estate income during the rebellion and civil war. In 1649 Ranelagh lowered his demands in the light of the Chichesters' predicament, but the first Earl, who had just succeeded his father, must have felt that earlier achievements were then in jeopardy. That he had to pay Ranelagh after regaining his property in 1656 gave him a further reason for subsequently neglecting his brother's family.[10]

Yet Viscount Chichester left a less indebted situation in 1648 than he had inherited in 1625, which was quite an achievement,

[9] *Complete Peerage*, op. cit., vol. iv, pp. 389-90; *Peerage of Ireland*, op. cit., pp. 332-6; PRONI D 389/11; D 509/31, being the settlement of 15 June 1692 which recites earlier developments.

[10] PRONI D 389/4, 5; D 509/26; D 1932/8/12, 13; G. Benn, *A History of the Town of Belfast* (2nd ed., London, 1877), vol. i, pp. 104, 130.

for besides devising sizeable legacies and annuities, his predecessor, the former Lord-Deputy, also left large debts, one
account alone amounting to £10,000. Viscount Chichester had
been obliged to sell the family's house in Dublin and mortgage
parts of the Ulster estate.[11]

Debt, therefore, ran like a seam through the Donegalls'
affairs for over 250 years. By the early eighteenth century in-
cumbrances were annually consuming more than half their
estate income. This situation did not stem from human foibles
and frailty, rich though the family's history is in such phenomena. Its origins lay in the background from which they
came to landownership, in the manner in which they fashioned
their estate, and in the circumstances peculiar to Ulster with
which they had to grapple.

III

Sir Arthur Chichester was a younger son of an insubstantial
Devonshire squire.[12] While an undergraduate he robbed a
Crown purveyor and fled to Ireland, but after being pardoned
returned to fight against the Armada. There followed ten
years' experience of war on land and at sea before he was
chosen for operations in Ireland. On returning there in 1599
Chichester was merely a professional soldier: thirty-six years
old and unmarried, he was wholly reliant on his pay and
expenses. Nor did his situation alter immediately. Before his
unexpected nomination as Lord-Deputy in 1603 he repeatedly
complained of inadequate pay and considered seeking his
fortune elsewhere. Thereafter a Crown grant of considerable
property along the northern coastline of Belfast Lough plugged
the gap between his heavy public responsibilities and his private
lack of substance. Chichester then used his position to augment
his estate. Fraudulently, in collusion with James Hamilton and
fellow servitors, he more than doubled his holdings in County

---

[11] PRONI D 389/3; D 509/12; T 712/26; G. Hill, ed., *The Montgomery Manuscripts*
(Belfast, 1869), p. 231.

[12] For elaboration of the following two paragraphs, see P. Roebuck, 'The Making
of an Ulster Great Estate: the Chichesters, Barons of Belfast and Viscounts of Carrickfergus, 1599-1648', *Proceedings of the Royal Irish Academy*, lxxix, section C, No. 1.
(1979), p. 22 of which contains a transcription of a rental of the family's estate, minus
Dungannon, for 1630 (PRONI. D 389/4).

Antrim within two years. Later he was the major single bene-
ficiary of the plantation, obtaining property at Dungannon and
almost all of Inishowen. In less than a decade and at negligible
cost he accumulated a vast estate.

Nevertheless, Chichester's rapid emergence as a major landowner and senior civil servant was not matched by an appropriate rise in his personal wealth. He persistently claimed that
his expenses as Lord-Deputy exceeded his income; subordinates
confirmed his use of private means to sustain his public position;
within a year of his appointment came the first of several pleas
to be made a 'private man'. The demands of office prevented
Chichester from devoting adequate attention to his property;
political developments periodically threatened to uncover his
collusion with Hamilton; his proprietorial rights were challenged,
and both he and his successor were obliged to surrender certain
properties. A final confirmation of the family's holdings was
not obtained from the Crown until 1668. Chichester's major
problems, however, stemmed from the nature of the environ-
ment in which his estate was situated. Development in Ulster,
the most underpopulated province of a lightly settled country,
was impeded by the lack both of security and of individuals
who commanded the capital it required. Immigrants were
few and insubstantial, and liable to overreach themselves. New
proprietors were in a weak position, with little room for man-
œuvre in attempting to generate income from property, and
were constrained to offer prospective lessees generous terms. In
all recorded instances Chichester gave either fee-farm grants,
perpetual tenancies, or lengthy determinable leases for rents
and fines which were exceedingly low in relation to the amounts
of property demised. This policy produced a rental (£3,731 in
1630) well below contemporary and later estimates, which,
because of the leasing structure, remained substantially un-
improved for many decades. From the start the vast majority,
if not indeed all, of Chichester's grantees and tenants were
middle men, who reaped profits from subletting to undertenants.

The leasing structure of the estate altered, but only slowly,
as the pace of change depended on the rate at which leases
dropped. Inevitably, therefore, rental income remained modest

—£4,500 in 1707, and around £7,000 in 1751.[13] During the later seventeenth century leases of urban property were generally for three, sometimes for four, lives; of rural property, usually for over fifty and at times for up to ninety-nine years. In the early eighteenth century, particularly towards the end of the trusteeship, terms were reduced to below fifty, and occasionally to below forty years.[14] A survey of Inishowen in 1741 reveals the difficulties under which the trustees laboured. Some 160,000 statute acres there were divided into 76 holdings. Fourteen were either out of lease, held under fee-farm grants or leases for lives, or for unknown numbers of years. Of the remaining 62 holdings, 15 were held by leases granted between 1721 and 1730 for under 40 years; 23 by leases granted between 1711 and 1730 for 41 to 50 years; and 4 by leases granted between 1701 and 1720 for 51 to 70 years. The remaining 20 holdings were all held under leases granted before 1700 for between 61 and 99 years. Although Inishowen was then valued at some £10,600 a year, the current rental of £1,766 remained largely unaltered until the 1770s.[15] A further document of about 1750 reveals the gap which had then developed between proprietorial and middlemen's incomes from the same property. Alexander McClintock leased seven-and-a-half townlands in Carnmoney parish in south County Antrim for an annual rent of £131 9s. 8d. He sublet this property in ninety-four separate holdings for £732 13s. 3d., earning £601 3s. 7d. in rental profits annually. Particularly in that region, near Belfast, many undertenants themselves let part of their holdings to others, so that there were often several tiers of tenancy.[16]

Why was a policy of granting lengthy leases adhered to for so long to the detriment of the family's income? Firstly, as conditions for proprietors had in many respects deteriorated in mid-seventeenth-century Ulster, many properties were let on even longer terms than had been the case forty or fifty years

---

[13] PRO London, C 107/16 (PRONI Mic 4B and T 455/1-2); House of Lords Record Office, Manuscript Estate Bill, 13 February 1752.

[14] For examples of leases, see PRONI D509/*passim*.

[15] PRONI D 835/3/2.

[16] PRONI D 354/285A. I am grateful to B. M. Walker for drawing my attention to this document.

previously.[17] Secondly, indebtedness perhaps encouraged short-term gains in entry fines in return for long-term losses in rents. Thirdly, a sudden change in policy was difficult, and became more so as a tradition of long leases was established; while a process of more gradual change, bolstered by settlements which successively placed tighter restrictions on the leasing powers of incumbents, was circumvented or ignored under the pressure of events.[18] Finally, departure from the current regional practice placed proprietors at the mercy of laws of supply and demand. From the outset the leasing structure of the Donegall estate was similar to that of most other properties in the province. Indeed, in eighteenth-century Ulster the three-life lease was the most common form of head tenancy: as its average length has been estimated at between fifty and seventy years, by 1760 Donegall leases were clearly somewhat less, rather than somewhat more, restrictive of growth in proprietorial income than was the case elsewhere in the province.[19] Nevertheless, the first Marquess faced severe difficulties on his succession. Ironically, the Private Estate Act of 1752 had departed from previous settlement restrictions so that building leases of three lives or ninety-nine years could be used to redevelop Belfast. Consequently, what should have been the most lucrative part of the Ulster estate became increasingly unremunerative; after the early 1750s any rise in the rental had to come from other property. The Hearts of Steel disturbances resulted from efforts to generate an increase from rural property near the city; the over-all rise in the rental to around £30,000 by the late 1790s came from rent improvement throughout the rest of the estate.[20]

Thus, although very low in relation to the size of his estate, the landed income of the family's founder, Sir Arthur Chi-

[17] G. Benn, *History of Belfast*, op. cit., vol. i, pp. 283-5, 289-90; PRONI D 509/13; D 778/4; D 2083/1/1. A study of the leasing policy of the Antrim family during the seventeenth century (PRONI D 265) supports this point.

[18] The successive settlements are PRONI D 389/8, 9 (1670); D 509/31 (1692); D 509/45 (1718); D 971/5/15 (1761). For an example of the 3rd Earl ignoring settlement restrictions in granting a lease, see D 572/21/9, 10.

[19] W. H. Crawford, 'Landlord-Tenant Relations in Ulster 1609-1820', *Irish Economic and Social History*, ii (1975), 8; Maguire, *The Downshire Estates*, op. cit., p. 33; Maguire, 'Lord Donegall and the Sale of Belfast', op. cit., p. 571; F. M. L. Thompson and D. Tierney, eds., *General Report on the Gosford Estates in Co. Armagh, 1821 by William Greig* (Belfast, 1976), p. 23.

[20] William Salt Library, M 521/4.

chester, placed him on a par with all but his wealthiest contemporaries in Britain; whereas the first Marquess, while still
owner of one of the largest estates in Britain or Ireland, succeeded to an income lower than that enjoyed by the average
British peer or great landowner.[21] Large has argued that from
1760 Irish rentals rose at a rate broadly comparable to that in
Britain.[22] In terms of income per acre, however, rent improvement in Ulster proceeded from a much lower base, and at a
much less even pace, than in Britain. It therefore remained
difficult for proprietors to oust debt from its position as a
common accompaniment to everyday life.

IV

Further scrutiny of the differing circumstances encountered by
British and Ulster proprietors suggests additional explanations
of heavy indebtedness among the latter. One important difference was the greater extent to which landownership and management in Ulster were disrupted by civil and political disturbances and associated factors. Having lost control of their Ulster
property in 1644, the Chichesters did not regain it until 1656;
they experienced a shorter dispossession following the William-
ite invasion.[23] Few details of either episode survive but they
undoubtedly contributed to the family's indebtedness. Although
some proprietors were permanently dispossessed in the seventeenth century, it would be a mistake in highlighting their fate
to ignore the impact on others of temporary dispossession.
While there was no revolution in landownership in Britain
between 1640 and 1660, debts accumulated through fines, re-
purchases of confiscated property, or both, created difficulties
(particularly for families indebted before 1640) which resulted
in property sales in later decades.[24] As contemporary disruption
in Ulster was at least comparable with that in Britain, it would

---

[21] L. Stone, *The Crisis of the Aristocracy, 1558-1641* (Oxford, 1965), pp. 760-1;
H. Perkin, *The Origins of Modern English Society 1780-1880* (London, 1969), pp. 18-19.

[22] Large, 'The Wealth of the Greater Irish Landowners', op. cit., 27-33. For an
examination of this contention, see P. Roebuck, 'Rent Movement, Proprietorial
Incomes and Agricultural Development 1730-1830' in Roebuck, ed., *Plantation to
Partition: Essays in Ulster History in Honour of J. L. McCracken* (Belfast, 1981).

[23] Benn, *History of Belfast*, op. cit., vol. i, pp. 104, 130.

[24] H. J. Habakkuk, 'Landowners and the Civil War', *Economic History Review*,
2nd Ser. xviii (1965), 130-51.

be surprising if the long-term effects were not proportionate. Moreover, in post-Restoration Ulster proprietors recognized a continuing need to insure against 'troubles': about 1680 the Conynghams surrounded their new house at Springhill in County Londonderry with the substantial defensive enclosure or bawn common on properties developed much earlier.[25] The experience of their neighbours, the Dawsons of Castledawson, provides evidence of the adverse effect on proprietorial incomes of subsequent public events. Their rents fell from £2,292 due in the three years 1686-8 (of which £1,004 were recorded in arrears) to receipts of merely £273 in 1690-2, and of £961 in 1693-5. A resetting in 1696 raised rents due to new levels— £2,326 for 1696-8, but only from 1699 did receipts substantially exceed those of the mid-1680s.[26] By previous standards Ulster was relatively peaceful in the eighteenth century; nevertheless it experienced a degree of unrest unknown in Britain which exacerbated problems of estate management. The establishment of a national Registry of Deeds reflected persistent concern about proprietorial rights and titles; the surcharge on British interest rates was in practice higher than that prescribed by law, with many potential sources of credit remaining unavailable on Irish securities; and the widespread and frequent occurrence of rent arrears contributed substantially to proprietorial indebtedness.[27]

Another consideration concerns the chronology and extent of regional development in Ulster. Settlement in peripheral areas was often so low that development was delayed; for much of the seventeenth century there were proprietors who obtained little income, even from sizeable acreages. Although heavy immigration in the 1680s and 1690s, particularly from Scotland, ameliorated this situation, marked regional variations in levels of economic activity persisted, not least because Ulster experienced the falling agricultural prices which affected much of

---

[25] M. Bence-Jones, *Burke's Guide to Country Houses*, vol. i, *Ireland* (London, 1978), p. 263.

[26] PRONI D 1470/3/3. I am grateful to W. Macafee for drawing my attention to this document.

[27] P. Roebuck, 'The Irish Registry of Deeds: A Comparative Study', *Irish Historical Studies*, xviii (1972); Large, op. cit., 23-4, 42; for examples of eighteenth-century rent arrears in Ulster, see PRONI T1175 (Charlemont); D 1939/17 (Balfour); D 2624 (Langford-Rowley); D 2433/32 (Caledon).

north-western Europe in the early eighteenth century. The Bath and Barrett-Leonard estates in County Monaghan and the Balfour estate in County Fermanagh provide evidence of tenants' difficulties down to the early 1730s; while on the Gage estate at Magilligan in County Londonderry rents were reduced by 25 per cent from 1714 and did not exceed previous levels until the early 1740s. Some tenants migrated to America, others to more prosperous parts of the province, though even on the Brownlow estate in east-central Ulster upward rent movement was not sustained in the first and third decades of the century. As late as 1749 one agent in south Ulster spoke of nursing tenants like 'a hen that gathers her chickens'.[28] If in these circumstances he was already heavily indebted, a proprietor was tempted to settle for a low but realizable income, irrespective of possible future consequences. Thus, having encouraged Scots to settle on part of their estate in County Monaghan in the 1690s (by granting determinable leases for sixty-one years, with the first three years rent-free and the remainder set at less than a shilling per acre), the Massereene family subsequently let the whole of their 22,000 statute acres there on perpetuity leases, for renewal fines which averaged only half a year's rent. Thereby they increased their rental income from £261 in 1713 to £1,082 in 1752, but, besides being exceedingly low, the resultant average rent of 5p. per acre was unimprovable thereafter.[29] The Antrim family adopted a similarly shortsighted solution to their financial problems in the eighteenth century.[30] In the decade 1740-9 *new determinable lettings* on the Brownlow estate averaged 30p. per statute acre, and on the Downshire estate 15p. but even on well-managed properties it was only by mid-century and beyond that *gross*

---

[28] W. H. Crawford, 'Economy and Society in South Ulster in the Eighteenth Century', *Clogher Record*, viii (1975), 241-4 (quotation, p. 243); Crawford, 'Landlord-Tenant Relations', op. cit., 13; G. Kirkham, 'Landholding and Economy in the Parish of Magilligan (County Londonderry) in the Eighteenth Century', unpublished BA dissertation, New University of Ulster, 1979, chapter II; B. H. Slicher van Bath, *The Agrarian History of Western Europe A.D. 500-1850* (London, 1963), pp. 206-20.

[29] PRONI D 207/1/1; D 562/834; D 1739/3/9.

[30] *Belfast News Letter*, 10 April 1761. For a list of the fee-farm grants and perpetuity leases of the Antrim estate granted down to 1810, see PRONI D 1375/5/2.

average head rents approached the former figure or rivalled the latter.[31]

Apart from the manner in which estates were organized and income mobilized, a major reason for the contrast in Ulster between owned acreage and rental income was the poor quality of much of the land. Estate surveys conducted all over the province from the early eighteenth century onwards testify to this, as do rentals and valuations. Almost half of the 13,279 statute acres of the Balfour estate in County Fermanagh was described as mountain and bog in 1723; despite the substantial intervening rise in prices, average rents of determinable leases of the property rose from 21p. an acre in 1770 to only 35p. in 1815.[32] The *current value* of the 239,000 statute acres of the Antrim family was recorded as 6p. an acre in 1734: this was not merely a reflection of the estate's numerous fee-farm grants and perpetuity leases, for in 1798 its 44,000 statute acres of determinable lettings brought in only 13p. an acre.[33] Nor was this problem encountered merely on extensive properties. At Corky in County Antrim 3,885 statute acres, comprising half of the Macartney family's holdings, were rented at ¾p. an acre in 1759, reducing gross average rents on their estate from 7½p. to 4p. an acre.[34] The Watt family's 2,500 statute acres in the barony of Raphoe in County Donegal fetched a mere 17p. an acre in 1827.[35] Moreover, the province was not well endowed with non-agricultural resources. Timber was exploited to near exhaustion in the early seventeenth century. Thereafter owners assiduously prospected for minerals and were not slow to invest when they were found, but at no stage did profits from industrial or commercial ventures approach either the scale or variety of those increasingly available to many British landowners as the period progressed.[36] At the cost of promoting subdivision the

[31] Crawford, 'Landlord-Tenant Relations', op. cit., 13; Maguire, *The Downshire Estates*, op. cit., p. 39.

[32] PRONI D 1939/2/17; D 1939/17/10/50, 57.

[33] PRONI T 904, f. 35. The figures for 1798 are calculated from PRONI D 1375/3/26/43, 44; D 1375/5/2/14; T 2325/6.

[34] PRONI D 1375/5/2/2.

[35] PRONI T 2107/5.

[36] See for example PRONI T 2541/1A1/1A/8 (Abercorn); Craig, *The Volunteer Earl*, op. cit., pp. 146, 149; H. J. Habakkuk, 'The Economic Functions of English Landowners in the Seventeenth and Eighteenth Centuries', *Explorations in Entrepreneurial History*, vi (1953); G. E. Mingay, *English Landed Society in the Eighteenth Century* (London, 1963), pp. 189-201.

linen industry helped to maintain and then to increase rent levels, but was relatively unimportant to landowners as a means of supplementing or diversifying direct income.[37] Thus, Ulster proprietors were persistently and overwhelmingly dependent on rent rolls, whose growth was restricted by long leases. Indeed, especially with the enfranchisement of Catholics in 1793, owners were reluctant to discard life-tenancies because of the political consequences which this entailed.[38] Only in the two decades before 1815, when prices were at their highest, did lettings solely for terms of years or 'at will' become prevalent.[39] It was then too late for, by its very nature, this was a change of policy which could not be speedily implemented.

In regard to net or disposable income, there was a further difference between the Ulster and the British experience. On larger estates in both Ulster and Britain a hierarchy of estate officials—stewards, receivers, bailiffs, etc.—was established at an early date; the system gradually percolated through to smaller properties until by the early nineteenth century it was virtually universal. The rapid economic diversification of landed property which was a significant feature of industrialization from the later eighteenth century onwards in Britain led to greater professionalism among estate employees there, and to financial rewards more commensurate with the complexity of their duties.[40] Before then, however, estate officials in Britain had rarely matched the earnings of their Ulster counterparts. During the minority (1706-15) of the fourth Earl of Donegall no less than £2,630, or almost 6 per cent, of the gross rental of £48,500 was devoted to salaries, wages, and fees; a substantial outgoing from a relatively fixed income, most of which went to a chief agent and a few subordinates.[41] In Britain costs were generally lower, partly because payment on commission was rarer, and partly because those who performed these tasks (local

---

[37] Cullen, *Economic History of Ireland*, op. cit., pp. 59-64 and *passim*.

[38] Maguire, *The Downshire Estates*, op. cit., pp. 121-2.

[39] This statement is based on a study of the following estate surveys: PRONI D 1939/2/17 (Balfour); D 1939/14/2 (Cole Hamilton); D 1939/18/9/34 (Erne, Co. Donegal); T 1176/3 (Charlemont); T 2325/6 (Antrim); T 3059/1 (Sandwich).

[40] G. E. Mingay, 'The Eighteenth-Century Land Steward' in E. L. Jones and G. E. Mingay, eds., *Land, Labour and Population in the Industrial Revolution* (London, 1967); F. M. L. Thompson, *English Landed Society in the Nineteenth Century* (London, 1963), pp. 161-2, 164-6.

[41] PRO London, C 107/16 (PRONI Mic 4b and T 455/1-2).

attorneys or able tenant farmers) worked for less than the substantial individuals commonly employed on Irish estates. In Ulster the size of many properties, the difficult circumstances in which they were administered, and the substance of many head tenants required the employment of agents who had as much presence and authority as skill and experience. The Donegalls' was not the only eighteenth-century Ulster estate to be administered by an Irish MP; petty gentry, merchants, and ex-army officers were particularly prominent in this capacity.[42] Together with the commission system of payment, the social gap between agents and less substantial tenants made good relations between the two difficult to achieve, particularly when attempts were made to rationalize tenancies. First and foremost, however, the terms of service enjoyed by Ulster agents created a wide margin between gross estate income on the one hand and net or disposable income on the other.

A serious charge against Irish landowners is that little of their disposable income was devoted to estate improvement: to many this renders their indebtedness inexcusable, if not inexplicable. In the absence of sufficient case-studies it is impossible to be conclusive on this count, though the history of the Donegalls throws up points for consideration. Success for a plantation landowner, as Lord-Deputy Chichester never tired of reiterating, was heavily dependent on the level of his capital investment, not just in estate improvement, but also in the provision of security. His personal record in this respect was impressive. Many of the English-type farmhouses, outbuildings, and accompanying enclosures on his estate were erected at his expense. Belfast Castle was rebuilt on a massive scale; new towns were laid down both there and at Dungannon, where a fort was also erected; and, in addition to building his own house at Carrickfergus, he had new ramparts raised.[43] The family was ordinarily resident in Ulster during the seventeenth century and both the first and third Earls improved facilities

---

[42] William Macartney was an MP while agent of the Donegall estate (PRONI T 2873/2), as was Arthur Dobbs while agent of the Conway estate (PRONI D 162/33). See also E. Hughes, 'The Eighteenth-Century Estate Agent' in H. A. Cronne, T. W. Moody, and D. B. Quinn, eds., *Essays in British and Irish History* (London, 1949); W. H. Crawford, ed., *Letters from an Ulster Land Agent* (Belfast, 1976).

[43] Roebuck, 'The Making of an Ulster Great Estate', op. cit., 16-17.

in and around Belfast and Carrickfergus.[44] Significantly, in comparison with British landowners, proprietors in Ulster were faced with a much wider range of needs and options for investment. If, once the initial period of plantation was over, they concentrated investment in public utilities rather than in agriculture, this was because until late in the seventeenth century the prime need remained to attract more people to the province, not to increase the economic viability of those already established there. In Britain, agricultural improvement gathered momentum primarily because it promised to be profitable; for under a system of much shorter leases rentals kept broadly in step with the pace of investment. In Ulster, on the other hand, the early establishment of very long leases left proprietors with no alternative to minimum returns from programmes of estate improvement. Any consideration of this aspect of proprietorial performance in Ulster must pose the question: could landowners reasonably be expected to have invested in estate improvement, given the strictly uneconomic level at which rents remained before the later eighteenth century? Sizeable investment in public utilities occurred none the less.

Finally, settlement charges appear to have been the major long-term cause of indebtedness on the expenditure side. The use of family settlements was widespread; when British and Ulster families married the terms of trade were generally unfavourable to the latter; Ulster proprietors and their heirs had fewer opportunities than British proprietors of marrying into commercial wealth, and Irish interest rates were higher than in Britain.[45] There were, moreover, further dimensions to this matter. Throughout much of western and southern Europe the desire to practise primogeniture whilst providing for those members of a family who did not inherit property inevitably boosted the burden of debt. But the system was particularly precarious where land was not easily alienated, where rents were less buoyant, and where families had less chance of diversifying their incomes.[46] If Ulster landowners were not seriously

---

[44] Benn, *History of Belfast*, op. cit., vol. i, pp. 144-9, 292-3, 533.

[45] Large, 'The Wealth of the Greater Irish Landowners', op. cit., pp. 23-4, 37-42.

[46] J. P. Cooper, 'Patterns of Inheritance and Settlement by Great Landowners from the Fifteenth to the Eighteenth Centuries' in J. Goody, J. Thirsk, and E. P. Thompson, eds., *Family and Inheritance: Rural Society in Western Europe, 1200-1800* (Cambridge, 1976).

disadvantaged in the first of these respects, they were in the second and third. Given that they were, notwithstanding, as lavish in their settlement provisions as in other items of expenditure, the evidence suggests why indebtedness was commonly heavy and frequently unmanageable.[47] Emulation was a major motive force in polite society; generous settlements were a ready means of aping British landowners; and in general Ulster proprietors behaved not according to their means, but according to how they saw society's expectations of them. This was particularly true of families like the Donegalls who, though from insubstantial backgrounds and in financial difficulties, were raised to honour and title at an early date.[48]

V

In this brief essay it has been possible only to indicate some of the major causes of proprietorial indebtedness in Ulster before 1815. Moreover, in view of the preoccupation in the past with patterns of expenditure, discussion has been concentrated on matters relating to proprietorial incomes. No doubt further research will both qualify and extend the judgements expressed here and reveal how far, for example, they are appropriate to an understanding of the circumstances, policies, and performance of Irish landowners generally. At this stage, however, it seems reasonable to emphasize the comparatively weak position, financially and economically, of Ulster proprietors; and in the light of this to suggest that long-term analysis of the rural problem of nineteenth-century Ireland is advisable.

[47] See Large, op. cit., 37-42; Maguire, *The Downshire Estates*, op. cit., and Maguire, 'The 1822 Settlement', op. cit., *passim*; PRONI D 1375/3/26/43 (Antrim).

[48] On this point see C. R. Mayes, 'The Early Stuarts and the Irish Peerage', *English Historical Review*, lxxiii (1958).

7. Irish Agriculture and the Great Famine*

J. M. Goldstrom

The subject of the Great Famine of 1845-51 is of consuming interest to all who study Ireland's history. In the popular imagination this vast national calamity stands as the great divide; before the Famine there is the 'old economy', and after it, the 'new'. The popular imagination views Ireland before the Famine as inhabited by small farmers[1] who cultivated potatoes, grew some cereals, reared a pig or two, and, if they were affluent, owned a cow. These farmers lived at a bare subsistence level on milk and potatoes, selling their pigs and cereals to pay the rent and to earn cash for buying any other necessities. In the years prior to 1845 increasing pressure of population obliged them to subdivide the land to provide a livelihood for their many sons, who in turn, given a scrap of land, married early. Thus was the birth-rate further increased and the pressure on occupiers of land to subdivide reinforced.

The only crop capable of supporting a large family which held mere scraps of land was the potato. Such a dependence on one crop became progressively more dangerous because the harvest failed from time to time in various parts of Ireland and sooner or later there was bound to be a nation-wide failure. This danger was exacerbated by the introduction of high-yielding varieties of potatoes which were less resistant to disease. The Famine is interpreted thus as an inevitable and classic Malthusian check upon a population which had outstripped its resources.

The popular story continues with a representation of how the Irish learned a bitter and unforgettable lesson from the Famine. They were determined that they would not leave themselves so vulnerable again and for the farmer this meant

* My thanks are due to Brenda Collins, the late Miriam Daly, Cormac Ó Gráda, Líam Kennedy, and Joel Mokyr for their most helpful criticisms. I alone am responsible for the views expressed here.

[1] In the absence of an agreed meaning for the term 'peasant', the term 'farmer' has been used.

many unpalatable alterations to his traditional way of life. Abandoning the potato as the means of self-sufficiency signified a new kind of farming involving substantially larger units. Such a change-over obliged all but one of the farm children to leave the land and emigrate. The sons who remained postponed marriage, and if they did marry at all, they married prudently, with an eye to enlarging their holding. The long-term effect on Ireland of these enormous upheavals was a population decline which left the survivors with larger and more viable holdings.[2]

Thus reads the popular story. It is an account of two very different Irelands, so different they might be separate nations. The destructive force of the Famine snapped all links between them so that economic and social developments are invariably given a pre-Famine or a post-Famine label. It is a story feelingly retold over the years by popular historians, novelists, playwrights, and journalists. It is much loved by schoolteachers and schoolchildren because it is easily expounded.

Professional historians who wrote in the first half of the twentieth century have been far from clear as to how they stood when they were dealing with the impact of the Famine, and superficial readers might be excused for seeing resemblances between popular and academic accounts of the Famine's role. In 1921 George O'Brien chose as the title for his major textbook *The Economic History of Ireland—from the Union to the Famine* and this is typical of the pattern into which writers of specialist books and articles fell. Book titles and chapter headings have for years implied the Famine as the watershed and historians have fallen naturally into seeing Irish history in this mould. It is only upon a close reading of their works that it can be seen how difficult they have found the task of forcing the facts into the mould. There are so many qualifications to the Famine watershed theory when topics such as emigration, consolidation of land, and late marriage prior to 1845 are discussed, that their schematic framework is progressively eroded.[3] Adams,

---

[2] Roger J. McHugh, 'The Famine in Irish Oral Tradition', R. Dudley Edwards and T. Desmond Williams, eds., *The Great Famine, Studies in Irish History 1845-52* (Dublin, 1956), pp. 391-435.

[3] See K. H. Connell, *The Population of Ireland, 1750-1845* (Oxford, 1950); George O'Brien, *The Economic History of Ireland from the Union to the Famine* (London, 1921); John O'Donovan, *The Economic History of Livestock in Ireland* (Cork, 1940). Connell sees

writing on pre-Famine emigration, was the only economic historian at this period to raise doubts. He saw emigration as a continuous process from 1815, and he charted economic developments from this period too.[4] Perhaps it was his choice of subject which made it easier for him to see the longer, underlying processes at work in Ireland.

Not until the 1960s was the watershed theory subjected to close scrutiny. At Queen's University, for example, the views of a nineteenth-century economist who had never subscribed to the traditional interpretations, Neilson Hancock,[5] were now closely read and discussed in seminars. In other universities scholars were working independently, and were coming to similar conclusions. Cousins demonstrated that the kind of society which the Famine had supposedly destroyed was largely intact in the west of Ireland in the late nineteenth century.[6] It remained for R. D. Crotty, who published his seminal work *Irish Agricultural Production* in 1966, to take a really radical stand and assert that the Famine caused 'not a tremor' in agricultural development. Crotty argued that fundamental processes of change in agriculture were well under way before 1845 and he attributed these processes to steam transportation and the buoyant demand for livestock. His section on the Famine was fiercely assailed by Lee in 1969, and Ó Gráda's research has seriously weakened it. Crotty's book, nevertheless, strengthened the position of those stressing a continuity of economic development.[7]

---

the Famine as the watershed, yet he devotes considerable space to pre-Famine emigration and land consolidation. O'Brien argues (p. 3) that the Famine initiated emigration and contradicts himself on page 208. O'Donovan ends the first section of his book in 1845, yet it is clear from the text that 1815 or 1830 would have been a better dividing-point.

[4] William Forbes Adams, *Ireland and Irish Emigration to the New World from 1815 to the Famine* (Yale, 1932).

[5] W. N. Hancock, *Report on the Supposed Progressive Decline of Irish Prosperity* (Dublin, 1863).

[6] S. H. Cousens, 'The Regional Variations in Population Changes in Ireland, 1861-1881', *Economic History Review*, 2nd Ser., xvii (1964), 301-21.

[7] Raymond D. Crotty, *Irish Agricultural Production, its Volume and Structure* (Cork, 1966); Joseph Lee, 'Irish Agriculture', *Agricultural History Review*, xvii (1969), 64-76; Cormac Ó Gráda, 'On Some Aspects of Productivity Change in Irish Agriculture 1845-1926', a paper prepared for the Agricultural History Session of the International Economic History Congress, Edinburgh, 1978. Typescript.

From the early 1960s we have travelled to a point where no historian would argue that all change stemmed from the Famine, and scholars are at present confronted with a voluminous and contradictory mass of information when trying to quantify underlying trends in the pre-Famine era. Before a better understanding of the influence of the Famine can be developed a number of issues need clarification. The changes in agriculture and population need to be quantified. Were farmers producing potatoes, cereals, pigs, butter, and eggs in increasing quantities right up to 1845 rather than switching to beef and sheep? How far had subdivision progressed before the Famine? What evidence is there of consolidation before the Famine? Was the population rising at a steady rate up to 1845? How was it affected by emigration? What was happening to the age at marriage and to the marriage rate?

Resolution of the arguments concerning the timing and location of changes must depend ultimately on appeal to statistical data. A newcomer to Irish economic history, seeing just how extensive this is, might be excused for wondering how any scope for argument remains. The first complete Irish Census dates from 1821; the 1841 Census is much more detailed than the British Census. Furthermore, Ireland was subjected to numerous parliamentary inquiries. Particularly useful is the Drummond Commission which investigated the feasibility of a railway system for Ireland, in the course of which it collected export figures for the year 1835. The Devon Commission of 1845 which investigated Irish agriculture in massive detail just before the Famine is also of great value.[8] The 1841 Census provides us with the size of landholdings, a livestock census, estimates of births and deaths, and emigration estimates. Unfortunately registration of births and deaths is not available until 1864 so direct evidence on the age and rate of marriage is lacking. The systematic collection of agricultural-production statistics begins in 1847 though some limited indicators for the earlier period from the 1841 Census onwards are available as well as export data. The customs and excise figures provide a complete annual series of cereal exports for the first half of the

---

[8] For an excellent bibliography of official publications see James S. Donnelly, Jr., *The Land and the People of Nineteenth-Century Cork, the Rural Economy and the Land Question* (London, 1975), pp. 393-404.

nineteenth century and for the period up to 1825 customs and excise figures for the export of all agricultural produce are available.[9] For the year 1835 there are the estimates of agricultural exports collected by the Drummond Commission.[10] There also exists a good series of Dublin cereal prices but no equivalent, unfortunately, for livestock. For these it is necessary to rely on scattered farm accounts, the Ballinasloe Fair (for West of Ireland prices), and other miscellaneous sources.[11]

Twentieth-century scholars have added to our statistical knowledge. But, while adding to what we know they have also made historians particularly conscious of the treacherous nature of the data. The censuses of 1821, 1831, and 1841 have been shown to be deficient in certain respects. Bourke has made adjustments to some aspects of the 1841 Census and Solar has published a critique of the Drummond Commission.[12] The estimates of birth- and death-rates used by the 1841 Census Commissioners are probably an underestimate and the emigration figures, too, are deficient.[13] The material collected by the Drummond and Devon Commissions cannot readily be compared or used with the Census material because it was collected in each case under different terms of reference. To confuse matters further, Irish and English acres are of a different size and it is not always clear which unit is being used.[14] Nor should it be assumed that collectors of data in these various areas of statistics were necessarily disinterested. Respondents, perhaps fearing the tax collector, did not always give an honest

[9] The MS ledgers are in the Public Record Office, London. Annual series are printed in G. R. Porter, *The Progress of Nations in its Various Social and Economical Relations from the Beginning of the Nineteenth Century* (London ed., 1851), p. 345. More accurate figures based on five-yearly averages are in Donnelly, p. 32. See also Crotty, pp. 276-7.

[10] *Second Report of the Commissioners Appointed to Consider and Recommend a General System of Railways for Ireland*, P.P., 1837-8 (145), XXXV, 813-36.

[11] For prices taken from *The Irish Farmers' Journal* and *Freeman's Journal* see Crotty, p. 283. See also *Thom's Irish Almanac and Official Directory, with the Post Office of Dublin City and County Directory for the Year 1849* (Dublin), p. 173 and R. Montgomery Martin, *Ireland Before and After the Union with Great Britain* (London, 1843), pp. 128-9.

[12] W. E. Vaughan and A. J. Fitzpatrick, *Irish Historical Statistics: Population, 1821-1971* (Dublin, 1978), p. xii. P. M. Austin Bourke, 'The Agricultural Statistics of the 1841 Census of Ireland: a Critical Review', *Economic History Review*, xviii (1965), 376-91. Peter M. Solar, 'The Agricultural Trade Statistics in the Irish Railway Commissioners' Report', *Irish Economic and Social History*, vi (1979), 24-40.

[13] See p. 164 below.

[14] P. M. Austin Bourke, 'Notes on Some Agricultural Units of Measurement in use in pre-Famine Ireland', *Irish Historical Studies*, xiv (1965), 236-45.

answer. Ó Gráda does not exaggerate when he describes the pre-Famine period as a statistical Dark Age.[15] Post-Famine figures are more reliable but these, too, have to be treated with caution.[16]

Since the export figures are the most detailed of all, they represent the best starting-point. If we were to pursue the

Table 7.1   Irish exports of wheat, barley, and oats to Great Britain (Qrs.)[17]

Years	Oats and oatmeal	Wheat and wheat flour	Barley and barley meal
1815	597 537	189 544	27 108
1816	683 714	121 631	62 254
1817	611 117	59 025	26 766
1818	1 069 385	108 230	25 387
1819	789 613	154 031	20 311
1820	916 250	404 747	87 095
1821	1 162 249	569 700	82 884
1822	569 237	463 004	22 532
1823	1 102 487	400 068	19 274
1824	1 225 085	356 408	45 872
1825	1 629 856	396 018	165 082
1826	1 303 734	314 851	64 885
1827	1 343 267	405 255	67 791
1828	2 075 631	652 584	84 204
1829	1 673 628	519 493	97 140
1830	1 471 252	529 717	189 745
1831	1 655 934	557 520	185 409
1832	1 890 321	572 586	123 068
1833	1 762 519	844 201	107 519
1834	1 713 971	779 504	217 568
1835	1 813 101	661 773	156 176
1836	2 126 693	598 756	182 867
1837	2 274 675	534 465	187 473
1838	2 742 807	542 583	156 467
1839	1 904 933	258 331	61 675
1840	2 037 836	174 440	95 954
1841	2 539 380	218 708	75 568
1842	2 261 434	201 998	50 286
1843	2 648 033	413 466	110 449
1844	2 242 300	440 153	90 655
1845	2 353 985	779 113	93 095

[15] Ó Gráda, p. 1.

[16] The police collected the agricultural statistics. Elderly farmers still living recall that the policeman deputed to collect the data stationed himself at the local public house to do so.

[17] Porter, p. 345.

argument, that same argument explored by Crotty, that export figures are a guide to the volume of Irish agricultural production, it ought to be possible to judge the volume of total output over a period of time. There can be no doubt that Irish exports of oats, wheat, and barley expanded dramatically after the Napoleonic war period. As the table shows this expansion came to an end in the latter part of the 1830s and exports levelled off. Figures for individual years show that wheat exports peaked in 1833, barley in 1834, and oats in 1838.[18] Exports fluctuated sharply thereafter as one would expect of crops dependent on the vagaries of the weather. For example, wheat exports were almost as high in 1845 as they were in 1833. But if the export figures reflect what was happening to agriculture as a whole (Crotty's underlying assumption), there are reasonable grounds for assuming that arable production had peaked in the 1830s and was probably in decline before the Famine.

It can be said with confidence that live-pig and bacon exports rose in the years up to 1835. Butter exports over the same period are also thought to have risen though Solar has cast doubt on this point.[19] There are no export data for any of these products between 1835 and the Famine, and we have only one lead in the quest for data after 1835, Donnelly's work on Cork. He thinks that butter exports from that city were stable between 1835 and the Famine and his export figures for live pigs for 1843 show little change from 1835. It cannot, however, be assumed that Cork typified what was happening in the rest of the country.[20]

If the above export data reflect what was happening in rural Ireland it would not be unreasonable to assume that the traditional interpretation of an expanding arable sector in Ireland is valid to at least 1835. Cereals, pigs, and butter were products in the main of small farms and production increases are consistent with spreading subdivision of land and the extension of potato culture. However, the traditional explanation requires

---

[18] *Thom's Irish Almanac* 1846, p. 172 has a table closely resembling Porter's table. It is reasonable to assume that, while both tables have inaccuracies, these are sufficiently minor to discount. See also footnote 9.

[19] Solar, p. 32; O'Donovan, p. 193.

[20] Donnelly, pp. 41, 43.

cereal, pig, and dairy products to have been produced in ever-increasing quantities right up to 1845, and for this there is no evidence in the export data. The apparent levelling-off of exports appears to support Crotty's contention that the turning-point was somewhere in the mid-thirties and Crotty's view that Irish farmers were switching from arable farming at this stage gains further credence when the sluggish arable export sector is compared with the buoyant performance of the export of live cattle.

Table 7.2   Export of live cattle[21]

Period	Annual Export
1815	33 809
1816	31 752
1817	45 301
1818	58 165
1819	52 175
1820	39 014
1821	26 725
1822	34 659
1823 .. ..,	46 351
1824	62 314
1825	63 519
1835	98 150
1846	192 846

But export figures, however detailed, and accurate, are mere indicators to the performance of Irish agriculture as a whole. It is here that Crotty's thesis comes into question. There is no reason for supposing that the ratio of exports to the total volume of production remains constant. The levelling-off of cereal exports could have conflicting explanations. The demand from the increasing population for more food might have meant the diversion of land to potato-growing.[22] Alternatively, the rise in

[21] *Report from the Select Committee on Agriculture, Reports from Committee*, P.P. 1833 (612), V, 630; *Second Report ... System of Railways for Ireland*, 91; *Return of the Aggregate Amount of Provisions imported from Ireland into England in the three last years ending 1846*, P.P. 1847 (24), LIX, 523. (The figure for 1846 is for exports to England only.)

[22] The extent of the pre-Famine potato crop is subject to dispute. Crotty thinks it was 1.2 to 1.3 million acres out of a total 20 million acres of farmland. Bourke thinks it was 2.5 million. The difference arises because it is not known whether statistics collected by the police on the potato acreage in 1846 were in the form of statute or

living standards for some sections of the population might have meant that cereal production was being diverted to home consumption. A further complication is the fluctuating harvest— the years 1838 to 1842 are said to have been particularly bad.[23]

The rising export of live cattle, at first sight indicating a switch from arable to pasture, is similarly open to contradictory explanations. Following the collapse of the provision trade, cattle that had been exported in the form of salt beef were now being exported on the hoof, so accounting in part for the rise in exports. But it should not be assumed that increased beef production necessarily entailed a switch of land from arable use. Higher beef prices might well have encouraged more intensive rearing on east-coast farms, where the farmers conceivably supplemented fodder by cereal. Since the figures are inconclusive and can be interpreted in so many different ways, that part of Crotty's argument which is based on export figures cannot be disproved but neither can it be relied on, and his case must remain not proven.

Further difficulties arise with his argument if the pre-Famine agricultural-production figures are studied. Ó Gráda's recent attempt to quantify agricultural output in the period 1840-5

Table 7.3   Irish agricultural output (gross value added) (in current prices £mil)[24]

	1840-4	%
Potatoes	11.0	24.1
Crops (all others)	17.9	39.2
Cattle	4.7	10.3
Butter and milk	5.6	12.3
Pigs	3.4	7.5
Sheep and Wool	1.3	2.8
Eggs	0.9	2.0
Other	0.8	1.8
£mil	45.6	100.0

Irish acres, (1 Irish = 1.62 Statute). The yield per acre is also in dispute. P. M. Austin Bourke, 'The Extent of the Potato Crop in Ireland at the time of the Famine', *Journal of the Statistical and Social Inquiry Society of Ireland*, xx (1959), 1-35; Crotty, pp. 308-18.

[23] Lee, 'Irish Agriculture', p. 69; Donnelly, p. 32.

[24] Ó Gráda, amended version of Table 1. This Table was kindly provided by Ó Gráda. I have rearranged the contents slightly.

suggests that livestock farming was only a small part of total production—the value of cattle, sheep, and wool output was only 13 per cent of Irish agricultural output. He comes to the conclusion that tillage farming increased right up to the Famine. Even if Ó Gráda grossly underestimated livestock production the switch from arable to pasture must still have been in its early stages, so if the argument about the Famine as a watershed was confined to the agricultural-production figures, the traditional interpretation is plausible. Let us see how far this plausibility is sustained when the influences of population change and market forces at work on the economy are examined.

Clearly under way before the Famine was a reversal in population trends. The 1841 Census gives Ireland's population as 8.175 million and it has been said by O'Brien in a most curious passage in his book that, but for the Famine, this figure would have jumped to 9.01 million by 1851.[25] Such an argument ignores important factors, notably the rising tide of emigration. In his work on emigration before the Famine Adams demonstrates a steady upward trend in emigration in the 1830s to North America. Between 1841 and 1845 he shows that this trend was accelerating and that the numbers leaving Ireland for British North America and the United States averaged in excess of 60,000 a year. In addition there was a substantial outflow to Great Britain, which Mokyr estimates to have been of the order of 42,000 per annum in the 1840s.[26] The total per year from 1841 to 1845 could not have been less than 100,000 and was likely, given that Adams's figures are usually conservative, to have been an underestimate.[27]

Births per year at this time were substantially higher than the numbers leaving the country, approximately 270,000 births

[25] O'Brien quotes the 1851 Census Commissioners who calculated this figure on the assumption that immigration and emigration were equal (p. 208). Elsewhere in his book he points out that this was not the case (p. 246). This figure is often quoted in popular works, for example, Cecil Woodham-Smith, *The Great Hunger* (London, 1962), pp. 31, 411.

[26] Joel Mokyr, 'The Deadly Fungus: An Econometric Investigation into the Short-Term Impact of the Irish Famine, 1846-1851', in Julian L. Simon, ed., *Research in Population Economics* (Greenwich, Conn.), vol. ii, p. 246.

[27] Adams, pp. 413-14. Even after the Famine there is evidence of underrecording. Cormac Ó Gráda, 'A Note on Nineteenth-Century Irish Emigration Statistics', *Population Studies*, xxix (1975), 143-5.

per annum if the Census Commissioners' estimates of a birth-rate of 33 per 1,000 are accepted; 285,000 if Lee's estimate of 35 per 1,000 is accepted; and 325,000 if Mokyr's of 39.7 per 1,000 is accepted. The Commissioners' figure, as Connell has shown, is definitely too low. Lee's figure is an informed guess and Mokyr's, though the highest, is probably the most reliable, being based on careful calculation. The death-rate which the Commissioners put at 22.2 per 1,000 per annum and Mokyr at 23.5 per 1,000 sets the total deaths per year at 180,000 on the Commissioners' estimates, and 190,000 on Mokyr's.[28]

It is unlikely that there will ever be agreement on the figures for births, deaths, and emigration, but that does not mean that a rough estimate of what was happening to the population cannot be made. The natural increase was diminished by 100,000 every year between 1841 and 1845 by emigration. Approximately 185,000 people died each year. If births were 325,000 per annum there would therefore be a slight increase in the population, and in 1845 the figure was probably about 8.3 million.[29] Clearly it was levelling off. It is even possible that the population was declining. Adams noted that the populations of many towns outside Ulster were shrinking in the 1830s, and more recently F. J. Carney, generalizing from his study of the Trinity College Estates, suggests that 'the population in Ireland was adjusting in such a way that the beginning of either a falling population, or at least stability in the rate of growth, may have set in before the Famine'.[30]

That the long-term trend of growth was downward is indisputable, and this must be attributed to emigration and its associated effects. Once emigration is the common custom in a country, it will tend to increase. This happens because the established emigrants send remittances to their relatives for fares and with the knowledge gained from the letters of emigrants there develops increasing confidence for those at home

[28] *Census of Ireland for the year 1851, General Report*, Part II, P.P. 1856 [2134], XXXI, xvi; Lee, 'Irish Agriculture', p. 65; Mokyr, op. cit., p. 243; Connell, p. 31.
[29] The figure of 8.3 million is too low if there was underenumeration in 1841. See G. S. L. Tucker, 'Irish Fertility Ratios before the Famine', *Economic History Review*, 2nd Ser. xxiii (1970), 267-84. A more likely figure if such is the case is 8.4 million. The argument is not affected either way.
[30] Adams, p. 211; F. J. Carney, 'Pre-Famine Irish Population: the Evidence from the Trinity College Estates', *Irish Economic and Social History*, ii (1975), 36.

in the possibilities of a new life. Shipping companies seek emigrant business and travel agencies increase, which has the effect of making emigration easier and cheaper. Emigration ceases to be a step in the dark and becomes an institution.

The Irish emigrants did not constitute a cross-section of Irish society. Generally single, two-thirds of them over fifteen and under thirty-five,[31] their departure had a profound effect on the population that remained. Because they married and had their children abroad, the crude birth-rate was dampened down. A further indication of the downward turn population was to take is the increase in the countryside of the mercenary marriage. Statistics by which to measure or even estimate the extent of these late marriages and the linked practice of non-partible inheritance before the Famine are quite unreliable. But the existence of late marriage in the east is indisputable, and it was probably a custom that was growing.[32] The consequences of refusal to subdivide are reduced marriage opportunities; the consequence of late marriage is a reduction in average family size.

If Ireland is viewed in the context of European historical development population decline seems inevitable. The principal ingredients of rural depopulation were there. She was one of the first countries to be affected, and was particularly hard hit because of the dearth of industries. Where other countries experienced a redistribution of the population, Ireland suffered a massive loss. Even without the Famine there is every reason to suppose that the population of Ireland would have been smaller in 1861, even 1851, and substantially smaller by the turn of the century.

It is clear from Ó Gráda's work that the process of consoli-

---

[31] Adams, p. 389.

[32] Michael Drake, 'Marriage and Population Growth in Ireland, 1750-1845', *Economic History Review*, xvi (1963), 301-13. See also Crotty, pp. 40-1. A contemporary observer notes: 'The people of Wexford county generally, are said to be a money-getting people: and in the system which prevails extensively with regard to marriages, among the rural population, there is considerable evidence of this. The disposal of farmers' daughters is matter of regular traffic—acre for acre, or pound for pound—and so great is the difficulty of marrying girls without portions, that it is no unusual thing to find farmers, who are in comfortable circumstances, living as poorly as the common labourer, or the rack-rented tenant of a few acres, in order that they may save a few hundreds for *fortuning off* their girls.' Henry D. Inglis, *A Journey Throughout Ireland, during the Spring, Summer, and Autumn of 1834* (3rd ed., London, 1835), vol. i, pp. 45-6.

dation accompanying the swing from arable to pasture could not have progressed very far, given the relatively small pastoral sector in Irish farming.[33] But because the swing was slow it would be wrong to assume, as the traditionalists have done, that between 1845 and 1851 the pattern of agriculture changed out of all recognition. Subdivision before the Famine was not so extensive as the Census Commissioners have led us to believe. Bourke's analysis of the 1841 Census material suggests that the Commissioners were mistaken in two respects. Farms were larger than stated, and the number of farms was considerably fewer. His argument is that the Commissioners obtained their returns in the form of Irish acres but recorded them as English acres, having omitted to convert by 1.62. He considers that wasteland was excluded from the 1841 calculations but included for the years 1847 and 1851. His estimate for the actual number of farms over one and under five acres at the onset of the Famine is 181,950 compared with the Census estimate for 1841 of 310,375.[34] Bourke's thesis means that holdings under five acres declined over the Famine years to about half, and not a quarter of their previous number. On that basis it must be concluded that holdings were not so extensively subdivided as previously thought, and the transition from small to larger holdings was less dramatic.

Furthermore, it is misleading to attribute to the Famine all the consolidation that took place between 1841 and 1851. Connell noted that in pre-Famine Ireland, consolidation was under way on the eastern seaboard, particularly in Leinster where it was 'most pronounced'.[35] The Devon Commission investigated the extent of consolidation and although it was not quantified the Commissioners found many instances where consolidation had taken place. They questioned witnesses closely on consolidation in their own areas, and the replies lend themselves to content analysis. The evidence of 287 witnesses was sufficiently clear for it to be possible to conclude that consolidation was not unusual. Their evidence is classified below under five headings:

[33] See Table 7.3.
[34] P. M. Austin Bourke, 'Irish Agricultural Statistics of the 1841 Census', p. 380.
[35] Connell, p. 172.

Table 7.4   The extent of consolidation[36]

Consolidation	No. of witnesses	%
None	10	3.5
Rarely	70	24.5
Not in recent years	17	6.0
Not unusual	158	55.0
Extensive	32	11.0
	287	100.0

Consolidation required initial capital outlay for those farmers who took the step; clearly they had accumulated money to be able to undertake it. Equally clearly their investment brought about benefits. Farmers who enlarged their holdings would in due course have a larger income. They figured amongst the numbers in the population who enjoyed a modest level of affluence before the Famine. Taking the quality of housing as one indicator of living standards it is instructive to see that 23 per cent of the population lived in first- and second-class houses and the majority lived in accommodation that was deemed reasonable by the standards of that time. The Census-Commissioners classified houses as first, second, third, or fourth class:

Table 7.5   Quality of houses[37]

	1841	1851	Increase
First class	40 080	50 164	25%
Second class	264 184	318 758	20%
Third class	533 297	541 712	1½%
Fourth class	419 135	135 589	

[36] Calculated using content-analysis techniques from *Report from Her Majesty's Commissioners of Inquiry into the State of the Law and Practice in Relation to the Occupation of Land in Ireland* [*Report, Evidence, Appendix*], P.P. 1845, XIX-XXII.

[37] *The Census of Ireland for the Year 1851* Part VI, xxiii. Whether the additional first-, second-, and third-class houses were built before 1845 or after has not been determined. I am inclined to the former view, but Connell, in private conversation, thought they were built after 1845, financed by 'Famine profiteers'.

It is remarkable that, despite the ravages of the Famine decade, by 1851 the number of people living in second-class housing had risen from 264,000 to 318,000.

Rising prosperity for a substantial section of the community is corroborated by other sources. The ten years before the Famine saw a substantial increase in the value of livestock. The amount of money deposited in Trustee savings banks and in bank deposits increased steadily until 1845. Between 1830 and 1845 the volume of exports and imports measured by tonnage moving between British and Irish ports nearly doubled, and the volume of canal traffic increased considerably. The breweries and flour mills flourished and increased in number. True, many industries declined and some disappeared, but industry in the north-east expanded.[38]

Historians have dwelled extensively upon that very large sector of society which was poor. The images of the soup kitchen and the mud-cabin eviction have between them dominated Irish history. But at the very height of the Famine a majority, albeit a small one, survived that terrible time without recourse to the soup kitchen[39] and were able eventually to find a secure future in their own country. Too many British historians have seen early nineteenth-century history through the eyes of the hand-loom weavers, and too many writers of Irish history have permitted the plight of the starving peasant to determine their perspectives.

An understanding of how structural changes in the Irish economy and in Irish society were making their appearance before the Famine is made clearer if Ireland is looked at from the outside. Her proximity to the first industrializing nation in the world had a profound effect. As the urban populations of nineteenth-century Britain swelled, their need for food was helped in part by exports from Ireland. Initially, during the Napoleonic-war period, the demand was for cereals and Irish farmers responded to demand by increasing output. This expansion continued after the war despite the fact that prices were falling sharply. Falling prices should, as Crotty has pointed

[38] *Thom's Irish Almanac* 1859, p. 200; Porter, pp. 345-6; T. W. Freeman, *Pre-Famine Ireland: a Study in Historical Geography* (Manchester, 1957), p. 89; Hancock, pp. 45, 50-1.

[39] At the height of the Famine the numbers obtaining government relief were just over three million. Thomas P. O'Neill, 'The Organisation and Administration of Relief' in Edwards and Williams, *The Great Famine*, p. 241.

out, have induced farmers to abandon their labour-intensive arable production, but Irish holdings were on the whole so small that cereal production was the only option available to them, and they could not readily switch to the more attractive opportunities for profit that were offered in meat and dairy production in the post-war period.[40]

The initial disadvantages for Ireland of small holdings, a lack of capital, and poor transport facilities slowed the inevitable transition from arable to pasture farming. Conditions for livestock production were very favourable; mild winters allowed grass to grow almost all the year round and cattle required little shelter; it was efficient transport that was lacking. Before the days of the steamship Irish cattle would arrive at their English destinations on sailing vessels which were slow and often delayed by adverse weather. The cattle lost weight in transit and prices obtained were depressed. The arrival of steam transportation and, later, of the English railways, had far-reaching consequences.[41] In 1818 the first regular steam service between Belfast and Glasgow was introduced and in the 1820s there were services to British ports from northern, eastern, and southern ports. By 1845 both Belfast and Dublin were linked with a number of British ports. Waterford, Wexford, Drogheda, Newry, Dundalk, and Londonderry also had regular steam services to Britain.[42]

There was a greater incentive for the Irish farmer than for the British to change to livestock. The British farmer saw livestock prices rising relative to cereal, as did the Irish. However, the disadvantages under which the Irish producer had laboured initially were steadily diminishing and, with his cattle arriving in better condition and his transport costs dropping, he was able to see the gap between his selling price and that of his British counterpart narrowing. In these promising circumstances those farmers who could switch to livestock production did so, and the export figures testify to the fact. The process had not gone very far by the time the Famine struck but the

---

[40] Crotty, chapter 2.

[41] O'Donovan, pp. 213-14.

[42] D. B. McNeill, *Irish Passenger Steamship Services Northern Ireland* (Newton Abbot, 1969); D. B. McNeill, *Irish Passenger Steamship Services South of Ireland* (Newton Abbot, 1971).

new trend was by then firmly established. It was concentrated in the main along the eastern seaboard, where sea transport was readily accessible, but as railway transport improved in the late 1840s and the 1850s, a larger area of Ireland came into the orbit of the trading economy.

Since the publication of Crotty's work scholars have been more guarded. Cullen writes of the Famine 'it has been given a more decisive role in changes in Irish social and economic life than it merits'.[43] Lyons suggests that what the Famine did was to 'accentuate the existing tensions in Irish rural society and to hasten the transformation of which the faint beginnings could be discerned even before the catastrophe had struck'.[44] Caution is the keynote. In one respect only may caution be set aside, and that is when it is said with certainty of the Famine that its effect upon agriculture was to speed trends which were already established before its onset. Subsequent research is unlikely to undermine our new perception of the Famine as an accelerator rather than an initiator of change. What that research will accomplish is the sifting and evaluating of the often conflicting findings that come from variations in the pattern of farming and the behaviour of people over the crucial years. Such research does not lend itself to the bold generalizations that are associated with the earlier historians.

---

[43] L. M. Cullen, *An Economic History of Ireland since 1660* (London, 1972), p. 135.
[44] F. S. L. Lyons, *Ireland Since the Famine* (London, 2nd ed., 1973), p. 15.

8. Regional Specialization, Railway Development, and Irish Agriculture in the Nineteenth Century*

Líam Kennedy

I

A characteristic feature of economic progress in peasant societies is the movement from self-sufficient farming to a situation where the bulk of farm output is marketed. A concomitant of this transition is an increase in specialization in production, both at the level of the individual holding and at a regional level. This essay is primarily concerned with the latter development in nineteenth-century Ireland. Of particular interest is the period between the Great Famine and the Great War. These seven decades of *laissez-faire* policy enclose a remarkable period in the history of United Kingdom agriculture. With the repeal of the corn laws in 1846 and the revolution in transport costs in the second half of the nineteenth century, United Kingdom agriculture—hitherto sheltered by long centuries of protectionist measures—found itself increasingly exposed to the force of international competition. In the following century the long-run tendency for state intervention in agricultural trade reasserted itself, as a new wave of protectionism broke in Britain and Ireland. Thus this free-trade interlude offers a unique opportunity to observe the uninhibited response of farmers to radically changing market conditions. One important aspect of this response is changing regional patterns of production within Ireland.

Change in the spatial distribution of agricultural activity has a certain intrinsic interest, most obviously for geographers. Our primary concern, however, is with underlying economic processes. Changing patterns of land use are viewed here as

* The helpful comments of Peter Solar on an earlier version of this essay are gratefully acknowledged. I alone am responsible for the views expressed here.

essentially surface phenomena, the causes and consequences of which must be explored on the economic and social planes. The first part of the essay introduces some theoretical issues relating to regional specialization and goes on to present impressionistic evidence on regional farming-patterns in pre-Famine Ireland. In the following section the course of regional specialization in the second half of the nineteenth century is traced using the agricultural statistics of the period. Thereafter the so-called transport revolution in Ireland and its impact on farming patterns is considered. The arguments are then summarized.

II

Regions with different natural-resource endowments or different factor proportions may gain from specialization in those lines of agricultural activity for which they possess a comparative advantage. Whether in fact inter-regional trade takes place depends crucially on the level of transaction costs, transport costs in particular. The latter may be so high that despite very considerable variation over space in the costs of producing commodities, trade and specialization do not occur. Cost-reducing innovations in the transport sphere help erode the physical barriers that separate different producing regions, thus expanding opportunities for trade. Normally the extension of trading relationships brings about a reallocation of resources, new production and consumption patterns, and a greater volume of traded output.[1]

The most visible expression of these processes in agriculture is the emergence of regions and subregions dominated by the production of one or a few commodities; in contemporary times the most casual observer is struck by the great wheat fields of East Anglia, the sheep-raising areas of north-west Scotland, or the cattle-fattening districts of eastern Ireland. The structure of production apparent in such areas is the outcome of long historical processes. To take the particular case of Ireland: it is clear that well before the Great Famine a considerable degree

---

[1] The implications of these changes for the welfare of different socio-economic groups are by no means as straightforward as is sometimes assumed. The output elasticity of employment, for example, could be negative in the new situation, thus producing unemployment or underemployment among labourers.

of specialization had taken place. Wakefield's description in 1812 of the various stages of cattle production and the associated regional linkages bears comparison with accounts of the cattle trade in twentieth-century Ireland:

> In Ireland, calves, when yearlings, are often collected by jobbers, who carry a great number of them to Connacht, where they are grazed during the course of some years, but without any view of being fattened ... Under this system, cattle, when four years old, are driven to Ballinasloe fair in October, where they are offered for sale in a half-fattened state by some of the graziers, and purchased by others, for the purpose of finishing them, or fattening them into beef. The latter are occupiers of the rich pastures in Limerick, Tipperary, Roscommon and Meath, which are the chief grazing counties in Ireland. The banks of the Fergus in Clare, some parts of Cork, the Queen's County, Westmeath, a small part of Louth and Kildare, are all in some degree held by persons engaged in the occupation of grazing bullocks.[2]

Thompson, writing a decade earlier about Meath graziers, relates how these are 'under the necessity of going to other parts of the kingdom for the major part of the cattle fatted by them'.[3] Store cattle bought at fairs in Munster and Connacht were densely stocked on the rich pasture lands of Meath, fattened, and then sold either on the Dublin market or at local fairs to buyers from the north of Ireland and England. Some indication of the magnitude of this trade is suggested by the scale of operations of farmers involved in livestock fattening. Many of these were engaged in the cattle business in a very substantial way, finishing from 'three to five hundred cows in the summer season, beside numbers of bullocks and sheep'.[4] It should be noted also that despite the natural advantage possessed by counties such as Meath and Westmeath in livestock farming, production patterns were responsive to price as well as environmental factors.[5]

---

[2] E. Wakefield, *An Account of Ireland, Statistical and Political* (London, 1812), vol. i, pp. 310-11. See also *Report of the Commissioners appointed to inquire into the state of the Fairs and Markets in Ireland*, P.P. 1852-3, XLI, 86, 234.

[3] R. Thompson, *Statistical Survey of the County of Meath* (Dublin, 1802), p. 218.

[4] Ibid., p. 219. Large specialist farmers such as these, who formed the core of the rural middle class in pre-Famine Ireland, might sometimes also be middle men. Cesar Otway who toured Connacht in the 1830s makes the interesting (if somewhat loose) claim that the more progressive types of middle men—engaged not only in subletting great tracts of land but also farming directly themselves—were the 'principal stockfarmers who supply Ballinasloe fair with the sheep and black cattle that are so much in demand'. C. Otway, *A Tour in Connacht* (Dublin, 1839), p. 127.

[5] Thompson estimates that while a few decades earlier three-quarters of the county of Meath had been under grass 'not more than about two-thirds is at present so

In Ireland generally in the late eighteenth and early nineteenth centuries tillage was expanding relative to pasture in response to changes in relative prices (including the price of land which was rising, partly as a result of demographic pressures). This broad movement is reported by observers in widely separated parts of Ireland—Dublin, Cork, Clare, Kilkenny, and Londonderry.[6] Even in such apparently remote districts as Burrishool and Murrisk—two baronies running along the Atlantic coast of south-west Mayo—the bulk of the farmland was in tillage at the beginning of the nineteenth century.[7] In the former barony it was estimated, on the basis of the increase in tithes, that 'agriculture must have extended itself, to one-third more than it had been ten years ago'.[8]

In the linen-weaving districts of Ulster, in the county of Armagh in particular, it is clear that land-use patterns were directly responsive to economic factors, though the effects of agricultural prices seem to have been swamped by those of the domestic linen industry. Given that most farms in Armagh were smaller than five acres in size,[9] the agricultural surplus on such holdings must have been slight and sometimes negative. 'There is not one extensive market for grain in the county', Coote reported in 1804, 'indeed little is reared for sale'.[10] However, this should not be interpreted as an indication of subsistence living. M'Parlan whose *Statistical Survey of the County of Sligo* was published in 1802 helps complete the picture. 'This whole country may, strictly speaking, be called a tillage country', he observed, 'and together with Mayo is the principal granary

---

occupied', the buoyant demand for corn having induced 'a great many who, before that period, invariably grazed their lands, to break up, and turn into tillage, large tracts of ground, which had not for some ages felt the iron hand of the husbandman'. Ibid., p. 208. A half-century later both Meath and Westmeath still had large tillage acreages. In 1851 31 per cent of farm land in Meath and 27 per cent of that in Westmeath were under tillage.

[6] J. Archer, *Statistical Survey of the County Dublin* (Dublin, 1801), pp. 11-16; H. Townsend, *Statistical Survey of the County of Cork* (Dublin, 1810), pp. 451, 543; H. Dutton, *Statistical Survey of the County of Clare* (Dublin, 1808), pp. 69-70; W. Tighe, *Statistical Observations relative to the County of Kilkenny* (Dublin, 1802), p. 260; W. S. Mason, *Statistical Account, or Parochial Survey of Ireland* (Dublin, 1816), vol. i, p. 333; R. D. Crotty, *Irish Agricultural Production: Its Volume and Structure* (Cork, 1966), pp. 23-4.

[7] J. M'Parlan, *Statistical Survey of the County of Mayo* (Dublin, 1802), pp. 40-4.

[8] Ibid., p. 28.

[9] C. Coote, *Statistical Survey of the County of Armagh* (Dublin, 1804), p. 136.

[10] Ibid., p. 181.

and potato support of the manufacturing counties of the north, in times of scarcity'.[11] Thus a symbiotic relationship between Ulster counties and North Connacht had developed, involving a division of labour as between manufacturing and agricultural pursuits. The degree of specialization in different types of economic activity in the early nineteenth century was, of course, limited. The domestic textiles' industry had spread widely through Connacht,[12] as a supplement to agricultural activity, while even the strongly manufacturing districts of Ulster produced considerable quantities of oats, potatoes, and flax.[13]

Inter-regional links in the dairying industry are also apparent in this period. The Revd Townsend knew 'some persons, under the name of cow jobbers, who made a livelihood by purchasing cows in the county of Limerick, and selling them in the neighbourhood of Cork'.[14] There was also, of course, a crucial nexus between the dairying and the cattle trade. Wakefield noted that 'in most of the dairy districts calves are reared, and frequently sold when yearlings, to persons who graze them till they are three or four years old'.[15] They were then resold to graziers for fattening, thus completing the chain of production.[16]

Before concluding this section it may be helpful to summarize contemporary accounts of the spatial distribution of different types of agricultural activity in the early nineteenth century. In relation to dairying, Wakefield found extensive tracts of dairy farms in Cork, Kerry, and Waterford, while parts of Kilkenny, Carlow, Meath, Westmeath, and Longford also had considerable clusters of dairy farms.[17] In addition, dairying was carried on in the mountainous areas of Leitrim and Sligo, and in parts of the neighbouring county of Fermanagh.[18] Mountainous districts, such as in Kerry, Tipperary, Waterford, King's

[11] J. M'Parlan, *Statistical Survey of the County of Sligo* (Dublin, 1802), p. 14.

[12] Ibid., p. 122; M'Parlan, *Mayo*, pp. 28-30.

[13] J. Dubourdieu, *Statistical Survey of the County of Down* (Dublin, 1802), p. 85; Coote, *Armagh*, pp. 171, 174; J. Dubourdieu, *Statistical Survey of the County of Antrim* (Dublin, 1812), p. 173.

[14] Townsend, p. 582.   [15] Wakefield, p. 308.   [16] Ibid., p. 308.

[17] Ibid., pp. 323, 327; Townsend, pp. 577-82; Tighe, p. 383. See also J. S. Donnelly, Jr., 'Cork Market: Its Role in the Nineteenth Century Butter Trade', *Studia Hibernica*, xi (1971), 130-63.

[18] M'Parlan, *Sligo*, p. 31; Wakefield, p. 322.

County, and Leitrim, were the principal nurseries for the 'immense droves of young cattle'[19] that formed the basis of the internal cattle trade. 'In regard to sheep bred for fattening, Galway and Clare', according to Wakefield, 'rear a far greater number than any other parts of Ireland'.[20] Elsewhere, along the steep, exposed hillsides of Donegal, Sligo, Antrim, the Mourne country, and Kerry, great flocks of sheep subsisted under harsh natural conditions.[21]

Although tillage was increasing relative to pasture in pre-Famine Ireland, specialized grazing districts were maintained in the fertile region of north Munster—Limerick, east Clare, parts of Tipperary, and north Cork.[22] The eastern counties of Kildare, Queen's County, Meath, and Westmeath, as well as Roscommon in the west of Ireland, also displayed somewhat similar patterns, though to varying degrees.[23] The limestone plains of Roscommon, for instance, seem to have been devoted very largely to grazing and livestock production while, by contrast, Meath contained both cattle-fattening and extensive corn-growing areas.[24] While, in general, it is difficult to discern sharp regional patterns in relation to tillage in the early nineteenth century, it is clear that districts in the south-eastern corner of Ireland, the valley of the Slaney in particular, were well-established corn-growing areas.[25] Other districts producing substantial grain surpluses were to be found in east Cork, Tipperary, King's County, Queen's County, and north

---

[19] T. Newenham, *A View of the Natural, Political, and Commercial Circumstances of Ireland* (London, 1809), pp. 66-7. It is worth noting that regional specialization in the cattle industry, and the associated movement of large herds of cattle from one district to another had important consequences for urban development. For example, Navan, Athboy, Kells, and Nobber—towns on the drove roads from the north and west into Meath—owed their existence, in considerable part, to the cattle trade. See T. J. Hughes, 'East Leinster in the Mid-Nineteenth Century', *Irish Geography*, iii (1958), 227-41.

[20] Wakefield, p. 341.

[21] Newenham, pp. 66-7; Dubourdieu, *Antrim*, p. 338; Dubourdieu, *Down*, pp. 204-5.

[22] Wakefield, p. 387.

[23] Ibid., p. 311; T. J. Rawson, *Statistical Survey of the County of Kildare* (Dublin, 1807), pp. 103-4; Thompson, pp. 218-19; I. Weld, *Statistical Survey of the County of Roscommon* (Dublin, 1832), pp. 665-70.

[24] Weld, pp. 665-70; Wakefield, p. 387; Thompson, p. 208. See also Hughes, p. 229.

[25] H. D. Inglis, *Ireland in 1834: A Journey throughout Ireland, during the spring, summer, and autumn of 1834* (3rd ed., 1835, London), vol. i, pp. 43-4.

Mayo.[26] By contrast, counties such as Leitrim, Roscommon, and Limerick seem to have had comparatively little land in tillage.[27] In relation to potatoes, largely a subsistence crop, one need only remark that they were grown widely throughout the island,[28] and in increasing quantities, especially in the west of Ireland in the decades before the Great Famine. Indeed it is possible that the subdivision of holdings and the spread of potato culture actually reduced the scope for farming specialization in the west in this period. In eastern Ulster, spade-cultivation of potatoes, oats, and flax formed the backbone of the tillage economy of the tiny farms.[29] 'The quantity of oats, sown in the northern counties of Ireland', according to Dubourdieu, 'is great in proportion to that of any other grain'.[30] Oatmeal and potatoes, he added, formed the 'principal food of the great body of the people'.[31]

III

Detailed agricultural statistics became available in the parliamentary papers from 1847 onwards, and it is therefore possible to develop quantitative measures of regional specialization for the post-Famine period. A convenient index or measure for our purposes is provided by the coefficient of variation.[32] This may be used to show the degree of dispersion of different crop acreages (or livestock numbers) over the thirty-two counties. A high value for the coefficient indicates that production of the commodity varies markedly over space, i.e. that production tends to be concentrated in particular regions (counties). The outstanding example, with reference to the commodities examined in tables 8.1 and 8.2, is flax. The degree of regional specialization is very pronounced, as is indicated by the high values assumed by the coefficient of variation. Conversely, a low value for the

---

[26] Townsend, pp. 232, 605-11; Inglis, pp. 130, 180; Wakefield, p. 398; M'Parlan, *Mayo*, pp. 28-30.

[27] Wakefield, p. 387; M'Parlan, *Leitrim*, pp. 26-7.

[28] See, for example, Townsend, pp. 195, 221; Newenham, p. 63.

[29] Dubourdieu, *Down*, pp. 42-3, 75, 85; Coote, pp. 171-4; Dubourdieu, *Antrim*, pp. 173-4, 181, 220.

[30] Dubourdieu, *Antrim*, p. 173.

[31] Ibid., p. 173.

[32] The coefficient of variation is the standard deviation of a data set (in the present instance crop acreages or livestock numbers for each of the thirty-two counties of Ireland) divided by the arithmetic mean of the data set.

coefficient, as shown for example by potatoes, implies a low level of regional specialization.

Before proceeding to a discussion of changes in post-Famine agriculture, a brief comment on the reliability of the agricultural statistics is in order. There are a number of likely sources of error. Data on land-use patterns were based on farmers' judgements of the relative extent of different farm enterprises. A certain casualness in making these estimates is consistent with our knowledge of rural society and its relations with the representatives of state bureaucracies. Estimation of the extent of land other than agricultural land (bog, barren mountain, etc.) was recognized by nineteenth-century commentators as being highly problematic.[33] Calculation of the average produce per acre of the various crops presented difficult sampling and other problems.[34] Furthermore, the efficiency of the enumerators in seeking out and recording information was unlikely to have been wholly uniform across space and time. There is also the fact that, owing to typographical or computational errors, there are inconsistencies in the data between different volumes of the agricultural returns. Thus the total wheat acreage for 1877 is reported, in the agricultural returns for that year, as being 139,297 acres.[35] A few years later the considerably lower figure of 113,297 acres is given.[36] Assuming the county totals for wheat are correct, it is the earlier estimate that should be accepted. The total number of sheep under one year in Queen's County in 1847 is given in one report as 159,729.[37] This absurdly high figure—roughly one-third of the total for Ireland— is clearly a mistake. A check on the internal consistency of the calculations shows that the correct figure for Queen's County should be 15,972.[38] According to the agricultural statistics for 1880, the total of sheep (under one year) for the thirty-two counties was 1,601,151 in the year 1873.[39] However, the county

---

[33] R. M. Barrington, 'The Drought of 1887, and some of its effects on Irish Agriculture', *Journal of the Statistical and Social Inquiry Society of Ireland*, ix (1888), 239-40.

[34] Ibid., p. 236; W. N. Hancock, *Report on the Supposed Progressive Decline of Irish Prosperity* (Dublin, 1863), p. 30.

[35] *The Agricultural Statistics of Ireland for the year 1877*, P.P. 1878, LXXVII, 542. This series is cited hereafter as *A.S.*

[36] *A.S., 1880*, P.P. 1881, XCIII, 732.

[37] *A.S., 1870*, P.P. 1872, LXIII, 374.

[38] As indeed was reported in *A.S., 1847*, P.P. 1847-8, LVII, 123.

[39] *A.S., 1880*, P.P. 1881, XCIII, 750.

totals presented in the report add to only 1,597,296.[40] Again in relation to sheep, one finds in the agricultural returns for 1910 that the sum of the county totals comes to 1,600,296 and not the printed figure of 1,597,296 for the year 1907.[41] Nevertheless, it seems more reasonable to commend rather than to criticize the agricultural statisticians for their work. After all, manipulating and presenting such great masses of data was a very formidable task in an era when the numbers-weary clerk was obliged to rely on mental rather than mechanical processes. It is the internal consistency of the arrays of tables, rather than the occasional lapses, which leaves the stronger impression. Furthermore, for the particular purposes for which the data have been used, the deficiencies are not of such a magnitude as to vitiate the findings. Essentially the work consists of constructing aggregate indices which are not highly sensitive to error.

The peak year for tillage in post-famine Ireland was 1851. This was followed by a decline in the area under tillage and then recovery to reach a second and somewhat lower peak in 1857. Taking the period 1850-1914 as a whole, the picture presented in Table 8.1 is one of dramatic decline in the tillage acreage. In 1850 the area under tillage crops was 4,558,000 acres; by 1910 it had declined to roughly half this level. A particularly noteworthy feature of Table 8.1 is that such radical change was not matched by comparable changes in the degree of regional specialization. To take the example of potatoes, while the acreage grown was halved between 1855 and 1910, the coefficient of variation varies within very narrow limits. This implies that potatoes continued to be grown widely across the country and that inter-county trade in this commodity was only weakly developed. Very probably on many medium-sized and small farms, in most parts of the country, potatoes for home consumption continued to be grown.

Of the crops under consideration, flax-growing shows the highest degree of regional specialization, both at the beginning and the end of our period. In 1851 just under 90 per cent of

[40] An earlier report presents figures for sheep numbers at county and national levels for the year 1873 that are, in fact, internally consistent. See *A.S., 1873*, P.P. 1875, LXXIX, 211. The national total of 1,601,151 seems to be correct.

[41] *A.S., 1910*, P.P. 1911, C, 687.

Table 8.1 National acreage of selected crops, and the degree of regional specialization for the period 1850-1910

YEAR	Cereals		Wheat		Green Crops		Potatoes		Flax	
	Acres ('000)	C. of Var.	Acres ('000)	C. of Var.	Acres ('000)	C. of Var.	Acres ('000)	C. of Var.	Acres ('000)	C. of Var.
1850	3 150	0.502	605	0.944	1 318	0.617	875	0.628	91	1.631
1855	2 833	0.556	446	0.972	1 444	0.562	982	0.516	97	1.559
1860	2 639	0.551	466	0.986	1 608	0.576	1 172	0.540	129	1.759
1865	2 216	0.572	267	1.221	1 502	0.568	1 066	0.554	251	1.649
1870	2 174	0.587	260	1.014	1 499	0.575	1 044	0.574	195	1.584
1875	1 917	0.621	159	1.290	1 370	0.574	901	0.584	101	1.806
1880	1 766	0.601	149	1.230	1 247	0.557	821	0.589	158	1.737
1885	1 595	0.628	71	1.384	1 219	0.561	797	0.574	108	1.757
1890	1 515	0.636	92	1.158	1 214	0.558	781	0.568	97	1.825
1895	1 439	0.656	37	1.345	1 152	0.580	710	0.581	95	1.832
1900	1 347	0.696	54	1.243	1 098	0.595	654	0.586	47	1.966
1905	1 271	0.707	38	1.255	1 044	0.601	617	0.604	46	1.985
1910	1 300	0.719	48	1.210	1 011	0.600	593	0.605	45	2.046

land under flax was located in Ulster, the major producing counties being Antrim, Londonderry, and Tyrone. It is also apparent that the degree of specialization varied through time. High prices for flax in the 1860s stimulated a rapid expansion of the flax-growing area; the contraction of the flax acreage after the peak of 302,000 acres in 1864 was accompanied by an even more marked regional pattern of production.

The decline of the wheat acreage is truly remarkable; in 1900 it stood at barely 11 per cent of its 1851 level. The three major wheat-growing areas in 1851 were Cork, Tipperary, and Wexford (in that order). By 1900 few counties had in excess of 2,000 acres of wheat. Down had the single largest area under wheat—10,000 acres—and was followed by counties Cork and Wexford. It is evident from Table 1 that the uneven distribution of the wheat acreage was more pronounced at the end than at the beginning of the period. However, production had not developed such a strong regional character as one might, perhaps, have expected. The contrast with flax is instructive. While at the turn of the century wheat and flax had roughly similar total acreages, flax-growing none the less showed a much more concentrated regional pattern.

Other cereal crops were grown widely throughout the island in the second half of the nineteenth century, though the total acreage of cereals declined quite substantially. (It should be mentioned that the cereals totals in Table 8.1 contain small acreages of beans and peas.) Oats, the most important corn crop over the whole period, was grown more frequently for home consumption than either wheat or barley.[42] While there were substantial acreages of oats in virtually every county, barley-growing was more strongly associated with the southern counties. Cork had the relatively massive total of 46,000 acres under barley in 1851. Lagging some distance behind Cork in terms of relative significance were the counties of Wexford, Limerick, Clare, and Tipperary. By the end of the century the ordering had changed considerably, Wexford, Kilkenny, Queen's County, and Tipperary being the main barley-producing areas. Of the more northerly counties only Louth had a strong barley-growing tradition.

---

[42] Barrington, pp. 236-7.

The other major group of tillage crops, apart from cereals, was green crops. This category was dominated by potatoes and turnips throughout the period 1850-1914. As green crops were an important element—both as human- and animal-feed inputs—in the mixed economy of small farms, it is hardly surprising that their cultivation does not bear a strong regional character, as indeed is evidenced by the fairly low values over time for the coefficient of variation. It is worth noting also that at mid-century the cereal acreage was more than double that of green crops. However, the acreage of green crops declined only slowly through time; by the first decade of the twentieth century these two forms of tillage occupied roughly equal land areas. Turnips, which with hay constituted the major winter feed for livestock, experienced a relatively mild decline in area through time. The resilience of the turnip crop is, of course, an indication of the increasing livestock orientation of the agricultural economy. It cannot be interpreted as some kind of rearguard action against the forces which so radically undermined the tillage economy of pre-Famine Ireland.[43]

In relation to livestock, it appears from Table 8.2 that in the mid-nineteenth century the degree of regional specialization in the production of young cattle was low.[44] By the turn of the present century a less uniform spatial pattern had emerged. Certainly by 1900 calf production was strongly associated with the southern dairying counties of Cork, Kerry, Tipperary, and Limerick. These four counties held just under one-third of all cattle aged under one year in the country. As regards older cattle (aged two years and upwards), these were most numerous in the extensive grazing districts of Meath, Tipperary, Galway, and Kildare. Meath alone held over 10 per cent of the country's total in 1900.

---

[43] Tillage crops dominated the agricultural economy of the 1840s. One quantitative estimate is that by Ó Gráda, who suggests that on the eve of the Famine over 60 per cent of gross value added in Irish agriculture was accounted for by tillage output. See Cormac Ó Gráda, 'On Some Aspects of Productivity Change in Irish Agriculture, 1845-1926', paper prepared for the Agricultural History Session of the International Economic History Congress, Edinburgh, 1978, Table I. (Amended version of the Table he presented at Edinburgh.) Livestock production is, of course, more land intensive than tillage production, thus the structure of agricultural output is only a rough guide to land-use patterns on the eve of the Famine.

[44] This feature is subjected to closer scrutiny on p. 190.

Table 8.2   Total numbers of livestock, and the degree of regional
specialization for the period 1850-1910

Year	Cattle*		Sheep*	
	No's ('000)	C. of Var.	No's ('000)	C. of Var.
1850	503	0.422	483	0.836
1855	679	0.500	1 106	0.895
1860	581	0.489	1 184	0.920
1865	740	0.536	1 309	0.892
1870	772	0.567	1 493	0.893
1875	836	0.578	1 498	0.869
1880	841	0.680	1 267	0.913
1885	981	0.671	1 339	0.954
1890	1 023	0.707	1 785	0.925
1895	1 017	0.694	1 564	0.898
1900	1 086	0.700	1 801	0.868
1905	1 092	0.693	1 555	0.928
1910	1 111	0.727	1 625	0.900

* less than one year old

By contrast with young cattle at mid-century, sheep aged less than one year were distributed much more unevenly over the thirty-two counties. In 1851 major lamb-producing areas, as in pre-Famine Ireland,[45] were located in the western counties, Galway and Mayo in particular. The counties of Cork, Tipperary, and Kildare were also major producers. By 1900 there had been some change in the order of importance of different lamb-producing counties, though Galway, Mayo, Cork, and Tipperary still dominated. Just over 20 per cent of the national total was accounted for by Galway and Mayo.

IV

The evidence given above on regional specialization provides a useful vantage-point from which to form an impression of the impact of railways on the agricultural economy. And while the approach used here is, admittedly, rough by comparison with the data and labour-intensive techniques of the econometric historians of the railway,[46] it has at least the advantage of being economical in terms of time and source material. If a transport

---

[45] Wakefield, p. 341; Newenham, pp. 66-7.
[46] A useful assessment of this literature is P. O'Brien, *The New Economic History of the Railways* (London, 1977).

innovation, such as the introduction of railways in Ireland, had a major impact, then one would expect a considerable shift in the spatial distribution of agricultural activity to result. This proposition, that transport development and regional specialization are intimately linked, is readily derived from the theoretical considerations touched on earlier in the essay. The historical experience of a number of countries reinforces this view. Metzer in his study of railways and the rural economy in Tsarist Russia concludes that the construction of a rail network gave the single most important impulse to internal trade in agricultural produce.[47] The result was a sharp increase in marketed output and in regional specialization. In the case of the United States, it has been argued that high transport costs constituted one of the most formidable obstacles to economic growth in the early decades of the nineteenth century. The Appalachian mountain barrier effectively divided the country into two economic regions, each 'spatially and functionally compartmentalised'.[48] As R. W. Fogel points out, cheap transport was a necessary condition for the development of regions specializing in different commodities.[49] First, internal waterways, and later railways, made possible the emergence of new spatial patterns of agricultural production (with all the developmental effects that flowed from market integration and specialization in production). Among the discernible effects of transport innovation on West African trade in the late nineteenth and twentieth centuries noted by Hopkins is that of locational changes in production.[50]

What of Ireland and its 'transport revolution'?[51] If the coming of the railways had a strong impact on Irish agriculture this is

---

[47] J. Metzer, 'Railroad Development and Market Integration: the Case of Tsarist Russia', *Journal of Economic History*, xxxiv (1974), 529-50.

[48] H. H. Segal, 'Canals and Economic Development' in Carter Goodrich, ed., *Canals and American Economic Growth* (New York, 1961).
See also L. E. Davis, R. A. Easterlin, *et al.*, *American Economic Growth: An Economist's History of the United States* (New York, 1972), p. 513.

[49] R. W. Fogel, *Railways and American Economic Growth: Essays in Econometric History* (Baltimore, 1964), p. 110.

[50] A. G. Hopkins, *An Economic History of West Africa* (London, 1977), pp. 195-7.

[51] The term is that of K. B. Nowlan. See K. B. Nowlan, 'The Transport Revolution: The Coming of the Railways' in Nowlan, ed., *Travel and Transport in Ireland* (Dublin, 1973). Note also Joseph Lee, 'The Railways in the Irish Economy' in L. M. Cullen, ed., *The Formation of the Irish Economy* (Cork, 1969), p. 87.

not immediately apparent from a comparison of the chronology of railway growth and the course of regional specialization.[52] In the period between 1850 and 1910—by the latter date railways had penetrated even the remote areas of the country—there is a positive association between regional specialization (RS) and time. This is apparent from Table 8.3 where regional

Table 8.3   The relationship between regional specialization
(as measured by the coefficient of variation)
and time, in the period 1850-1910[§]

Cereals*	RS = 5.084 + 0.084 TIME (0.046) (0.003)	R^2 = 0.97 n = 25
Wheat*	RS = 10.141 + 0.122 TIME (0.401) (0.027)	R^2 = 0.47 n = 25
Greens*	RS = 5.525 + 0.025 TIME (0.154) (0.010)	R^2 = 0.20 n = 25
Potatoes*	RS = 5.545 + 0.016 TIME (0.084) (0.006)	R^2 = 0.27 n = 25
Flax*	RS = 15.539 + 0.173 TIME (0.257) (0.017)	R^2 = 0.81 n = 25
Cattle*	RS = 4.605 + 0.118 TIME (0.123) (0.008)	R^2 = 0.90 n = 25
Sheep	RS = 8.796 + 0.012 TIME (0.117) (0.008)	R^2 = 0.10 n = 25
Cows*	RS = 6.944 + 0.053 TIME (0.069) (0.005)	R^2 = 0.84 n = 23

* The relationship is statistically significant at the 95 per cent confidence level.

§ The number of observations used in each of the equations, with the exception of that relating to milch cows, is twenty-five. Rather than calculate the coefficient of variation for a particular product for every year between 1850 and 1910—an unnecessarily tedious procedure—somewhat longer time-intervals were adopted. The first observation related to the year 1850, the second to 1853, the third to 1855, the fourth to 1857, the fifth to 1860, and so on for the succeeding decades. There are only twenty-three observations for milch cows, beginning with the year 1855. This is because cows do not appear in the agricultural statistics as a separate category until 1854.

    To avoid working with very small values the coefficient of variation has been multiplied by ten throughout. Standard errors are in parentheses.

---

[52] Some useful material on the historical development of Irish railways is contained in the following: *Royal Commission on Railways: Appendices to Evidence taken before the Commissioners*, P.P. 1867, XXXVIII; *Second Report of the Royal Commission on Irish Public Works*, P.P. 1888, XLVIII, 188-92, 940-1; Grimshaw, 346-7. A remarkably dull history is J. C. Conroy, *A History of Railways in Ireland* (London, 1928).

specialization is related to time for each of the eight farm enterprises. In some instances there is a very smooth increase over
time in the degree of specialization. Thus, for example, in the
case of cereal-growing there is a steady tendency towards a
more concentrated pattern of production as is indicated by the
high value for the coefficient of determination ($R^2 = 0.97$). By
contrast, the degree of specialization in wheat-growing increases
less regularly over time (R^2 value of less than 0.5). Much of
this unexplained variation is presumably in response to short-
term economic and climatic factors. Sheep—no friends of the
pattern-making statistician—display even more erratic tendencies (the value for R^2 being extremely low). None the less,
in all cases regional specialization and time are positively correlated. More significant, however, is the *pace* of change. The
value of the regression coefficients in all the equations is low,
suggesting a gentle rate of change in regional specialization. A
good illustration of this point is provided in the case of cows.
While specialization increases fairly smoothly in the time period
under consideration, as indicated by the high value for R^2, the
degree of change per unit of time (indicated by the regression
coefficient) is low. For crops such as potatoes and green crops
there is very little change indeed.

The point we are emphasizing may be seen more clearly
perhaps by reference to Table 8.4. This shows that the index
of specialization for crop and livestock products in the period
1905-10 is higher in every case than in the opening period
1850-5. However, with the exception of cattle (under one
year)—a special case, as it will be argued later—the pattern of
change is not especially marked over these six decades. And of
course factors other than railway development served to promote regional specialization, in part accounting for these
observed changes. Technological change in the butter industry,
for example, gave an impulse towards greater specialization in
the dairying industry in the late nineteenth century.[53] More
generally it may be assumed that some of the forces making for
more efficient spatial patterns of production in pre-Famine
Ireland were also operative after 1850, thus further deflating
the explanatory role of the railways.

[53] Líam Kennedy, 'Agricultural Co-operation and Irish Rural Society, 1880-1914',
(unpublished D.Phil. thesis, University of York, 1978), p. 107.

Table 8.4   Regional specialization in 1850-5
compared with 1905-10[54]

	1850-5	*1905-10*	*change*
Cereals	0.526	0.714	36%
Wheat	1.000	1.220	22%
Greens	0.582	0.639	10%
Potatoes	0.567	0.601	6%
Flax	1.590	2.00	26%
Cattle	0.469	0.711	52%
Sheep	0.868	0.908	5%
Cows	0.683*	0.798	17%

* refers to the period 1855-60

It may be objected that the impact of the railway is being
diluted by using such a long time perspective. But even if one
takes a shorter time-interval, for example the first phase of
major railway development in the late 1840s and the early
1850s, it is difficult to resist the conclusion that the 'iron horse'
did not radically alter the course of Irish agriculture. In 1847
less than 150 miles of railway-track had been laid. By 1851 the
pace had accelerated rapidly to produce a fourfold increase in
the length of track opened. A few years later the framework of a
national rail-communications system was firmly established.
Dublin and Belfast had been linked; Dublin was also connected
to the west and the south of the island through its rail links with
Galway and Cork.[55] Yet there is no indication of a strong
impetus towards regional specialization in these years. The coefficients of variation for wheat in the years 1847, 1850, 1853,
and 1855 are 1.06, 0.94, 1.08, and 0.97 respectively. Variability
in the index of specialization, rather than a uniform pattern or
trend, is all that is apparent. Inspection of the data on the total
corn acreage points to a similar conclusion. Nor is the case for
the railways borne out if we shift our attention from tillage to
livestock farming. The coefficient of variation for sheep aged
less than one year is 0.92 in 1847, 0.84 in 1850, 0.87 in 1853,

[54] The value of the coefficient of variation for the period 1850-5 is taken as the
simple average of the values for 1850, 1853, and 1855. The value of the coefficient for
1905-10 is similarly calculated from the values for 1905, 1907 and 1910.
[55] Conroy, p. 38; Nowlan, p. 101. A total of 580 miles of track was open in 1851,
1,420 miles in 1861, 1,990 miles in 1871, and 2,440 in 1881. See Grimshaw, p. 347.

and 0.90 in 1855. Two years later it had dropped back to 0.87. The statistical evidence for calves is more problematic for the case that is being developed here. The values for the coefficient of variation are 0.38, 0.42, 0.49, and 0.50 for the years 1847, 1850, 1853, and 1855 respectively. It would seem, therefore, that a fairly consistent increase in regional specialization in the production of calves took place between 1847 and 1855—a period of major railway development. This interpretation, however, is open to serious objection. Quite simply, the values calculated for the period are likely to be misleading on the issue of specialization. This is because the slaughter of young calves was a feature of Irish agriculture in the pre-Famine period and later.[56] This is most likely to have occurred in calf-surplus (dairying) districts, thus lopping off numbers in peak areas and so creating the impression of a high degree of uniformity across the regions. The rise in store-cattle prices over the period 1845-55 would have pulled up the price of calves,[57] reduced gradually the practice of slaughtering, and so allowed regional variations to emerge more clearly. Given the tentative nature of this explanation, it is reassuring to find that the regional pattern of production for cattle aged between one and two years fails to show any clear tendency in this period.[58] If the growth of the railway system had a major impact on the store-cattle trade then one could reasonably expect this to be reflected in an upward trend in the index of specialization. A comparison of the degree of regional specialization of cattle or sheep for the two years 1841 and 1856 strengthens our findings regarding the

[56] T. Barrington, 'A Review of Irish Agricultural Prices', *Journal of the Statistical and Social Inquiry Society of Ireland*, xv (1926-7), 266-7; Crotty, p. 85. See also Thompson, pp. 221, 614.

[57] Barrington, p. 266.

[58] The values of the coefficient of variation are 0.41, 0.46, 0.47, 0.46, 0.49, 0.49, 0.47, and 0.46 for the years 1848-55 inclusive. There is, however, a factor which makes more hazardous the task of drawing comparisons between years in this period. This is that the agricultural returns were not taken in the same month each year. This is unlikely to affect estimates of the spatial distribution of tillage crops, but in the case of livestock the situation is clearly complicated to the extent that cattle movements took place during the course of the year. One notes, for example, that the agricultural returns for 1853 were collected nearly eight weeks earlier than in 1852. See *A.S., 1853*, P.P. 1854-5, XLVII, xxi. However, the broad pattern, as distinct from estimates for livestock in particular years is unlikely to be greatly affected.

impact of railways on spatial patterns of production.[59] Only slight change is apparent between these pre-Famine and post-Famine dates.[60]

A review of regional patterns of production in pre-Famine Ireland suggests that inter-regional linkages, particularly in the livestock trade, were firmly established in the early nineteenth century. There is little comfort here for any remaining advocates of a dual economy in Ireland in this period.[61] One might also add that while commodity production advanced in the post-Famine decades, it is clear that the Famine itself does not represent a watershed in terms of the diffusion of market relationships in rural Ireland. It is concluded also that the role of transport constraints on agricultural development has been exaggerated.[62] Professor Lee, never one to qualify his assertions out of existence, claims that the transport system prior to 1845 'was grossly inadequate to the country's needs'.[63] We would suggest that the degree of adaptation to a pre-railroad technology—whether it was sliding-cars to transport butter in mountainous areas, canals and navigable rivers in the wheat-growing eastern counties, new roads linking the more remote towns and villages, or sea transport in coastal areas of the south-east and the north-west—has been substantially underestimated.[64] The corollary to this part of the argument, as put

[59] The coefficient of variation for cattle in 1841 is 0.47; in 1856, well over a decade later, it is 0.51. The values for sheep for the years 1841 and 1856 are 0.95 and 0.97 respectively. The year 1856 is taken for purposes of comparison with 1841 as the returns were collected in early June in both years. The 1841 census did not ennumerate calves of that year. To make the 1856 cattle data more directly comparable cattle aged less than one year have been eliminated.

[60] It should be pointed out, though, that a heterogeneous category such as cattle (or sheep) is far from satisfactory. There could, for instance, be mutually offsetting shifts in different counties, as between different types of cattle production. The index of specialization would fail to reveal such changes.

[61] A recent, but unconvincing attempt to reinstate the dual-economy thesis is S. J. Nicholas and M. Dziegielewski, 'Supply Elasticities, Rationality, and Structural Change in Irish Agriculture, 1850-1925'. *Economic History Review*, 2nd Ser. xxxiii (1980), 411-14.

[62] For comment on the backwardness of the transport network prior to 1850, and the adverse implications for agricultural development, see Ó Gráda, p. 3. Nowlan, in the course of a rather vague essay, manages to convey the impression of both backwardness and progress on the transport front. See Nowlan, pp. 104-7.

[63] Lee, p. 87.

[64] Inglis, pp. 321-2; Newenham, pp. 17-18; Wakefield, p. 309; Townsend, pp. 230-1; M'Parlan, *Mayo*, p. 27; Rawson, p. 41; Hughes, p. 231. The important role of the Shannon waterway in the pre-railway transport system is reviewed in the *Second Report of the Commissioners on a General System of Railways for Ireland*, PP. 1837-8 (145),

forward here, is that the impact of railways on the agricultural sector is easily overstated. The data on regional specialization suggest that the loci of production were not strongly affected by this particular transport innovation. If strong locational effects did not follow the development of a railway system then it may be seriously doubted whether, in fact, railways had a major impact on the agricultural sector.[65] More generally, we should be sceptical of the sweeping benefits predicted by contemporary advocates of the new transport system, benefits resplendently itemized by one set of official inquirers under the heading 'On the influence of railroads in developing the resources of a country, and improving the condition of its inhabitants'.[66] It should be pointed out, though, that we are talking exclusively of rail transport *within* Ireland. Certainly the revolution in transport abroad, coupled with other changes in the international economy in the second half of the nineteenth century, had a profound effect on Irish agricultural production, most obviously in relation to the tillage/pasture balance. Thus in tracing the impact of changing transport technology on Irish agriculture, it is steam navigation, refrigeration, and foreign railway systems—not railway development within Ireland—which should constitute the primary focus of inquiry.[67]

XXXV, 563-4. Road development over wide areas of the country is reported by Lewis for the early decades of the nineteenth century. See S. Lewis, *A Topographical Dictionary of Ireland* (London, 1837), pp. 183, 185-6, 369, 455, 615; also J. H. Andrews, 'Road Planning in Ireland before the Railway Age', *Irish Geography*, v (1964), 17-41. In making any economic assessment of transport arrangements it should be borne firmly in mind that the opportunity cost of labour tied up in the provision of transport services was low in pre-Famine Ireland.

[65] It is of course possible that lower transport costs, while failing to produce strong locational effects, were none the less crucial for the intensification and development of Irish agriculture, most notably in relation to the live cattle trade. This possibility may be worth exploring further, though it should be emphasized that the expansion and intensification of the live cattle trade was well under way by the early 1840s, that is, prior to the emergence of an extensive rail system. It may also be added that while one would not anticipate shifts over time in the spatial distribution of production in Ireland of the same order as that of major land areas such as Russia, for example, none the less there is sufficient diversity in topographical and other natural conditions within Ireland to allow for substantial regional variations.

[66] Benefits anticipated ranged from the moral to the economic welfare of the people. See *Second Report of the Commissioners on a General System of Railways*, pp. 560-6.

[67] On declining transport costs and their impact on supply conditions in the British market for agricultural produce, see P. J. Perry, ed., *British Agriculture 1875-1914* (London, 1973) and R. Perren, *The Meat Trade in Britain 1840-1914 (London, 1978).*

Comparing the 1850s with the 1900s it is apparent that the degree of regional specialization increased in all of the lines of production examined here, though to varying degrees. The spatial distribution of items largely for home consumption, such as green crops or potatoes, shows only a very gradual change over time. Where a very high proportion of a particular output was marketed, as in the case of wheat, flax, and cattle, production became considerably more specialized in terms of location. These locational shifts imply a more efficient distribution of resources, and partly account for the increasing productivity of labour and land that has been noted in Irish agriculture in this period.[68] Our measures of regional specialization do not, however, increase monotonically; fluctuations in the index for a particular farm product indicate, not irrationality on the part of producers, but rather responsiveness to price and other economic variables.

[68] Ó Gráda, *passim*.

9. Irish Emigration to Dundee and Paisley during the First Half of the Nineteenth Century

Brenda Collins

The conventional view of urbanization and modernization has been that these processes involve major changes in the life-styles of the individuals concerned, particularly when the migration is from rural to urban communities. Discussion of integration and assimilation of an immigrant community has frequently relied on a comparison of the immigrant community with its host, on the assumption that modernization is a one-way process by which pre-industrial peasants are transformed into modern urban dwellers.[1] More recently, however, research in this area has tended to stress not only comparisons between immigrant and host communities but also the continuities between migrants and the communities which they have left. It is possible that the degree to which individuals and families were able to carry their cultural traditions into urban life was important for their settlement and may have been a major reason for the selection of their destination in the first place.[2]

The emigration of the Irish to other parts of the British Isles and across the Atlantic during the first half of the nineteenth century has been well documented. Customarily the topic is viewed separately from either end of the migration process. There are numerous studies on the economic and social conditions in Ireland which led to emigration, and those dealing with the Irish as immigrants abroad discuss them in terms of assimilation to, and differences from, supposedly given patterns of urban living.[3] This essay considers Irish migration into two Scottish towns, Dundee and Paisley, as a process involving not

[1] An example is W. I. Thomas and F. Znaniecki, *The Polish Peasant in Europe and America* (New York, 1927).

[2] V. Y. McLaughlin, *Family and Community - Italian Immigrants in Buffalo 1880-1930* (London, 1977). For a recent Irish example see L. H. Lees, *Exiles of Erin* (Manchester, 1979).

[3] For the former see, for example, W. F. Adams, *Ireland and Irish Emigration to the New World* (New Haven, 1932); for the latter, an example is J. A. Jackson, *The Irish in Britain* (London, 1963).

just the destinations of particular migrant groups but also their origins and the attributes which they brought with them.[4]

In the year 1851, the base year from which the quantitative data in this essay are taken, the decennial census recorded the highest ever proportion of Irish-born people in Great Britain. Between 1841 and 1851 the total number of Irish-born resident in Great Britain increased by 74 per cent to almost 750,000. Allowing for mortality and remigration it is possible that half a million Irish immigrants entered Britain in that ten-year period, of whom perhaps 110,000 entered Scotland. In 1851 the proportion of the Scottish population which was Irish-born was over 7 per cent, more than twice the proportion in England.[5]

The immigration of the 1840s was a continuation of a movement of migrants across the Irish Sea which had developed at least two generations earlier. The seasonal harvest migrants were the most easily identifiable of all the Irish immigrants to Great Britain in the 1820s and 1830s because, as the fundamental object of their migration was to move from harvest to harvest and from one agricultural region to another through stable rural communities, they were immediately visible as strangers.[6] However, during the first half of the nineteenth century the Irish migration stream became, increasingly, one of permanent urban settlers rather than transient migrants. There was considerable overlap between the two; the Irish who came over to fulfil a specific job contract in seasonal grain-harvesting or potato-picking often stayed and took up contract work in the construction sector or petty trading in the towns. Similarly, the Irish who were settled in the towns went out to nearby country areas in the summer-time to take advantage of harvest work.[7]

---

[4] See B. Collins, 'Aspects of Irish Immigration to Two Scottish Towns (Dundee and Paisley) during the Mid-Nineteenth Century', M.Phil. (Edinburgh, 1978). The quantitative data are based on stratified samples of the Irish, Scots migrant, and non-migrant groups in both towns from the 1851 census-enumeration schedules. These are held in New Register House, Edinburgh; vols 201-20 (Dundee), vols 460-75 (Paisley).

[5] M. Flinn, ed., *Scottish Population History* (Cambridge, 1977), p. 457.

[6] E. J. T. Collins, 'Migrant Labour in British Agriculture in the Nineteenth Century', *Economic History Review* 2nd Ser. xxxix (1976), 48-9.

[7] E. J. T. Collins, p. 48. The Irish were not alone in doing this. See B. Lenman, C. Lythe, and E. Gauldie, *Dundee and its Textile Industry* (Abertay Historical Society Publications, 1969), p. 57; also R. Samuel, 'Comers and Goers' in H. J. Dyos and M. Wolff, eds., *The Victorian City - Images and Realities* (London, 1973), p. 133.

There is, however, one useful analytical distinction to be made between transient and permanent Irish immigrants, based on the demographic differences in the composition of the migrant streams. Almost all contemporaries considered that the transient Irish harvesters were young adult males, but as early as 1836 a government commission drew attention to two main groups of Irish urban migrants in Great Britain: first, 'those who come over here with their families, with a view of obtaining labour for their children as well as themselves, so as to prevent starvation'; second, the single people who were 'young and healthy and who, because their parents have no means of supporting them, have no ties to keep them at home'.[8] Employment opportunities were the major determinant of settlement patterns and this was why permanent Irish settlement was almost entirely confined to urbanized and urbanizing areas.

The towns with the highest proportions of Irish-born in 1851 were, in descending order, Liverpool, Dundee, Glasgow, Manchester, Paisley, and Bradford.[9] In Scotland, although Glasgow had a much higher number of Irish-born, there were proportionately more in the population of Dundee. The pattern of Irish settlement in Glasgow and Liverpool (and also London) is explained by the fact that these were major ports of entry. The other towns were textile centres and these offered the best work opportunities for women, adolescents, and children as well as adult men.[10]

Dundee's economic expansion and population growth began in the 1820s with the impetus given by mechanized yarn production to an established linen-weaving centre. This expansion continued throughout the nineteenth century. In the decade 1841-51 the population increased by over 25 per cent to nearly 80,000 and the in-movement of Irish people was at its height.

[8] *Poor Inquiry (Ireland) Appendix G. Report on the State of the Irish Poor in Great Britain*, P.P. 1836 [40], XXXIV, 81.

[9] Proportions of Irish-born were: Liverpool 22 per cent, Dundee 19 per cent, Glasgow 18 per cent, Manchester and Salford 13 per cent, Paisley 13 per cent, Bradford 9 per cent. *1861 Census, England and Wales, General Report*, P.P. 1863 [3221], LIII, pt. I, Appendix to Report, table 126, 160 (England); *1851 Census, Great Britain: Ages, Civil Conditions, Occupations, Birthplaces*, P.P. 1852-3 [1691-II], LXXXVIII, pt. II, 1041 (Scotland).

[10] For statements in this respect on Paisley see *Report from the Select Committee on Distress (Paisley)*, P.P. 1843 (115), VII, q. 474; *Poor Inquiry (Ireland) Appendix G*, P.P. 1836 [40], XXXIV, 133, statement of Alex. Carlile.

By 1851 the Irish were 19 per cent of the population of Dundee; their immigration during the previous ten years had accounted for more than half of all migrants coming into the town.[11]

At this time the linen (and, from the 1840s, jute) manufacture of Dundee relied on a work-force which used both mechanized and hand technology, a duality with important consequences for labour requirements. The combination of both forms of technology was most clearly seen in the hand-loom production of cloth and the mechanized mill production of yarn. It was not until the 1860s that power looms were widely used in the Dundee area so much of the expansion in cloth production before this time was met by an increasing number of hand-loom weavers. Thus the hand-loom linen weavers in Dundee in the 1840s and 1850s were operating within a seller's market. This was, however, true only within the local context.[12] Although the hand-loom weavers played an important part in the expansion of textile production, their numbers were far exceeded by workers in the flax and jute spinning mills. The textile industry employed over one-quarter of the population by 1851. Between 1841 and 1851 actual numbers employed in textiles almost doubled; female employment increased by a factor of 2.5 and male employment by 1.6. Thus the town was dominated by an industry which offered work not only to adult males but also to women, particularly young women, and to adolescents.[13]

In contrast to Dundee, the population of Paisley during the mid-nineteenth century was stable. Paisley's initial growth was based on the production of fine handwoven fabrics of muslins and silk gauzes for the fashionable market. The peak of its growth and prosperity occurred immediately after the Napoleonic Wars and it continued to be a prosperous town until the 1830s.[14] By then its staple manufacture was the Paisley shawl,

[11] *1851 Census Great Britain: Numbers of Inhabitants 1801-51*, P.P. 1852-3 [1632], LXXXVI, 60. For a discussion of the expansion and increasing dominance of the linen and jute industry in Dundee see A. J. Warden, *The Linen Trade Ancient and Modern* (London, 1864, reprinted 1967), pp. 578-657.

[12] N. Murray, *The Scottish Hand Loom Weavers* (Edinburgh, 1978).

[13] *Report on the Changes in the Employment of Women and Girls in Industrial Centres. Part I. Flax and Jute Centres*, P.P. 1898 [C. 8794], LXXXVIII; see also William M. Walker, *Juteopolis* (Edinburgh, 1979).

[14] For an introduction to the Paisley shawl industry and its origins see C. H. Rock, *Paisley Shawls* (Paisley Museum and Art Gallery, 1966), and M. McCarthy, *A Social Geography of Paisley* (Paisley Public Library, 1969).

a finely patterned silk, wool, or cotton shawl woven on a harness loom. The designs originated in Kashmir in the late eighteenth century; by the 1820s Paisley and Lyons were the two main producers. About half the adult male labour force in Paisley were hand-loom shawl-weavers working on a domestic basis or in small weaving shops. The technology of the harness or draw loom used until the mid-century required each weaver to employ a draw-boy or weaver's assistant to raise the warp threads in order to produce the pattern. In addition, many women and children were engaged in the finishing side and in the silk and cotton spinning mills which provided yarn for the weavers.

Because it was subject to changes in fashion, the Paisley shawl trade was vulnerable to periodic depression, and during the most serious depression of 1841-3 nearly 15,000 people, 30 per cent of the population, applied for poor relief from a special disaster fund.[15] During the 1840s and 1850s the only points of stability in the economy were the silk and cotton-thread mills and the dyeing, bleaching, and calico-printing industries which manufactured printed shawls more cheaply than the woven patterned ones. The transformation of the economic base of the town in the 1840s was reflected in stagnation of the population between the 1830s and the 1870s with out-migration of weavers, skilled craftsmen, and labourers to other parts of Scotland and to America.[16] The number of Irish-born in Paisley remained around 5,000 between the prosperous years of the 1820s and 1830s through the depressed years of mid-century to the 1870s.[17] Thus, although there was sufficient in-movement of Irish migrants to counteract the losses through mortality or out-migration, the large Irish immigrant movement into Scotland in the 1840s did not settle in Paisley.

An examination of the timing of Irish immigration into any town rests on an analysis of family movements derived from

[15] T. C. Smout, 'The Strange Intervention of Edward Twistleton: Paisley in Depression, 1841-3' in T. C. Smout, ed., *The Search for Wealth and Stability* (Edinburgh, 1979), pp. 218-42.

[16] R. Brown, *History of Paisley*, vol. ii (Paisley, 1886), p. 443; M. Blair, *The Paisley Thread* (Paisley, 1907), p. 117; *Report from the Select Committee on Distress (Paisley)*, P.P. 1843 (115), VII, q. 531.

[17] *1831 Census*, P.P. 1833 [149], XXXVII, 1020; *1851 Census, Great Britain*, P.P. 1852-3 [1632], LXXXVI, 106; *1861 Census*, P.P. 1862 [3013], L, 153; *1871 Census*, P.P. 1873 [C841], LXXIII, clii.

census enumeration-schedules.[18] But there are limitations in measuring migration through census material. At any one time there is only a static picture of past family movements although it could be argued that the aggregate patterns of family-migration decisions, taken together, reflect changing social and economic circumstances. A second, practical limitation is that the earliest families to move to a community stand a far greater chance of 'disappearing', either through mortality or the break-up of the family unit as the members form independent households. A third limitation is the necessity of relying on family movements as a surrogate measure for all migration because the proportion of families in the total migration stream can vary over time and between groups.

Despite the inherent limitations, this form of analysis high-lights the contrasts in Irish migration patterns to Dundee and Paisley. The rate of movement of Irish families to Dundee increased substantially between the years 1835 and 1851, whereas in Paisley the in-movement of Irish families decreased sharply during the depression years of the early 1840s and scarcely increased at all during the post-1845 period. More-over, while in mid-nineteenth-century Dundee most Irish-headed families had all their co-residing children born in Ireland, a majority of the Irish-headed families in Paisley had sons and daughters born in Scotland. Analysis of the Roman Catholic marriage and baptism registers confirms that in Paisley there had been a rapid but short-lived increase in the Roman Catholic population during the 1820s and early 1830s. It seems probable, therefore, that the majority of the Irish headed families resident in Paisley in the mid-nineteenth century were the descendants of earlier Irish immigration; those who were parents in 1851 had themselves been brought over to Scotland as children. In contrast, the Roman Catholic parish registers of Dundee show a steady increase in the annual totals of baptisms and marriages from about 1830, while, to cope with the potential congregations, additional Roman Catholic churches were opened in the late 1840s.[19] Irish mi-

---

[18] See C. Richardson, 'Irish Settlement in Mid-Nineteenth Century Bradford', *Yorkshire Bulletin of Economic and Social Research*, xx (1968), 40-57, and T. Dillon, 'The Irish in Leeds 1851-61', *Thoresby Society Publications*, liv (1973), 1-28.

[19] Scottish Record Office (hereafter SRO) Roman Catholic parish registers: Dundee RH21/39/1-7, Paisley RH21/8/1-10.

gration into Dundee was therefore concentrated in the fifteen years up to mid-century and particularly in the second half of the 1840s. Research on the Irish in other British towns has also dated Irish immigration to these years (and has correlated the timing of the movement with the Irish Famine and increasing poverty) but the earlier migration and relatively long-standing Irish residence in Paisley is an entirely different phenomenon.

However, if instead of considering the chronology of Irish immigration it is examined from the perspective of the families, there are patterns of similarity between Dundee and Paisley.[20] On the basis of the mid-nineteenth-century census data, typical migration profiles can be delineated for both groups of family migrants. These show that at the time of heaviest immigration to each town the largest categories of family migrants were those with several children ranging in age from infancy to adolescence. The prime impetus for migration seems to have arisen when the families had children ranging in age from complete dependency to those capable of helping to increase family earnings.

In addition, there was an element in the Irish migration stream to Dundee in the 1840s which was scarcely evident in Paisley and which confirms the importance of employment opportunities in attracting specific types of migrants. This was an in-movement of young unmarried migrants, particularly girls and women. Their influx completely distorted the sex ratios of the adolescent groups in the town. While the sex ratio of the total population of Dundee was 833 males per 1,000 females, the sex ratio of the group aged 15-24 years was 738 males per 1,000 females and the sex ratio of Irish people in this age group was 551 males per 1,000 females.[21]

Analysis which takes account of the family life-cycle and the life course of individuals is therefore relevant on two counts for an understanding of the Irish experience in Dundee and Paisley. First, the longer the period of residence and settlement of a migrant group the more probable it is that its distinctive demographic elements will disappear. The long-established Irish

---

[20] For a discussion of the conceptual advantages of this form of analysis see T. K. Hareven, 'Family Time and Historical Time', *Daedalus*, 106 (1977), 57-70.

[21] *1851 Census*, P.P. 1852-3 [1691-II], LXXXVIII pt. II, 898 and samples of enumeration-books.

community in Paisley had, by 1851, little to distinguish it demographically from the other residents of the town. In contrast, the Irish migration to Dundee continued at a high level during the mid-nineteenth century and was composed mainly of single girls and families with adolescent children. Second, this form of analysis is useful in explaining the movement out of Ireland to these towns. Both migration streams were primarily moves from a situation in Ireland where there were more mouths to feed than there were resources to feed them.

What were the areas of Ireland from which the Irish migrated to Dundee and Paisley? The geographical areas of origin overlapped only a little. In Dundee, over one-third of the Irish whose county birthplace was recorded in the census enumeration-books in 1851 came from Cavan and Monaghan, 20 per cent from Leitrim, Fermanagh, and Sligo 15 per cent from Donegal, Tyrone, and Londonderry, and 12 per cent from King's County.[22] An analysis of the birthplaces of Irish marriage partners in Dundee in 1855 reveals a similar pattern.[23] In Paisley, in contrast, in 1851, almost 70 per cent of those in the census samples came from Donegal, Tyrone, and Londonderry. Moreover, an early Roman Catholic marriage register of 1808-12 indicates that the Donegal-Londonderry link had been equally evident one generation earlier.[24] In both towns initial settlement led to the establishment of networks of chain migration.[25]

The domestic textile production of linen yarn and cloth, which was widespread throughout the north of Ireland by the late eighteenth century,[26] was common to all the counties supplying migrants to Dundee and Paisley. Domestic linen production took place within the context of a landholding society. The most simple unit of production was that described by Arthur Young in County Meath in the 1780s: 'Every farmer has a little flax from a rood to an acre and all the cottages a spot. If they have any land they go through the whole process

---

[22] Samples, 1851 census enumeration-books.
[23] SRO 282/1-3.   [24] SRO RH21/8/1.
[25] For examples see E. Gauldie, ed., *The Dundee Textile Industry 1790-1885* (Edinburgh, 1969), p. 122. Also *Poor Inquiry (Ireland) Appendix G* P.P. 1836 [40] XXXIV, 157. See also *Poor Law Inquiry (Scotland) Appendix pt. III*, P.P. 1844 [565], XXII, 174, case 2.
[26] W. H. Crawford, *Domestic Industry in Ireland* (Dublin, 1972).

themselves and spin and weave it.'[27] The family acted as a complete production unit and, instead of the growth of the industry stimulating the growth of a labour force independent of agriculture, weaving remained a rural occupation. The farming, cloth-producing family could therefore combine spinning and weaving with work on other agricultural crops for other sources of income. Thus, although the agrarian system encouraged the growth of domestic textile production it also determined its limits.

One potential check on the development of family-based industry was the adequacy of its labour supply within an individual family or small group of families. Because there was division of labour between the sexes for spinning and weaving, and because several spinners were needed to supply one weaver, age and sex ratios were crucial.[28] Within the constraints of domestic industry it was only by manipulating those ratios that production could be extended. Thus weavers without adult sons employed journeymen or apprentices because they required enough male household members to engage in domestic weaving 'by which employment is afforded to the females and children and the most profitable way of disposing of the flax produce, the consumption of potatoes and other produce without carrying them to a distant market'.[29] In the other domestic textile processes sufficient labour was equally important. Independent weavers bore all the costs incidental to weaving such as winding the yarn; 'one winder can attend two looms and usually the weavers employ their own children, either boys or girls. When the weaver has not any children he is forced to hire a winder who for plain goods is paid 6d or 8d per week, for checks 10d-1/- per week.'[30] The possibility of raising total household income was therefore dependent on the combined work of all household members. This meant there was a willingness to expand the household by taking in relatives or strangers, who would extend the production and income of the household while reducing the

[27] A. Young, *A Tour in Ireland 1776-79* (Cambridge, 1925 ed.), p. 10.
[28] E. Wakefield, *An Account of Ireland, Statistical and Political* (London, 1812), vol. i, pp. 685-6.
[29] *General Report on the Gosford Estates in Co. Armagh, 1821 by W. Greig*, introduction by F. M. L. Thompson and D. Tierney (Belfast, 1976), pp. 197-8.
[30] *Poor Inquiry (Ireland). Third Report*, P.P. 1836 [35], XXX, Appendix C pt. 1, Drogheda, 47.

marginal cost (in terms of living space) of the addition of each new member.[31] The utility of extra household members varied with the proportion of dependents to producers within the family and this itself varied with the life-cycle stage of the family. Moreover, in order to retain the services of journeymen and adult sons wishing to marry, the farmer-weaver had every incentive to accommodate them within his own farm holding, by subdividing a piece of land. Thus, because of the flexibility of its labour organization, rural domestic industry could support large numbers of young, single people and provide opportunities for family formation which were not regulated by the transmission of land.[32]

By 1800 a regional pattern of production developed as households in the peripheral counties of linen production concentrated on the provision of yarn on a commercial basis to the linen-producing counties of south-east Ulster.[33] Flax cultivation and yarn spinning became the chief aspect of domestic textile production in north-west Ireland. In Sligo Arthur Young had found spinning prevalent in the 1770s. By 1812, Wakefield reported, 'there were many parts of Ireland where [linen] manufacture extended no farther than to spinning and ... markets were held in these places solely for yarn... Flax is spun in Tyrone and Derry but only a small part of the yarn is wove in these counties; the yarn is sold and is wove in Armagh, Down and Antrim.'[34] The flax crop fitted well into the limited crop rotation practised by small farmers in the north-west of Ireland. Flax and potatoes were complementary crops, while there was increasing specialization in food production with grain, root crops, and cattle produced for sale in the eastern counties. Household income from female employment in spinning was of considerable importance. In domestic tasks

[31] Examples from the surviving census enumeration-schedules of Armagh and Cavan in 1821 indicate that co-residing kin invariably held domestic textile occupations. Public Record Office of Northern Ireland, Mic 5A.

[32] W. H. Crawford, 'Economy and Society in South Ulster in the Eighteenth Century' *Clogher Record*, 8 (1975), 253-4. For other European examples see H. Medick, 'The Proto-Industrial Family Economy: the Structural Function of Household and Family during the Transition from Peasant Society to Industrial Capitalism' *Social History*, 3 (1976), 303-4, and D. Levine, *Family Formation in an Age of Nascent Capitalism* (London, 1978).

[33] C. Gill, *The Rise of the Irish Linen Industry* (Oxford, 1925) pp. 36-8, 153.

[34] Wakefield, vol. i, p. 689.

its monetary value was implicit, but in the households of farmer-weavers it was made explicit. 'The poor farmer finds it more convenient to grow a small bit of flax, and employ the otherwise unavailable labour of the female and younger portion of his family, on the several processes required for converting it into yarn or cloth...'.[35]

Regional specialization meant that competition from machine-spun production of cotton yarn in the early years of the century and of machine-spun linen yarn from the 1820s was felt first in the north-west counties of Ulster, Donegal, and Londonderry. The market for hand-spun yarn from the Londonderry area was destroyed and the prices obtainable there for cloth woven from hand-spun yarn were reduced.[36] The decline in income from hand spinning affected the viability of the family farming unit. During the 1820s and 1830s many smaller farms were consolidated and the population loss, particularly of youth, was extensive.[37]

However, in the counties of north-central Ireland, particularly Cavan and Monaghan, the rural domestic textile industry benefited in the short term by the changes which destroyed it in the north-western counties. During the thirty years before the Famine the area became increasingly more integrated as an internal economic unit within the framework of an extra-local economy. Raw flax was sent from the rural areas of Cavan, Monaghan, and Armagh to the spinning mills of nearby towns such as Drogheda, Navan, and Belfast to be processed while putting-out manufacturers and agents supplied the machine-spun yarn to rural weavers over a wide area.[38] Flax grown here was also sold to the spinning-mill owners of Dundee. During the 1830s flax grown in Cavan was exported through Drogheda to Dundee to be machine spun and the spun yarn was then shipped back to Drogheda for weaving into cloth.[39] Hence the extension of flax machine-spinning both

---

[35] *Handloom Weavers, Reports from Assistant Commissioners, pt. III, Ireland*, P.P. 1840 [220], XXIII, 650-1.

[36] Gill, pp. 323-8. *Handloom Weavers, Reports*, 711.

[37] S. H. Cousens, 'The Regional Variation in Emigration from Ireland between 1821 and 1841', *Transactions of the Institute of British Geographers*, 37 (1965), 21. *Handloom Weavers, Reports*, 725.

[38] *Second Report of the Railway Commissioners on a General System of Railways for Ireland. Appendix B no. 4*, P.P. 1837-8 (145), XXXV, 16, 19, 22, 25-7.

[39] *Second Report of the Railway Commissioners,* 15.

in this area of Ireland and in Dundee benefited those at both ends of the production chain—the flax producers and the weavers organized by putting-out manufacturers—while the output of the independent farmer-weavers of Donegal and Londonderry became increasingly irrelevant to this tightly meshed economic chain.

The availability of two sources of livelihood—textiles and farming—hid the potential disaster which would arise from the failure of one or the other. If this happened one response was a return to peasant farming, which occurred, to some extent, in the north-western counties during the 1820s and 1830s. An alternative response was a shift to full wage labour outside agriculture, which entailed migration; during the 1830s and early 1840s emigration increased from north-central Ireland, intensifying after the failure of the potato crops in the mid-1840s.[40]

For people moving away from Cavan and Monaghan, Dundee was a logical choice because it enabled them to retain the multiple employment of family members in textile production. The trading links between Dundee and Drogheda had made possible detailed knowledge of the conditions of employment in the Dundee textile industry, and had acquainted Irish families with the relatively superior standards of Dundee weavers with regard to housing and clothing.[41] Mill owners in Aberdeen and Dundee advertized in the north of Ireland for both weavers and spinners so adult men and girls were aware of the opportunities for work.[42] Finally, 'in some cases, hands for working in the spinning mills were sent for'.[43] During the 1830s and 1840s Dundee became the dominant area in Britain for production of coarse linen and cloth and these trading exchanges bound north-central Ireland closely to the economic expansion of Dundee.

[40] S. H. Cousens, 'The Regional Pattern of Emigration during the Great Irish Famine 1846-51', *Transactions of the Institute of British Geographers*, 28 (1960), 119-34. His analysis shows the greatest level of loss to have been from the counties of north-central Ireland, but his explanation rests on the level of the poor rate and the high proportion of the population liable to pay it, rather than on changes in the linen industry.

[41] *Poor Inquiry (Ireland). Third Report*, P.P. 1836 [35], XXX, Appendix C pt. 1, Drogheda, 47.

[42] W. F. Adams, *Ireland and Irish Emigration*, p. 142.

[43] *Poor Inquiry (Ireland) Appendix G*, P.P. 1836 [40], XXXIV, 157.

The migration to Paisley from the north-west counties of Ireland at an earlier period began under different circumstances. General connections between the north of Ireland and the west of Scotland were already well established. The extension of steamboat services from Londonderry and Belfast in the 1820s and the low cost of the journey brought emigration within reach of a wide range of society, and one of the cheapest routes was that from Londonderry city to Glasgow, only six miles from Paisley.[44] From Glasgow, migrants simply moved within the west-of-Scotland region until they found jobs and accommodation. The Irish in Paisley were part of an Irish population dispersed throughout the west of Scotland. The earliest figures available, those for 1841, show that in the county of Renfrew there was a higher proportion of Irish-born than there was in Paisley itself.[45] Renfrew's proportion of Irish people was exceeded only in Wigtownshire, the county geographically nearest to Ireland. The first-generation Irish immigrants from the farming-weaving communities of Donegal were not equipped with skills particularly relevant to Paisley. The specialized skills of shawl-weaving restricted recruitment into the industry to a father-son tradition and there is little evidence of migrants (Irish or Scots) taking up the trade.[46] However, the prosperity which the shawl trade brought to the town in the 1820s provided expansion in commerce, canal- and building-construction, and in the ancillary textile processes such as bleaching and dyeing. When the woven-shawl trade declined this general economic expansion was curtailed.[47] By the mid-nineteenth century the Irish male labour force in Paisley was absorbed in the general employment structure. In 1851 one-fifth were skilled craftsmen and shopkeepers, while 46 per cent were in semi-skilled and unskilled labour. Irish women and children continued to work in the cotton-spinning mills and dyeworks which remained after the shawl trade declined.[48]

Thus two factors structured the Irish experience in Paisley: first, the changing economy and society in Ireland which

---

[44] J. E. Handley, *The Irish in Scotland 1798-1845* (Cork, 1943), pp. 30-3.
[45] Handley, pp. 89-90.
[46] Samples of enumeration-books, 1851.
[47] McCarthy, *Social Geography of Paisley*, pp. 72-83; Handley, p. 98.
[48] Samples of enumeration-books, 1851.

prompted the beginning of emigration to the west of Scotland in the 1820s, and second, the economic depressions in Paisley culminating in the 1840s, which ensured that the Irish community did not increase at a time when almost all other towns in Britain were experiencing an influx of Irish. The integration of the farming-weaving households of Donegal and Londonderry into the economy of Paisley did not involve the retention of a household form of textile production but an abandonment of that way of life. Paisley may have been a short-term destination for those whose ultimate goal was America.

Knowledge of the timing of migration to Dundee is relevant for an understanding of the Irish experience in the town because it explains why half the labour force in the textile industry in the mid-nineteenth century was Irish.[49] Among Irish men the proportion employed in hand-loom weaving was 60 per cent, while it was 9 per cent among the male Scots migrants and 12 per cent among the non-migrants. The industry in Dundee was expanding at precisely the time at which the proto-industry in Ireland was declining. Moreover, although the industry in urban Dundee had severed all links with landholding and flax production, it nevertheless encompassed several employment patterns which used a household form of organization.

The participation by children in woven-cloth production continued even after most weaving had moved from domestic shops into handloom-weaving factories. In the factories the loom and equipment were supplied to the weaver who was paid a piece-work rate. His work task was reduced to that of throwing the shuttle with none of the extra tasks involved at the beginning and end of the domestic weaving-process. The one aspect which continued from the days of domestic weaving was the necessity of employing someone to wind the weft yarn on to pirns or bobbins.[50] Weavers preferred to employ a member of their family rather than pay an outsider. The work was generally done by children below the age of full-time mill employment because, unlike the spinning mills, there were no legal

---

[49] Estimated from the census samples, 1851, using a weighted total population.

[50] *Handloom Weavers, Scotland and Continental Europe. Assistant Commissioners' Reports. Dr. Harding's Report*, P.P. 1839 (159), XLII, 187. *Children's Employment Commission (Trades and Manufactures). Second Report. On the Handloom and Hosiery Manufactures in Ireland and Scotland by Mr. J. E. White*, P.P. 1864 [3414], XXII, 22.

restrictions on the age of children working in domestic loom-shops or hand-loom factories.[51] About 30 per cent of the Irish children in the 9-12 age group were employed in this way in 1851 (the minimum age for full-time mill employment was 13 years) and most Irish children in Dundee would have spent some time at this work before graduating to adult textile employment.[52] Because the children's labour was within the family it did not bring in additional earnings but was rather in the nature of saving on outgoings and allowing family forms of labour recruitment to exist. However, because not all weavers had children of a suitable age at any particular time there were opportunities for other people's children to be employed. In addition, manufacturers employed the home-based labour of women and children to wind the warp bobbins which they gave out to the weavers.

The number and age distribution of a weaver's children were factors of importance to him because, as in Ireland, their earnings or dependency could have considerable implications for the family's standard of living. Contemporaries acknowledged that weavers especially relied on the labour of family members. 'It is only when they can carry on until their children become fit to go into the spinning mills that they can recover from their [financial] embarrassment, and there are a good many cases in which they do so at a distance of twenty years from the time of their marriage.'[53] Over half of the families of Irish-born weavers in Dundee were clustered in the life-cycle stages where the ratio of dependants to income earners could be greatly altered by the children entering work. There was an average of two working children, adolescent or young adult, in these families. Over 70 per cent of sons and daughters aged over 15 years were in weaving or mill work.

The explanation of this pattern of family migration lies in a combination of the attributes of the industry and the attributes which the migrants brought with them. Textile towns gave families the opportunities for young adults to enter employment while remaining at home. As Anderson found in Preston,

---

[51] B. L. Hutchins and A. Harrison, *History of Factory Legislation* (London, 1926), chapters VII and VIII.
[52] Samples of enumeration-books, 1851.
[53] *Poor Law Inquiry (Scotland) Appendix pt. III*, P.P. 1844 [565], XXII, 30.

it was possible for them to live at home with their parents until they were married. This situation contrasts with that of the children of landless labourers in rural Lancashire who could not be employed at home and had to seek work elsewhere.[54] Co-residence of adolescent and adult children was equally a feature of the proto-industrial linen production in Ireland. When linen workers migrated to Dundee they were able to continue this form of family economy. Moreover, Irish labourers and their families, whose survival in Ireland frequently entailed seasonal migration, could also exploit mechanized textile work in this way.

Two other types of Irish immigrant attracted by the age-and sex-specific employment in Dundee were groups of young single women and widows and their families. Most female workers in the mills and associated processes were single; 63 per cent of the Irish single girl textile workers were aged 15-24. They moved to Dundee when domestic industry in north-central Ireland declined. Through domestic textile work their labour, previously underemployed, had been given a monetary basis. This monetary basis existed in part because the hand spinners of Cavan and Monaghan had been competing against the mechanized mill output from Dundee.[55] By migrating to Dundee these girls moved within a framework of opportunities with which they were familiar, even if their work changed from a domestic to a mill setting. These adolescent and young adult girls migrated in sibling groups of two, three, or four. Many lodged with other Irish families; those with daughters in mill work were particularly likely to take in girl mill workers as lodgers. The extent of this age-and sex-specific immigration can be seen by the fact that Irish girls living in lodgings accounted for more than half of the Irish female textile workforce.[56]

Widows and their families migrated because their economic position and family circumstances were more precarious than

---

[54] M. Anderson, *Family Structure in Nineteenth Century Lancashire* (Cambridge, 1971), chapters 5 and 7; L. A. Tilly, 'Individual Lives and Family Strategies in the French Proletariat' *Journal of Family History*, 4 (1979), 137-52.

[55] *Poor Inquiry (Ireland). Appendix D (supplement). Earnings of Cottiers, Women and Children*, P.P. 1836 [36], XXXI, answers to q. 9, Ballymore, Co. Armagh, (Mr R. McMeehan), 288, Monaghan parish (Revd Chas. Evatt), 376.

[56] Samples of enumeration-books, 1851.

those of others. There is some evidence that rural widows, Scottish and Irish, may have perceived towns which offered textile employment, such as Dundee, as places likely to provide the basis for sustaining a family single-handed.[57] Widows constituted just under one-fifth of all Irish household heads in Dundee. Nearly 70 per cent of Irish widows' families were clustered in life-cycle stages where the ratio of dependants to income earners could be crucially altered by textile work.[58] These widows had an average of just under three co-residing, working adolescent children—even more than the households headed by Irish men. Moreover, instead of relying entirely on their children for support, Irish widows boosted family income by taking in lodgers. Over the whole family life-cycle Irish widows had more co-residing kin and lodgers than other groups, although there was also variation over the family life-cycle as the need for extra income changed. As their children became older and started work, widows stopped taking in extra-familial members, but when children left home and the number of co-resident, working children declined, Irish widows again turned to lodgers for their rent payments as well as for companionship.[59] They were able to do this because of the constant influx of Irish immigrants requiring accommodation.

The experience of the Irish migrants in Dundee and Paisley underlines the necessity of extending any consideration of the integration of an immigrant community to include, not merely the migrants' responses to the places where they settled, but also the attributes of the migrants themselves. It was the interaction between the economic developments in the two towns and the consequent work opportunities for specific sections of the potential migrant group which led to Irish settlement in the

---

[57] T. C. Smout, *History of the Scottish People* (London, 1969), p. 408; *Factories Inquiry Commission. Second Report. Medical Report by Sir D. Barry*, P.P. 1833 (519), XXI. A3 (Northern District), 10, 37; *Report from the Select Committee on Distress (Paisley)*, P.P. 1843 (115), VII, q. 1320; *Poor Law Inquiry (Scotland) Appendix pt. III*, P.P. 1844 [565], XXII, q. 1750.

[58] This was not explained solely by the age at which widowhood was reached. The proportion of Irish widows whose children were all Irish-born (those who most probably moved to Dundee after their husbands' deaths) and whose families were in the life-cycle stages referred to in the paper constituted 56 per cent of all Irish widows and 10 per cent of all household heads in the Dundee sample. The equivalent figures for Paisley were 21 per cent and 4 per cent.

[59] Samples of enumeration-books, 1851.

towns in the first place. When the work opportunities declined, as in Paisley, the rate of Irish immigration declined, even at a time during the 1840s when there was a high level of Irish migration to Britain. In Dundee the expansion of the linen and jute industry provided the greatest possibility of advancement to migrant families because they could exploit the age and sex divisions of the textile labour force according to their household-membership patterns. Moreover, the Irish migration into Dundee had a considerable effect on the subsequent development of the linen and jute industry. The characteristics of the Irish immigrant labour force, such as its domination by young adult women, became the characteristics of the textile labour force as a whole. In addition, the retention of hand-weaving technology into the 1860s and 1870s alongside the mechanized spinning sector was related to the nature of Irish family-employment patterns. The females in mill employment were the daughters and kin of male hand-loom weavers. As long as the Irish influx into Dundee consisted of hand-loom weavers' households with unbalanced sex ratios, there were advantages to manufacturers in the retention of hand-loom-weaving production. Thus, far from integrating into the economic and social structures of mid-nineteenth-century Dundee, the Irish families played a large part in determining the nature of those economic and social structures.

10. Thomas Barbour and the American Linen-Thread Industry*

E. R. R. Green**

Thomas Barbour, who was born in 1832, was the fifth son of William Barbour of Hilden, near Lisburn in County Antrim. His grandfather was John Barbour, who had moved from Paisley in Scotland in 1784 to begin manufacturing linen thread there. In the early years of the eighteenth century the production of fine linen thread became well established around Glasgow and Paisley and the local spinners were highly skilled. None the less, sewing and embroidery thread continued to be imported entirely from Holland for many years. The pioneer in making thread of this type in Scotland was apparently Christian Shaw of Bargarran in the parish of Erskine, who obtained a twelve-spindle Dutch twisting machine in 1722. The secrets were in turn learned in Paisley which in due course became the chief centre of fine thread-making.[1]

The genealogy of the Barbours has never been firmly established beyond John, the founder of the Irish family. There were in fact a number of families of the name in the Paisley linen-thread trade in the eighteenth century but their exact relationship with one another is unclear. The Barbours of Kilbarchan, who entered the linen trade in 1739, are the most likely origin of the Irish family, especially as that district had a trade with Dublin in lawns and cambrics.[2] The connections between the

* The individuals and institutions on both sides of the Atlantic who helped with the research for this essay are far too numerous to be mentioned individually but an exception should be made for Mr Tom Barbour in New York City and Mr Sam Smyth in Lisburn. The author also had the good fortune to be employed on the Great Falls-SUM Survey in the summer of 1973. This work was carried out jointly by the Historic American Engineering Record, a programme of the National Park Service, and the Great Falls Development Corporation of Paterson, NJ and a report on the first summer's work has been published.
** Unfortunately Professor Green died before the publication of this Volume.

[1] *The Statistical Account of Scotland*, ix (1973), 74-5.
[2] *The Barbours of Hilden, their Scottish Ancestors and their American Relations* (privately printed, 1907), p. 10; *The Statistical Account of Scotland*, xv (1795), 503.

textile industries of England, Scotland, and Ireland in the eighteenth century are insufficiently appreciated. Not only did John Barbour buy yarn in Ireland but the country was also an important market for this thread. There is a possibility that the proper regulation of yarn offered for sale in Ireland compared with Scotland was a determining factor in his decision to move. Certainly, many of the usual inducements for a manufacturer were present—an existing market for his product, access to raw material at lower cost, and cheap labour.

John Barbour either came of substantial people or had been remarkably successful in business for he cannot have been much over thirty years of age when he came to Ireland with ample capital to invest in his thread-making enterprise. The thread manufactory which John Barbour established at Lisburn was in reality an industrial settlement for which the name which he chose, the Plantation, was quite appropriate. The machines were installed in the workers' houses and no use was made either of water- or steam-power. These houses are now gone, but the dwelling-house survives and there are also the remains of an interesting circular building in which machinery was worked by animal power.[3]

When John Barbour died in 1823, the Plantation occupied about seventy-eight acres. Employment was given to 172 people and about 200,000 hanks of thread produced annually. There was also a bleach-works and a warehouse on the property.[4] Barbour had furthermore been a pioneer of the sewn-muslin trade, once of such great importance in the north of Ireland. The sewing of muslin by hand was again introduced from Scotland and teachers had to be brought over to instruct the women and girls.[5]

Barbour was succeeded at the Plantation by his eldest son John, who survived him by only seven years. William, the second son, was the more effective business man. He had been determined to mechanize, and for that reason leased an old bleach-green on the river Lagan at Hilden in 1824. When his elder brother died in 1831, he abandoned the Plantation and concentrated production at the new site. By 1837 there were

---

[3] E. R. R. Green, *The Industrial Archaeology of County Down* (Belfast, 1962), p. 26.
[4] A. Atkinson, *Ireland exhibited to England* (2 vols., London, 1823), vol. ii, pp. 27-8.
[5] [Hugh McCall], *Ireland and her Staple Manufactures* (3rd ed., Belfast, 1870), pp. 541-3.

300 people employed at Hilden. A single water-wheel drove 900 spindles for twisting thread and drove the beetling and winding machinery in a three-storey, slated building, seventy-one feet in length. There were in addition a boiling-house, drying-houses, dipping-shed, stores, and workshops.[6]

By this time, William Barbour was buying mill-spun yarn from John Marshall of Leeds. Flax had been spun by power in Leeds as early as 1790, but it was not until the invention of the wet-spinning process in 1825 that fine yarns could be produced. Soon after, power spinning began in Belfast and in County Down but for many years, until the development of textile engineering in Belfast, the machinery continued to be imported from Leeds. The mechanization of spinning began a great expansion of the linen-thread trade by providing abundant supplies of yarn and by enlarging the market through reducing the cost of the finished article. It was on the river Bann in County Down that the most important initial development took place. Hugh Dunbar and William A. Stewart formed a partnership in 1834 to build a mill at Gilford which when completed was one of the largest in the country. F. W. Hayes of Seapatrick, another large firm, concentrated exclusively on making linen thread after 1835.[7] William Barbour, on the other hand, did not embark on power spinning until 1842. The first wet-spinning frames were brought over from Leeds in 1845. It was about this time that the first steam-engine, 16 hp and built by Victor Coates of Belfast, was installed at Hilden. This engine was destroyed by an explosion in 1848 and replaced by a 40 hp one from the same maker.[8]

Despite the relatively modest scale of the undertaking, William Barbour had one great advantage. He had been blessed with a large family of seven sons and six daughters. No fewer than five of these sons were men of conspicuous business ability. The availability of these young men in combination with the technical innovations in the trade ensured a rapid expansion of the business. Thomas was the fifth son, although only eight years younger than John Doherty Barbour,

---

[6] Detailed descriptions of the Hilden threadworks are given in the Valuation Survey Fields Books, Public Record Office of Northern Ireland, Val. IB 172, Lambeg South, pp. 114-15 and in the Ordnance Survey Memoirs, Royal Irish Academy, Dublin, Box 14, Lambeg.

[7] Green, p. 13.   [8] *Barbours of Hilden*, pp. 24-5.

the eldest of the family. He was sent to New York by his father in 1849, as a youngster of seventeen, to serve his time with A. T. Stewart at a salary of a hundred dollars a year.[9] Stewart, the pioneer of the modern department store, was also a Lisburn man. He had emigrated to the United States around 1820 as a very young man and began by teaching school. His success was achieved in a line of business which he entered almost by accident when he took the advice of a friend and invested a legacy in Irish laces rather than remit the actual cash.[10]

In 1852, Thomas Barbour rented a loft at Exchange Place in New York City in the store of a firm of linen importers and began dealing in threads and twines on his own account, particularly in his father's goods. His name now appears in the New York directories as an importer and as a dealer in shoe thread.[11] Thread was still sold by auction, like so many other imported commodities in the New York of those days, and his nephew, Sir William Barbour, recounted a tradition of how he was supposed to have got around a system which he regarded as inconsistent with stable prices:

So he conceived an idea, and he sent over an order for 200-yard spools which should be made of tow yarns and the more towy they were the better they would serve the purpose. He got these out to New York and sent them into the auction room of course without any name on them. The result was after that people who bought thread wanted to know what they were buying, and they wanted to know the maker's name.[12]

So important was the American market for the Barbour business that Thomas's older brother Samuel was sent out to New York at twenty-three years of age in 1855 and remained there until 1864. As a consequence of Samuel Barbour's arrival in New York, the firm of Barbour Brothers was formed to act as selling agents for the Irish house. Then in 1862 Thomas and Samuel were taken into full partnership under the firm name of William Barbour & Sons, their father being now sixty-five years of age.[13]

[9] W. Woodford Clayton, *History of Bergen and Passaic Counties, New Jersey* (Philadelphia, 1882), p. 461.
[10] *Dictionary of American Biography*, xviii, 3-4.
[11] *New York City Directory*, 1853-4 and 1854-5.
[12] Lecture by Sir Milne Barbour at Hilden Discussion Circle, 5 October 1949. MS in private possession.
[13] Clayton, pp. 460-1.

The decision to begin manufacturing in the United States was taken in 1864. The problem which confronted William Barbour & Sons was the high wartime American tariff, likely to become permanent in any case because of the strength of protectionist feeling in the United States. Adding to the incidence of the tariff was the depreciation of the dollar in consequence of the Civil War which still further raised the price of imported goods. The argument for manufacturing in the United States was clinched by the fact that the tariff of 1864 allowed the import free of duty of 'any machinery designed for and adapted to the manufacture of woven fabrics from the fibre of flax or hemp, including all the preliminary processes requisite therefore'.[14]

Suitable premises were found at Paterson, New Jersey, about twenty miles from New York. Paterson is a place of such importance in the industrial history of the United States that something must be said about its origin and development. The idea of a manufacturing centre, such as Paterson, came from Alexander Hamilton, Secretary of the Treasury in Washington's administration. Hamilton was a man of brilliant intellect and a firm believer in the industrial future of his country. In his eyes, the Federal Constitution was merely the outline of a great common market in which industry must follow the spread of settlement and the expansion of agriculture. He committed his ideas to paper in a famous report on manufactures which he prepared for Congress and he was also involved in practical schemes. It was for the furtherance of these schemes that Hamilton and his associates secured an act of incorporation from the New Jersey legislature at the close of 1791 for the Society for Establishing Useful Manufactures (SUM).[15]

A site at the great falls of the Passaic was chosen in the following year and duly named Paterson in honour of the governor of the state of New Jersey. Major Pierre L'Enfant, who laid out the city of Washington, DC, was engaged by the Society, but his grandiose scheme for the town and his poor performance as an engineer soon led to his dismissal. His place was taken by Peter Colt, who was state treasurer of Connecticut

[14] *Statutes at Large*, First Session, 38th Congress, c. 171.
[15] The standard account of the SUM is in J. S. Davis, *Essays in the Earlier History of American Corporations* (2 vols., Cambridge, Mass., 1917), vol. i, pp. 349-503.

and also had some experience of woollen mills. The latter qualification was important as it had been decided at a very early
stage that the main concern of the SUM should be the 'manufacturing of cotton ... and printing the same'.[16] A cotton mill
was opened early in 1794, as soon as the dam had been completed above the falls and the first canal to the proposed mill
sites constructed. It was, in fact, the second cotton mill on the
North American continent, the first having been started at
Pawtucket in Rhode Island by Samuel Slater in 1790.

Nevertheless, little progress was made at Paterson in the first
twenty years of its existence. The cotton mill closed within two
years and at that time the dissolution of the Society was seriously
considered. It was the import starvation caused by embargo
and eventual open war between Great Britain and the United
States which finally gave an infant manufacturing centre like
Paterson its chance. The power canals had already been extended between 1804 and 1807 and more mill sites were now
available. The old cotton mill reopened about 1800, and when
it burned down some six years later two new cotton mills were
built in 1808 and 1809. Although Paterson developed primarily
as a cotton-manufacturing town in the war years, there were
already signs in the machine-shops and rolling-mills of the
later engineering industry.[17]

While Paterson undoubtedly benefited greatly from easy
access to the New York capital market, the town also enjoyed
the vigorous leadership of Peter Colt's younger son, the re-
doubtable Roswell. He began buying up depreciated shares of
SUM stock as early as 1808 and soon acquired a controlling
interest, formalized by his appointment as governor in 1814.
Roswell Colt at once turned the Society into a utility and
development company which sold power and made available
sites, buildings, and finance.[18] Other members of the Colt
family were also outstanding innovators in a community remarkable for its contribution to American industrial advance.
Samuel Colt is the best known even if the significance of his
pistols in the development of standardization and the use of

[16] Davis, vol. i, p. 398.
[17] L. R. Trumbull, *A History of Industrial Paterson* (Paterson, NJ, 1882), pp. 73-4, 104.
[18] Davis, vol. i, p. 507.

interchangeable parts is not so widely appreciated. He began making pistols in the Old Gun Mill in 1836.[19]

The attraction of Paterson for Thomas Barbour was its connection with the manufacturing of flax, hemp, and jute. As early as 1791, a letter of Alexander Hamilton to the directors of the SUM refers to the engagement of an 'ingenious mechanic' who had patented a flax mill.[20] John Colt, Roswell's elder brother, began manufacturing yarn and twines from American flax at the Passaic No. 1 Mill as early as 1814. Soon afterwards, he successfully branched out into the weaving of linen duck for sailcloth. About 1824, Colt apparently became the first individual to successfully substitute cotton for flax in making duck and consequently ceased being a flax manufacturer.[21] The Phoenix Manufacturing Company, which did not go over completely from flax to cotton until as late as 1854, was a much larger concern than John Colt's. This firm originated in 1817 when John Vasquez acquired one of the very earliest Paterson mills and began manufacturing linen sailcloth, sail twines, and flax-tow gunny bagging. By 1825, the year the company was formed, the mill had 1,188 flax spindles and used three tons of flax a week, seven-eighths of which was imported from Ireland.[22] This early specialization in sailcloth in Paterson may well indicate a willingness to diversify and to develop new lines and so explain why the town later became the centre of the American silk industry.

The individuals concerned in the formation of the Dolphin manufacturing Company in 1846 were mainly from Dundee and the president was a Scots flax and jute broker in New York City. The superintendent, John B. Meldrum, was said to have spun the first jute yarn made in Dundee in 1832. Although the company was initially mainly concerned in producing sailcloth, hence the name, it later became the leading American manufacturer of jute.[23] The original Barbour mill was alongside the

---

[19] W. Nelson and C. A. Shriner, *History of Paterson and its Environs* (3 vols., New York and Chicago, 1920), vol. i, pp. 333-5.

[20] H. C. Syrett and J. E. Cooke (Eds.), *The Papers of Alexander Hamilton* (11 vols., New York, 1961-6), vol. x (1966), p. 345.

[21] Trumbull, p. 268.

[22] W. Wright, 'The Manufactures of Paterson' in *Scientific American* (1859), 298 and 314, and S. Fisher, *Census of Paterson, New Jersey, 1824-1832* (reprinted Paterson, NJ, 1877), xxxix, liv.

[23] Trumbull, pp. 268-9.

Dolphin mill in Paterson, and even more interesting is the fact that Meldrum appears as treasurer and secretary of the Barbour Flax Spinning Company in the local directory between 1875 and 1878.[24] John Swinburne also manufactured jute yarns, twine, and cordage in Paterson between 1856 and about 1877.[25] Paterson possessed the only American manufacturer of hemp and flax machinery in the Todd and Rafferty Machine Company which originated as early as 1847.[26] The presence of such firms meant that Paterson must have been familiar to Thomas Barbour in carrying on his business in New York and an obvious choice for a manufacturing plant.

The Passaic No. 2 Mill on Spruce Street was acquired in December 1864 for $60,000.[27] This mill had been built in 1832 by the SUM on the new upper tier of mill lots completed three years before. The mill was acquired by John Colt and was described in 1859 as a substantial four-storey, stone building containing 5,000 spindles and 65 looms and employing 120 people. Part of the output went to the Duck Mill and the rest for weaving muslin and other types of cloth. From John Colt the mill passed to his son, E. Boudinot Colt, and from him to the Passaic Manufacturing Company which made the sale.[28]

There is a good description of Belfast Mill, as it was renamed, in an American industrial history published in 1868. It was 140 feet long and five storeys high. There was a large dye-house and a new brick office-building. A three-storey, wooden building was used for spooling and labelling the machine thread and for papering and packing the shoe thread, and the building contained a shop for printing the labels. The power was developed from a water-wheel of 120 hp. The value of the product was estimated at $662,000 a year. The machinery had all been brought from Ireland. The flax used was also imported from there, arriving already sorted and prepared. About a quarter of the 450 people employed had been brought from Ireland. This compares with the adjoining Dolphin Mill where three-quarters of the workers were from Scotland.[29]

[24] *Paterson Directory*, 1875-6, 1876-7, 1877-8.   [25] Trumbull, p. 272.

[26] C. A. Shriner, *Paterson, N.J.* (Paterson, NJ, 1890), p. 195.

[27] New Jersey, Passaic County, Deeds, Book V 2, p. 12.

[28] Wright, p. 314.

[29] J. Leander Bishop, *A History of American Manufactures from 1608 to 1860* (3rd ed., 3 vols., Philadelphia, 1868), vol. iii, pp. 232-3; *Ninth Census* (1870), III, 548.

Thomas Barbour had no experience of manufacturing and when the Paterson venture was decided upon his brother Robert, seven years his senior, came out to run the mill. It was also thought necessary to organize the Barbour Flax-Spinning Company for this purpose. The company was owned by Barbour Brothers whose stock was in turn owned by the parent firm of William Barbour & Sons. Thomas Barbour remained president of the flax-spinning company until 1875 when he was succeeded by Robert. In effect, there was little change as Thomas exercised general control from the New York office.[30]

Despite the fact that the Barbour business was the child of the US tariff and that Thomas Barbour's son became a vociferous protectionist, all was not plain sailing initially so far as the American authorities were concerned. Thomas Barbour had a resounding encounter with the United States Customs which created considerable interest at the time. The root of the trouble was an Act of Congress of 1863 which required the importer to invoice his goods at their actual cost to him as well as at their market value in the country of origin. The entire value of an importation falsely declared was subject to forfeiture, half going to the head of the custom house as his fee and to cover legal expenses. This moiety system, as it was called, combined with the difficulties of complying with an exceedingly difficult method of valuation, bred a whole tribe of spies and informers who made a fat living by entrapping and blackmailing business houses. These miscreants were protected in their operations in the Port of New York by the fact that Chester Arthur when head of the Custom House there had deliberately turned it into an extension of the Republican Party organization. Officials were expected to contribute from their salaries to party funds and to help generally as party workers.[31]

The New York Chamber of Commerce took up the grievances of the importers in 1872 but deemed it prudent to delay action during the presidential election in the following year. When the Chamber's committee finally did report in March 1874 it roundly denounced the existing system as a 'hideous tyranny'. Thomas Barbour, although not a member of the

---

[30] Clayton, pp. 460-1; Trumbull, p. 276.
[31] Matthew Josephson, *The Politicos* (New York, 1938), pp. 95-6.

Chamber, took a leading part in the agitation for revenue reform.[32] The Chamber for its part was so impressed by the oppression suffered by his firm that they reprinted his statement of 23 March 1874 from the *Tribune* as a pamphlet with the forthright title of *Appraisers, Spies and Informers*.

Barbour Brothers' troubles had begun when rumours reached them that their customers believed they were in difficulty with the Custom House. They assumed that it was a business rival who had started the rumours and stirred up the revenue informers. A consignment of goods which arrived by steamer in New York was not delivered as usual on payment of duty. Goods which had been received a month previously and on which duty had been paid were also recalled. This meant that supplies of flax, yarn, dye, bleaching materials, and wrapping paper were all kept back. Thomas Barbour found that the charges on which the detentions were based came from the Special Revenue Detective Bureau and his efforts to get satisfaction from it dragged on for fourteen months. The detained goods were released eventually, but then the same trouble started all over again with the invoices for the imports for the spring trade. The invoices entered consisted of flax, yarns, threads ready for market, and threads in the bundle ready for spooling. The flax was advanced ten per cent and detained for undervaluation even though it paid a specific duty. The same happened with the yarns although they too paid a specific duty of five cents per pound.

Barbour refused a compromise even though, according to him, the penalty came all the way down from a quarter of a million dollars to five hundred. Eventually the firm was declared innocent and the invoices correct, but Barbour claimed that during those fourteen months the mills were interrupted, the workers scattered, the assortment of goods broken up, and many customers lost. He also asserted that work had to be stopped on the new mill for which the foundations had already been laid and that machinery had to be taken out and shipped back to Ireland. This new factory would have represented on his estimate an investment of half a million dollars. Barbour addressed a special meeting of the Chamber of Commerce in

---

[32] *Fourteenth Annual Report of the Chamber of Commerce of the State of New York* (New York, 1874), pp. 84-6; *Sixteenth Report*, pp. 10, 106, 115, 165-72.

Steinway Hall at which he vociferously stated his grievances against the Revenue authorities. The consequence of this powerful agitation was that Congress repealed the moieties in June 1874.[33] There was rejoicing in Belfast as well as New York and Barbour was guest of honour at a public banquet in the Music Hall there in October.[34] The episode is an interesting illustration of the special difficulties which a firm may encounter in extending operations abroad and of the political hazards surrounding a high tariff policy. It might well be of course that Barbour Brothers' difficulties were not entirely due to the nefarious activities of customs spies and informers at a time when the country was still experiencing the full effects of the 1873 depression.

Thomas Barbour presided over the Paterson Board of Trade, inaugurated during the depression, for the first two years of its existence. The Board did valuable work in attempting to help the town and its industries out of their difficulties. It gave $2,000 for relief, secured a reduction in fire-insurance rates by overhauling the water supply, and established better relations with the Erie Railroad. One of its projects was a history of Paterson industry which was planned in 1875. Although the idea was not carried through at that time, Shriner's book on Paterson when it appeared in 1890 was published under the auspices of the Board. The work of historians like Turnbull and Clayton which had appeared some years before must also have benefited from the interest aroused by the proposal.[35]

Nor did Barbour lose touch with his fellow countrymen, being an active member of the Society of the Friendly Sons of St. Patrick of New York. He was secretary in 1860-4 and president in 1875-7.[36] He seems, unlike his son and grandson, to have taken little interest in state or national politics, although he did entertain President Grant on one occasion at his country home, Warren Point.[37]

The great expansion of the Barbour thread enterprise came after the country had recovered from the 1873 depression. On

---

[33] Statutes at Large, First Session, 43rd Congress, c. 391.

[34] *Belfast News Letter*, 30 Oct. 1874.

[35] Shriner, pp. 29-30.

[36] R. C. Murphy and L. J. Mannion, *History of the Friendly Sons of St. Patrick in the City of New York* (New York, 1962), pp. 297, 333.

[37] C. A. Shriner, *Random Recollections* (Paterson, NJ, 1941), pp. 205-6.

the demand side, the main stimulus was from the boot and shoe industry which was now being effectively mechanized and placed on a factory basis of production. As a promotional pamphlet issued by Barbour Brothers in 1882 stated, the sewing-machine was 'the great agent in the rapid manufacture of boots and shoes, and in other work of a similar nature. These machines necessitate the use of a thread which is not only strong, but is above all, even in quality. Hence the development of the industry of linen threads.'[38]

Thomas Barbour had purchased a very large site on Grand Street, away from the old industrial centre on the power canals and close to the railroad, from the SUM at a cost of $28,150 as early as 1866.[39] It was here that the foundation stone of a four-storey, fire-proof mill of 200 feet in length was laid in September 1876. The mill was doubled in length the following year and when completed in August 1877 was estimated to have cost some $700,000.[40] A Paterson newspaper wrote in simple admiration, 'there is nothing like it in Paterson, if there is in the state'.[41] An architect, E. J. M. Derrick, had provided the design which was perhaps the reason for a contemporary comment that 'the style of the whole structure is far more elaborate than is usually seen in factory buildings in this country'.[42] In 1879 a fire started in the adjoining Rogers Locomotive Works and destroyed the Spruce Street mill which was immediately rebuilt on the model of the new Grand Street mill. The rebuilt mill was 180 feet in length and four storeys high.[43]

Land was also bought on Garret Mountain and a reservoir built so as to guarantee a constant supply of pure water for bleaching. The Highland Water Company, in which Thomas and Robert Barbour held equal shares, was formed in 1882 to own this water supply. The certificate of incorporation gave the company powers similar to those of the SUM of supplying water, buying and selling land, and of building and renting mills and factories.[44] This seems to have been the origin of the

---

[38] Barbour Brothers, *Imperial Macramé Lace Book* (8th ed., New York, 1882), p. 46.
[39] New Jersey, Passaic County, Deeds, Book C 3, p. 315.
[40] *Paterson Daily Press*, 31 Aug., 13 Sept. 1876.
[41] *Paterson Daily Guardian*, 15 Aug. 1877.
[42] Trumbull, p. 276.   [43] Ibid.
[44] New Jersey, Passaic County, Certificates of Incorporation, Book A, p. 300; *Paterson Daily Press*, 8 Oct. 1879.

Granite Mill, built by the Barbours on a site on Grant Street adjoining the Spruce Street mill, and originally leased to silk manufacturers. The mill was built of stone from their own quarries and was 400 feet in length.[45]

The growth of the Barbour enterprise in the United States is clearly shown by comparing the information available in the censuses of 1870 and 1880; between those dates the value of the annual product had virtually doubled from $662,000 to $1.2 million. The labour force had grown from forty male employees over sixteen to 200 and from 200 females over fifteen to 730. No children or youths were employed in 1880 although there had been 200 ten years before.[46] The American mills contained about 12,000 spindles or half the number in the parent mills at Hilden. They were still the only linen-thread producers in the United States although other firms from the United Kingdom were soon to expand across the Atlantic. The principal demand was for shoe thread though sewing-thread and fine twines were also made. They dyed and bleached their own products. The principal offices and stores were in New York with branches in Boston, Chicago, and San Francisco.[47] There is an interesting contemporary comment on the labour force:

Nearly all the hands who have been employed in the mills in the past eighteen years have been brought over from Lisburn and vicinity, or at least a large proportion of them, as there has not been a sufficient local supply of help of this character. The company engages them in the old country, pays their passage out, and allows them to refund the advance by weekly deductions from their wages. They own a number of tenement houses in which some of these hands live.[48]

The energy and success which had marked Thomas Barbour's business career in the United States came to a tragically early end. The first sign of failing judgement was the disaster of the Barbour Twine Company which he formed in 1881. The idea of expanding into the manufacture of harvesting or sheaf-binding twine was sound enough. John Appleby had patented his twine binder in 1878 which effectively solved the problems of mechanical binding with the device of the knotter. The

[45] Trumbull, p. 277; Shriner, *Paterson*, p. 208.
[46] *Ninth Census* (1870), III, 548; *Tenth Census* (1880), II, 154.
[47] Clayton, pp. 458-60.
[48] Clayton, p. 460.

project had a fanfare of publicity in the Paterson press in late 1880 and was hailed as the 'establishment of another great new industry'.[49] It was announced that the output would be ten tons of twine a day, manufactured from Kentucky hemp. Comment was made on the large capital required as production during most of the year would be for stock although it was granted that this factor also reduced the possibility of competition from other manufacturers.[50] An incredible blunder was made of importing $100,000 worth of machinery without having any buildings in which to instal it. The end of the melancholy venture was noted in the *Paterson Daily Press* in March 1883. 'The heavy machinery imported from Belfast, Ireland, for the Barbour Twine Company, which never went into operation, is being removed from the Granite Mill ... The machinery is of the most costly description, and ... is almost totally useless in its present form for any other than the twine manufacture.'[51] Over the years, Thomas Barbour had built up a considerable personal fortune and as early as 1868 made over real estate to the Barbour Flax Spinning Company for $150,000, a large part of which was similarly reinvested.[52] Now, in June 1882, he had to make over property to the amount of almost $160,000 to his brother John D. Barbour to cover his losses.[53]

The family took alarm at the possible damage which he might do and in consequence formed Barbour Brothers Company into a corporation in May 1882 for the 'importation and selling on own account and on commission of linen thread, flax, products of flax, hemp and other textile fabrics' and to conduct business in New York City and in Paterson. The authorized capital of $300,000 was divided equally between John D., Robert, and Thomas Barbour.[54]

Clearly, this measure was not enough for in March 1883 Robert Barbour gave his brother the clear choice of returning to Ireland or leaving the board of Barbour Brothers. This he agreed to do and went back to Lisburn to live in a house called the Fort which had formerly been Robert's residence. In July

[49] *Paterson Daily Press*, 15 Jan. 1880.
[50] *Paterson Daily Press*, 16 Nov. 1880.
[51] *Paterson Daily Press*, 14 Mar. 1883.
[52] New Jersey, Passaic County, Deeds, Book V 2, p. 351.
[53] New Jersey, Passaic County, Deeds, Book D 7, pp. 200, 224.
[54] New Jersey, Passaic County, Certificates of Incorporation, Book A, p. 312.

1883 the Irish firm, William Barbour & Sons, was turned into a limited company. Thomas Barbour was a director and continued to take part in the affairs of the company although not without complaint about his lack of competence to take business decisions. The problem did not continue for too long for his health was gone beyond hope of recovery and he died on 19 January 1885 at the early age of fifty-two.[55]

Thomas Barbour had only one child who survived to adult life, a son, William, born in 1857. The boy had an entirely American upbringing apart from three years which he spent in Hanover and Tours, studying German and French. The letters which he wrote from Europe show a particularly close relationship between father and son. He wrote to his mother in 1878 that 'I never expect to be as good a man of business as Father, for we both know that he is the best of a family of 6 or 7 sons.'[56]

Yet William Barbour clearly inherited the business ability of the previous generation in full measure and came to enjoy greater independence in the conduct of his affairs and more influence over the enterprise as a whole than his father had ever done. That did not seem to be the case when his father died; he was then twenty-eight years of age and apprehensive that his financial situation might prove to be seriously imperilled. His fears on the latter score proved groundless as his share in the business more than covered his father's debts of perhaps $180,000. Then the death of his uncle in November 1892 placed him effectively at the head of the American branch of the firm. Robert Barbour did have a son but he was no rival and eventually sold out in 1909 and went to Allenton, Pa., to run the mill which he had inherited from his father.[57]

William Barbour was active in politics at both state and national level as his father never had been. No doubt it was inevitable that a family like the Barbours should belong to the Republican Party whose policies so nearly coincided with their own business interests. Barbour was a delegate to the Republican National Convention in 1884 and to every subsequent convention for the rest of his life. In 1901 he ran for Congress

---

[55] *Report of the Barbour Will Case* (Belfast, 1885), pp. 32, 56.
[56] William Barbour to Sarah Elizabeth Barbour, Hanover, 5 March 1878. MS in private possession.
[57] Nelson and Shriner, vol. i, p. 359.

and was defeated by an Irish-born lawyer, William Hughes, who had once worked in the Paterson silk mills. He was Treasurer of the Republican National Committee in 1911. From 1910 he was President of the American Protective Tariff League. The importance he attached to politics is shown by his preference for being known as Colonel Barbour, the honorary rank conferred on him by Governor John W. Griggs of New Jersey after the election of 1895.[58]

As might be expected in the second generation, William Barbour was more interested in organization and consolidation than his father and had wider business interests. He became president of another ten corporations and a director of more than twenty. Of particular interest is the part which he played in the creation of the United Shoe Machinery Corporation in 1899. Machinery for boot and shoemaking was perfected in the decade after 1870 and was normally leased by the makers rather than sold. The patents of the two chief inventors, Charles Goodyear Jr. and Gordon McKay, came to be held by the three main companies which were now combined.[59]

The most important event in William Barbour's business career was the formation of the Linen Thread Company which brought together the leading firms on both sides of the Atlantic. The initial discussions were between the Barbours and the Marshall Thread Co. of Newark, New Jersey, an offshoot of the historic Leeds firm. Next, an approach was made to Finlayson, Bousfield, & Co. of Johnstone in Scotland but with works at North Grafton, Mass., as well. This went well and Barbour was then able to carry the idea further on one of his regular visits to Ireland. It was at this point that W. & J. Knox of Kilbirnie showed interest in what was going on and were invited to Belfast to discuss the matter. The consequence was a meeting in Glasgow at which the four firms concerned were amalgamated.[60]

It would be wrong to regard the formation of this combine simply as a consequence of the trust movement in America, for

---

[58] W. Nelson (ed.), *Nelson's Biographical Cyclopedia of New Jersey* (New York, 1913), pp. 618-19.
[59] W. B. Kaempffert (ed.), *A Popular History of American Invention* (New York, 1924), vol. ii, pp. 409-11.
[60] Sir J. Milne Barbour, Formation of the Linen Thread Co. Ltd. (1938), pp. 1-2. MS in private possession.

the merger in the linen-thread industry was very closely connected with the rapid advance of combination in cotton thread
where J. & P. Coats had acquired Clark & Co. to create one
giant firm in Paisley. In the same year, 1898, thirteen cotton-
thread firms in the States were combined in the American
Thread Co.[61] Nor was it only a matter of example for J. & P.
Coats had a half-interest in Finlayson Bousfield. Particularly
interesting is the fact that the arbiter appointed by the firms
concerned was Otto E. Philippi of J. & P. Coats who had been
particularly successful in handling the merger with Clarks.[62]

Colonel Barbour gave an interesting account of the origin
and nature of the Linen Thread Company to the United States
Industrial Commission in 1901. He was insistent that it was
'a separate corporation, and the corporations which it represents are still in existence and were never dissolved'. In fact,
it was a selling corporation formed to distribute more economically the products of four American linen-thread mills. He
emphasized particularly the company's dependence on the
protected American market and also the size of that market. As
much linen thread was made in the States as in the rest of the
world. The company sold more carpet yarn in Philadelphia
alone than was used in the whole of England. All the flax was
imported; rough flax from Canada, but for the finer grades flax
already hackled as there was no market in America for yarns
spun from the tow. The Linen Thread Company also continued
to depend on imported labour. 'We have not a spinner' Barbour
said 'in any of our mills that is an American born'. The explanation was that women brought up in the United States would
not do such work. Immigrant labour was reconciled by being
three times better-off. Spinners earned $1.00 to $1.10 compared
with 35 cents or the equivalent in Belfast. Interestingly enough,
the employees worked on identical machinery, speeded the
same, and achieved the same production. So it was the tariff,
in his eyes, that made such wages possible.[63] A correspondent
of the *Newark Advertiser* saw the advantage in a somewhat different way—'a pay-roll of a thousand operatives transferred,

[61] H. W. Macrosty, *The Trust Movement in British Industry* (New York, 1907),
pp. 126, 130.
[62] Barbour, p. 3.
[63] *Report of the Industrial Commission*, XIV (1910), 723-6.

greatly to the advantage of America, from the Old World to the New'.[64]

The American linen-thread industry was the child of protection. To begin with, a vacuum existed from the lack of any industry based on flax; in 1860 a mere 528 people were employed and less than 1,000 tons of raw material used.[65] On the demand side, there was a vast and growing market where high living standards meant large sales of thread for clothing, footwear, and furnishings. In such a case, the tariff had the desired result. The leading firm in an industry localized in Ireland and Scotland was forced to undertake manufacturing within the protected market. The problems encountered bore some resemblance to those which have to be overcome in an underdeveloped country. The machinery was so specialized that it had to be brought over from Ireland, so did the labour although not because of any special skill, and it would not be too fanciful to regard the collision with the US customs as analogous to a problem of political instability.

It must not be forgotten that Thomas Barbour was a member of a closely knit family enterprise and that complete financial control remained in Ireland. Samuel Barbour was in partnership with him in New York for about seven years and Robert came out to America immediately the decision was made to embark on manufacturing. None the less, Thomas Barbour was the dominant figure and if his career had not ended at the age of fifty-two he might have hoped in the ordinary course of nature to achieve much of what was done by his son.

---

[64] *Paterson Daily Press*, 3 Jan. 1878.
[65] *Eighth Census* (1860), VIII, ciii.

11. Thomas Newenham, 1762-1831

H. D. Gribbon

Typical of the 'classical' school of Irish economic historians, Newenham saw English political influence and commercial jealousy as wholly inimical to Ireland. For him, British reaction to Pitt's Commercial Propositions of 1785 was all of a piece with the seventeenth-century Cattle Acts and the suppression of the Irish woollen industry. Grattan's parliament, on this view, had offered the best hope of real prosperity for Ireland; the years between 1782 and 1800 saw the peak of economic achievement; and the Union could not have been other than the backward step which his figures in 1809 demonstrated it to be. A member between January 1798 and February 1800 of the parliament in College Green, Thomas Newenham was referred to as 'one of the steadiest anti-Unionists'.[1] Writing in 1825 he still maintained that, 'The legislative Union of Great Britain and Ireland has certainly not as yet proved beneficial, in almost any respect, to the latter.[2]

In his own day Newenham met with both praise and criticism, the second probably better informed and more soundly based than the first. In the early years of this century O'Brien not unnaturally regarded him as a kindred spirit—'Newenham, whose views on Irish affairs are of such value ...';[3] 'Newenham, who was by far the most enlightened writer on Irish economic affairs ...'[4] Much, however, has been written on Irish economic history since O'Brien's day; political, economic, and social influences have been disentangled; available statistics have been more carefully evaluated, and perhaps a better-balanced picture has emerged. Thus, the present tendency is to regard Newenham (if not indeed O'Brien) as somewhat 'dated'. But

---

[1] Barrington, Sir J., *The Rise and Fall of the Irish Nation* (Paris, 1833), p. 482.

[2] Newenham, T., *A Series of Suggestions and Observations relative to Ireland Submitted to the Consideration of the Lord President of the Council* (Gloucester, 1825), p. 26.

[3] O'Brien, G., *The Economic History of Ireland in the Eighteenth Century* (Dublin, 1918), p. 396.

[4] Ibid., p. 400.

he cannot be wholly dismissed. Connell made use, with approval, of his work on Irish population;[5] in another context Bowen
says, 'Thomas Newenham was right when he perceived that ...
[theological] issues mattered little to most people ...'[6] Lee has
praised the remarkable accuracy of Newenham's estimate of
population in 1804, noting that he 'showed striking natural
intelligence in eking out sparse demographic data by analyzing
the implications for population change of a mass of material on
consumption and trade. He made effective use of scattered
ad hoc parochial returns. He organized some local surveys and
appreciated the importance of the double check in this treacherous type of investigation.'[7] Who then was this man? What
training had he as a writer on Irish economic affairs? What
weight should be attached to his opinions? A glance at Newenham's published work adds point to the interest in his background, for the population study and the review of the Irish
economy are only the best known of a series of writings.[8]

An Obstacle to the Ambition of France, with preface dated from
Oswestry, April 1803, was a straightforward argument for
Catholic Emancipation: the suggestion that disaffection in
Ireland might furnish opportunity for a French incursion was
simply a peg on which to hang a lengthy discourse on a subject

[5] Connell, K. H., *The Population of Ireland 1750-1845* (Oxford, 1950).

[6] Bowen, D., *The Protestant Crusade in Ireland 1800-70* (Dublin, 1978), p. 142.

[7] *Pioneers of Demography: the Population of Ireland before the Nineteenth Century* (Westmead, 1973). Introduction by J. Lee.

[8] These are:

(i)   *An Obstacle to the Ambition of France; or Thoughts on the Expediency of Improving the Political Condition of His Majesty's Irish Roman Catholic Subjects* (London, 1803).

(ii)   *The Warning Drum, a Call to the People of England to Resist Invaders* (London, 1803).

(iii) *A Statistical and Historical Inquiry into the Progress and Magnitude of the Population of Ireland* (London, 1805).

(iv)   *A View of the Natural, Political and Commercial Circumstances of Ireland* (London, 1809).

(v)   *An Address on the Subject of Catholic Emancipation to the Protestant Noblemen and Principal Protestant Gentlemen of the County of Cork* (Cork, 1811).

(vi)   *The Christian's Treasure: being a Synthetical Arrangement of the ... Doctrines ... of the Apostles ... Comprising near 350 Texts of Scripture drawn from the Douay Translation ... for the Use of Pastors of the Church of Rome by one of whom the Texts and Notes have been Revised* (Cork, 1811).

(vii) *A Letter to the Roman Catholics of Ireland* (Dublin, 1823).

(viii) *Letters on a Re-union of the Churches of England and Rome from and to the Revd. Dr Doyle, R.C.Bp. of Kildare, John O'Driscol, Alexander Knox and Thomas Newenham Esqrs.* (Dublin, 1824).

(ix)   *A Series of Suggestions and Observations relative to Ireland Submitted to the Consideration of the Lord President of the Council* (Gloucester, 1825).

which evidently moved the writer deeply. Not that Newenham made an impassioned plea; such was not his style. Rather he put forward a reasoned case in which equity and political expediency appeared in about equal proportions. Claiming that not all Irish Roman Catholics were disaffected, indeed that some were amongst the steadiest supporters of Grattan's parliament, he referred to that parliament's failure to grant Catholic Emancipation: '... measures were continued after the reason for them had ceased'.[9] He held that political power could safely, and ought to be, distributed without discrimination between Protestants and Catholics, and concluded, 'After all, I strongly suspect that government only waits for a dutiful and humble submission of the wishes of the Roman Catholic nobility, gentry and merchants, through the medium of a petition to the legislature. But it would be more noble and prudent to anticipate their known wishes than to comply with them when expressed.'[10] The argument was an obvious mixture of political naivety (or was it ignorance of the strength of the forces opposing Catholic Emancipation?) and far-seeing common sense. Yet there was a measure of cynicism rather than idealism in such comments as ' ... most men of reflection are loyal in proportion as they find it in their interest to be so'.[11]

The Warning Drum, also published in 1803, was no more than sixteen pages of sententious and gratuitous propaganda telling the English people (with whom Newenham identified himself) what to expect from a successful Napoleonic invasion. Based on the experience of other conquered peoples, the invaders would conscript all the men they did not kill, rape all the women, and seize all public and private property. It would therefore be prudent to resist them. Why Newenham should have thought it necessary to write such a pamphlet a few months after the publication of his earlier and more creditable book is hard to imagine. The *British Critic* did its duty, marginally: 'Throughout the little tract now before us we find sentiments unexceptionable, expressed in language forcible and clear.'[12] At least it was modestly priced, at 3*d*. or 2/6 per dozen.

[9] *An Obstacle to the Ambition*, op. cit., p. 9.
[10] Ibid., p. 36.
[11] Ibid., p. 7.
[12] *The British Critic*, 22 (1803), 51.

Newenham's *Population of Ireland*, dated from Ellesmere, Shropshire, November 1804, was a work of quite a different calibre. Its initial purpose was to inform the British public, which since the Union was more intimately concerned in Irish affairs, of the true magnitude of the Irish population. Newenham feared not only that the best available figures were considerable underestimates, but also that some 'respectable and influential' commentators had minimized even these. Secondly, he thought that, using traditional investigative methods, the result of any official inquiry would be unlikely to approach the truth. He stressed his own disinterested position, 'I really have no other object in view than the welfare of a country to which I am naturally and habitually, but not exclusively, attached',[13] and concluded his preface with the words 'not being in pursuit of literary fame, but merely solicitous to distribute among my fellow subjects the information I have endeavoured to collect, I shall take no pains to introduce those ornaments and critical niceties of style which embellish and render acceptable the writings of others'.[14] Despite the florid introduction there followed a work of industry and scholarship.

On Newenham's conclusions and his methods of reaching them there has already been adequate comment. It is sufficient to say that he made critical use of previous population studies, added to them the results of his own researches, mainly in Munster, and by way of comparison or illustration, cited from some thirty or more wide-ranging works on politics, trade, and economics. Adam Smith and Arthur Young were mentioned frequently, with approval. For purposes of probing his own mind, however, the following is particularly illuminating:

During near three-fourths of the last century, the trade of Ireland was illiberally and unwisely shackled; its manufactures were very few, and, with the solitary exception of the linen, insignificant and languishing. One restraint succeeded another; and the utmost vigilance appears to have been employed in order to prevent that country from enjoying the benefits of trade. The spirit of commercial jealously operated without control.[15]

---

[13] *A Statistical and Historical Inquiry ... Population of Ireland*, op. cit., p. xvi.
[14] Ibid., p. xix.
[15] Ibid., p. 37.

Speaking highly, and sympathetically, of the attitude of most Catholic clergy during the 1798 rebellion he said of the bishops, ' ... the exertions of these Bishops, in support of the throne, have probably superseded the necessity of sending to Ireland an additional force of 20,000 men ...'[16] Newenham's admiration for John Foster appears from: ' "Can those who now hear me", said Mr Foster, "deny that since the period of 1782, Ireland has risen in civilization, wealth, and manufactures, in a greater proportion, and with a more rapid progress than any other country in Europe?" Certainly not; thanks to *his* zeal and abilities.'[17] In his conclusion, which included, unexpectedly, the view that Ireland's prospects under the Union *could* be bright, he wrote something of lasting relevance; 'Surely Irishmen, of all sects, have sufficiently experienced the diversified mischiefs of religious animosity; and must languish for its utter and final extinction.'[18] Rather strangely, although he knew that the population of Ireland was growing rapidly, although he was aware of the poverty, unemployment, or gross underemployment of great numbers of the people, and although he himself commented on the increasing reliance on the potato, Newenham seemed never to have considered what would happen if the potato crop failed in the conditions which his own predictions rendered sooner or later inevitable.

With *A View of the Natural, Political and Commercial Circumstances of Ireland* published in 1809 Newenham joined the ranks of Ireland's foremost historical apologists—men like Swift, Molyneux, or Lord Sheffield—not necessarily in scholarship, and certainly not in literary ability, but undoubtedly in forthright approach. Here was no nostalgia for a passing Gaelic civilization, no reference to an isle of saints and scholars. The book was, rather, an appeal to hard facts—geographical, historical, and statistical. In terms of volume, if not of selectivity or understanding of the mass of material assembled, it was a major work; but the style was execrable. A modern reader might be forgiven for thinking the author a tedious, sententious, self-opiniated bore.

---

[16] Ibid., p. 25.
[17] Ibid., p. 75.
[18] Ibid., p. 355.

Starting from the thesis that British statesmen had insufficient knowledge of Ireland to enable them to discharge properly the duties and responsibilities devolving upon them as a consequence of the Union, Newenham proceeded to enlighten them. He may be allowed the eulogy on harbours, rivers, climate, fertility of the soil, roads, and fisheries, even on productivity as illustrated for instance by exports. He was factual on wages, living conditions, and population. He detailed the 1807 religious divisions of Cork city street by street. His appendices are convenient and valuable. But his strictures on government, landlords, and English/Irish relationships were not calculated to win friends. Bearing in mind that even if few men who had been active in public life before 1782 were still alive in 1809 their families certainly were, and it was scarcely prudent to write, for instance, of monies granted for harbour improvement:

How much of the foregoing sum ... was faithfully expended in the different works to which it was appropriated, it would be difficult to conjecture. We may suspect however, that little more than half, if so much, was thus expended; it being well known that among those in the Irish community who were capacitated to enjoy the patronage of government, there has almost uniformly been, with a few individual exceptions, not only a shameful want of public spirit, but an inveterate propensity to outrageous jobbery.[19]

(Curiously, Newenham supported the system of grand-jury presentments for road construction and repair.) Returning to and developing a theme introduced in *Population of Ireland*, the following was typical of his argument:

To cramp, obstruct and render abortive the industry of the Irish, were the objects of the British trader. To gratify commercial avarice, to serve Britain at the expense of Ireland ... were the unvarying objects of the British minister. To keep down the papists, cost what it would, and to augment their own revenue by the public money ... were the objects of the reputed representatives of the Irish people ...[20]

As for the Irish civil list in the period 1729-86, it was 'scandalously lavished on prodigals, parasites, pimps, prostitutes and foreign princes ...'[21] The Established Church did not escape Newenham's pen—'The Roman Catholic Irish were required

[19] *A View of the Natural, Political and Commercial Circumstances of Ireland*, op. cit., p. 14.
[20] Ibid., p. 97.   [21] Ibid., p. 151.

to relinquish their ancient form of worship and follow the new one of the Protestant English, without being previously alienated from the former by a perception of its errors or allured to the latter by the virtues, talents or examples of its ministers.' Of these Newenham remarked, 'They did not propagate it by superior zeal, learning or address. They were neither competent, nor do they appear to have been even solicitous to forward its reception'.[22] In marked contrast, whilst he stigmatized the Catholic clergy of earlier times, he referred glowingly to those of his own day:

The pastoral zeal, the moral worth, the piety, the ardent patriotism, the just sentiments of loyalty, the extensive erudition, the generosity, the politeness and the apparent liberality which at this day are so frequently found amongst the Roman Catholic clergy, in every diocese in Ireland, and which have raised them to an exalted place in the esteem of every unprejudiced Irish Protestant ...[23]

Not surprisingly, in view of such sentiments, he renewed his advocacy of Catholic Emancipation, expressing unflattering views on those who disagreed with him.

On purely economic matters *A View ...* was severely criticized by D'Ivernois as to both its motives and its conclusions.[24] Newenham replied at length in a letter dated from Ludlow, Shropshire, March 1810.[25] Malthus also criticized Newenham, claiming that the data which he used did not support the conclusions which he drew from it.[26] More pertinently, the writer of a substantial pamphlet in 1811 pointed out that Newenham's figures for imports and exports on which he based the assertion that post-Union Ireland had an adverse balance of trade, were 'official' and not 'real' values.[27] Of the book in general he said, 'From that mass of garbled statements and ignorant inferences every flaming agitator has been enabled to borrow material for invective and misrepresentation. From thence

---

[22] Ibid., p. 165.   [23] Ibid., p. 181.

[24] D'Ivernois, Sir F., *Effects of the Continental Blockade upon the Commerce...* (Translated from the 3rd French ed., Dublin, 1810).

[25] Public Record Office of Northern Ireland, Belfast (hereafter PRONI) T.2534/2.

[26] *Edinburgh Review*, xiv, no. 27 (April, 1809), 151-70.

[27] *Sketches of Irish History and Considerations on the Catholic Question, together with an Answer to the Misrepresentations of Messrs Newenham and Cobbett Respecting the Affairs of Ireland* (London, 1811), p. 40. D'Ivernois had made the same point, but in his study it was an incidental rather than a main ground of criticism.

every disaffected journalist has transferred into his columns the substance of Mr Newenham's unjust and unfounded specu- lations'.[28] William Greig in 1817 renewed the attack on the discrepancy between the official (notional) and actual values of Irish exports as cited by Newenham for the period 1799-1805.[29] Other peculiarities are worth noting. Newenham commented on the difficulties and failures in Ireland's canal system, but not on the successes, for example the Newry Canal. He as- cribed to corn bounties the substantial increase in Ireland's production and export of grain after 1784, ignoring apparently the effect of scarcity and trade disruption caused by the Nap- oleonic war in enhancing prices. He was distinctly simplistic about Catholic attitudes to tithes. He used an extraordinary argument to demonstrate that absentee rents ' ... can never prove, in any considerable degree, detrimental to Ireland';[30] although elsewhere, of course, he pointed out that landlords were seldom interested in improvements, preferring to extract the maximum rents from short leases rather than to improve the productive capacity of their land. His own family back- ground and connections may help to explain the ambivalent attitude to landlords.

In his *Address on the Subject of Catholic Emancipation...* Newenham commenced rhetorically, 'Whoever suspects you of entertaining sentiments hostile to your Roman Catholic countrymen, betrays great ignorance of your general character.'[31] But he regretted that, while absence of hostility was one thing, enthusiasm for Catholic Emancipation was quite another. Hence he advanced arguments in favour of emancipation and tried to allay the fears of those opposing it.

On constitutional grounds, my Lords and Gentlemen, the Roman Catholics have, indisputably, as well warranted a claim as the Protestants to the political benefits which the latter still exclusively enjoy. To withhold from them, on account of their religious sentiments, any civil or political right exercised by their fellow subjects is, in truth, a monstrous and intolerable outrage on the principles of the constitution, however it may have been

---

[28] Ibid., p. 45.

[29] *The Irish Farmers' Journal and Weekly Intelligencer*, v, no. 21 (18 January, 1817).

[30] *A View ...*, op. cit., p. 293.

[31] *An Address on the Subject of Catholic Emancipation to the Protestant Noblemen and Principal Protestant Gentlemen of the County of Cork*, op. cit., p. 1.

palliated by the exigencies of former times. To withhold the right of re-presentation from those who exercise the right of election cannot be justified on any principle of policy or common sense.[32]

A hypothetical fifty Irish Catholic MPs at Westminster could pose no threat to the Protestant succession or the British constitution when counterbalanced by 618 Protestant members. Even at local level, the granting of Catholic Emancipation could not lead to the exercise of county patronage while Protestants owned the greatest part (estimated at 95 per cent) of the land. Time to procrastinate, however, was not necessarily on the side of those addressed. 'It has been suspected my Lords and Gentlemen, that the Roman Catholics are anxious for separation from England. How far they may ultimately become so, in the event of a continued resistance to their just constitutional claims it is not easy to conjecture.'[33]

The contents of *The Christian's Treasure* ... (1811) are fully described by the title. In this work Newenham left the realms of history, politics, and economics for others in which he must have considered he had something to contribute—unless he had some proselytizing intent. But his approach was uncharacteristically oblique and his expectation, as a layman, of being read by, let alone of influencing, professional clergy somewhat unrealistic.

Twelve years later in *A Letter to the Roman Catholics of Ireland* Newenham's pro-Catholic sympathies seemed to have undergone a change; undoubtedly he was aware of increasing resentment at the delay in granting Catholic Emancipation. He had heard rumours of a proposed re-enacted destruction of Protestants as in 1641 and of desires to terminate the Union by force. His main message to Catholics therefore was that, whilst they might have certain grievances, they were not ill-governed to an extent which would justify insurrection. In any case, military success against Britain would not be possible; and Britain would certainly fight, for—'be assured, my dear countrymen, that while she has gold to spend and blood to shed—and she is well supplied with both—she never will, because, in truth, she never safely can, loose her present hold of our valuable country'.[34]

---

[32] Ibid., p. 5.   [33] Ibid., p. 12.
[34] *A Letter to the Roman Catholics of Ireland*, op. cit., p. 3.

He identified Britain's interests, other than strategic, as absentee rents, and support for her co-religionists and British descendents in Ireland. On balance, however, Newenham was inclined to discount the more alarmist rumours as emanating from no more than a lunatic fringe amongst Irish Catholics.

On 6 May 1824 Alexander Robertson, speaking in the House of Commons during a debate on the Church Establishment in Ireland, had mooted the possibility of a reunion of the Churches of England and Rome.[35] On 13 May Dr James Doyle, Roman Catholic bishop of Kildare and Leighlin, wrote to Robertson expressing interest in the matter, at least to the extent of saying he would welcome discussion of theological points of difference between the two communions.[36] The correspondence, reported in the *Morning Chronicle* of 18 May, came to the notice of Thomas Newenham who wrote to Dr Doyle on 7 June:

> The promptness and alacrity with which your lordship appears to have concurred with Mr Robertson's project of uniting the Churches of England and Rome, certainly indicates no ordinary perspicacity, penetration and foresight on the part of your Lordship. I frankly confess, my Lord, that when my attention was first directed to that project ... I regarded it as puerile, visionary, vain and impracticable. Candour, however, now compels me to acknowledge ... a complete change of my opinion ...[37]

He went on to suggest the selection of names of ten divines from each side who might exchange views, possible items for discussion, and appropriate background material. On receipt of Newenham's letter, which was subsequently published, Dr Doyle promptly and prudently withdrew. The two men parted with expressions of regret and mutual esteem, Newenham promising to pay a courtesy call on the bishop when next in Ireland.

What appears to have been the last document from Newenham's pen was published in 1825 and is also the most illuminating from the point of view of his thinking and personality. In the first half of 1824 a select committee of the House of Lords had considered the state of Ireland and called Thomas

---

[35] *Hansard*, 2nd Ser. vol. xi, col. 568, 1824.
[36] *Letters on a Re-union of the Churches of England and Rome*, op. cit., p. 1.
[37] Ibid., p. 12.

Newenham to give evidence. He was unable to attend but submitted a document, which does not appear in the appendices to the minutes of evidence.[38] He repaired the omission by having it printed in 1825. In it he still appeared as an advocate of Catholic Emancipation but 'no longer considers it as having a prominent and effectual tendency to increase tranquility in Ireland'.[39] Whereas in the past there had seemed a probability that the majority of Catholics would support the constitution he queried whether this was any longer the case. He had 'no doubt that if the existing dissatisfaction of the Irish Roman Catholics were only analysed, religion would be found the principal ingredient in it; in other words that a large majority of even the more educated Roman Catholics are at least as solicitous for the extinction of Protestantism as for an extension of their political rights'.[40] For this anti-Protestant animus he blamed the Jesuits, referring to their 'zeal, activity, dissimulation, duplicity, plausible language, insinuating manners and conciliatory address'. Their object he claimed was 'to extirpate Protestantism, if possible, *per fas atque nefas'*.[41] Newenham recommended the reformation of the Established clergy, the general reading of the Bible in charity schools, the exposure of the errors of Rome in the press and by learned, pious, undaunted, itinerant missionaries of the Established Church, provision from the public purse for 'such Roman Catholic priests of unblemishable character as might desire to conform to the established religion';[42] the dissolution of parochial unions; and the expulsion of Jesuits from the United Kingdom. Estimating Irish population at 7 million, of whom about 1.4 million were Protestants, Newenham believed that the ratio of Catholics had increased markedly over the last hundred years. This he attributed to 'the unwearied diligence in proselytism' of the priests, abolition in 1735 of tithe agistment (and consequent reduction in numbers of Protestant clergy), non-residence of Established clergy, and the negligence of those actually in residence.[43]

---

[38] *Minutes of Evidence taken before the Lords Select Committee appointed to inquire into the state of Ireland* 1825 (18) (521), IX, 1;249.

[39] *A Series of Suggestions and Observations relative to Ireland ...,* op. cit., p. 1.

[40] Ibid.   [41] Ibid., p. 9.   [42] Ibid.   [43] Ibid., p. 6.

On economic matters he said comparatively little. He considered wages of agricultural labourers too low and wages of country artificers (masons, carpenters, and slaters) disproportionately high. He noted the damaging effects of combinations among workers in the cities. 'Agriculture', he argued, 'is at present, generally speaking, little understood in Ireland, rural economy still less'.[44] Noting that there were no sown grasses, that pastures were overgrown with thistles and weeds, and that fields had few fences and fewer gates, he recommended ample premiums, agricultural schools, and restraints on landlords increasing rents on improvements.

The causes of commercial poverty in Ireland, he believed, 'may latterly be attributed in a very great degree to the feverish, unsettled state in which she has been most imprudently suffered to remain ...'[45] Reverting to one of his earlier themes, he still considered that the Union had been injurious to Ireland's commercial interests, but, 'that the case however will soon be otherwise, they who contemplate the liberal and prudent measures of the King's present Ministers can scarcely entertain a doubt'.[46]

The author of these nine works, spread over the first quarter of the nineteenth century, was a member of a family established in Ireland since the Commonwealth. Edward Newenham was a Cromwellian settler whose son John was Sheriff of Cork in 1655 and Mayor in 1661. He bought the estate of Coolmore, at Carrigaline some ten miles outside the city in 1672. A Thomas Newenham was Lord Mayor of Dublin in 1694.[47] Branches of the family later engaged in banking, shipping, and the woollen industry.[48] Thomas Worth Newenham of Coolmore (1729-66) married the eldest daughter of William Dawson, son of Joshua Dawson of Castledawson. Their elder son, William, inherited the estate. The younger son, Thomas, born at Coolmore on 2 March 1762, was sent to Trinity College, Dublin in 1777.[49] After graduating, he continued his education

[44] Ibid., p. 20.   [45] Ibid., p. 25.   [46] Ibid., p. 26.

[47] *DNB*; *Burke's Irish Family Records* (London, 1976); Crone, J. S., *A Concise Dictionary of Irish Biography* (Dublin, 1928).

[48] Tenison, C. M'C., 'Old Provincial Private Banks', *Journal of the Institute of Bankers in Ireland*, vii, no. 1, Jan. 1906, 12. PRONI, D562/5932.

[49] *DNB*; Burke, op. cit.; Burtchaell, G. D., and Sadlier, T. U., eds., *Alumni Dublinenses ... 1593-1860*, New edition with supplement (Dublin, 1935), p. 617.

at the Middle Temple to which he was admitted in 1782.[50] He was not called to the Bar, indeed such was probably not the intention, and he may have spent only a year in London, for he married, on 24 April 1783, Mary Anne Hoare, the daughter of another extensive landowning County Cork family, also with commercial interests.[51] As a young county gentleman he obtained a commission as major in the North Cork County Militia[52] and later referred to having been quartered in Co. Mayo[53] (possibly about the time of the French landing at Kilalla Bay). His political career was brief. Entering the Irish parliament as Member for Clonmel (a borough in the gift of his kinsman the Earl of Mountcashel) in January 1798, he resigned on appointment as 'Escheator of Munster' in February 1800. As a parliamentarian he was overshadowed by, and on the opposite side of the political divide from, his better-known uncle, Sir Edward Newenham.[54] It is possible that Thomas Newenham might have been less hostile to the Union than Barrington suggests, indeed he claimed himself that he did not so much oppose the Union in principle as disagree with its terms. Perhaps there was an attempt between January 1799 and February 1800 to get him to change sides. In any event, Bolton records' ... it was suggested that George Sandford's employment as Barrack Master of Dublin could profitably be conferred on Thomas Newenham, one of Lord Mount Cashel's members, who was believed to differ from his anti-Unionist patron'.[55]

After the Union Thomas Newenham moved to England and lived on the Welsh border, moving to Gloucester some time before 1824 and finally Cheltenham where he died. But he retained a close connection with Coolmore, where the old house had been pulled down and rebuilt by his brother in 1788. *A View* ... was dated from Coolmore, May 1808; he was probably there in 1811 since *The Christian's Treasure* was published in

---

[50] For this information I am indebted to The Librarian, The Honourable Society of the Middle Temple, London.

[51] *Hibernian Chronicle*, 24 April 1783; Hoare, E., *Early History and Genealogy of the Families of Hore and Hoare* (London, 1883), p. 25.

[52] *DNB*; Hoare, op. cit.

[53] *A View* ..., op. cit., p. 54.

[54] *DNB*; *Commons' Journals (Ireland)*, XIX, 37; Crone, op. cit.

[55] Bolton, G. C., *The Passing of the Irish Act of Union* (Oxford, 1966), p. 102.

Cork; and he was certainly there in 1818.[56] The puzzle is how he derived his livelihood and on what means he managed to raise and educate two sons and one daughter. Possibly there was a settlement on himself or his wife out of Coolmore,[57] possibly he found some employment in England; more likely he simply married money. When he died aged seventy-three at his residence in Paragon Terrace, Cheltenham on 16 October 1831, the *Cheltenham Journal* referred to him as 'a gentleman eminently distinguished by his literary attainments, and by his ardent devotion to theological pursuits and the diffusion of Scriptural knowledge'. He had, it appeared, been knocked down by a galloping horseman, and the newspaper concluded with a condemnation of reckless driving![58]

It is clear that Thomas Newenham was brought up fairly typically as an eighteenth-century, county-family younger son. He entered Trinity and the London Inns at a period when matters of political, social, and economic liberty were exercising mens' minds. He turned out to have something of a flair for scholarship. His writings indicate extensive knowledge of a wide range of authorities, particularly in commerce, economics, and history. He evidently had access to the statutes of the English and Irish parliaments and to their respective journals. His style was heavily influenced by the Greek and Latin classics, overlaid unfortunately with the contemporary verbosity of English polite society. *A View* ..., particularly, contains sizeable quotations from Latin authors which Newenham does not translate, evidently believing that anyone intelligent enough to read his book would not need translation. Apart from his acquaintance with published material (including for instance the quite recent work of Dubourdieu[59] and Tighe[60]) his excellent relations with the Catholic clergy enabled him to conduct his own parochial survey. From references to books in his possession one can infer that he had a respectable library.

[56] From Newenham correspondence in possession of Cork Archives Council, by courtesy of the Archivist.

[57] The estate was heavily encumbered in 1833. Donnelly Jr., J. S., *The Land and People of Nineteenth-Century Cork* (London, 1975), p. 68.

[58] For the *Cheltenham Journal* extract I am indebted to the Divisonal Librarian, Cheltenham Library, Cheltenham.

[59] Dubourdieu, J., *Statistical Survey of the County of Down* (Dublin, 1802).

[60] Tighe, W., *Statistical Observations relative to the County of Kilkenny* (Dublin, 1802).

Newenham's work contains some shrewd observations, for example on agriculture, land tenure, family size, wages, and living standards. He had forward-looking views on drainage and the poor law. But on the whole, as an economic commentator he must be treated with caution. In the first place, he did not speak or claim to speak from an unbiased point of view. In English attitudes to Irish trade and industry he saw not merely commercial rivalry but positive malignancy. Secondly, there is reason to doubt his grasp of monetary concepts and practices, such as rates of exchange, the balance of trade, and bills of exchange; in this area he tended to cite a variety of contradictory authorities. He had no understanding whatever of technical industrial processes. His descriptions of the general Irish character were shrewd and his references to the living conditions of the lower classes sympathetic, but one wonders how close were his actual contacts with them. Finally, and this seems inexplicable, he was aware of the differences between official values of goods used for customs purposes and real values, but chose to use the former in putting forward conclusions as to the balance of trade in the period after 1800. He told D'Ivernois that he did so because no others were available,[61] but it remains a mystery why, when he was able to make effective use of estimates in his population study, he did not do so, at least in a footnote, for trade figures. In general, he seems to have used economic observations to support his own particular political views. On social matters his background did not dispose him to question the possession by a Protestant minority of more than 75 per cent of Irish land. Nor did he doubt the place of the Established Church in a properly organized society, as he saw it, sustained by tithes to which Catholics, equally with Episcopalians and Dissenters, were obliged to contribute.[62] He could see that society as organized (he would probably have said 'ordained') had many ills, but these could be cured by just and honest men without fundamental change to the structure itself.

Newenham was naturally concerned like many of his contemporaries with the important question of Catholic Emanci-

---

[61] Letter to D'Ivernois, 10 Mar. 1810. PRONI, T 2534/2.

[62] His only comment on that was that at least tithes were less onerous in Ireland than in England. *A Series of Suggestions and Observations*, op. cit., p. 18.

pation; but he had too many hobby-horses, of which a more evangelical role for the Established Church and the need to redress the population imbalance between Catholics and Protestants were but two, and these by no means consistent with his avowed ecumenical feeling. Religion formed a large, and came to form an increasing, element in his thinking and, coincidentally, his attitude towards Catholics changed. Not unexpectedly his eldest son entered the Church.[63] But Thomas Newenham's was a robust rather than a contemplative form of Christianity—he liked to be known as an ex-military man and retained the title of Major throughout his life.

Although much of what he wrote was confused, even contradictory, this is not to say he may be ignored. He put into writing what many others thought and felt—men like those who formed the Dublin Society, some of the improving landlords, or men like Power le Poer Trench of the evangelical wing of the Established Church. In spirit he was close to Grattan, in economic interests to John Foster. Before the reformed parliament at Westminster had instituted the plethora of committees and commissions which provided so much information on Ireland, Newenham's writings conveyed a mass of material and sentiment for use by those sympathetic to Ireland's interests. In the political speeches of men like Hume one feels that Newenham's *A View ...* had been well studied, although the source was not acknowledged. Thus, in the early years of the century, directly or indirectly, he exerted a considerable influence on the climate of public opinion favourable to Ireland. Had he possessed the geniality of, for example, his contemporary Barrington or the accommodation of Foster he might have found more acceptance personally. Unfortunately his eccentricities were becoming more marked or better known,[64] and it is not perhaps surprising that the Lords' Select Committee of 1824 chose not to publish his written submission. But it was rather unfair that the reports of neither that Committee nor the Commons' Committee of the following year[65] should have

---

[63] *The Christian Herald* was founded by the Revd. Edward Newenham Hoare, Limerick, in 1830.

[64] See his letters to Peel of 30 April and 31 May 1824, in British Library Add. MSS 40,364, f.195, and 40,365, f.221.

[65] *Report from the Select Committee appointed to inquire into the disturbances in Ireland*, H. C. 1825 (129), VIII, 1.

made any passing reference to Newenham, whilst Shaw Mason treated him with apparent condescension.[66] In any event, his work faded from view for the greater part of a century before being used again by O'Brien and later by Connell.

There is a portrait of Thomas Newenham in Coolmore House,[67] painted around or a little past middle life. It reveals a man of upright stance, with a high forehead and somewhat narrow face, a scholar's spectacles, and regular features. The over-all impression, however, is of a man almost totally without humour. And that, on reflection, is the element uniformly absent from his works.

---

[66] *Select Committee ... into the state of Ireland*, H. C. 1825 (521), IX, 294-8.

[67] I am indebted to Mr and Mrs W. P. W. Newenham for their courtesy during a visit to Coolmore House, June 1979, and for an opportunity to see the portrait.

12. Ireland's Crystal Palace, 1853*

Alun C. Davies

I

The first international industrial exhibition held in Ireland, in 1853, was born out of the convergence of two ideas. In the upheaval following the Famine emerged an industrial movement seeking to reverse the decline of domestic, rural-based industries. It was closely associated with the efforts of the Royal Dublin Society to stimulate agriculture and industry through the series of exhibitions they promoted, trienially, after 1834. By the 1880s the movement became institutionalized in the Irish Industries Association and, at the turn of the century, in the Industrial Development Association.[1] In the 1850s, however, it was in its infancy.[2] Indeed, 'movement' might be too strong a word to describe the efforts of those who believed that Ireland's economic (and perhaps political) woes would disappear if 'industry' could be reinvigorated. The second idea came from outside Ireland; it was the belief, derived from the dramatic success of the Great Exhibition of 1851, that international exhibitions could induce economic growth by starting a chain reaction leading to industrialization and prosperity. Such a simple notion confused cause with effect. It was part of a widespread belief in the inevitability of progress and a reflection

---

[1] For the role of the Royal Dublin Society in promoting industrial education and exhibitions see R. Kane, *The Industrial Resources of Ireland* (2nd ed., Dublin 1845), pp. 412-15, and H. Berry, *A History of The Royal Dublin Society* (London, 1915), pp. 271, 280. For the movement in the 1880s see L. M. Cullen, *An Economic History of Ireland since 1660* (London, 1972), p. 148, and T. E. Fitz-Patrick, *Irish Industrial Enterprises past and present: especially in connection with the approaching exhibition of native industries designed for their revival and extension* (Dublin, 1881). [I owe the latter reference to the late Professor K. H. Connell.] The industrial Development Association is noted in E. J. Riordan, *Modern Irish Trade and Industry* (Dublin, 1920), pp. 265-75.

[2] J. F. Maguire, *The Industrial Movement in Ireland, as illustrated by the National Exhibition of 1852* (Cork, 1853), pp. 7-18, 429-37.

of imperfect contemporary understanding of the nature of industrialization and economic growth. Following the Great Exhibition, country after country acted as host to international exhibitions, partly as an exercise in cultural self-expression, partly in the hope that an exhibition would prove the magic first step on the ladder of industrialization. Ireland was early in the race.[3] A small national exhibition in 1852 served as a prologue to a much larger enterprise arranged for Dublin in 1853. The present paper is concerned with this hitherto neglected event. It examines its origins, organization, and exhibits, and shows that despite its failure to achieve its objectives the exhibition nevertheless provides much useful empirical evidence about social and economic life in the early 1850s.

II

Paxton's glass and iron building erected in Hyde Park in 1851 contained an extraordinary assembly of raw materials, machines, and manufactured goods from all over the world. But Ireland's contribution had been negligible, understandably so considering her shattered economy. Out of 13,000 exhibitors fewer than 300 were Irish.[4] Yet the Great Exhibition made a direct impact on Ireland, for it prompted some Irish visitors who already subscribed to the idea of an industrial movement to turn a regional trade fair, to be held in the following year, into a national industrial exhibition. Held in Cork in 1852, it proved moderately successful: 140,000 visits were recorded, costs were covered, and public attention directed towards three developments promising economic benefits, namely the growth of flax to supply Ulster's thriving linen industry, the introduction of sugar-beet as a staple, and the revitalizing of Ireland's once-thriving provisions trade through the newly discovered

---

[3] K. Luckhurst, *The Story of Exhibitions*, (London, 1951); R. Poirier, *Des foires, des peuples, des expositions* (Paris, 1958); and J. Allwood, *The Great Exhibitions* (London, 1977). *The Times*, 13 May 1853, noted that 'The Dublin exhibition now stands at the head of a long series of similar spectacles actually in preparation or in course of projection. We have found in the arts of industry and in the departments of trade a glorious embodiment of the spirit of modern civilization. That is the secret of these exhibitions that are now rising in all the great capitals'.

[4] *The Great Exhibition of 1851: Reports of the Juries* (3 vols., London, 1852), i, 67, 231; ii, 766, 809, 1241; *First Report of the Commissioners for the Exhibition of 1851* (London, 1852), App. XL, 180-95.

supplies of salt.[5] Although modest in scope the Cork exhibition was sufficiently successful to vindicate its organizers' beliefs, and to further the idea that industrialization would best be served by a bigger and better exhibition, international in scope. Among those involved in demonstrating the potential of the sugar-beet and flax enterprises was William Dargan, Ireland's leading railway magnate. Even before the Cork exhibition closed he formally proposed a full-scale international exhibition for Dublin for 1853, to display 'the materials of manufacturing arts, with a view to practical results in the development of national industries'.[6] Such an Irish Crystal Palace, it was hoped, would 'give an impetus to industrial enterprises ... would show the Irishman his strengths and weaknesses as regards production ... would become a centre whence a stream of new industrial life would flow back into every valley and over every plain'.[7]

Already elected Lord Mayor of Dublin for 1853, Dargan was propitiously placed to give the enterprise an organizational and ceremonial lead. As Ireland's most celebrated non-political contemporary ('one of the demi-gods of modern Irish mythology') he was a rich railway contractor reputed to employ daily between 40,000 and 50,000 workers.[8] If one man might shape Ireland's industrial future then Dargan was he, and his promise to underwrite the initial financial cost sufficed to sweep away objections. Moreover, a small exhibition of industry was already scheduled for Dublin for 1853, one of the series sponsored by the Royal Dublin Society. Dargan proposed to advance between £15,000 and £20,000 to expand this into a full-scale international exhibition, to be explicitly modelled on the Great Exhibition of 1851. His terms were generous. No interest on the initial loan was to be paid unless or until there was a profit. Then, 5 per cent of the first £20,000 of profit would be returned

---

[5] A. C. Davies, 'The First Irish Industrial Exhibition: Cork, 1852', *Irish Economic and Social History*, ii (1975), 46-59.

[6] *Atheneum*, 3 July 1852.

[7] Ibid., 4 February 1854. *The Times*, 23 May 1853, hoped it would end Irish migration to 'the already overcrowded labour markets of England'.

[8] For Dargan see K. A. Murray, 'William Dargan', *Journal of the Irish Railway Record Society*, 2 (1950-1), 94-102; J. Lee, 'The Construction Costs of Irish Railways, 1830-1853', *Business History*, ix (1967), 103-7; J. Lee, 'Railway Labour in Ireland, 1833-1856', *Saothar: Journal of the Irish Labour History Society*, 5 (1979), 10-12.

to him, along with the principal.[9] No one believed that Dargan's loan was really at risk. Once started, the enterprise would be self-supporting, indeed self-perpetuating, and 'Dargan would not lose a shilling'.[10] *The Times* speculated that when returned the stake would again be available 'for other objects calculated to promote the social and material welfare of his countrymen'.[11]

Dargan and the Royal Dublin Society jointly nominated a committee of twenty-five to look after organization.[12] Cusack P. Rooney, one of Dargan's close associates, was appointed to the key post of secretary, with John C. Deane as assistant. The committee's headquarters was 3 Upper Merrion Square, a comfortable town house. A separate information office was opened at the terminus of the Dublin and Kingstown railway, thus encouraging exhibitors and visitors to use Dargan's company to transport themselves and their wares. The exhibition site was on the grounds of the Royal Dublin Society, whose premises had been adequate for previous triennial exhibitions but were too small for the present purpose. As no other Dublin building was large enough, and after brief consideration of the possible erection of a gigantic permanent structure at Phoenix Park (which might afterwards be used for 'flower shows, bazaars, fêtes, and promenades'), it was decided to erect a temporary structure on the Society's grounds. A public competition to choose the design, with prizes of £50, £30, and £20, was won by John Benson, county surveyor of the East Riding of Cork, and engineer to the Cork Harbour commissioners.[13] His blueprint bore little resemblance to Paxton's masterpiece. Only in the use of iron pillars for girders to support a large semi-circular roof was there any similarity. Whereas Paxton had used glass in a revolutionary way, Benson relied on wood, the only glass being a strip along the top of the dome sufficient to light the building. In area Benson's original design was about a third of the size of the London Crystal Palace. It com-

[9] J. Sproule, *The Irish Industrial Exhibition of 1853* (Dublin, 1854), pp. 5-6; *The Proceedings of the Royal Dublin Society*, lxxxviii [1851-2] (Dublin, 1852), pp. 90-1; lxxxix [1852-3] (Dublin, 1853), pp. 1-9, 33-8, 43-9.

[10] *The Art-Journal* (1853), pp. 161-2.

[11] *The Times*, 23 May 1853.

[12] Sproule, p. 6; H. Parkinson and P. L. Simmonds, *The Illustrated Record and Descriptive Catalogue of the Dublin International Exhibition of 1865* (Dublin, 1866), p. 77.

[13] Sproule, p. 36.

prised a grand central hall with smaller halls or aisles on each side. Subsequently these were augmented by two smaller avenues, making in all five parallel halls (the centre being higher and bigger than the rest), plus an extra extension at the back of the original area to house displays of agricultural implements, carriages, and other large objects.[14] The building was constructed quickly, within six months of the laying of the foundation-stone, despite a set-back on Christmas morning, 1852, when a violent storm blew down the southern dome and damaged the partially erected northern gallery. Between 1,000 and 1,500 construction workers gained temporary employment and shared in some of the first practical economic benefits so freely promised by press and pundits.[15]

As construction progressed the committee set about collecting exhibits. Invitations were sent to each firm in the British Isles that had exhibited in 1851, and to the mayors or principal magistrates of every corporate town. Rooney himself visited firms in half-a-dozen major English and Scottish manufacturing centres; he then left his assistant in charge of co-ordinating English contributions whilst he proceeded to the Continent to recruit support in Paris, Brussels, The Hague, and Berlin.[16] The visit proved disappointing, even counterproductive. First, Rooney's efforts to secure European exhibits met with competition from Charles Buscheck, agent for the rival New York Crystal Palace, able to offer a more promising market for intending European industrial exhibitors.[17] Second, Rooney's inability to arouse the enthusiasm of European manufacturers led the organizers to solicit frantically for additional contributions from Ireland itself, in order to fill up space in the exhibition hall. They especially welcomed 'Fine Arts and

---

[14] *Atheneum*, 14 and 21 May 1853.

[15] *Freeman's Journal*, 19 April 1853; T. D. Jones, *Record of the Great Industrial Exhibition 1853, being a brief and comprehensive description of the different objects of interest contained in that Temple of Industry* (2nd ed., Dublin, 1854), p. 23.

[16] Royal Dublin Society, Dublin, MS Letter Book, 1853-4, contains samples of printed letters from the committee soliciting exhibits. For Rooney's trip, see *The Art-Journal* (1853), p. 65, and *Atheneum*, 29 January 1853.

[17] New York Historical Society, New York, Crystal Palace MSS, Box 48A, C. Buscheck to T. Sedgewick, 5 November 1852: 'The Belgians, as good men of business, know very well which of the two undertakings is most to their interest.'

Antiquities' though these had no connection with manufacturing. As a result what had originally been intended as a
selective display of art became so swollen in size that it dominated the exhibition. The idea that exhibits should be restricted
in number and selective in quality was abandoned, and a wide
range of domestic art and lesser items began to pour in. Instead
of a shortage of exhibits, there was soon a shortage of space.
Everything was accepted. Dargan's generous guarantee to
underwrite the exhibition's cost simply compounded the
problem, for it removed any lingering restraint on the part
of the organizers. Freed from the necessity to raise public
money they blithely sanctioned new extensions to the building.
The two additional halls produced a final effect, according to
one critic, of 'five Brobdignagian vegetable marrows laid side
by side'.[18] Dargan's loan of £20,000 was supplemented by
another of £6,000 and then by other sums. The display area
was twice that intended in the first design, and building costs
soared to over £60,000, more than two-thirds of all expenditure.
As receipts came to just over £69,000, this left a net deficit of
more than £18,000 to be found, as promised, by Dargan.[19]

Although not all exhibits were in place by the appointed day
the opening ceremony went ahead on schedule. It produced
a magnificent social occasion. Led by the Lord Lieutenant,
representatives of the Church, bench, university, army, city
corporation, and guilds assembled in the central hall, which
had been draped for the occasion with 160 heraldic banners
'which added much to the picturesque appearance of the whole'
and incidentally helped conceal the incompleteness of the
exhibition. Thus the exhibition's purpose was 'somewhat
hidden by the ceremony which was to usher it into the world ...
the means overlaid the end'.[20] Dublin's commercial activity
was suspended for the day and 15,000 people flocked, in
glorious sunshine, to attend the musical fête at the centre of the
inauguration ceremonies. A choir and an orchestra, each of
a thousand performers, rendered the national anthem, twice.

---

[18] Allwood, p. 26.
[19] *Atheneum*, 11 February 1854, commented that the financial loss was 'in part if not
entirely a consequence of over-lavish expenditure on the structure, which grew daily
larger under the committee's hands'. See also Jones, pp. 32-3, and Sproule, pp. 21 ff.
[20] *Atheneum*, 21 May 1853.

Popular works by Beethoven, Mozart, Haydn, and Mendels-
sohn were performed and, inevitably, the Hallelujah Chorus
from Handel's *Messiah*. The resulting volume of sound was
'sufficiently powerful to fill this building ... the sensation produced thereby was eminently calculated to rouse devotional
feelings even in the minds of the most thoughtless'. The concert
over, the Lord Lieutenant declared the exhibition open. Then,
indeed, 'all was hope, curiosity, and expectation, and the genius
of Erin hovered in ecstacy over the splendid specimens of artistic
and scientific enterprise that greeted her view'.[21]

   In their anxiety to emulate the Great Exhibition the committee adopted the system of classification devised by Dr Lyon
Playfair for 1851. Exhibits were grouped into four broad
categories, 'Raw Materials', 'Machinery', 'Manufactures',
and 'Fine Arts and Antiquities'; further subdivisions resulted
in thirty separate classes. In theory everything could be allocated
to an appropriate place. In practice the very shape of the exhibition building and the unevenness in size and quantity of the
various contributions made neatness impossible. On the central
hall's ground floor articles were placed without reference to
design or class, as samples of what was in adjacent bays and
side halls. Banners signposted different classes of exhibits. To
the north there were the main British and Irish displays; in an
adjoining court was 'a rich and splendid assortment of machinery in motion'. Elsewhere were displays of jewellery, precious
metals, and various foreign exhibits. Smaller bays contained
colonial and oriental collections, and larger halls and courts
held fine arts, antiquities ('The Medieval Court'), and bulky
machines and carriages. Finally, separate first- and second-
class refreshment rooms dispensed 'malt liquors of all sorts ...
where probably whiskey is not a stranger'.[22]

   A number of publications helped visitors identify exhibits
in the six-and-a-half acre display area. An *Official Catalogue*
(unavailable until three weeks after the opening, when at last
the late exhibits had been classified) listed and described the
1,833 separate exhibits (some containing many items); a separate entry listed pictures and sculptures.[23] The *Catalogue* cost a

[21] Jones, p. 27.   [22] *Atheneum*, 21 May 1853.
[23] *Official Catalogue of the Great Industrial Exhibition in connexion with the Royal Dublin
Society, 1853* (Dublin, 1853) [hereafter *Catalogue*]. *Atheneum*, 4 June 1853; Sproule, p. 26.

shilling, ran through four editions, and sold 50,000 copies. The system of giving each exhibit a number and a brief description in the catalogue, although claiming to be one that 'explained itself at once to the most careless and least systematic mind', in reality simply reflected the jumbled way in which the exhibits were generally arranged. A briefer and therefore more practical guide to agricultural and industrial exhibits was the *Synopsis* by C. C. Adley, superintendent of machinery, offered as 'a companion to the official catalogue'.[24] The independent *Art-Journal* performed a similar service for the arts, cumulating its issues to form a souvenir *Illustrated Catalogue*.[25] Of all publications the most popular was printed in the building itself, the *Exposition Expositor*, a 'newspaper' that ran for the twenty-five-weeks lifetime of the exhibition. Priced at 2*d.* unstamped and 3*d.* stamped, copies could be bought as they rolled off the press. They contained lengthy technical articles and descriptions, copious illustrations, advertisements from exhibitors, and selected extracts from other British and Irish newspapers; edited by John Sproule, the *Expositor* formed the basis for his official record of the exhibition, published in 1854.[26]

III

The range and quality of the first category of exhibits, 'Raw Materials', was disappointing. The organizers made little effort to obtain an adequate representation of Ireland's mineral resources, and assembled a random rather than systematic collection of lead, iron, copper, sulphur, coal, silver, gold, and 'granulated charcoal made from peat for household purposes'.[27] Samples were presented with little accompanying information

---

[24] C. C. Adley, *Synopsis of the contents of the Great Industrial Exhibition of 1853 in connection with the Royal Dublin Society, and guide to its internal arrangements* (Dublin, 1853).

[25] *Illustrated Dublin Exhibition Catalogue: the Exhibition of Art-Industry in Dublin* (London, 1853). There was also a sixpenny *Supplement to the Official Catalogue of the Great Industrial Exhibition (in connexion with the Royal Society), 1853: the Gallery of Old Masters with a short sketch of each artist* (Dublin, 1853).

[26] *The Exposition Expositor and Advertiser* (Dublin, 1853. Twenty-five issues). The exhibition also inspired at least two anonymous religious tracts, namely, *Thoughts on the Dublin Exhibition Building* (Dublin, 1853) and *Good News! or Free Admission to the Great Exhibition* (Dublin, 1853). The standard guide-book was refurbished: W. F. Wakeman, *Dublin: What's to be seen and how to see it, with excursions to the country and suburbs* (2nd ed., Dublin, 1853).

[27] W. K. Sullivan, 'Mining and Mineral Products', in Sproule, p. 44.

to show their extent, quality, and economic potential. Some items, such as foreign minerals, specimens of gold from Virginia and California 'with an ingenius gold-digging tool possessing a moveable handle', were interesting but irrelevant to Ireland's needs.[28] Yet raw materials with a clear economic potential, such as samples of different marble, were displayed as scientific curiosities rather than shown for their economic importance, exhibited 'not by private traders, as commercially remunerative, but by the Royal Dublin Society'.[29] A potentially important subgroup, 'Chemical and Pharmaceutical preparations', was 'very imperfectly represented ... some of the chief chemical manufacturers in Ireland displayed nothing'.[30] Whereas the raw-materials collection at Cork in 1852 had at least publicized the likely benefits to be derived from sugar-beet, salt, and flax-growing, the Dublin exhibition added nothing to what was already known about these or other of Ireland's raw materials. Even samples of animal and vegetable matter that might be used as food for manufacture were far from extensive 'particularly in a country where raw materials contributed the chief source of her wealth, and whose manufacturing industry, in many branches, may be said only to be in embryo'.[31]

Whereas 'Raw Materials' disappointed, the next two categories, 'Machinery' and 'Manufactures', showed the uneven impact of industrialization on the Irish economy. They covered a wide spectrum of exhibits and vividly illustrated the yawning gap between primitive production methods used in most trades and industries in Ireland compared with those used elsewhere in the British Isles. The least popular of all displays was agricultural machinery, ironically the one with the greatest relevance to Ireland's economy. It comprised a comprehensive collection of modern agricultural implements and machines. Most came from England for, as *The Times* pointed out, there were 'not half a dozen good implement makers in all Ireland'.[32] There were ploughing, digging, sowing, haymaking and threshing machines, and dairy utensils of all kinds, many previously shown in the 1851 exhibition, their presence in Dublin

[28] Jones, p. 182.
[29] *The Times*, 23 May 1853.
[30] Sullivan in Sproule, p. 103.
[31] Sproule, p. 158.
[32] *The Times*, 28 May 1853.

a testimony to Rooney's early and successful soliciting of English firms. Merely the exposure to Irish eyes of these products of advanced technology, it was assumed, would encourage their adoption. The implements most likely to induce desirable changes in Irish agriculture, suggested *The Times*, were some hoes, drills, and the portable steam-engine of which there were numerous examples.[33] The newspaper was silent, however, about how precisely these labour-saving devices might best be diffused within a poor agricultural economy with an abundance of labour. Thus agricultural machinery sharply emphasized Ireland's retardation compared with Britain. The trials of farm machines, at Malahide, Co. Kerry, under the auspices of the Royal Agricultural Improvement Society of Ireland, further underlined the backwardness of Irish agricultural-machinery makers, and exposed the vulnerability of the Irish market to English competition.[34]

Unspecified but benign economic consequences were also assumed likely to emerge from simply viewing exhibits of wood-working machinery. Furniture making, one of the smaller trades in Ireland, was a good example of the kind of manufacturing activity the exhibition organizers hoped to save. Labour-intensive, with modest capital requirements, it was a trade that provided a wide range of products. Irish firms, mostly small-scale, still used handcraft methods to make mainly ornamental products for a small luxury market. The Irish exhibit included 'very few articles suited for the less wealthy of our citizens; scarcely a parlour chair, a parlour table, or an article of bedroom furniture was to be seen ... ornamentation more than utility formed the basis of every exhibitor's endeavour'.[35] Although there were abundant carved and gilt 'ducal chairs', and 'a gorgeous display of the richest and most costly furniture fitted only for the mansions of the great', the same firms were evidently no longer able to compete effectively in the production of furniture for a mass market in the face of competition from machine-made products from England. The exhibits of the mortising, tenoning, boring, and circular-sawing machines, argued the *Expositor*, would help Irish firms to 'compete with

---

[33] Ibid., *Catalogue*, pp. 47-9 give details of examples or models of about a dozen steam-engines.
[34] Sproule, pp. 205-6, 214-16.   [35] Jones, p. 147.

the various branches of cabinet and carpentry work of our neighbours, who, by their machines, are enabled to undersell us at our own doors'.[36]

If agricultural and wood-working machines emphasized the weaknesses of Ireland's primary and processing industries, the special hall containing 'machinery in motion' dramatically, and noisily, illustrated the industrial changes occurring in the north-east of the country. Power from two 25 horsepower high-pressure steam-engines (made by Fairbairn of Manchester) was transmitted by a shaft supported by a line of cast-iron pillars, along the hall's length, to a number of machines worked by bands running over drums placed on the shaft. It worked the printing press which churned out the *Exposition Expositor*, and other machines, such as flour millers. There were several examples of spinning machines and looms, 'some weaving the coarsest articles, others ribbons and poplins'.[37] By 1853 the power loom had already been applied to the manufacture of flax by twelve of the largest producers in the north, and one English manufacturer of flax machinery, Lawson of Leeds, was forming a branch factory in Belfast.[38] Not surprisingly the products of this one modernized sector of Irish industry made an impressive display in the exhibits of 'goods made by machines'. Linen, 'Ireland's healthiest and most prosperous commercial interest', seemed to have made very considerable progress even in the short time since the Hyde Park exhibition: 'the goods shown are finer in quality and better in design'.[39] An adjacent exhibit unwittingly revealed the continuing decline of woollen manufacture, from its position at the end of the eighteenth century. (In 1838 it was supplying only 14 per cent of the domestic market.)[40] Unable to compete in its own home market either in price or quality with the products of England and Scotland, by 1853 the industry seemed doomed to sink beyond the reach of even the most ardent proponent of the industrial movement: 'the [Irish] blankets were high-priced, and tweeds have to contend with the almost overwhelming

[36] *Exposition Expositor*, vi, p. 6.
[37] Sproule, p. 158; *Atheneum*, 14 May 1853; *Exposition Expositor*, xi, p. 4.
[38] *The Times*, 5 September 1853.   [39] Ibid., 23 May 1853.
[40] Cullen, pp. 105-6.

rivalry of Scotland ... the finer cloths were inferior to the products of Yorkshire and the West of England'.[41]

At the opening of the exhibition the general range of products made in Ireland on view had been very limited apart from linens. There were no ceramic manufactures 'or at least none worth mentioning of native growth; and the display in the gallery appropriated to them is entirely English'.[42] Hardware, too, emphasized the extent of recent de-industrialization; the only home-made products were a few razors, a kitchen range, bells, and 'some indifferent chandeliers', all showing up badly against the comprehensive selection of hardware sent by 'many first-rate English firms' with attendants to explain the goods, issue catalogues, convey information and prices, and take orders.[43] Consequently after a few weeks the committee recruited extra contributions to swell the collection of 'Irish manufactures'. Local makers and retailers of lace, poplin, and tabinets—chief among them Pim, Fry & Co., Atkinson, Kealery, and Deal—rallied to the call, and Messrs Fry erected an elaborate Jacquard loom, for weaving in front of the visitors 'a newly invented brocaded poplin which has not before been produced'.[44]

The branch of Irish industry that gained the greatest stimulus, at both Cork and Dublin, was lace, embroidery, and crochet-making. This industry was organized through aristocratic patronage, or by institutions such as workhouses and gaols, or by commercial firms employing thousands of women and children, 'as a public benefit ... [to do] the kind of manufacture that in England has been displaced by machinery'.[45] Production was through the domestic, or 'putting-out' system, or in proto-factories. Thirty-four patronesses of such 'industrial schools' had exhibited at Cork;[46] at Dublin two of the largest of the organizations which co-ordinated production, 'The Ladies' Industrial Society of Ireland' and 'The Seamstresses' Society of Dublin', mounted extensive displays of lace, embroidery,

[41] *The Times*, 25 May 1853.
[42] Ibid., 25 May 1853.
[43] Ibid.; *Exposition Expositor*, viii, pp. 1-5, 'Iron and General Hardware', and advertisements.
[44] *Atheneum*, 14 May 1853.
[45] *The Times*, 25 May 1853.
[46] Davies, pp. 55-6.

and needlework. Similar work from pauper children from forty-three poor-law unions and from the inmates of five gaols illustrated the extent in Ireland of hand labour with the needle, the worst paid of all employments, 'the most helpless when periods of pressure and difficulty overtake the trade of a country'.[47] The exhibitions of the 1850s, far from hastening the decline of this kind of handcraft work, greatly helped to publicize it. Thereafter both charity and commercial organizations extensively used international industrial exhibitions to develop export markets, especially in the United States.[48] This branch of handcraft industry was able to survive the initial impact of the sewing-machine because exhibitions helped to stimulate special luxury demand for hand-made lace and embroidery. Although the exhibition contained machines made by the Lancashire Sewing Machine Company and displayed by a Mr Spackman of Belfast (described as 'the first person to introduce the sewing machine to Ireland')[49] they could not displace handcraft labour in embroidery and lace-making. They did, of course, cause fundamental changes in the making of clothes and shoes, and the exhibit of sewing-machines in Dublin was welcomed by *The Times* because one could do the work of thirty to forty tailors 'far more efficiently'. Sewing-machines were thought likely to supersede 'a miserable, ill-paid, unhealthy occupation and, by removing the necessity from a class properly regarded as fractious of humanity, will eventually prove a great gain to the cause of industry and the permanent interest of labour'.[50]

'Machinery' also included a number of consumer as well as capital goods, products aimed at the luxury market, such as pianos, clocks, and other musical and horological items. Specialist scientific exhibits of 'philosophical and surgical items' included telegraphic machines, and Grubb's telescope, 'the second largest achromatic telescope ever mounted'. Photography was popular, with daguerreotypes of the 1851 exhibition and some of the earliest photographs of Dublin streets. Various branches of engineering contributed practical displays, and

[47] *The Times*, 25 May 1853; *Catalogue*, pp. 100-2.
[48] Elizabeth Boyle, *The Irish Flowerers* (Belfast, 1971), pp. 83-105.
[49] Sproule, p. 185.
[50] *The Times*, 5 September 1853.

civil and naval engineers sent maps, drawings, and models.[51] The military exhibit included a collection of small arms sent by Colonel Samuel Colt. After gaining great publicity in 1851 Colt quickly realized the advertising benefits industrial exhibitions conferred. His Dublin exhibit produced a modest return, for twenty revolvers were sold to the Director of Convict Prisons in Dublin.[52]

In a court outside the main building, with agricultural machines, were over sixty examples of carriages. Bianconi cars dominated the collection. They were apparently identical in construction, differing only in upholstery and decoration, an illustration that one Irish firm, at least, tried standardized production and model styling in an attempt to widen its market. In 1853 high transport costs still protected regional markets for road-transport vehicles, and sheltered small manufacturing firms, for eighteen of the thirty-two carriage-makers were Irish.[53]

IV

If the exhibition had confined itself to Irish raw materials, machines, and manufactures and to examples of the best machinery and products from Britain, then its educational purpose would have been straightforward. Information about the best available technology and practice would have been made available for general discussion. Strengths and opportunities, as well as weaknesses, would have been exposed, ultimately to the benefit of the Irish economy. That this undoubtedly was the motive of the industrial movement and the exhibition's organizers makes it all the more ironic that the economic lessons of the exhibition were largely obscured in the public mind by unusual, exotic foreign displays, and by a vast collection of art and Irish antiquities.

Only a few of the foreign displays were commercial exhibits from independent manufacturers; most were prestige displays

---

[51] Sproule, pp. 226-60; *Catalogue*, pp. 53-62.

[52] H. C. Blackmore, 'Colt's London Armoury', *Gun Digest* (1958), reprinted in S. B. Saul, ed., *Technological Change: The United States and Great Britain in the 19th Century* (London, 1970), p. 190.

[53] Bianconi's car factory was at Clonmel: T. P. O'Neill, 'Bianconi and his Cars', in Kevin B. Nowlan, ed., *Travel and Transport in Ireland* (Dublin, 1973), p. 89.

of luxury products sent as good-will gestures by various royal courts. This was simply because the Irish market, as one German manufacturer explained, was of 'so little importance'.[54] Thus the Zollverein exhibit contained curiosities, such as fine iron ornaments, terracotta wares, and examples of royal porcelain. The Belgian collection comprised random samples of raw materials, marble fireplaces, and some household-manufactured textiles, the latter hardly likely to break into an oversupplied Irish market or even to serve as a model for Irish manufacturers.[55] Ironically, the one Belgian exhibit relevant to contemporary Irish needs provoked hostile comment. A display of cheap footwear, wooden sabots, elicited a contemptuous comment from an official that 'our peasantry and workpeople will never be induced to adopt so barbarous a covering for the feet. These wooden shoes have only one merit, that is their durability'.[56] Much more welcome was the large, well-organized French display showing the exquisite craftsmanship of the great imperial manufactories at Sèvres, Gobelins, and Beauvois. Yet the French provided the most successful of all commercial exhibits, one which exposed the existence of an Irish market for cheap clocks. Minoy Frères, of Paris, sent £10,000 stock of clocks and fancy castings in zinc and bronze of which they sold £7,000 worth. Their display contained 'articles suited to the wants and purses of all classes, including a range of cheap clocks, set in zinc, for the less opulent purchaser'.[57] Their salesman admitted that the exhibition was a means of establishing direct commercial ties between Ireland and France, independently of London middlemen. But apart from Colonel Colt and Minoy Frères no other foreign manufacturers used the exhibition as a spring-board for commercial expansion. The United States section was particularly disappointing in view of the importance of the American exhibit at London in 1851. Preoccupied with their own Crystal Palace, Amercians saw little attraction in the rival Dublin exhibition, and their country was represented by random exhibits only,

---

[54] Quoted in Jones, p. 81.
[55] *Atheneum*, 14 May 1853; Adley, pp. 45-7.
[56] Jones, p. 71.
[57] Ibid., p. 78.

such as specimens of gold and other minerals, a hydrostat, and a straw, hay, and vegetable cutter.[58]

Unquestionably the foreign contribution which made the greatest popular impact was the oriental display, three collections representative of life in India, China, and Japan that found their way to Dublin largely through the good offices of the London Society of Arts.[59] The Indian exhibit was the residue of the East India Company's display at the Great Exhibition; it had subsequently been presented to the Royal Collection at Windsor Castle, and from there it had been sent on to Ireland for further viewing. With a Chinese collection from the Royal Asiatic Society, an exotic display was formed. Precious stone and metal ornaments, suits of armour, pottery, carvings, rare and beautiful dresses, models of Ceylonese and Hindu temples, 'a large two-edged sword used by Tippo Saib at the siege of Seringapatan'—all proved more attractive to visitors than the farm equipment in the back court. The most remarkable oriental exhibit was from Japan, a country which was in 1853, on the eve of Commodore Perry's expedition, still almost entirely hidden from western eyes. The Japanese exhibit was drawn from the Oriental Museum at The Hague, sent as a good-will gesture by the Dutch government. Holland was the only country to have had any contact with Japan, through its trade with Batavia, and the collection of Japanese arms, ornaments, musical instruments, and clothing aroused the greatest excitement and curiosity of visitors, becoming the central attraction in the exhibition.[60] The press strained to make constructive connections between such exhibits and the purported objective of the exhibition. *The Times* drew on stereotyped English views of Ireland: the Irish, like Orientals, it mooted, had 'a strong bias towards expensive and ornamental rather than useful production'. Hence the oriental collections offered Irish people 'a fertile field for the study of those principles of form and

[58] Ibid., p. 182; *Catalogue* p. 113. For the rival Crystal Palace in New York see I. D. Steen, 'America's First World's Fair', *The New York Historical Society Quarterly*, xlvii (1963), pp. 256-87; and C. Hirschfeld, 'America on Exhibition: the New York Crystal Palace', *American Quarterly*, ix (1957), pp. 101-16.

[59] A. C. Davies, 'The Society of Arts and the Dublin Exhibition of 1853', *Journal of the Royal Society of Arts*, cxxii (1975), 433-6; Royal Society of Arts, London, MS Minutes of Committee, 1852, pp. 33ff., 107 ff.

[60] *Atheneum*, 14 May 1853; Adley, pp. 44-5.

colour applied to decorative purposes which seem to be a natural instinct among Eastern nations'.[61]

Similar specious claims were made to justify the incongruous presence of a vast collection of art and antiquities in an exhibition intended to stimulate economic activity. The committee claimed that 'it was not easy to draw the line of demarcation between objects which come within the strict limits of Fine Arts and those which are purely utilitarian in their character'.[62] 'Fine Art' comprised about a thousand oil and water-colour paintings, frescoes, drawings and engravings, and about four hundred sculptures and carvings. More than half the paintings were hung in the main picture gallery, a room more than 100 yards long and 40 feet wide. Undoubtedly an extraordinarily fine collection, it was the best to date that had been assembled in Ireland 'at one time and under one roof'.[63] The paintings included an alleged Leonardo, two Van Eycks, several Correggios and Titians (including Titian's portrait of Caesar Borgia), a Dürer, Holbein's portrait of Henry VIII, and representative works by a pantheon of great artists including del Sarto, Tintoretto, Rubens, Velasquez, Watteau, Hogarth, Canaletto, Reynolds, Gainsborough, Holbein, Turner, and Rembrandt. Works of lesser quality by English and Irish artists, were 'noteworthy for a large number of portraits and pictures illustrating Irish history'.[64] The collection of statues was much less impressive than the paintings, but it did include Baron Marochetti's enormous equestrian statue of Queen Victoria, which dominated the centre of the grand hall, and busts by the leading Irish sculptor, John E. Jones; his subjects were drawn from Irish public life and included the secretary and chairman of the exhibition, three successive Lord Lieutenants, and Mr and Mrs Dargan.[65]

Splendid as the fine-arts exhibition undoubtedly was, it was quite inconsequential to the exhibition's purpose. Equally irrelevant was the collection of antiquities, borrowed mainly from the Museum of the Royal Irish Academy and the Royal

---

[61] *The Times*, 5 September 1853; cf. Ned Lebon, 'British Images of Poverty in Pre-Famine Ireland', in D. J. Casey and R. E. Rhodes, eds., *Views of the Irish Peasantry, 1800-1916* (Hamden, Conn., 1977), pp. 62-4.

[62] Sproule, pp. 9-10.   [63] *Atheneum*, 14 May 1853.

[64] *Catalogue*, pp. 136-58.   [65] *Atheneum*, 22 October 1853.

Dublin Society. As these ancient treasures were already in the city it seemed even to contemporaries difficult to justify their relocation in an expensive, temporary exhibition building. Yet the collection included casts of two great crosses from Monasterboice, the Book of Armagh, the banner of the O'Donnell family, the Psalm of St Columb, and examples of ancient and medieval ecclesiastical fittings and vestments, painted glass, iron, brass, and silver work, wood carvings, and ornamental tiles. As contributions to this category of exhibit flowed in, the committee found it easier to ask Dargan for more money to expand the building than to refuse exhibits; one natural-history enthusiast sent a display comprising 257 speciments of the birds of Ireland, together with their eggs.[66] The *Atheneum*, desperately trying to justify it all, suggested that antiquities could collectively be viewed as a lesson in ornamental art: 'the Irish have a fertile fancy and great aptitude, and this portion of the exhibition may dispose them to produce articles of ornament, as the artworkmen of the Middle Ages did, by application of taste and skill to materials of comparatively little worth'.[67] *The Times* was less generous but more accurate, dismissing the collection as 'a very curious and highly interesting but extremely useless collection of Irish antiquities ... How is it that when Mr Dargan offers them a building in which to collect everything that may stimulate the industry and develop the resources of the country, the committee appropriates a very considerable portion of it to such objects as the harp of Brian Boroihme and Rorie More's horn ...?'[68]

V

With machinery and manufactures relegated to the sidelines, obscured by paintings, sculpture, exotic oriental and luxury European exhibits, it is not surprising that the exhibition failed to reach the very people whose lives it was intended to change. The official attendance figures of 1,149,365 visits in six months conceals the reality that 'not one in every twenty of the inhabitants from Dublin ever entered the building', and that visitors

[66] *Catalogue*, p. 82.
[67] *Atheneum*, 21 May 1853.
[68] *The Times*, 3 September 1853.

from other parts of Ireland were very few.[69] One-sixth of total visits was accounted for by the daily attendance of officials and exhibitors themselves. For the rest, high admission prices placed the exhibition beyond the reach of all but the well off. As a result it became a social meeting-place for the metropolitan upper classes. Thirteen thousand season-tickets were sold, initially at 3 guineas for men and 2 guineas for women; they accounted for 367,000 visits, an average of 28 per ticket. Of the remaining half-million individual visits most were probably made up by people who, although not season-ticket holders, came several times, for the daily admission fee of 5*s*. and 2*s*. 6*d*. was simply beyond the reach of most of the population. Attendance in the first few weeks fluctuated between 300 and 1,000 daily in an exhibition building which had a comfortable capacity for 15,000 visitors. Even when admission was dropped to a shilling on weekdays (with half-crown days on Wednesdays and Saturdays), daily attendance barely reached 2,000. In vain, editorials in the *Exposition Expositor* lamented the prohibitively high cost of admission.[70] The building became an amusement centre for the social élite: 'it is pleasant for visitors to meet in the great Centre Hall, as a place of common rendezvous, to enjoy a conversation with their friends and acquaintances, and perchance listen to the inimitable performance of Dr Steward on the Grand Organ ... [but] ... if one can judge from the promenade which takes place during the afternoon ... one sees the same persons day by day walking up and down, apparently with a view of exhibiting themselves rather than with that of becoming acquainted with the objects around them'.[71]

To boost popular interest and avert a complete fiasco the committee managed to arrange a royal visit.[72] At the end of August, Victoria, Albert, and two of the royal children arrived in Dublin. Their presence, noted *The Times*, would 'suppress some murmurings at the little countenance extended by the

[69] Jones, p. 36; Sproule, pp. 21-6.

[70] Editorials in *Exposition Expositor*, issues iii-viii, xii, xv, and xx.

[71] Ibid., xii, p. 1.

[72] The visit received extensive press coverage; see *The Times*, 24 August, 3, 6, and 7 September 1853. For a collection of clippings from the Irish press see: Royal Irish Academy, Dublin, MS 23Q22.

government towards the exhibition here, while a pompous Commission is sent to report upon that of New York'.[73] The royal party stayed a week, went to the exhibition four times, reviewed the fleet at Kingstown, examined model schools and farms and the zoo, and visited the Earl of Howth and the home of Mr and Mrs Dargan, the latter event a celebrated courtesy call to acknowledge Dargan's generosity in underwriting the enterprise. Royal patronage brought benefits, not least the purchase of ten season-tickets, 'a business-like tribute to the self-supporting character of such undertakings', and the Queen was so attracted by the lace display of Messrs Forest of Grafton Street that she bought the entire exhibit.[74] The royal visits were made early in the morning, before the public was admitted, but they stimulated subsequent ticket sales as people flocked to examine those of the Queen's purchases not already removed. Outside the exhibition building the benefits of the royal visit were less certain; business in Dublin was suspended for a week during 'one continued holyday', prompting the *Freeman's Journal* to advise people to return from 'holy-day making' to work out 'the problems of self-reliant industry'.[75]

Eventually, at the end of September, the exhibition committee relented and lowered admission to sixpence. Daily attendance doubled, to four or five thousand a day, and then doubled again to about eleven thousand during the exhibition's last week. This showed 'the absolute oversight', in the words of the treasurer, 'of not having done so two months previously'.[76] Lower prices at last brought in some of the 'middle-classes, artisans, farmers and labourers' from in and around Dublin.[77] Few ordinary people from elsewhere in Ireland could afford the journey until, after considerable pressure, the Midland Great Western Railway offered special excursion fares, at 5s. each, (third-class return journey, including admission) from points as far as Belfast and the South of Ireland. Until the very end the railway companies had seemed 'more bent upon carrying

[73] *The Times*, 13 May 1853. For the importance of the 'pompous Commission's' report, see N. Rosenberg, ed., *The American System of Manufactures* (Edinburgh, 1969), pp. 20 ff.

[74] *The Times*, 5 September 1853.

[75] Cited in *The Times*, 6 September 1853.

[76] Jones, pp. 28-9.

[77] *The Art-Journal* (1853), p. 302.

tourists away from [the exhibition] than in bringing people to it'.[78]

Although the exhibition failed to attract popular support and cover its costs, and although it probably hastened the decline of some rural industries by exposing their vulnerability to competition from imports, the exhibition did confer minor benefits. In the short term it provided employment for construction workers, stimulated some business for the tourist trade, and produced sales for some exhibitors, especially those of lace and embroidery. It also left two legacies. The more tangible arose from the art display: a public testimonial to thank Dargan resulted in £5,000 being allocated towards the erection of a Public Gallery of Art, which in 1864 became the National Gallery. And with all its shortcomings the exhibition served as an example, a model for subsequent exhibitions sponsored by movements to reinvigorate Irish industry.[79] Yet despite the flood of enthusiastic press rhetoric accompanying the exhibition's closure, encomiums mainly directly towards the displays of art and antiquities, a few perceptive observers recognized that the committee had erred in allowing culture to dominate industry. Guillaume Lambert, secretary of the Hainault Society of Arts, was an informed outsider able to compare the Irish and American Crystal Palaces; he disposed of the Dublin exhibition in a few words: 'malgré le titre dont elle avait été décorée, cette exposition était plûtot artistique qu'industrielle'.[80] Other assessments drew unfavourable comparisons with the Great Exhibition, perhaps unfairly. Despite much formal resemblance the objectives and spirit of the two were very different. England's Crystal Palace was an exercise in confident cultural self-expression, as well as a demonstration of economic and industrial hegemony. Ireland's

[78] Ibid., p. 302. Tourists from Great Britain were able to take advantage of special excursions organized by Thomas Cook: see W. Fraser Rae, *The Business of Travel* (London, 1891), p. 48, and J. S. Pudney, *The Thomas Cook Story* (London, 1953), pp. 108-9, 120.

[79] Subsequent exhibitions were held in Dublin in 1865 and 1872, in Cork in 1883, at Olympia, London, in 1888, and Glasgow in 1901, and again in Dublin in 1895 and 1907: see 'International Exhibitions', *Journal of the Royal Society of Arts*, liv (1907), pp. 1140-6.

[80] G. Lambert, *Voyage dans L'Amérique du Norde, en 1853 et 1854, avec notes sur les expositions universelles de Dublin et de New York* (Brussells, 2 vols., 1855), i, p. 12.

Crystal Palace was intended as a direct effort to create and foster trade and manufacture. To *The Times* 'England entered the lists as champion; poor Ireland accepts defeat for the instruction it conveys', an evaluation echoed in the *Atheneum's* comment that 'the exhibition was not so much a trophy as a lesson'.[81]

[81] *The Times*, 7 September 1853; *Atheneum*, 14 October 1854.

13. Sir Horace Plunkett and Agricultural Reform*

Cyril Ehrlich

Plunkett was a puzzle. He devoted his life to the service of his fellow creatures collectively; and personally he disliked them all ... He took the chair as a matter of course at all meetings in which he was interested. I have perhaps more experience of public meetings than most people; and I can testify that he ranked first among the very worst chairmen on earth. He went round the Congested Districts to persuade Irish farmers whose farms were uneconomic to move into better holdings: a task which would have taxed the persuasive powers of a barrister earning £20,000 a year, and took with him small schoolmasters of the £150 type, who could only make Plunkett's offer in the baldest terms, and when it was refused say no more than "Well, you are a very foolish man ..." And yet with all this against him he was an amiable man whom nobody could dislike, a highly talented writer with a sense of humour, great political intelligence, and tireless public spirit: the greatest political Irishman of his time'

G. Bernard Shaw, letter to M. Digby
16 June, 1948

The extensive literature about Plunkett's co-operative movement was, until recently, almost wholly panegyric. With varying degrees of fervour enthusiasts subscribed to the belief that Sir Horace 'galvanized the economic life of Ireland'.[1] Some writers were less devout and more cautious, but even they conveyed a general impression of considerable achievement.[2] Recent comment, however, has been more sceptical. With few exceptions,[3] current interpretation ranges from a muted recognition

---

* I wish to thank Líam Kennedy for drawing my attention to a number of sources, and for his most helpful comments.

[1] M. Digby, *Horace Plunkett, An Anglo-American Irishman* (Oxford, 1949), p. 295; cf. R. A. Anderson, *With Horace Plunkett in Ireland* (London, 1935). L. Smith-Gordon and T. C. Staples, *Rural Reconstruction in Ireland. A Record of Co-operative Organization* (London, 1917).

[2] F. S. L. Lyons, 'Sir Horace Plunkett: A centenary appreciation of his life and work', *The Irish Times*, October 20 ff. 1954. J. C. Beckett, *The Making of Modern Ireland* (London, 1966), pp. 409-10.

[3] The principal recent exception is Paul L. Rempe's revival of the heroic view: 'Sir Horace Plunkett and Irish Politics, 1890-1914', *Eire-Ireland*, 13 (1978), 3-20. Professor Rempe is presumably not responsible for an editorial note which attributes Ireland's present 'glaring affluence' to Plunkett's 'policies and ambitions'.

of limited success[4] to outright rebuttal of the old creed: 'as a force for rural regeneration the Irish co-operative movement was a failure'.[5] The present essay is intended as a postscript rather than a challenge to that significant revision. If the movement's ultimate achievement was indeed modest, what were its principal weaknesses and why were they so frequently glossed over?

The economic climate was, at first glance, propitious. During the closing decades of the nineteenth century there was an enormous increase in the quantity of foodstuffs entering international trade, and a particularly remarkable growth in United Kingdom imports of bacon, eggs, and butter which 'ceased to be special luxuries on the [English] working class table'.[6] This 'retailing revolution', which involved the geographical realignment of vastly expanded markets and their increasing standardization and sophistication, offered farmers a challenge of great risk and opportunity. In Denmark, for example, the combined influence of cream-separators, folk high-schools, and cooperatives converted butter-making into a modern remunerative industry with a homogeneous, reliable, and highly competitive product, fully able to exploit new market opportunities.[7] Here, it seemed, was an ideal model for Irishmen, who were urged by Plunkett to create forthwith a 'Denmarkised Ireland'.[8] Nor was he alone in this desire: even Andrew Carnegie assured him that 'a second Denmark was the only possibility'.[9]

Within Ireland, however, the difficulties of attempting to modernize food production and marketing were more apparent than the opportunities. If old problems of land tenure were nearly solution, those of land *use* were barely recognized in a country whose agriculture was allegedly the most backward in Europe. Productivity was low and the quality of products frequently poor. Irish butter was a joke of legendary bad taste, fit only, it was said in Parliament and elsewhere, to adulterate

---

[4] L. M. Cullen, *An Economic History of Ireland since 1660* (London, 1972), p. 155; Joseph Lee, *The Modernisation of Irish Society* (Dublin, 1973), pp. 125-7; F. S. L. Lyons, *Ireland since the Famine* (London, 1973), pp. 207-16.

[5] C. Ó Gráda, 'The Beginnings of the Irish Creamery System, 1880-1914', *The Economic History Review*, 2nd Ser. xxx (May 1977), 301.

[6] J. B. Jefferys, *Retail Trading in Britain, 1850-1950* (London, 1954), p. 146.

[7] E. Jensen, *Danish Agriculture, its Economic Development* (Copenhagen, 1937).

[8] Digby, op. cit., p. 88.   [9] Ibid., p. 105.

good margarine. To 'Denmarkise' such products, Plunkett argued, would require nothing less than a complete remoulding of agrarian life, and that could be achieved solely through the elixir of co-operation: 'without this agency of social and economic progress small landholders in Ireland will be but a body of isolated units having all the drawbacks of individualism, and none of its virtues, unorganised and singularly ill-equipped for that great international struggle of our time, which we know as agricultural competition'.[10] He insisted that Ireland was the only European country where peasant landholders had no 'form of corporate existence', such as the French village commune, or the Russian *mir* (field commune: a singularly ill-chosen model, incidentally, since Stolypin was about to break its outmoded authority in a desperate attempt to modernize Russian agriculture).[11] Moreover, Ireland's transition from landlordism to peasant proprietorship had deprived its people of even 'that slight social coherence which they formerly possessed as tenants of the same landlord'.[12] Therefore 'coherence' must be recreated by a fundamental reappraisal and reshaping of economy and society.

The details of Plunkett's analysis and programme did not receive their complete exposition until the publication of his book in 1904, but their main features emerged during the preceding fifteen years. The diaries, extending from 1881, when he was twenty-seven, until his death in 1932, are a useful source for his ideas during these formative years, but he also published widely and with devastating frankness. In 1888, for example, he argued that 'the initiative must be taken by the upper classes' because, except in the North, Ireland lacked 'that intelligent class earning regular wages' which had created the English co-operatives.[13] Here we meet, for the first time, an element in Plunkett's thought and behaviour best described, perhaps, by the phrase *de haut en bas*. Patrician authority which assumes an innate implicit superiority is not remarkable in a man of Plunkett's class and time, but it is surely alien to the

[10] Horace Plunkett, *Ireland in the New Century* (London, 1905, Popular Ed. with an Epilogue), p. 44.
[11] A. Gerschenkron, *Continuity in History* (Harvard, 1968), pp. 236-40.
[12] Plunkett, op. cit., p. 45.
[13] Plunkett, 'Co-operative stores for Ireland', *The Nineteenth Century*, September 1888, 415.

ideology of co-operation: an observation which could be dismissed as trite, were it not ignored by both apologists and critics. Nor is the trait rendered any less apparent by its repeated disavowal, for Plunkett persisted in a sincere and confusing belief that his movement was based on self-help: thus in a typical letter he describes the 'horrible fight of paternalism *versus* Plunkettism'.[14] The appeal to the gentry culminated in 1908 with the pamphlet *Noblesse Oblige*, in which he begged expropriated landowners to stay in Ireland and work for a noble neighbourliness. 'It will be said that, however desirable it may be for the Irish farmers to receive guidance, they will not accept it from their landlords.' But, since country gentry are no longer landlords 'the interests of both classes are the same'. The paramount need was now for a great 'philanthropic endeavour'.[15]

In 1889, after stumping the country and, on his own admission, delivering many a lamentable speech, Plunkett's fifty-first attempt to form a co-operative creamery succeeded—at Drumcollagher, Co. Limerick. Within five years there were thirty-three societies, mostly creameries, but including a few 'agricultural' co-operatives whose main purpose was the joint purchase of requirements such as fertilizers and seeds. The next step was to establish a formal institution. In 1894 the Irish Agricultural Organisation Society was formed, as a 'philanthropic non-political organisation', with £10,000 raised by a few generous subscribers. It aimed 'to improve the condition of the agricultural population of Ireland by teaching the principles and methods of co-operation as applicable to farming and the allied industries, to promote industrial organisation for any purpose which may appear to be beneficial, and generally to counsel and advise those engaged in agricultural pursuits'.[16]

A commitment to avoid politics and embrace co-operation as the sole basis of agrarian reform was thus unequivocal. Dependence upon paternalism and philanthropy was modified only by an abortive hope that, after five years, the IAOS would be transformed into a democratic federal body financed by the affiliation fees of its constituents. Thus throughout our period the IAOS was based upon a paradox: it was created to meet an

[14] Plunkett to M. J. Bonn, 23 September 1909.
[15] Horace Plunkett, *Noblesse Oblige: an Irish Rendering* (Dublin, 1908).
[16] Irish Agricultural Association, *Rules* (Dublin, n.d.).

alleged need for a self-supporting spontaneous and democratic federation of co-operative farmers, yet its status and financial arrangements were essentially those of a charitable society.

The year 1895 was an eventful one. New forms of co-operative were launched including some ill-fated credit societies modelled upon the Raiffeisen and Schulz-Delitzsch system which had been so successful in Continental Europe.[17] An excellent farmers' newspaper, the *Irish Homestead*, was launched, with an annual subscription of 6/6*d*.: 'it is the organ of the Co-operative movement in Ireland; its party is Ireland; its creed the welfare of all; it goes to cottage and castle alike'.[18] Most important however was a sequence of events which led to the appointment of the 'Recess Committee'. Plunkett initiated this movement with 'a proposal affecting the general welfare of Ireland' arguing that Home Rule was in suspense and public men could therefore best employ themselves by uniting to promote useful non-contentious legislation. The committee that resulted was a triumph of practical politics, its report a considerable document of educational propaganda, which assembled massive evidence of the contemporary interaction between agrarian self-help and state aid in Europe.[19] One of its sixteen appendices contained a blueprint for an Irish Ministry of Agriculture, drawn up by no less a person than the French Director-General of Agriculture. The Report was a notable success, leading directly to the 1899 Agricultural and Technical Instruction Act which established a department of agriculture designed, the IAOS announced, 'to foster in every way possible the spirit of self help, which this Society has sought to engender in Irish farmers by its teachings'; ' ... to do for farmers what they are capable of doing for themselves, would be to misapply the resources of government and to demoralise the people'.[20] An attempt was also made to link the department with the new representative machinery of local government which had been created by the 1898 Irish Local Government

---

[17] Cf. F. C. Helm, *The Economics of Co-operative Enterprise* (London, 1968), pp. 3-4. J. H. Clapham, *Economic Development of France and Germany* (Cambridge, 1961), pp. 326-8.

[18] *The Irish Homestead*, 3 February 1906.

[19] For Plunkett's account of the Recess Committee see *Ireland in the New Century*, chapter VIII.

[20] IAOS *Annual Report* (Dublin, 1899), p. 33.

Act, by establishing a Council of Agriculture, though this was dismissed by some enthusiasts as a mere 'debating society'.[21] Thus by 1900 Plunkett and his men could claim much of the credit for providing Ireland with an administrative framework for a new agrarian society and, what was more important in their eyes, an ideology which they regarded as essential for its future success. It is arguable that his appointment as Vice President of the Department in that year marks the apogee of his career, though few of his disciples would have accepted that judgement.

During the following decade there was a considerable increase in the number of co-operative societies and in their turnover, as shown in Table 13.1.

Table 13.1   Growth of the Irish co-operative movement

	Number of Societies	Turnover ('000)	
		Dairy	Other
1889	1	4.4	
1890	1	8.5	
1895	76	184.9	
1900	477	703.9	327.8
1905	835	1 195.5	238.4
1910	880	1 903.3	630.4
1915	991	3 167.7	1 441.1
1920	1 114	8 247.8	6 326.6

Educational propaganda and marketing improvements also began to have some effect. It was observed that farmers who previously had described all fertilizers as 'guano' and judged its quality by smell, the more evil the better, were now beginning to discriminate between them 'in a way that would do credit to a professor of agriculture'.[22] Costs were also being forced down: inferior fertilizers had once sold at anything from £4 to £15 a ton; now, thanks to the activities of the Irish Agricultural Wholesale Society, which handled about 12,000 tons a year, the best fertilizer became available at £3 a ton. General standards of marketing were still commonly far below the best

---

[21] Anderson, op. cit., p. 119.
[22] E. A. Pratt, *The Organization of Agriculture* (London, 1904).

Continental levels, but at least there was a growing awareness of new requirements and opportunities. Thus a 'leading Dublin merchant' is interviewed by the *Irish Homestead*: Danish and Irish Methods of packaging and presentation are contrasted, and prominence is given to the 'absolute necessity for regularity and reliability as between the creameries and their wholesale customers'.[23] The Irish fowl, whose 'chief characteristic was a ripe and unprofitable old age'[24] and whose miniscule products were dirty, ungraded, and badly packed, is subjected to a short course in Denmarkisation: Mr Viggo Schwartz, an expert on egg grading and packing, is recruited by the IAOS, and distributes a plentiful supply of packing material.

The new techniques and ideology were not always accepted with docile acquiescence. To reinforce AE's admonition that 'experts should be on tap and not on top'[25] there were occasional indications of healthy scepticism among the pupils. 'A farmer' complained in 1906 that 'tillage is decreasing and nearly every kind of stock except asses ... they publish everything except the one thing farmers are anxious to know, viz,: what system of farming pays best? Surely they do not imagine Professor Wilson's 23 tables would convince anyone. To check them a farmer would want a laboratory in his field, a spring balance on his hay fork, and a ready reckoner in his pocket.' And he concluded with a wounding tilt at 'a President who has tried to improve everything from our faith to our cabbage'.[26] In gentler mood Countess Fingall later reminisced: 'while Horace was Vice President of the Department, we tried out his schemes', doing 'everything that the Department advised ... cider ... Fingall gave up his best horse paddock to make an orchard ... but we never toasted each other or Ireland in the Bottle of the Boyne'. Tobacco ... 'the smell of it was beautiful on a summer evening ... but it would have killed a smoker'. Her gardener threatened to quit, so she gave up the tobacco and kept him instead. 'Now our orchards have gone back to grass, and Oliver puts his horses in the paddocks where his father put his. And

[23] *The Irish Homestead*, 8 January 1898.
[24] Smith-Gordon and Staples, op. cit., p. 155.
[25] AE, *Co-operation and Nationality: A Guide for Rural Reformers from This to the Next Generation* (Dublin, 1912), p. 81.
[26] *The Irish Homestead*, 3 February 1906.

our schemes have a dream-like quality when I look back on them.' An old woman remembered how the Countess was 'always pestering us to have gardens and hens ... *and* ducks ... and she had us *desthroyed* with goats!' So, says Countess Fingall, 'our great efforts and thirty years of work are remembered by those who endured them'.[27]

Catalyst or irritant, the work of agricultural extension was rapidly overshadowed by internecine strife which revolved around two incidents—the publication of Plunkett's *Ireland in the New Century* in 1904, and a squabble between the IAOS and the Department of Agriculture. It should have been obvious that Plunkett's book would provoke opposition and harm his cause. Moritz Bonn, who was staying with him during the weeks before publication, later described it as 'a book whose brilliance broke his political career. I tried hard to prevent him from publishing it. But he could be very obstinate.'[28] Its reception could hardly have been more antagonistic, one critic publishing a 506-page review, which, as Plunkett later remarked, was a book about a chapter instead of the customary reviewer's chapter about a book.[29] John Redmond, who had co-operated on the Recess Committee and had 'once entertained some belief in the good intentions of Sir Horace Plunkett and his friends' denounced a work which 'full as it is of undisguised contempt for the Irish race, makes it plain to me that the real object of the movement in question is to undermine the Nationalist Party and divert the minds of our people from Home Rule, which is the only thing which can ever lead to a real revival of Irish industries'.[30] Another typical attack, in the *Freeman's Journal*, declared that Plunkett had 'demonstrated his unfitness for his position by wantonly and deliberately insulting the character and religion of the great majority of the Irish people, to whom he appeals for co-operation'.[31]

Plunkett's reaction was characteristically urbane and, in the eyes of his detractors, supercilious: the immediate publication

---

[27] E. Fingall, *Seventy Years Young. Memories of Elizabeth, Countess of Fingall, Told to Pamela Hinkson* (London, 1937), pp. 255-6.

[28] M. J. Bonn, *Wandering Scholar* (London, 1949), p. 104.

[29] M. O'Riordan, *Catholicity and Progress in Ireland* (Dublin, 1905).

[30] Letter to the *Irish World of New York*, quoted in Plunkett, *Ireland in the New Century*, op. cit., pp. 310-11.

[31] *Freeman's Journal*, 26 June 1904, quoted in Plunkett, ibid., pp. 297-8.

of a 'popular' second edition, with an added epilogue in which he quotes a selection of attacks and reiterates condemnation of his countrymen's 'lack of moral fibre'. The historical origins of this weakness were clear, he argued, and its excuse 'more than plausible', but it remained the 'chief present evil of Irish life'.[32] His opponents were upset because they had confused *morale* with *morals*, whereas he was castigating defects of character which were 'not ethically grave, but economically paralysing'.[33] Yet a few pages later he repeats the confusion and gives fresh ammunition to his opponents: 'the plain truth is that the *moral* atmosphere in Ireland is not yet considered, either at home or abroad, favourable for industrial enterprise ... I am driven to the conclusion that our comparatively backward industrial state is due to the *moral* conditions, which, however caused, it is the first duty of Irishmen to improve.'[34] To be sure there was evidence for such belief. Two examples of fecklessness and irresponsibility may serve to illustrate a theme which had evidently come to dominate his thinking. The farmer-secretary of a co-operative writes to AE 'please come down and hold a meeting which I have fixed for about Thursday'.[35] The second incident is described by Bonn who accompanied Plunkett on a visit to a place which had been ravaged by soil erosion 'where the islanders had cut off the sod and dried it for fuel; this was more convenient for them than going to the mainland to cut turf, but it was not an agricultural improvement. We were greeted by an angry, disappointed crowd. They were expecting a relief boat ... bringing goods for which they did not have to pay, to save them from starvation. As one of them explained to us afterward, "if it were not for the famine, nobody could live here". Horace resented this attitude, the absence of any attempt to help themselves, the reliance on permanent grievances.'[36] Such incidents were, perhaps, sufficiently frequent to account for Plunkett's concern. But a public attack upon the 'moral fibre' of those he wished to reform was scarcely likely to further his cause.

[32] Plunkett, ibid., p. 301.
[33] Ibid., p. 304.
[34] Ibid., p. 308.
[35] *Yearbook* (Dublin, 1936), p. 14 (referring to an incident *c.*1900).
[36] Bonn, op. cit., p. 85.

Linked with the uproar over his book, and equally damaging, was the growing friction which led ultimately to a complete break between the IAOS and the Department of Agriculture, a dispute in which personalities, politics, and policies were inextricably intertwined. T. P. Gill, the Department's first Secretary, was loathed and distrusted by Plunkett's lieutenants: R. A. Anderson described him as a 'bureaucrat of bureaucrats'. Gill and such other interested knowledgeable men as H. F. Montgomery, were, at best, dismissed by the true believers as sceptics for whom co-operation was 'nothing more than a system of business in which sentiment had no place' and the making of character 'pure moonshine'.[37] The politics of the row were diffuse and acrimonious, but at least two themes are fairly clear. First there was inevitable antagonism between shopkeepers and co-operators. The former, many of whom were active in nationalist politics, were vehement in their opposition to *trading* co-operatives, and particularly to any prospect of public money being used for their promotion; the latter did nothing to appease their rivals or to allay their fears. Denigration of traders is common in agrarian societies,[38] but in the Irish co-operative movement it became an obsession. *Paddy the Cope* is an excellent good-humoured guide to gombeen demonology.[39] Anderson is more succinct and venomous: 'Ireland has always suffered from a plague of small shopkeepers ... a parasitical class.'[40] Whatever the merits of their case it is hardly surprising that the co-operators met powerful opposition from traders. The second factor in the dispute was a continuous undercurrent of suspicion, sometimes openly expressed, as in Redmond's letter, that co-operation was fundamentally antipathetic to Home Rule; at best an attempt to kill it with kindness.

So much for personalities and politics. The *policy* implications of the conflict were both economic and administrative. Two opposed approaches to agrarian betterment were at stake: must the Department of Agriculture work solely through co-operat-

---

[37] Anderson, op. cit., p. 40.
[38] Cf. P. T. Bauer's classic defence of 'parasitic middlemen' in *West African Trade* (London, 1963), Ch. 2.
[39] Patrick Gallagher, *Paddy the Cope: My Story* (Dungloe, n.d., c.1947).
[40] Anderson, op. cit., p. 101.

ives or could it not also deal directly with farmers as individuals? One can assume that while Plunkett remained in the
Department the cracks were papered over. But his resignation
in 1907 and the accession of T. W. Russell, 'a stalwart defender
of tenant-farmers',[41] was followed by open conflict. It has been
argued that Russell 'inaugurated a complete change of policy',[42]
but this is misleading, for the seeds of discord had been well
sown and were sedulously nurtured. In any case the outcome
was that Russell broke the remaining links, reducing and
finally abolishing grants to the IAOS, which, in the absence of
adequate support from its own (co-operative) members, remained until 1913, when grants were reinstated, mainly dependent upon private philanthropy, notably from Plunkett
himself.

The severing of relations between the IAOS and the Department of Agriculture was described in 1917 as a fundamental
set-back for agricultural development.[43] If this exaggerates the
co-operative movement's importance, any reassessment will
depend in part upon the period of time being discussed. Concentration upon the years before 1920 avoids obvious difficulties
but conveys a misleading impression of achievement: the wartime and post-war boom ensured an easy but tenuous prosperity which inevitably benefited co-operatives. In 1921 their
previous year's peak in turnover was halved, and never again
equalled until the next boom in 1944. Even if the attention
is focused on the period before 1920, it would be unwise to
emphasise Plunkett's quantitative achievement. Co-operative
creameries were a success, but butter accounted for less than
10 per cent of Irish exports of farm products, and less than
5 per cent of total exports. Exports of livestock and meat were
always at least five times as valuable as those of butter, and
here the co-operative movement was insignificant. Since co-
operative creameries accounted for at most half of the country's
total butter production, their contribution to over-all economic
activity should not be exaggerated. A rough comparison with
Denmark indicates that in a country with half the land area
and three-quarters of the population co-operatives handled

[41] Lyons, *Ireland since the Famine*, op. cit., p. 215.
[42] Smith-Gordon and Staples, op. cit., p. 201.
[43] Ibid., p. 200.

about eleven times as much produce. Nor is there much evidence of rural regeneration over a longer period. In 1940 a
leading authority reported 'no perceptible improvement' in
crop yields or dairy cattle over the previous half-century, and
advocated 'a more widespread and energetic agricultural
extension service'.[44]

Appraisal of Plunkett's achievement will also be influenced
by the historian's subjective valuation of co-operative ideology.
Many observers regard co-operation, though not always explicitly, simply as a form of business organization, to be judged
by rational criteria in terms of individuals getting 'more satisfaction from collective effort than from individual effort'.[45] It is
on this basis that the Parkinson Report reaches its conclusion
that the movement's achievement was 'poor in relation to efforts
at organisation' because of an 'inability to distinguish between
what co-operation could and could not be expected to do'.[46] At
the opposite pole are the devotees who, even when they concede
the movement's 'material' weakness, claim a vague but deeply
felt ideological achievement: 'a clear vision of what co-operation
should be'.[47] Some even reflect upon the ideal and then rebuke
their countrymen for failing to attain it, lamenting :the unhappy
fact ... that those for whom this was done have not been true
to the principles they professed'.[48]

No balanced appraisal is likely to bridge so wide an inter-
pretative gulf, but, confessing a preference for rational economic
criteria, some tentative conclusions can be attempted. Plunkett
failed to inspire an agrarian revolution for a variety of reasons,
some of which diminish his achievement as a practical reformer.
Contrary to his frequently expressed belief, the time was not
ripe. More recent experience of decolonization offers ample
evidence that the decade of incipient nationhood is no time for
economic reformers. 'Seek ye first the political kingdom' was
Nkrumah's creed in Ghana, and no group of agrarian re-

[44] P. Lamartine Yates, *Food, Land and Manpower in Western Europe* (London, 1940),
pp. 111-12.
[45] H. H. Bakken and M. A. Schaars, *Economics of Co-operative marketing* (New York,
1937), p. 199.
[46] J. R. Parkinson, *Agricultural Co-operation in Northern Ireland* (Cmd. 484), London,
1965, p. 37.
[47] Smith-Gordon and Staples, op. cit., p. 253.
[48] Anderson, op. cit., p. 75.

formers could distract men from such a challenge. The argument was well expressed, without rhetorical flourish, by a witness at a departmental committee of inquiry in 1906: 'The prejudice that exists against the Department and the want of co-operation from the people in general ... is due simply to its being part of the English government, and it will never gain our co-operation so long as it remains that.'[49] Plunkett was appalled at the 'political obsession of our national life'[50] but refused to recognize what Bonn termed the 'psychological aspect of land reform in Ireland' which reinforced his contemporaries' predisposition towards political rather than social and economic activity: 'it is human nature—not merely Irish peculiarity—to prefer an increased income from distribution rather than from production; especially when an experience of more than twenty-five years has shown that a unit of energy applied to legislative activities secures a bigger and safer return than a unit of energy spent on raising crops'.[51]

There are additional explanations, more charitable to the activities of Irish farmers. Their products were frequently of poor quality, but that does not prove that their farming was inefficient, measured by economic, as distinct from technical standards. Concentration upon quality, regardless of cost, is the occupational disease of technical experts and improvers. It is true that Irish dairying made only modest progress during the period, that there was probably little increase in the total volume of agricultural production, though exports of beef cattle increased greatly, and that all this was in marked contrast to contemporary development in Denmark, which was exporting to the same market. But the moral to be drawn was not necessarily that Ireland could or should have been 'Denmarkised' forthwith. It has been argued[52] that concentration upon cattle, far from being a feckless *pis aller*, was a rational response to the relatively higher prices of beef and the cost of necessary inputs.

[49] Department of Agriculture and Technical Instruction, *Minutes of Evidence taken before the Departmental Committee of Inquiry*, vol. 18, Dublin, 1907, p. 816. Evidence of Mr Joseph Dolan.

[50] Plunkett, *Ireland in the New Century*, op. cit., p. 62.

[51] M. Bonn, 'The Psychological Aspect of Land Reform in Ireland', *Economic Journal*, xix (1909), 374-94.

[52] H. Staehle, 'Statistical Notes on the economic history of Irish agriculture, 1847-1913', *Journal of the Statistical and Social Inquiry Society of Ireland*, xviii (1951), 444-71.

Similarly R. D. Crotty has advanced substantial arguments to prove that it was not in the best interests of Irish farmers to increase milk yields'[53] Thorough 'Denmarkisation' would have required expensive entrepreneurial and managerial skills, and a widespread ability to comprehend and satisfy sophisticated consumer tastes. Plunkett appreciated this relationship between economic development, education, and culture—hence his life-long advocacy of the 'three b's'—better business, better farming, better living. But such deficiencies would inevitably take more than a generation to overcome. Meanwhile even those practical needs which were paramount, and to which modest co-operative organization had something to contribute—were befogged by an all-embracing ideology, and almost overwhelmed by political naivety and intransigence. All co-operative movements attempt to blend sound business practice with idealism. In Ireland the latter was dominant, frequently utopian, and sometimes cranky. The enthusiasts were highly articulate and their rhetoric prob-ably harmed their cause. Thus AE expresses his contempt for 'the little groups who meet a couple of times a year and call themselves co-operators, because they have got their fertilizers more cheaply and have done nothing else. Why the village gombeen man has done more than that! ... and I say if we co-operators do not aim at doing more than the Irish Scribes and Pharisees we shall have little to be proud of.'[54] A strain of rural utopianism, divorced from the realities of economic develop-ment and the needs of a modernizing society, enabled such men to claim, without a trace of irony, that 'few would wish to see another Lancashire reproduced in Ireland'.[55] If Plunket was sometimes more practical than some of his followers, he nevertheless tended to share their distaste for the practical world of business. He was, for example, singularly unimpressed by Thomas Lipton, prime architect of that retailing revolution which he hoped to harness to the Irish economy. After trying to 'interest him in the IAOS' and believing initially that he had 'hooked him alright', he soon concluded that Lipton was a 'regular bounder', from whom nothing could be gained

[53] R. D. Crotty, *Irish Agricultural Production, its volume and structure* (Cork, 1966), pp. 86-7.
[54] AE, *Co-operation and Nationality*, op. cit., p. 86.
[55] Smith-Gordon and Staples, op. cit., p. 10.

'except promises to buy Irish butter and eggs if they were the best and cheapest to be had'.[56]

It is usually dangerous for the agricultural reformer to assume that existing practice is irrational and that *everything* must be changed *quickly*. But even if he is willing to progress slowly he must have considerable and appropriate resources available, and these must be unequivocally welcome to the men he wishes to improve. Plunkett failed because his claims for co-operation were transcendental, because he tried to build a utopia, encouraging cranks and discouraging practical men, and because he misjudged the power of nationalism. His achievement has been exaggerated because his admirers, bewitched by the oft-expressed idealism of his group, have confused aspiration and attainment.

[56] Plunkett Diaries, 26 July, 22 August, 25 September 1898. National Library of Ireland (microfilm 6586).

14. The Belfast Boycott, 1920-1922*

D. S. Johnson

I

Between mid-1920 and the outbreak of civil war in June 1922 a boycott of goods distributed from, or manufactured in, Belfast and other northern towns was undertaken in nationalist areas of Ireland—at first with the blessing of Dáil Éireann and then without it. Indeed it was an incident connected with the boycott, the seizure of motor cars distributed by a Belfast wholesaler, that sparked off the civil war, and the republican officer arrested on that occasion, Leonard Henderson, had been the first director of the Belfast Boycott Committee.[1] The purpose of this paper is twofold; first to examine the origins, establishment, and workings of the boycott as an example of adapting to a new situation a device long used in rural Ireland; second, to make an estimate, albeit an imperfect one, of the effect of the boycott in reducing trade between the six and the twenty-six counties before cross-border statistics became available in April 1923.

The boycott had two origins. In the first place it was a nationalist protest against the general tendency of British policy, which was quite clearly at this stage directed towards the partition of the country. But the boycott was aimed less at the United Kingdom government than at bankers, industrialists, merchants, and workers in the north of Ireland: its purpose was to illustrate the importance of the south as a market for northern goods and thereby to demonstrate the folly of the division of the country. The boycott therefore was not solely a protest against the sectarian disturbances occurring during the summer of 1920.[2] Some local councils had already decided on it as an anti-partitionist move earlier in the year. On 4 February, for

* I would like to thank Cyril Ehrlich and G. N. Gandy for their comments on previous drafts of this paper.

[1] P. Béaslaí, *Michael Collins and the Making of a New Ireland* (Dublin, 1926), vol. ii, p. 402.

[2] Dorothy Macardle, *The Irish Republic* (London, 1968), p. 356.

instance, Ballinarobe District Council appealed to all traders in the district to close accounts with north-east Ulster firms 'unless and until the latter declared themselves anti-partitionist'.[3]

But there is no doubt that the sectarian disturbances in Belfast in July and August 1920 provided the second and powerful driving force for the boycott by arousing sympathy among southern Catholics towards the plight of their co-religionists destined to remain, against their wishes, in the new state of Northern Ireland. In this sense the boycott was intended to end what was widely regarded as a 'pogrom' against Catholics in the north, and lead to their reinstatement in the shipyards and engineering factories from which they had been expelled. Although these industries could not be affected directly, it was hoped to put pressure on their leadership and thereby on the entire business community. The expulsion of Catholic workers from the shipyards and other important factories, such as the Sirocco engineering works, was regarded with particular hostility in the south as it was believed, almost certainly mistakenly, that employers were inciting their Protestant workers to violent action.[4] In fact loyalist workers had decided to exact their own vengeance on their nationalist neighbours for the campaign being waged against the British forces in Ireland, as the resolution passed in the Sirocco works makes clear: 'We decline to work with those men who have been expelled recently until the Sinn Féin assassinations in Ireland cease.'[5] Belfast was soon gripped by a cycle of terror and counter-terror which lasted until late 1922. The world depression which began in 1920 had worsened by the summer of 1921 and unemployment rose, so any possibility of reinstatement of Catholic workers in the shipyards became increasingly remote; with high unemployment amongst both religious groups it would have been a bold employer who reinstated Catholics whilst making Protestants redundant.

In response to these disturbances, on 6 August 1920 a petition representing the views of nationalist members of Belfast

---

[3] *Irish Times* (hereafter *IT*), 4 February 1920. O'Hegarty suggests the boycott started in Tuam early in 1920. P. S. O'Hegarty, *The Victory of Sinn Féin* (Dublin, 1924), p. 183.

[4] The chairman of the Sirocco works made strenuous attempts to reinstate Catholic workers. *Northern Whig* (hereafter *NW*), 11 August 1920.

[5] *Belfast News Letter* (hereafter *BNL*), 4 August 1920.

corporation, as well as other republicans, was presented to Dáil Éireann. This drew attention to the 'war of extermination' being waged against the minority. Presented by Sean MacEntee, the petition urged the Dáil to 'fight Belfast' in particular by 'a commercial boycott' adding (somewhat inaccurately, given the types of industry from which Catholics had been expelled) that 'the chief promoters of Orange intolerance here are the heads of the distributing trade throughout Ireland'. It further urged supporters to withdraw 'accounts from Banks having their Headquarters in Belfast and transfer them to Banks with Headquarters in other parts of Ireland'.[6] Opinion in the Dáil was divided. Ernest Blythe, a northerner himself, felt that a boycott 'would destroy for ever the possibility of any union', whilst Liam de Roiste felt it could only divert trade to England. The motion to impose a boycott was eventually defeated, and the Dáil contented itself with passing a motion declaring 'religious tests, as a condition of Industrial Employment in Ireland, illegal'.[7]

As the Belfast troubles intensified, opinion in Dublin hardened. On 11 August the Dáil Cabinet agreed to support a boycott confined to banks and insurance companies having headquarters in Belfast. This was not to be implemented through the Dáil but by the General Council of County Councils in an endeavour to achieve maximum involvement at local level.[8] The General Council met on 12 August. Two days later the *Irish Times* warned that the intended boycott would 'cause as much inconvenience to southern customers as loss to the banks' via the cessation of overdraft facilities. The Cabinet's strategy was evidently successful for between mid-August and mid-September resolutions supporting the boycott were passed by local authorities all over nationalist Ireland, and boycotting incidents were reported from various parts of the country. For example, a motor car full of Belfast goods was thrown into the Erne at Ballyshannon; in Sligo, it was reported, merchants had cancelled goods ordered from Belfast houses; and in Galway

---

[6] Dáil Éireann, *Minutes of Proceedings of the First Parliament of the Republic of Ireland: Official Record* (Dublin, 1921), 191.

[7] *Minutes of Proceedings*, 193-4.

[8] Dáil Éireann, *Ministry and Cabinet Minutes*, 11 August 1920, State Paper Office, Dublin (hereafter *SPO*).

the representative of a Belfast firm had been driven away by a volunteer.[9]

From the very beginning there was much confusion about the aims of the boycott, and insufficient organization. From its outset the boycott was unofficially extended beyond the banks and insurance companies. As early as 17 September a ministerial statement from the acting president, Arthur Griffith, referred to a general boycott against Belfast which was being 'stringently felt' in the north.[10] Nor was it confined to Belfast, in part because of a decision by the General Council of County Councils to extend it to other places, where there had been secretarian conflict, including Lisburn, Dromore, Banbridge, and Newtownards. In some southern towns, such as Naas, the local population decided that the boycott applied to the whole of the north and extended to selling, while along the border, such as in Monaghan, Catholics took to boycotting shops belonging to Protestant shopkeepers.[11] The general absence of clear direction can be partly attributed to the imprisonment of Leo Henderson, the director of the Central Belfast Boycott Committee in October 1920, and partly to the fact that most of the committee members were 'on the run'.[12] Not even the existence of some eighty local committees established at the beginning of 1921 could achieve adequate organization.[13]

Systematic planning of the campaign began in 1921 when Joseph Macdonagh assumed responsibility. He was appointed 'substitute Minister for Labour' in January 1921, after a session of the Dáil in which strong criticism of the conduct of the campaign had been voiced.[14] Before his appointment Macdonagh had urged the systematic circulation of lists of Belfast-based wholesalers, merchants, travellers, and distributors.[15] In another letter he argued that the boycott 'should be enforced ruthlessly or not at all', advocating the

---

[9] *NW*, 13 August 1920; *IT*, 14 and 16 August, 7 September 1920.

[10] *Minutes of Proceedings*, 212.

[11] *NW*, 16 September 1920, 12 and 19 October 1920; *IT*, 16 September 1920.

[12] M. Collins to A. Griffith, 21 October 1920, SPO DE 2/122.

[13] Résumé of Boycott. Memorandum 20 January 1921, SPO DE 2/110.

[14] *Minutes of Proceedings*, 258.

[15] J. Macdonagh to S. MacEntee, 18 January 1921, SPO DE 2/261. In the letter Joe Devlin is quoted as saying 'if we can stick it [the Boycott] another twelve months, a republic is certain'.

appointment of eight regional organizers and the wide circulation of handbills containing information on Belfast travellers, manufacturers, agents, merchants, and wholesalers:

It would be the business of the organisers to get in touch with all the sympathetic clergy and TDs and other people of influence and to have appointed a Boycott Committee in every town in Ireland. These committees could be composed of merchants, shop assistants and Transport Recorders. Vigilance Committees would have to be formed to spot goods on Railway Stations to find out if any shopkeepers are getting through other towns and to find out when Belfast travellers arrive in a town and give him [*sic*] notice to quit. I presume the hands of the I.R.A. are too full for the Minister of Defence to instruct them to do the cleaning out of the Commerical Travellers.[16]

On his appointment Macdonagh sent a circular to mayors and chairmen of local authorities, reminding them of the 'pogroms'. Whilst claiming that Belfast wholesalers 'who for the past fifty years have battened on the people of the rest of Ireland, have not, owing to the operation of the economic boycott, been able to retain five per cent of their trade', the circular stressed that **'THE NECESSITY FOR THE RIGID ENFORCEMENT OF THE BOYCOTT IS NOW MORE VITAL THAN EVER'**, and appealed to the councillors to **'MAKE THE BOYCOTT EFFECTIVE IN EVERY WAY. COMMITTEES SHOULD BE FORMED IN EVERY TOWN AND VILLAGE.'** Shopkeepers should also be assured that 'trading with Belfast means endorsing the Orange atrocities'.[17]

The precise response of local committees is difficult to determine as few boycott lists survive. One national list, obviously incomplete, concentrates on Dublin businesses and northern towns still distributing Belfast goods and on Scottish and English firms which were allegedly reconsigning to the south of Ireland goods previously received from Belfast.[18] More detailed is a list produced by the Derry Boycott Committee naming commercial travellers, shops, and factories in the area selling Belfast goods or dealing with firms handling them. It also lists those firms in Ireland, Scotland, and England stocking Belfast goods and contains a catalogue of articles made in Belfast and other

---

[16] J. Macdonagh to the Cabinet, 18 January 1921, SPO DE 2/261.
[17] Undated circular headed Belfast Trade Boycott, SPO DE 2/110.
[18] Dated 25 October 1921, SPO DE 2/110.

boycotted towns, with their producers' names.[19] Although few such documents appear to have survived, the Derry list is probably similar to many produced at the time.[20] De Valera later claimed at the Sinn Féin *Ard-Fheis* that 30,000 black lists had been distributed since the beginning of 1921.[21]

The increasing effectiveness of the boycott is reflected in police and newspaper reports. In January 1921 Royal Irish Constabulary county inspectors reported boycott incidents in only four counties, all in Ulster (Cavan, Monaghan, Tyrone, and Londonderry); by March there were incidents in nine counties and by April, in twelve.[22] In May the Inspector General of the RIC wrote that 'the Belfast boycott was spreading. It is useless to pretend that this is not extremely serious and it is significant to note that some large English firms are now yielding to it and promising to obey the orders of Dáil Éireann.'[23] Between February 1921 and September 1921 (when the constabulary reports ceased) boycott incidents were reported in every county of Ireland except County Antrim and, surprisingly, County Carlow.[24] Even large firms were affected. In September 1921 Dunlop advised customers to transfer their orders from Belfast to Dublin or Birmingham,[25] and shortly thereafter two Woolworth branches in Dublin and one in Kingstown were boycotted. They capitulated and displayed notices: 'No boycotted goods are sold in this store ...'[26] In the same month J. S. Fry and Sons and the oil companies ceased to distribute from Belfast.[27] Indeed so successful was the boycott against Belfast, that it was extended to a list of English goods,[28] a matter which was regarded seriously enough for questions to be asked at

[19] E. M. Stephens Papers, Trinity College, Dublin (hereafter TCD), TCD MS 4238, Box 5, File 4, 48-53.

[20] But see for example Public Record Office of Northern Ireland (hereafter PRONI) CAB 6/23 Strabane and District Blacklist, 5 December 1921.

[21] *IT,* 28 October 1921.

[22] Public Record Office (hereafter PRO) C.O. 904/114-5. Reports of the County Inspectors to the Inspector General of the RIC.

[23] PRO C.O. 904/115. Inspector General's Confidential Report for May 1921.

[24] PRO C.O. 904/114-6. Activity in Co. Antrim was largely confined to burning bread vans. *NW,* 20 May and 1 June 1921.

[25] Memorandum 7 September 1921, PRONI CAB 6/23.

[26] *NW,* 19 and 20 October 1921. See also Dáil Éireann, *Private Sessions of Second Dáil* (Dublin, 1922), 19.

[27] Craig to Lloyd George, 28 October 1921. PRO CAB 6/23.

[28] The complete list is given in the Derry document. TCD MS 4238 Box 5, File 4.

Westminster.[29] It was nevertheless an exaggeration for Mac-donagh to boast that 'except in Antrim and Down it was im-possible for a Belfast merchant to sell as much as a bootlace in any other part of Ireland'.[30] The more sober *Interim Report of the Proceedings of the Department of Labour* admitted that the boycott was not as complete as it should be, that there were still 'leak-ages' in Galway and Mayo, and that it was difficult to set up successful committees in Antrim, Down, and Londonderry, but testified both to the great enthusiasm of the 400 boycott committees, and the campaign's general effectiveness.[31]

During the course of 1921 it became quite clear in Ulster that the boycott could no longer be derisively ignored. From the outset the 'official' Unionist view had been to dismiss it as in-effective since the large staple industries of the north were not dependent upon Irish markets. This opinion was expressed by H. M. Pollock (later to become the first Minister of Finance in the government of Northern Ireland) to the Belfast Chamber of Commerce in March. Southerners did not realize 'that ninety-five per cent of the goods manufactured in Belfast and one hundred per cent of the output of the shipbuilding yards found their markets in countries outside Ireland' although he admitted that the boycott was 'disturbing to a number of those engaged in the distributing trades'.[32] In similar vein, he told the English journalist W. Ewart in May that the boycott 'does not hit Ulster very hard'.[33] But distributors were less complacent. At the annual meeting of the Belfast Chamber of Commerce there were complaints about the adverse effects of the boycott and it was pointed out that commercial travellers had been driven out of the southern and border counties. At an assembly of the Belfast Wholesalers, Merchants and Manufacturers Associ-ation, the chairman admitted that 'this Association, like all the others had been hard hit by the boycott, five sixths of the trade having gone off'.[34] By the autumn of 1921 wholesalers were becoming more militant: there were demands for retaliation

[29] *Hansard Parliamentary Debates*, 140, cols. 90-1, 5 April 1921.
[30] *NW*, 18 August 1921.
[31] Dáil Éireann, *Official Report for the Periods 16-26 August 1921 and 28 February to 8 June*, 1922 (Dublin, 1922), 31-3.
[32] *IT*, 16 March 1921.
[33] W. Ewart, *A Journey in Ireland 1921* (London, 1922), p. 157.
[34] *NW*, 5 and 8 April 1921.

and a deputation was sent to the Prime Minister. Privately Craig admitted that 'the matter was serious' though he questioned whether it was 'desirable to make a squeal' as this would be grist to Sinn Féin's propaganda mill.[35] Publicly the government remained unconcerned, the Prime Minister maintaining as late as December that 'the results of the boycott are not serious for Ulster'.[36]

A further indication of the force of the boycott is provided by evidence from the nationalist community whom it had been intended to help. Southerners were evidently unable to distinguish between goods made or distributed by Catholic businesses in Belfast from those made by Protestants. As a result the Belfast branch of the Boycott Committee was forced to write to the Dáil Ministry complaining at the damage done to nationalist firms. 'In the distributing trades ... boots and leather, fruit and groceries are barely able to keep afloat. They are firms with small capital and therefore cannot stand the strain of the Boycott as well as their competitors of the Garrison.' Peculiarly ironic was the experience of Denis McCullough, one of the organizers of the Irish Republican Brotherhood in Belfast and an original signatory to the petition urging the boycott in August 1920, a man 'employing only Republicans and interned because of his beliefs'. He was forced to close his bagpipe factory, as 'the Irish public because of the Boycott, buy British made pipes rather than support this purely republican firm'. Belfast nationalists advocated that certain towns should be provided with 'licences' so they might trade with the rest of Ireland, and hoped that 'by getting a stronger hold upon the commercial life of the city, this would help to Irishise Belfast and would be a compact force ready at all times to oppose foreign influence in the city'.[37]

It is clear therefore that by the end of 1921 the boycott was causing serious economic problems for Belfast. It was also creating inconvenience to commerce in the south. In December Craig informed Lloyd George that Belfast business men had

[35] *NW*, 28 October 1921. Deputation of Belfast Wholesale Merchants, 28 October 1921, PRONI CAB 6/23.

[36] PRONI CAB 6/23. Press cutting from *Daily Mirror* attached to letter from Belfast wholesalers, 15 December 1921.

[37] Undated paper, SPO DE 2/110.

been visited by the 'Sinn Féin minister for Economics' in response to pressure from southern traders. He 'gave the impression that he would be glad if something could be done to enable the boycott to be removed without Sinn Féin losing face by doing so'.[38] The problem was to the forefront of the agreement between Craig and Collins in January 1922, the second article of which stated that 'Mr. Collins undertakes that the Belfast boycott is to be discontinued immediately and Sir James Craig undertakes to facilitate in every possible way the return of Catholic workers without tests to the shipyards as and when trade revival enables the firms concerned to absorb the present employed'.[39] The agreement was welcomed wholeheartedly by Belfast merchants. The managing director of Robinson and Cleaver felt that the agreement 'ought to improve trade considerably and create a feeling of confidence hitherto lacking'. One Dublin representative of a Belfast firm expected the pact to 'restore the big distributing trade which existed in Belfast in pre-boycott times'. Another paid tribute to the boycott's effectiveness. 'If the Free State will be conducted as efficiently as the Belfast boycott was carried out', he said, 'I will be quite satisfied'.[40] But hopes raised by the agreement were soon disappointed, hardly surprising given the complete divergence of views between Craig and Collins on the role of the projected Boundary Commission and indeed on the long-term future of the six counties.[41] On the one hand the continuance of sectarian disturbances in Belfast, coupled with high levels of unemployment in the shipyards, made the reinstatement of Catholic workers both politically and economically difficult. On the other hand Collins proved unable or unwilling to confront those elements amongst the anti-Treaty forces who wished to continue the boycott. Indeed newspaper reports at the time suggested Collins half agreed with its continuation and that the Dáil Cabinet was seriously considering its official re-imposition.[42]

By March 1922 there was a systematic attempt to destroy

---

[38] Craig to Lloyd George, 2 December 1921, PRONI CAB 6/23.
[39] *IT*, 23 January 1922.
[40] *Ibid., 24 January 1922.*
[41] Macardle, pp. 599-600.
[42] *IT*, 22 March 1922.

those goods sent south by hopeful Belfast wholesalers in the days immediately after the pact. In some instances the traditional method of seizing and destroying goods was adopted.[43] In others a new, more sophisticated, tactic was adopted by the boycott committees, that of exacting the settlement of invoices for Belfast goods still coming south. This happened to the creditors of Ireland Bros., wholesale drapers of Belfast. A Dublin distributor wrote to the company explaining that they had been 'compelled by the I.R.A. to hand over a cheque for all the money which we owe to Belfast firms in return for which they handed us a form stating that "we were absolved from any further liability"'. For the Dublin firm this concluded the matter: 'at present we are afraid nothing further can be done'.[44] The newly established Provisional Government was annoyed, and circularized traders, stating that these demands for payment were being made 'without lawful authority and should be disregarded'.[45]

Relations between Craig and Collins deteriorated during the spring of 1922, despite what seemed to be a strengthening of the January pact by the agreement between the Provisional Government and the government of Northern Ireland reached on 30 March 1922.[46] Craig complained that the boycott was still in operation and commercial travellers were once more being expelled. Collins deplored the fact, but remarked bitterly that he understood that 'many of those most actively engaged in this work are themselves men who as a result of the troubles in Belfast during the last few years had been deprived of employment and forced to flee their homes'.[47] By the end of the month the dispute had become public, Collins and Craig accusing each other of failing to put the agreement into operation. Craig claimed *inter alia* that 'interference with our trade has been greater than in the whole period when the boycott was officially countenanced, and damage has been done to Northern

[43] Ibid., 30 March 1922, 4 April 1922.
[44] Ireland Bros. to Ministry of Commerce, 8 April 1922. PRONI COM 62/2/2. See also Gallahers to Ministry of Commerce 8 April, 12 June, 1 August, 3 August 1922. PRONI COM 62/2/18.
[45] Circular dated 6 April 1922, SPO Cabinet Papers D/T S1095/22.
[46] *The Times*, 31 March 1922.
[47] Michael Collins to Sir James Craig, 11 April 1921, PRO C.O. 906/26.

Irish goods aggregating in value many hundreds of thousands of pounds'.[48]

After nearly two years of boycotting, Ulster merchants began to organize a counter-boycott. The Ulster Trades Defense Association had been set up in the autumn of 1921 but had been restrained from action by the wishes of the government. If a counter-boycott, modelled on that existing in the south, were seen to be operating in Northern Ireland, it was feared that this would be politically damaging to Craig in his negotiations both with the British Cabinet and with Collins.[49] It was also feared that it was likely to prove ineffective. The Prime Minister himself stated in his *Daily Mirror* interview (cited above) that a boycott of stout would be impossible. Conceivably, if Craig had not been absent in London in mid-May 1922 the counter-boycott might never have started.[50] The campaign involved extensive use of press advertising. Handbills accused Ulstermen of 'supineness and fatuity', of 'holding up the other cheek' for far too long, and urged them to cease purchasing all southern goods, clothing, meat, butter, biscuits, furniture, and, inevitably, stout and whiskey.[51] Although there was some follow-up to this campaign—the Belfast branches of Mooney's, for example, were ordered to stop purchasing drink from Dublin—it was ironic that just as the counter-boycott was starting, the whole boycotting operation in the south was on the point of breakdown.[52] On 26 June, after several months of increasing hostility between the pro- and anti-Treaty forces, Leo Henderson, first director of the Belfast Boycott Committee, acting 'in accordance with the boycott of goods from the six counties', set out with others to seize sixteen cars, imported from Belfast by Ferguson's of Dublin. He was arrested by pro-Treaty forces. As a reprisal the pro-Treaty Deputy Chief of Staff, General J. J. O'Connell, was seized as a hostage for Henderson's release.

---

[48] *The Times*, 27 April 1922.

[49] True, Craig once expressed the view that 'such measures of anti-boycott as are strictly within legal lines would do no harm'. PRONI CAB 6/23. Spender to Haslett, 3 January 1922. In general the government urged restraint. See for example 20/21 April 1922, correspondence of Litchfield and Spender, PRONI CAB 6/23.

[50] Ibid., 10 May 1922, Fulton to Litchfield.

[51] Circular to wholesalers, PRONI COM 62/2/34/1. The advertisements appeared in the loyalist press from mid-May to the end of June.

[52] Ulster Trades Defense Association to Mooney & Co., 3 June 1922. SPO D/T S1095/22.

The next day the government decided to bombard the Four Courts: the civil war had begun.[53] This brought the *systematic* enforcement of the boycott to an end.

Although the boycott's effectiveness slackened after July, the Belfast distributing trade was slow to recover. At a meeting of the Ulster Trades Defense Association with prominent civil servants in October 1922, the deputation admitted that 'things have got better since the dealing with the Four Courts' but stated that 'none of the big firms have re-opened in Dublin yet'. The tobacco manufacturers Gallaher's, for example, 'were still sending no stuff to the South of Ireland' as they 'had opened up three times and each time they were raided again, so they are not going to run any more risks'.[54] Furthermore during 1923 the south was disturbed both politically, by civil war, and economically because of the depressed conditions of agriculture resulting from low prices and poor harvests.[55] The bitterness resulting from the boycott and the 'troubles' generally, which extended beyond 1922, is reflected in the evidence presented to the Boundary Commission.[56] Indeed a revival of the boycott was proposed as late as at the Sinn Féin conference in November 1925.[57]

II

Before attempting to quantify the effect of the boycott on Belfast's distributing trade, it is proposed briefly to examine its effects on the institutions against which it had been initially aimed, namely the northern-based banks. Although the solvency of these was never really threatened their business in nationalist areas was diminished. The banks were able to keep open their main branches but many sub-branches, less easy to protect, were closed: by 1922 all sub-branches belonging to the Belfast Bank in the twenty-six counties had ceased to operate, compared to 83 per cent of the Ulster Bank's and 75 per cent of the Northern's. These closures were sometimes a source of profit

[53] Macardle, pp. 677-9.
[54] UTDA deputation, 9 October 1922, PRONI COM 62/2/34/1.
[55] Denis Gwynn, *The Irish Free State 1922-7* (London, 1928), pp. 288-9.
[56] PRO CAB 61/81 Keady, Committee of inhabitants of Town End, PRO CAB 61/64, Fermanagh County Council.
[57] *IT*, 21 November 1925.

to banks based in the south; of the twenty-one sub-branches opened by the Hibernian and Munster and Leinster during 1921 and 1922, fifteen were in the border counties of Ulster, traditionally the preserve of Belfast.[58] Furthermore, during the period from late 1920 to late 1922 the deposits of banks based in the north fell by 6.1 per cent whilst those of banks based in the south rose by 9.3 per cent.[59] It is true that other factors may have been involved in bringing this about, including the difficulties of the northern staple industries and the transfer by southern farmers of wartime profits from chests to bank accounts. But it is doubtful if structural features alone can explain the different performances of banks based north and south of the border. The Ulster Bank had 53 per cent of its branches in the twenty-six counties, yet it experienced the largest fall in total deposits for all northern-based banks, 7.1 per cent. The Northern, with 35 per cent of its branches in the south, recorded a decline of 6.5 per cent, whereas the Belfast Bank, with 29 per cent of its offices there, experienced a fall of only 4.5 per cent. This is strong prima-facie evidence for the effectiveness of the boycott, for had it had no impact, and structural factors alone operated, the bank with the *most* branches in the south rather than the fewest would have been expected to have performed the best. It has, moreover, recently been estimated that, as a result of the boycott, the Belfast Bank lost one-fifth of its deposits outside Northern Ireland, a fact which greatly influenced the decision to sell its southern branches in 1923. Although it is impossible to make similar estimates of deposits lost by the two other banks, it is clear that, given the higher proportion of their business transacted in the twenty-six counties, losses of the same order of magnitude as those suffered by the Belfast Bank would have been even more damaging.[60] Thus the boycott had a significant effect on Northern Ireland's banking community while falling short of destroying its financial credibility.

The harm done to Belfast's distributing trade was probably greater. There are of course no statistics which directly show

[58] *Thom's Directory of Ireland 1920 and 1923* (Dublin, 1920, 1923), 995-1003, 1001-6.

[59] Figures provided for the author by the banks. The southern bank increases ranged from 2.6 per cent (Provincial Bank) to 15.1 per cent (Munster and Leinster).

[60] N. Simpson, *The Belfast Bank 1827-1970* (Belfast, 1975), pp. 247-55. The Northern and Ulster banks apparently do not possess this information.

the trade of Belfast with the south between 1920 and 1922. But many of the goods distributed by the city's merchants were imports, largely from Britain; in the late 1930s, when official import statistics first distinguished countries of origin (rather than consignment) a third of goods entering the south from Northern Ireland originated in the province.[61] The proportion prevailing in the early twenties was probably similar. Indeed, possibly because it became most convenient after the establishment of the Land Boundary to import *direct* to southern ports, the proportion may have been even higher. Thus the statistics of imports into Belfast, particularly of those goods likely to have been widely distributed, should provide a guide to the fortunes of the city's trade not only in the province but also more widely over the northern half of Ireland.

Import figures are available down to 1921 in the *Reports on the Trade in Imports and Exports at Irish Ports*. From these *Reports* it is possible to calculate the total value of imports into Belfast and elsewhere, including the value of those goods most likely to have been widely distributed throughout Ireland. Simple totals of imports are insufficient indicators of the boycott's effect because they do not allow for ultimate re-exports. This was particularly important in Belfast where the textile and shipbuilding industries were heavily dependent on imported raw material. However, if those imports most likely to have been processed in local manufacturing industry are omitted, then the residue could reasonably be said to show the importation of goods forming the bulk of each port's distribution trade, at least in so far as it depended on previously imported commodities. This is shown in Table 14.1

As can be seen from the table, Belfast's share, having averaged 36.7 per cent of Irish imports between 1912 and 1920 (with only a small degree of variability), fell markedly to 30.6 in 1921, a fall of nearly 17 per cent compared to both the average and the 1920 level.

It would simplify matters if it could be assumed that the fall was caused solely by the boycott, but there are two possible objections to this interpretation. First, it could be that *per capita* incomes in the six-county area fell more sharply between 1920

---

[61] Ireland, *Statistical Abstract 1938* (Dublin, 1939), 90. *Ulster Year Book* (Belfast, 1938), 93.

Table 14.1   Imports into Irish ports of goods likely to feature in the distributing trade [62]
(figures in £m and percentages)

	Belfast £m	%	Cork £m	%	Dublin £m	%	Others £m	%	Total £m
1912	18.82	35.9	5.32	10.1	16.79	32.0	11.51	21.9	52.44
1913	18.96	36.3	5.75	11.0	14.69	28.1	12.88	24.6	52.28
1919	40.14	37.8	10.01	9.4	37.88	35.6	18.3	17.2	106.33
1920	47.48	36.8	12.92	10.0	42.9	33.2	25.8	20.0	129.1
1921	27.14	30.6	8.31	9.4	32.52	36.7	20.58	23.2	88.55

[62] Goods deemed 'not widely distributed' are (1) all textile goods *except* drapery, woollen goods, hosiery, lace, hats, apparel, carpets, felt, velvet, mattresses, mats, matting. (2) Pig iron, scrap iron, bar and wrought iron, girders, beams and joists, plates and sheets, galvanized iron sheets, anchors and chains, bolts, rivets, and nuts. (3) Textile machinery plus a third of 'unclassified machinery', a sizeable category, made up of textile, agricultural, and general machinery. (4) Coal.

and 1922 than in the rest of Ireland, thus causing imports through Belfast to fall more than elsewhere. Second, it might be that there had been a sizeable reduction in the distribution of goods from Belfast to the rest of the six-county area rather than to the south. These two objections will be considered in turn.

Unemployment in Belfast was high throughout 1921, rising from 16 per cent in January to 32 per cent in June, falling again to 26 per cent at the end of the year; the average was approximately 24 per cent.[63] Although comparable unemployment figures are not available for other Irish towns it is doubtful if they were as high because of differences in the industrial structure. There is therefore a prima-facie case for a greater proportionate fall in northern incomes than those in the south; but two factors offset this. First, the unemployment insurance acts of 1920 and 1921 greatly extended the provision of unemployment benefits, benefits which were geared to conditions in Britain where wage levels, particularly for the unskilled, were higher than in Belfast.[64] Moreover, although the benefits were not generous, their real value rose as prices fell throughout 1921. Some Belfast employers were worried that they were too generous. One large employer argued that 'there is no shirking the fact that the "dole" is a potent factor in keeping the percentage [of unemployed] higher, particularly among the thousands who have always taken their work in homoeopathic doses'.[65] It is thus probable that the provision for the unemployed in 1921 mitigated the worst effects of rising unemployment. The second and more important factor tending to reduce the effect of higher northern unemployment on relative income levels in the north and south, was the fall in agricultural incomes over the period. Of course this fall occurred throughout Ireland, but it had a greater effect on the south where 51.3 per cent of

---

[63] *Report of the Ministry of Labour for the Years 1923-4*, Northern Ireland Command Paper, Cmd. 41, p. 35. These figures cover all industrial workers except those employed in agricultural and domestic service. They are based on the percentage totally unemployed plus a half of those on short-time working. In the absence of figures for January 1921, the assumption is that Northern Ireland rates of unemployment were 150 per cent of the national average. See A. C. Pigou, *Aspects of British Economic History* (London, 1947), p. 221.

[64] See *Standard Time Rates of Wages Hours and Labour in the United Kingdom at 31 December 1920*, Cmd. 1253, 1921.

[65] *NW*, 30 December 1921.

the gainfully employed depended on agriculture compared to 26 per cent in the north.[66] It was suggested in March 1922 that losses in farmers' gross income from cattle alone were £100 per capita during the course of 1921 and early 1922. Further evidence corroborates this. Between December 1920 and December 1921 the average price of agricultural produce sold at fairs and markets in Ireland fell by between 45 to 51 per cent: since the fall in the cost of living was only 28 per cent over the same period, this would suggest a fall in net farming income of rather under 20 per cent.[67] Falls in income in Belfast brought about by unemployment were probably of the same order of magnitude. If it is assumed that 22*s.* per week (for a man, his wife, and two children) represents approximately one-third of the income of a man in work, then with an average unemployment rate of 24 per cent this would indicate a fall in income to wage earners of 16 per cent.[68] The real wages of the employed were largely maintained, indeed the Ministry of Labour index for the whole of the United Kingdom shows a 7.5 per cent rise between December 1920 and December 1921.[69] Thus it is likely that because of insurance benefits on the one hand, and the fall in agricultural incomes on the other, the *relative* income positions of the Belfast area and that of the twenty-six counties remained reasonably stable despite the former's high unemployment rate. It is unlikely, at all events, that there was any differential income movement sufficient to account for the large fall in the share of Belfast's imports of those goods involved in the distributing trade, shown in the table.

Coming to the second objection there could have been a decline in the distribution of goods to areas of the six counties

[66] K. S. Isles and N. Cuthbert, *An Economic Survey of Northern Ireland* (Belfast, 1957), p. 53; J. Meenan, *The Irish Economy Since 1922* (Liverpool, 1970), p. 41.

[67] *Times Trade Supplement*, 18 March 1922; *The Statist*, 11 February 1922. If it is assumed that farmers' income from sales fell by 47.5 per cent and their cost of living by 28 per cent this implies a fall in income of 27.1 per cent. However, many items produced on farms were for the farmers' own use, thus a fall in their market value did not affect their real income.

[68] The unweighted average wages of shipwrights, labourers, linen-loom workers, firemen, and engineers was 72*s.* Figures for wages from Cmd. 1253 reduced by average rate of wage decreases during 1921 given in Pigou, p. 232. Unemployment benefits for a family of four from P. Cohen, *Unemployment Insurance and Assistance in Britain* (London, 1938), pp. 20, 23. The estimate of the fall in incomes consequent upon a rise in unemployed is exaggerated as it presupposes no unemployment in 1920.

[69] Pigou, p. 232.

outside the main industrial conurbation. This might have been caused by either a disproportionate decline in incomes in the agricultural areas of the north, or by a boycott of Belfast goods within this area. The former is unlikely. The fall in prices of the main agricultural commodities was fairly uniform; as mentioned earlier they all fell between 45 and 51 per cent; thus it is reasonably certain that decreases in agricultural income, north and south, were very similar. The second cause—a 'Northern Ireland boycott' of Belfast—is potentially more serious. If this had been extensive, then the figures of losses attributable to the boycott cannot be accurately designated as cross-border losses. It is certainly true that attempts were made, particularly in nationalist areas in the west of the province, to boycott Belfast goods. Incidents were not uncommon in parts of Londonderry, Tyrone, South Armagh, and, to a lesser extent, Fermanagh. But the boycott was often directed less against goods distributed from Belfast than at Protestant traders.[70] Apart from the area traditionally served by Londonderry, Londonderry itself, the Foyle Valley, and, to a lesser extent, the Omagh area, there was no real alternative to goods imported through Belfast. Sometimes it appears a compromise was reached with local boycott committees whereby goods sent from Belfast were allowed in, in return for a contribution 'for the relief of men thrown out of employment as a result of the boycott'.[71] For the bulk of the nationalist population, perhaps 80 per cent or more, there was no alternative to Belfast-distributed goods. Only in the Londonderry area, perhaps, could there have been some switching in the direction of purchases; even here there were difficulties.[72]

Given that the fall in percentage trade of Belfast does, despite the problems involved, show the losses in the trade of Belfast with the twenty-six county area, it is possible to obtain some

[70] For example, undated memorandum from Castlederg traders, PRONI CAB 6/23.
[71] In Strabane the local manager of the Pallidrome cinema was allowed to show a Charlie Chaplin film distributed from Belfast on condition that he made a donation. Mr Cooper to Strabane Boycott Committee 20-21 December 1921. PRONI T1962/1/2-8.
[72] An attempt to boycott the nationalist-controlled corporation for ordering spare parts for local buses from Belfast had to be withdrawn. *NW*, 9 November 1921. In any case the government was committed to 'clear out every shred of the boycott in Ulster'. 28 October 1921, Craig to deputation of Belfast wholesalers, PRONI CAB 6/23.

indication of the absolute amounts of trade involved. A reasonable approximation of this can be obtained by comparing what Belfast imports would have been had Belfast's share of Irish imports for 1921 been maintained at the average level of the years 1912, 1913, 1919, and 1920. This is justified because of the small deviations from the average during these years. If Belfast's share had remained at its average level of 36.7 per cent (incidentally almost exactly equal to the level of 1920) then instead of Belfast's 'distribution' imports being £27.14m they would have been £32.5m—£5.36m higher. Thus the losses attributable to the boycott during 1921 can be estimated at something in excess of £5m at 1921 prices. This figure fits in remarkably well with valuations given by the Ulster Trades Defense Association of anything from £5m to £10m.[73] Since this refers to the period July 1920 to July 1921, the lower estimate can reasonably be compared with the conclusion derived from the import statistics. It might be expected that the wholesalers' upper estimates would be higher, not only because of natural bias, but also because some goods affected by the boycott had been manufactured in the province rather than imported. No doubt the wholesalers' figures also include an allowance for distribution costs and profit margin which our estimate does not. The loss to the distributing trade estimated above as £5.36m can be seen in perspective when it is compared with the total of £7.40m for goods exported across the Land Boundary in the year 1924.[74]

It is difficult to estimate the extent to which markets lost during the boycott had been recovered by 1924. The border was an undoubted nuisance, particularly in the period immediately after its establishment until railway companies and hauliers evolved methods of reducing its impact. Furthermore, from 12 May 1924 the Free State introduced a range of tariffs though these were of minor significance in cross-border trade.[75] Thus

[73] Minutes of Ministry of Commerce, 19 December 1922. PRONI COM 62/2/34/1.

[74] It should be born in mind that the figure of £7.4m includes wholesalers' profit and distribution costs; it includes also goods manufactured within Northern Ireland and commodities imported to Londonderry and Newry, and sent thence across the border.

[75] In the five months before the tariff was imposed the export of these goods was valued at £114,000. In the rest of the year goods valued at £86,000 were imported into the Free State.

it is possible that the imposition of the land boundary immediately hampered north-south trade. Nevertheless the balance of probability is that Belfast's trade never recovered to its pre-boycott level. Evidence presented to the Boundary Commission by H. M. Customs and Excise suggests that in 1924 approximately £2.3m of £7.40m exported to the Free State from Northern Ireland came from Londonderry or Newry, leaving £5.1m originating elsewhere.[76] If it is assumed that, as was the case in the 1930s, a third of these goods were the produce of Northern Ireland, then £3.4m consisted of previously imported commodities. If a deduction of a third is made to allow for distribution costs and traders' profits within the province then the value of the goods as landed would have been approximately £2.3m, or £2.7m expressed in 1921 prices. This is to be compared to losses to Belfast's distributing trade in 1921 of over £5m. Whether the £2.7m reflects commerce that had been recovered after the end of the boycott, or whether it represents a bedrock of trade which had been unaffected by it, is impossible to say. But, whichever was the case, it would appear that before 1921 Belfast's trade with the twenty-six counties was almost certainly double that existing in 1924.

Thus the effects of the boycott appear to have outlasted its ending. The 1924 level of exports from Northern Ireland to the Free State was never exceeded during the inter-war period: Belfast never regained the trade it had lost between 1920 and 1922. The considerable reduction of the city's market in the twenty-six counties is the mark of the boycott's success—hardly surprising given the long experience of boycotting as an economic and political weapon in Ireland. But it came nowhere near achieving its wider objectives. Even its more limited aim, that of bringing about the re-employment of Catholics, particularly in the shipyards, was flying in the face of the harsh economic realities of the period. Unemployment was high amongst both religious groups in the north and it was hardly within the power of the Northern Ireland government, or of employers, to give preference to Catholics over Protestants as the situation deteriorated, less still to dismiss Protestants and

---

[76] PRO CAB 61/88. Evidence of T. J. Large. Includes exports to the Free State cleared at customs in Londonderry (£1.38m), Newry (£0.3m), and two-thirds the clearances at Strabane (£1.00m × 0.66 = £0.66m).

replace them with Catholics. In its broader aim, that of bringing about Irish unity by the economic intimidation of Ulster Unionists, the boycott was almost certainly counter-productive. Although it cannot be isolated from the general atmosphere of bitterness and violence within which partition took place, the boycott helped worsen the situation. P. S. O'Hegarty writing in 1924, admittedly from the viewpoint of the pro-Treaty party after a bitterly fought civil war, had no doubts about its damaging effects.

It raised up in the South what never had been there, a hatred of the North, and a feeling that the North was as much an enemy of Ireland as was England ... It probably inflicted some damage on the Ulster majority, but it was an utter failure inasmuch as it did not secure reinstatement of a single expelled Nationalist, nor the conversion of a single Unionist.

Perhaps O'Hegarty shows insufficient understanding of the motives that led to the boycott, but his final assessment of its fundamental effect can scarcely be gainsaid: 'it was merely a blind and suicidal contribution to the general hate'.[77]

[77] O'Hegarty, pp. 52-3.

Bibliography of the Writings of Professor K. H. Connell

Compiled by M. Daly

I BOOKS

The Population of Ireland (Oxford, 1950)
Irish Peasant Society (Oxford, 1968)

II ARTICLES

'The Population of Ireland in the Eighteenth Century', *Economic History Review*, xvi, 1946

'Land and Population in Ireland, 1780-1845', *Economic History Review*, ii, 1950

'The Colonization of Waste Land in Ireland, 1750-1845', *Economic History Review*, iii, 1951

'Essays in Bibliography and Criticism: 17. The History of the Potato', *Economic History Review*, iii, 1951

'Some Unsettled Problems in English and Irish Population History, 1750-1845', *Irish Historical Studies*, vii, 1951

'Population Trends', T. W. Moody and J. C. Beckett, eds., *Ulster Since 1800: A Political and Economic Survey* (London, 1954)

'Marriage in Ireland after the Famine: The Diffusion of the Match', *Journal of the Statistical and Social Inquiry Society of Ireland*, xix, 1955-6.

'Peasant Marriage in Ireland after the Great Famine', *Past and Present*, 12, 1957

'Population', R. B. McDowell, ed., *Irish Social Life, 1800-45* (Dublin, 1958)

'The Land Legislation and Irish Social Life', *Economic History Review*, xi, 1958

'Illicit Distillation: An Irish Peasant Industry', J. Hogan, ed., *Historical Studies, III: Papers Read before the Fourth Irish Conference of Historians* (London, 1961)

'Peasant Marriage in Ireland: Its Structure and Development since the Famine', *Economic History Review*, xiv, 1962

'The Potato in Ireland', *Past and Present*, 23, 1962

'Ether Drinking in Ulster', *Quarterly Journal of the Study of Alcohol*, xxvi, 1965

'Land and Population in Ireland, 1780-1845', D. V. Glass and D. E. C. Eversley, eds., *Population in History: Essays in Historical Demography* (London, 1965)

'The Potato in Ireland', *Clogher Record*, v, 1965

Reproduced from *Irish Economic and Social History*, i (1974) by kind permission of the editors and of James Daly.

Index

oatcakes, 101
oatmeal,
  consumption of, 98, 102, 122, 123, 126,
    179;
  exports, 160;
  price, 118, 119, 123
oats,
  consumption of, 97, 100;
  cultivation of, 179, 183;
  exports, 160, 161;
  harvest, 98;
  production of, 177
O'Connell, J. J., 297
Offaly East, 49
Omagh, 304
Omey, 50
Ó Neachtain, Seán, 102
O'Sullivan, Humphrey, 98, 101, 115,
  118
Otway, C., 175

Paddy the Cope, 280
Paisley, 9, 195, 197, 198-9, 200, 201,
  202, 207, 208, 211, 212, 213, 229
Paisley shawls, 198-9, 207
Pale, the, 97, 107
Passaic Falls, 217, 219
Passaic Manufacturing Company, 220
Passaic Mill, 220
Paterson, NJ., 213, 217, 218, 219, 220,
  223, 225, 226
Pawtucket, Rhode Island, 218
peas, 97, 102, 106, 107, 109, 183
peasants, 8, 29, 86, 135, 195, 206, 273;
  see also labourers *and* farmers
pellagra,
  associated with Indian meal, 8, 113,
    124, 125, 127, 128;
  presence of in nineteenth-century
    Ireland, 8, 130, 132, 133;
  resemblance to typhus, 128;
  symptoms, 125, 127, 128, 129, 130,
    131, 133;
  vitamin deficiency disease, 124, 127
Penn, William, 59
Perry, M. C., 264
Petty, Sir William, 14, 15, 17-18, 21, 25,
  26, 103
Philadelphia, 114, 229
Philippi, Otto E., 229
Phoenix Park, 252
pig-meat, 104, 105
pigs, 104, 105;
  exports, 161;

  production of, 106, 155, 158, 161,
    162;
  trade in, 105, 155;
  value of output of, 163
Pim, Fry & Co., 260
Playfair, Dr L., 255
Plunkett, Sir Horace, 10;
  achievements, 271-2, 276, 277-8,
    281-2, 284-5;
  appointed Vice President of Depart-
    ment of Agriculture, 276;
  character, 271, 278;
  opinions of the Irish character, 278-9;
  resignation from Department of Agri-
    culture (1907), 281;
  views on Irish agricultural co-operation,
    272, 273-4, 284
Pollock, H. M., 293
poor-law unions, 261
population,
  affected by emigration, 158;
  age structure of, 30;
  and diet, 8, 31, 74, 81, 87-8, 89;
  decline of, 29-30, 35, 86, 165, 166;
  density of, 25;
  estimates of, 5, 7, 14, 24, 25-7, 29,
    38, 44, 55, 89, 90, 91, 232, 234,
    241, 245;
  growth of, 5, 7, 13, 15, 25-8, 29-30,
    34-5, 39, 85-6, 89-94, 96, 99,
    111, 112, 165, 235;
  Irish and British population growth
    compared, 15, 30;
  Irish and European population growth
    compared, 28;
  of Ireland, according to the censuses
    (1821-41), 26, 37, 45, 46, 53,
    54;
  pre-famine rise in, 158;
  pressure of, 155;
  pressure of on food supply, 162;
  pressure of on land prices, 176;
  relationship between growth and
    income, 111;
  rural depopulation, 166;
  urban, 124, 165, 169
pork, 95, 97, 104, 105
porridge, 97, 99, 102, 103
Portnehinch, 19
potatoes,
  and population growth, 31, 95;
  as animal feed, 31, 104;
  blight, 112;
  cheapness of, 105, 106;